new england

Edited by Jay Itzkowitz
Directed and Designed by Hans Johannes Hoefer

APA PRODUCTIONS

THE INSIGHT GUIDES SERIES RECEIVED SPECIAL AWARDS FOR EXCELLENCE FROM THE PACIFIC AREA TRAVEL ASSOCIATION.

NEW ENGLAND
Third Edition
© APA PRODUCTIONS (HK) LTD.
Published by APA Productions (HK) Ltd.
Printed by APA Press Pte. Ltd.
Colour Separation in Singapore by Colourscan Pte Ltd

APA PRODUCTIONS
Publisher and Chairman: Hans Johannes Hoefer
Marketing Director: Yinglock Chan
General Manager: Henry Lee
Administration Manager: Alice Ng
Editorial Manager: Vivien Kim
Executive Editor: Adam Liptak

Project Editors

Helen Abbott, Diana Ackland, Mohamed Amin, Ravindralal Anthonis, Roy Bailet, Louisa Cambell, Jon Carroll, Hillary Cunningham, John Eames, Janie Freeburg, Bikram Grewal, Virginia Hopkins, Samuel Israel, Jay Itzkowitz, Phil Jaratt, Tracy Johnson, Ben Kalb, Wilhelm Klein, Saul Lockhart, Sylvia Mayuga, Gordon MaLauchlan, Kal Müller, Eric Oey, Daniel P. Reid, Kim Robinson, Ronn Ronck, Robert Seidenberg, Rolf Steinberg, Sriyani Tidball, Lisa Van Gruisen, Merin Wexler.

Contributing Writers.

A.D. Aird, Ruth Armstrong, T. Terence Barrow, F. Lisa Beebe, Bruce Berger, Dor Bahadur Bista, Clinton V. Black, Star Black, Frena Bloomfield, John Borthwick, Roger Boschman, Tom Brosnahan, Jerry Carroll, Tom Chaffin, Nedra Chung, Tom Cole, Orman Day, Kunda Dixit, Richard Erdoes, Guillermo Garcia-Oropeza, Ted Giannoulas, Barbara Gloudon, Harka Gurung, Sharifah Hamzah, Willard A. Hanna, Elizabeth Hawley, Sir Edmund Hillary, Tony Hillerman, Jerry Hopkins, Peter Hutton, Neil Jameson, Michael King, Michele Kort, Thomas Lucey, Leonard Lueras, Michael E. Macmillan, Derek. Maitland, Buddy Mays, Craig McGregor, Reinhold Messner, Julie Michaels, M. R. Priya Rangsit, Al Read, Elizabeth V. Reyes, Victor Stafford Reid, Harry Rolnick, E.R. Sarachchandra, Uli Schmetzer, Ilsa Sharp, Norman Sibley, Peter Spiro, Harold Stephens, Keith Stevens, Michael Stone, Desmond Tate, Colin Taylor, Deanna L. Thompson, Randy Udall, James Wade, Mallika Wanigasundara, William Warren, Cynthia Wee, Tony Wheeler, Linda White, H. Taft Wireback, Alfred A. Yuson, Paul Zach.

Contributing Photographers

Carole Allen, Ping Amarand, Tony Arruza, Marcello Bertinetti, Alberto Cassio, Pat Canova, Alain Compost, Ray Cranbourne, Alain Evrard, Ricardo Ferro, Lee Foster, Manfred Gottschalk, Werner Hahn, Dallas and John Heaton, Brent Hesselyn, Hans Hoefer, Luca Invernizzi, Ingo Jezierski, Wilhelm Klein, Dennis Lane, Max Lawrence, Lyle Lawson, Philip Little, Guy Marche, Antonio Martinelli, David Messent, Ben Nakayama, Vautier de Nanxe, Kal Müller, Günter Pfannmuller, Van Philips, Ronni Pinsler, Fitz Prenzel, G.P. Reichelt, Dan Rocovits, David Ryan, Frank Salmoiraghi, Thomas Schollhammer, Blair Seitz, David Stahl, Bill Wassman, Rendo Yap, Hisham Youssef.

Distributors:

Australia and New Zealand: Prentice Hall of Australia, 7 Grosvenor Place, Brookvale, NSW 2100, Australia. **Benelux:** Uitgeverij Cambium, Naarder-straat 11, 1251 Aw Laren, The Netherlands. **Central and South America; Mexico; Portugal and Spain:** Cedibra Editora Brasileira Ltda, Rua Leonidia, 2-Rio de Janeiro, Brazil. **Denmark:** Copenhagen Book Centre Aps, Roskildevej 338, DK-2630 Tastrup, Denmark. **Europe (others):** European Book Service, Flevolaan 36-38, P. O. Box 124, 1380 AC Weesp, Holland. **Hawaii:** Pacific Trade Group Inc., P. O. Box 1227, Kailua, Oahu, Hawaii 96734, U.S.A. **Hong Kong:** Far East Media Ltd., Vita Tower, 7th Floor, Block B, 29 Wong Chuk Hang Road, Hong Kong. **India and Nepal:** India Book Distributors, 107/108 Arcadia Building, 195 Narima Point, Bombay-400-021, India. **Indonesia:** Java Books, Box 55 J.K.C.P, Jakarta, Indonesia.

Israel: Steimatzky Ltd., P.O. Box 628, Tel Aviv 61006, Israel (Israel title only). **Italy:** Zanfi Editori SRL. Via Ganaceto 121, 41100 Modena, Italy. **Caribbean:** Kingston Publishers, 1-A Norwood Avenue, Kingston 5, Jamaica. **Kenya:** Camerapix Publishers International Ltd., P. O. Box 45048, Nairobi, Kenya. **Korea:** Kyobo Book Centre Co., Ltd., P.O. Box Kwang Hwa Moon 1 658, Seoul, Korea. **Philippines:** National Book Store, 701 Rizal Avenue, Manila, Philippines. **Singapore and Malaysia:** MPH Distributors (S) Pte. Ltd., 601 Sims Drive #03-21 Pan-I Warehouse and Office Complex, S'pore 1438, Singapore. **Switzerland:** M.P.A. Agencies-Import SA, CH. du Croset 9, CH-1024 Ecublens, Switzerland. **Taiwan:** Caves Books Ltd., 103 Chungshan N.Road, Sec. 2, Taipei, Taiwan, Republic of China. **Thailand:** Far East Publications Ltd., 117/3 Soi Samahan, Sukhumvit 4 (South Nana), Bangkok, Thailand. **United Kingdom and Ireland:** Harrap Ltd., 19-23 Ludgate Hill, London EC4M 7PD, England, United Kingdom. **Mainland United States and Canada:** Graphic Arts Center Publishing, 3019 N.W. Yeon, P.O. Box 10306, Portland OR 97210, U.S.A. (The Pacific Northwest title only); Prentice Hall Press, Gulf & Western Building, One Gulf & Western Plaza, New York, NY 10023, U.S.A. (all other titles).

French editions: Editions Gallimard, 5 rue Sébastien-Bottin, F-75007 Paris, France. **German editions:** Nelles Verlag GmbH, Schleissheimer Str. 371b, 8000 Munich 45, West Germany. **Italian editions:** Zanfi Editori SLR, Via Ganaceto 121 41100 Modena, Italy. **Portuguese and Spanish editions:** Cedibra Editora Brasileira Ltda, Rua Leonidia, 2-Rio de Janerio, Brazil.

Advertising and Special Sales Representatives

Advertising carried in Insight Guides gives readers direct access to quality merchandise and travel-related services. These advertisments are inserted in the Guide in Brief section of each book. Advertisers are requested to contact their nearest representatives, listed below.

Special sales, for promotion purposes within the international travel industry and for educational purposes, are also available. The advertising representatives listed here also handle special sales. Alternatively, interested parties can contact Apa Productions, P.O. Box 219, Orchard Point Post Office, Singapore 9123.

Australia and New Zealand: International Media Representative Pty. Ltd., 3rd Floor, 39 East Esplanade Manly, NSW 2095, Australia. Tel: (02) 9773377; Tlx: IMR AA 74473.
Hawaii: HawaiianLMedia Sales; 1750 Kalakaua Ave., Suite 3-243, Honolulu Hawaii 96826, U.S.A. Tel: (808) 9464483.
Hong Kong: C Cheney & Associates, 17th Floor, D'Aguilar Place, 1-30 D' Aguilar Street, Central, Hong Kong. Tel: 5-213671; Tlx: 63079 CCAL HX.
India and Nepal, Pakistan and Bangladesh: Universal Media, CHA 2/718, 719 Kantipath, Lazimpat, Kathmandu-2, Nepal. Tel: 412911/414502; Tlx: 2229 KAJI NP ATTN MEDIA.
Indonesia: Media Investment Services, Setiabudi Bldg. 2, 4th Floor, Suite 407, Jl. Hr. Rasuna Said, Kuningan, Jakarta Selatan 12920, Indonesia. Tel: 5782723/5782752; Tlx: 62418 MEDIANETIA; Mata Graphic Design, Batujimbar, Sanur, Bali, Indonesia. Tel: (0361) 8073. (for Bali only)
Philippines: Torres Media Sales Inc., 21 Warbler St., Greenmeadows I, Murphy, Quezon City, Metro Manila, Philippines. Tel: 722-02-43; Tlx: 23312 RHP PH.
Thailand: Cheney, Tan & Van Outrive, 17th Floor Rajapark Bldg., 163 Asoke Rd., Bangkok 10110, Thailand. Tel: 2583244/2583259; Tlx: 20666 RAJAPAK TH.
Singapore and Malaysia: Cheney Tan Associates, 1 Goldhill Plaza, #02-01, Newton Rd., Singapore 1130, Singapore. Tel: 2549522; Tlx: RS 35983 CTAL.
Sri Lanka: Spectrum Lanka Advertising Ltd., 56 1/2 Ward Place, Colombo 7, Sri Lanka. Tel: 5984648/596227; Tlx: 21439 SPECTRM CE.

APA PHOTO AGENCY PTE. LTD.

The Apa Photo Agency is S.E. Asia's leading stock photo archive, representing the work of professional photographers from all over the world. More than 150,000 original color transparencies are available for advertising, editorial and educational uses. We are also linked with Tony Stone Worldwide, one of Europe's leading stock agencies, and their associate offices around the world:
Singapore: Apa Photo Agency Pte. Ltd., P.O. Box 219, Orchard Point Post Office, Singapore 9123, Singapore. **London:** Tony Stone Worldwide, 28 Finchley Rd., St. John's Wood, London NW8 6ES, England. **North America & Canada:** Masterfile Inc., 415 Yonge St., Suite 200, Toronto M5B 2E7, Canada. **Paris:** Fotogram-Stone Agence Photographique, 45 rue de Richelieu, 75001 Paris, France. **Barcelona:** Fototec Torre Dels Pardais, 7 Barcelona 08026, Spain. **Johannesburg:** Color Library (Pty.) Ltd., P.O. Box 1659, Johannesburg, South Africa 2000. **Sydney:** The Photographic Library of Australia Pty. Ltd., 7 Ridge Street, North Sydney, New South Wales 2050, Australia. **Tokyo:** Orion Press, 55-1 Kanda Jimbocho, Chiyoda-ku, Tokyo 101, Japan.

Muppet Studios, home of Kermit the Frog and Miss Piggy, may not seem the most likely place for the hatching of the book you now hold in your hands, but it was there that Apa Productions publisher **Hans Hoefer** and project editor **Jay Itzkowitz** first met. That meeting, held amidst furry puppets and assorted fantasti-cal creatures, ultimately resulted in *New England*, the latest title in Apa Productions series of highly acclaimed *Insight Guides*.

Itzkowitz   *Hoefer*

Apa, a Hong Kong and Singapore-based publishing house whose innovative approach to creating travel chronicles has been honored throughout the world since the company was established in 1970, introduced its first American title, *Hawaii*, in 1980. The success of *Hawaii* convinced Hoefer that American readers were ready for more *Insight Guides*.

As Apa became increasingly involved in the American arena, one region fairly cried out for the full *Insight Guide* treatment — New England, full of history and beauty, and currently being swept by one of its periodic fits of dynamism.

One who heard New England's beckoning call was Itzkowitz. Born in Turkey, he graduated from Harvard University in 1982. During his tenure at that illustrious institution he spent almost two years in Italy writing two editions of a bestselling budget guidebook, *Let's Go: Italy*. While Itzkowitz majored in Italian Renaissance History and Literature at Harvard, he was minoring in comedy as an editor of the university's most prestigious publication, the *Harvard Lampoon*.

With graduation approaching, Itzkowitz was trying to do almost anything to avoid going into one of the so-called honorable professions. He wrote to Hoefer and proposed an outline for an *Insight Guide* to Turkey, which was quickly accepted. But the Turkish project was put on hold and Itzkowitz was dragged, kicking and screaming, to Rutgers Law School. There, despite his apprehensions, he found torts, *res ipsa loquitur*, and *habeas corpus* much to his liking. He continued to write comedy, clawing his way up the laughter ladder to the point where he was finally able to write for animals — Jim Henson's *Muppets*.

Living a complex blend of law and comedy seemed to suit Itzkowitz just fine. But soon the travel bug, caught during a misspent youth following his father (a professor of Ottoman history at Princeton University) on research trips throughout the Near East and Europe, surfaced again.

Anderson

It was just about the same time that Apa Productions stepped up its timetable for new American titles. Apa managing editor **John Gottberg Anderson**, recalling that Harvard sits smack in the middle of New England, proposed the project editorship to Itzkowitz, who seemed to be a natural to take on the project. In fact, while at university, Itzkowitz had traveled widely in New England, exploring Maine, Martha's Vineyard and (of course) Boston. After meetings with Hoefer and Anderson in New York and in Princeton, New Jersey, Itzkowitz got the book rolling during the summer of 1983. The Harvard "old boy" network helped him to assemble a talented team of writers and photographers whose work has appeared in some of the world's leading publications.

Itzkowitz managed to complete work on *New England* despite a hectic schedule which included law school, a trip to Bombay and Goa to research Indian corporate law, and work in the Muppets' legal department. He is spending summer 1984 with the noted New York City law firm of Demov, Morris, Levin and Hammerling, where he hopes that a case involving comedy and travel will cross his desk.

One of Itzkowitz's major chores was coordinating the work of over 20 photograpers whose work graces these pages. The vast majority of images come from the cameras of a quartet of photographers.

The work of **Carole Allen** adds a special intimacy and magic to *New England*. A registered nurse-turned-professional image magician, Allen spent several years in Colombia where her husband served with the Peace Corps. Returning to the United States and seeking cooler climes, she adopted New England as her home, and has lived in Maine and New Hampshire for the past 10 years. Allen's work has appeared in *Audubon*, *Sports Illustrated* and *Yankee*, New England's leading regional magazine.

New York-based **Joseph Viesti** produced much of his work for this book while traveling through New England on assignment for UNESCO, the United Nations Educational, Scientific and Cultural Organization. Viesti, whose work has previously been represented in *Insight Guides* to *Florida* and *Southern California*, has shot for *Geo*, *Time*, *National Geographic*, Italy's *L'Expresso*, *Signature* and *Modern Photography*, among other publications. For the past seven years, he has specialized in photographing celebrations around the world; in 1984 his colorful collection was tapped for the UNICEF *Engagement Calendar*, the first time the work of a single artist has been used.

New England's other two principal photographers, **Ping Amranand** and **Hisham Youssef**, are natives of Thailand and Egypt, respectively, adding a unique vision of the region through the lens of latecomers from abroad.

Allen

Viesti

Amranand

Youssef

Amranand, who was born in Bangkok but holds a degree in Oriental history from London University, currently is based in Washington, D.C. His work has appeared in such publications as *Architectural Digest*, *Asia* and *Sawasdee*, the Thai International in-flight magazine. In 1983 he was awarded special commendation by the Pacific Area Travel Association (PATA) for a photo essay on Sri Lanka that appeared in *Serendib*, the Air Lanka magazine.

Youssef is a 1983 graduate of Harvard, where he was principal photographer and photo editor for *The Harvard Crimson*, campus newspaper; *What Is to Be Done?*, a campus arts weekly; and the *Harvard Lampoon's* 1983 parody of *Newsweek* magazine. He was also a teaching assistant in graphic design in Harvard's Visual and Environmental Studies Department. Youssef previously has worked on assignment to the Egyptian State Information Service in the Sinai Peninsula and for Sheraton Hotels International in upper Egypt.

This book's most prolific writer is **Peter Spiro**, who contributed more to New England than his sparkling historical introduction. Spiro added his insights on many details and critiqued several of the other contributors' pieces. A Harvard classmate of Itzkowitz, Spiro spent a summer working for the U.S. Department of State and may be the only Apa writer to have held a "Top Secret Clearance" from the United States government. He has written for *New Republic* and *The Christian Science Monitor*, and has

lived in Iceland, Germany, England, South Africa and Cameroon — but he finds New England especially enchanting.

Adam Nossiter, who wrote about "The New England Character," claims knowledge of and affection for New England from his days as a student at Harvard, where he studied history and literature. Nossiter's mother is a Boston native, and he himself has traveled extensively throughout the region. He is now a reporter for *The Anniston Star* in the southern state of Alabama; while he admits that Alabama is not much like Cambridge, he disagrees with the writer who

Nossiter

Muro

Brosnahan

said: "Alabama resembles Massachusetts about as much as Africa does."

Mark Muro's ties to Boston go back to the warm fall day he

Bastian

N. Sibley

showed up at Harvard fresh from the vastness of the Pacific Northwest. A native of Seattle, he has honed his knowledge of his adopted New England home as a staff writer for the region's preeminent daily newspaper, the *Boston Globe*. He characterizes himself as a traveler in two Americas: he loves the country's wilderness, but he also loves the American city at night, "glaring with neon and carlight." Another Harvard classmate of Itzkowitz, where he wrote for the *Crimson*, Muro has penned articles for the *Globe* on everything from politics to public restrooms.

Inez Sherman Keller and **Jonathan Keller**, residents of Cambridge, contributed sections on the North and South Shores (Greater Boston) and Central Massachusetts, animated by especially close New England ties. Inez is a graduate of Classical High School in Providence, Rhode Island, and Boston University. Jon, a lifelong Cambridgeite, hosts the popular "Jon Keller Show" on Boston's WRKO Radio, heard in all six New England states, and writes frequently for *People* magazine. He scored a major journalistic scoop by being the first reporter to tour the Martha's Vineyard home of Jacqueline Kennedy Onassis.

Tom Brosnahan was lured to New England from his native Pennsylvania more than 20 years ago. After graduation from one of Boston's many universities, he set out to see the world — in the process writing over a dozen travel guides to areas of the Middle East, North Africa, Europe, Latin America and Canada before "coming home" to

Spiro

Jon and Inez Keller

G. Sibley

Silber

Simmons

New England. He continues to free-lance for various magazine and book publishers. Among his recent publications is a book entitled *How to Beat the High Cost of Travel*. A regular contributor to one of the region's high-tech computer publications, his articles for *Insight Guide: New England* — "Cape Cod" and "Maritime New England" — were written on his faithful word-processing machine.

Molly Kuntz, who wrote on Martha's Vineyard and Nantucket and penned the special feature on "Architecture and Historic Preservation," has worked in recent years as a researcher-writer for Washington-based interest groups concentrating on

architecture, energy policy and public transportation issues. A graduate of American University in Washington, D.C., and a resident of Princeton, N.J., Kuntz visits New England in general and Nantucket in particular several times a year.

Julie Michaels, author of "The Berkshires" and "Connecticut," lives with her cat, Kitzel, on the outskirts of Northampton, Mass., where she is associate editor of *New England Monthly* magazine. Formerly a reporter for *The Berkshire Eagle* in Pittsfield, Mass., she claims Berkshire County is the single most beautiful piece of real estate east of the Mississippi River.

Kay Cassill is an identical twin. Her book *Twins: Nature's Amazing Mystery* (Atheneum, 1983) has received widespread critical acclaim. But the experiences of this book's Rhode Island specialist are widely varied: she is a former national synchronized swimming champion, and an accomplished artist whose works hang in the public collections of many museums including the Metropolitan Museum of Art in New York. She has lived many years in Providence where her husband, author R.V. Cassill, is a Brown University professor. Kay Cassill has had articles published in more than 20 periodicals, from *Smithsonian* and *Cosmopolitan* to *Physician's World*.

Kuntz   Michaels

Mark Bastian's early impressions of Vermont were formed on perennial family pilgrimages from their Merrimack River (Massachusetts) home to Aunt Polly Blennerhasset's camp at the tip of Hog Island, a patch of borderland in West Swanton, virtually unchanged since 1922. Bastian attended Phillips Exeter Academy in New Hampshire, where his acquaintance with New England was further deepened. After attending Princeton University in New Jersey, he returned to northern New England, where he writes travel articles for *Yankee* and other publications. He spends his weekends in Brattleboro, Vermont, gathering material for a book on New Age living.

To write "New Hampshire," **Norman Sibley** returned to the state of his birth after an extensive period of residence in Korea, where he and his wife, **Greta Diemente Sibley**, founded *Korea Quarterly* magazine and Dragon's Eye Graphics. While in Seoul, the Sibleys had their first experience with Apa Productions, contributing articles, photographs and drawings to *Insight Guide: Korea*, then acting as update editors for the
Continued on page 330

TABLE OF CONTENTS

TABLE OF CONTENTS

Cover
— by Carole M. Allen

Cartography
— by Nelles Verlag GmbH, Munich, West
  Germany

OTHER INSIGHT GUIDES TITLES

COUNTRY/REGION

ASIA
Bali
Burma
Hong Kong
India
Indonesia
Korea
Malaysia
Nepal
Philippines
Rajasthan
Singapore
Sri Lanka
Taiwan
Thailand

PACIFIC
Hawaii
New Zealand

NORTH AMERICA
Alaska
American Southwest
Northern California
Southern California
Florida
Mexico
New England
New York State
The Pacific Northwest
The Rockies
Texas

CARIBBEAN
Bahamas
Barbados
Jamaica
Puerto Rico
Trinidad and Tobago

EUROPE
Great Britain
France
Germany
Greece
Ireland
Italy
Spain

MIDDLE EAST
Egypt
Israel

GRAND TOURS
Australia
East Asia
California
Canada
Continental Europe

GREAT ADVENTURE
Indian Wildlife

NEW ENGLAND'S CALL

New England beckons. Listen and heed the call.

The call is one of a storied past and an exuberant present. Here is the richly endowed repository of America's most cherished memories: the Battle of Bunker Hill, the midnight ride of Paul Revere, the charisma of the Kennedy clan. It was here that the first cries of independence were heard, here that the movement to abolish slavery found fertile ground, here that education achieved its fullest flowering, here that American art attained its most refined aspect.

This is America's attic, crammed with marvelous antiques of every description. Here are the homes of Hawthorne, Emerson, Melville and Holmes; souvenirs of clippers and whaling ships from centuries past; houses and churches in whose gables and steeples can be read a national architectural history. The countryside abounds in inspiring vistas, enchanted with the bright golds and reds of autumn, slumbering beneath winter's heavy pure snows, bursting with the worshipful energy of spring's ritual rebirth, and joyful in summer's ceaseless vacation.

Heed the call of the Maine coast, its rocky promontories pointing to adventure; of New Hampshire's lakes, deep with silent wonder; of Vermont's mountains, shimmering in spring's verdant cloak and majestic in winter's whiteness. Heed the call of Newport's luxury, Cape Cod's peace and rolling dunes, Connecticut's celebrated colonial heritage, Boston's vibrant cityscape and quiet alleys, the Berkshires' charmed forests, Martha's Vineyard's quirky vision of quaintness.

Heed the call of New England. And reap the rewards.

NEW ENGL

The most remarqueable parts thus nam
by the high and mighty Prince CHAR
nowe King of great Britaine

THE PORTRAICTUER OF CAPTAYNE IOHN SMITH ADMIRALL OF NEW ENGLAND

Æta 37
A° 1616

Schooters hill
Sandwich
Dartmouth
Ipswich
P Kent
Snadoun hill
P Trevor
Boston
Poynt Davies
Hull
Smith Iles

These are the Lines that shew thy Face, but those
That shew thy Grace and Glory, brighter bee
Thy Faire-Discoueries and Fowle-Overthrowes
Of Salvages, much Civilliz'd by thee
Best shew thy Spirit, and to it Glory Wyn
So, thou art Brasse without, but Golde within

If so; in Brasse (too soft smiths Acts to beare)
I fix thy Fame, to make Brasse Steele out weare
Thine, as thou art Virtues
John Davies Heref

SouthHampton
P Wynthorp
Cape Anna

COGNITA
GENS IN

Bristow
Salem
Talbotts Bay
Fawmouth
Charles Towne
Frannces Ile
The River CHARLES
Charlton
Claiborus Ils.
London
P Saltonstale
Oxford
Poynt Sutliff

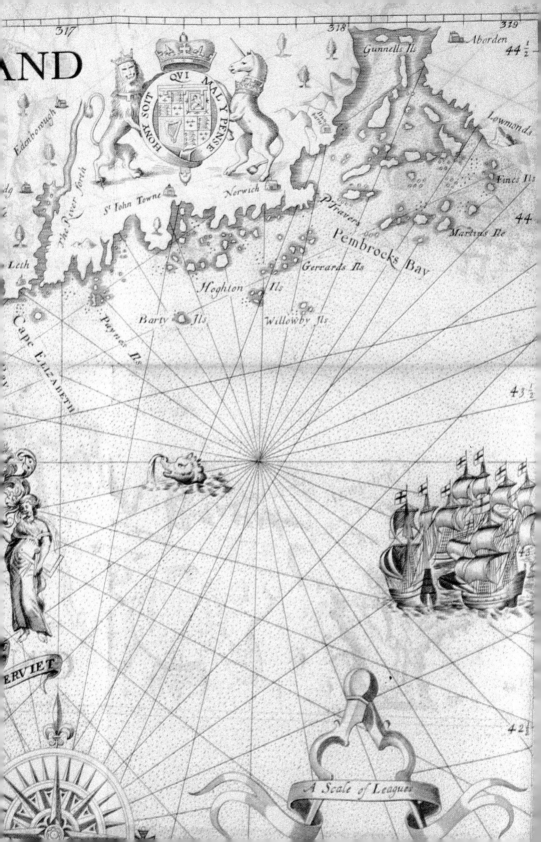

A Finished Place

New England is a finished place. Its destiny is that of Florence or Venice ... while the American empire careens onward towards its unpredictable end ... It is the first American section to be finished, to achieve stability in the conditions of its life. It is the first old civilization, the first permanent civilization in America.

— *Bernard DeVoto*

A crumbling stone fence in the middle of a forest: this is New England. Separating of a different age. The same urge that impelled the explorer to chart an unknown land, the freeman to stake his claim and the immigrant to make his fortune now lead the politician to guide the nation, the engineer to create new technology and the scholar to study the past and plan for the future.

And so the stone fence stands proud. Its people — the newly arrived and those with centuries of American lineage — embody the strength of diversity. Its history — a long trail of advance and retreat — provides an enduring example to inspire and teach. And

trees from other trees, this fence stands as a reminder of what man can and cannot do, of what the pioneers accomplished and what nature has reclaimed, of what New England was and what it is.

The frontier no longer faces the rolling hills and woodlands; the Indians no longer hunt and fish undisturbed; the white man no longer clears the forest to eke out a precarious life. Now, spruces and firs tower over this crumbling stone fence, dwarfing the achievements of those pioneers who toiled so hard in the excitement and uncertainty of a new land.

New England's work, for good or bad, has been done; its limits have been met. But its spirit lives on to grapple with the intricacies its landscape — the elegance of time-worn peaks, the tranquility of forests that will never be conquered, the lulling crash of ocean waves against sand and rock — draws countless visitors to its shores.

Lay of the Land

As defined today, New England encompasses 66,608 square miles (172,514 square kilometers) including the states of Massa-

Precedings pages: New Hamsphire Chelsea; White Mountains; Norwich Vermont; quiet road Jaffrey, N.H; Hampton Beach, New Hamsphire; early English map of region. Above left, a prehistoric inhabitant. Right, primitive tools unearthed in forests.

18

chusetts, Connecticut, Rhode Island, Vermont, New Hampshire and Maine. It is bounded by Canada to the north, the Atlantic Ocean to the east, Long Island Sound to the south, and New York to the west. Moving inland from the coastal lowlands in the south and east, the terrain gradually rises to forested hills and culminates in the weather-beaten peaks of the Appalachian system, represented by the White Mountains to the north and the Green and Taconic Mountains and Berkshire Hills to the west.

Perhaps 2 billion years ago, a vast ocean trough, under the pressure of more than 500,000 cubic miles (2.08 million cubic kilometers) of silt and sediment, was convulsed upward by an upheaval of the earth's crust. The mountains thus created were ancestors of the Appalachians. Its foundation a great buckling fold, the chain continued to shift and shudder.

The intense heat generated by the formation of these mountains metamorphosed sandstone and limestone deposits into the schists and marble now found in the southeastern lowlands and Berkshire Hills of Massachusetts and in Vermont's Green Mountains. Later, streaks of intrusive rocks formed, represented by the granite of Rhode Island, New Hampshire and Maine, and the reddish rocks found in the Connecticut River Valley.

About 200 million years ago, the thrusts from below the earth's crust stopped. The geologic revolution complete, the Appalachians towered about 30,000 feet (some 9,000 meters), the Himalaya of another time.

The elements, unopposed by new surges from below, went to work on the jagged landscape, until much of southern and central New England was no more than a featureless plain. Some outcroppings fared better against the wind and rain than others, accounting for the few scattered mounts that stand unescorted out of the lowlands — now called monadnocks after New Hampshire's Mount Monadnock. (Other examples are Mount Kearsage in New Hampshire and Mount Ascutney in Vermont.) About 8 million years ago, meanwhile, the rest of the flats were gently folded one final time into the hills we see today.

The great swamplands that surrounded the Appalachian core and the hot, muggy climate created the perfect habitat for dinosaurs, the

rulers of the day. Although nature mysteriously decided not to allow these impressive creatures to grace man with their presence, it thoughtfully left traces of their extended stay in New England. Between 200 and 300 million years ago, dinosaurs roamed the Triassic mud of the Newark Bed, which runs approximately along what is now the Connecticut River Valley. Such primitive dinosaurs as *coelophysia* (an early two-legged herbivore), *rhychosaurus* (a tusked four-legger with an eery rodent look) and more than 150 other species of reptiles and amphibians left tracks

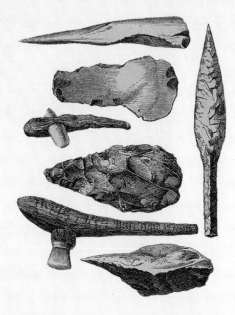

by the thousands in Smith's Ferry and South Hadley in central Massachusetts and, of course, at Dinosaur State Park in Rocky Hill, Connecticut.

Legacy of the Ice Age

The marauding glaciers of the Ice Age added the finishing touches to the landscape. About 1 million years ago, a sudden drop in the world's average summer temperature thickened already existing ice masses to 200 feet (61 meters). Under this pressure, their foundations spread outward, grasping for new ground. Conquering at a rate of 150 feet (46 meters) a year, the glaciers eventually claimed more than one-third of the globe's

total area. Ice swallowed up northeastern America on four different occasions during the Pleistocene Era, retreating and re-advancing over the millennia, finally leaving New England about 10,000 to 12,000 years ago.

This last flooding etched the New England landscape man admires today. Although the glaciers left unchanged the land's basic geologic make-up, they did leave reminders of their former supremacy. Working like steel wool, the glaciers, — often more than two miles (3.2 kilometers) deep — rounded out slopes and valleys from the underlying rock.

Carving scratches (glacial striations) on exposed rock, the glaciers left behind evidence of the path they traveled. Glacial till, the chaff that the ice scraped off the ground, was carried south. As the glaciers receded, this material was left behind; much of New England's bedrock is blanketed with a thin layer of this till, composed of clay, sand and broken rock. Rounded hills of glacial till, called drumlins, are found scattered throughout New England, with Bunker Hill in Boston the most famous.

A similar process gave birth to Cape Cod, Martha's Vineyard and Nantucket Island. Other dramatic legacies of the Ice Age include glacial cirques (large bowl-shaped depressions), glacial erratics (boulders, weighing as much as 5,000 tons, dragged for miles by the moving ice) and kettle lakes (crater-like indentations, of which Walden Pond is a good example). Like the towering Appalachians millions of years ago, many of these features are slowly wearing away. The erosion can only be measured in thousands of years, however, and the distinctiveness these features lend to New England's landscape will survive far into the future.

In 1848, workers laying railroad tracks in Charlotte, Vermont, more than 150 miles (241 kilometers) from the Atlantic Ocean, unearthed the skeleton of an improbable resident, a whale. How could this sea beast have strayed so far from home? When the glaciers melted in force, they released a vast amount of water, perhaps as much as 8 million cubic miles (33.3 million cubic kilometers) worldwide. The floods were great, and the oceans claimed many areas that are landlocked today. In parts of Maine, Atlantic waves crashed against shores up to 75 miles (121 kilometers) inland from the present coastline; Lake Champlain was then

"A Noble Savage": The native New Englander, from an 1876 American history. Most Indians welcomed the new arrivals from England.

a sea which transformed northern New England into an Atlantic peninsula. Evidence of marine activity has been found at points more than 500 feet (152 meters) above the present sea level. Hundreds of lakes and ponds once thrived where there are none today.

The waters gradually evaporated, and New England assumed its present configuration. Tundra plants and (later) trees took hold as the ice and sea receded. A flourishing fauna could live once again on the land but, this time, with a new creature in its midst — man.

Algonquians And
Frustrated Explorers

History remembers success more kindly than it does failure. Although, as the name suggests, it was the English who sowed the seeds of New England's fortune, they were by no means the first to gaze on these northern shores and forests.

Anthropologists generally agree that the first pilgrims to North America were a people of mixed Mongolian descent. Having trekked an overland route across Asia and over the then-frozen Bering Straits, they arrived on the continent between 12 and 25 thousand years ago.

The oldest fossil finds of human activity in New England, uncovered in Shawville, Vermont, and Wapunucket, Massachusetts, date respectively to 9000 and 4000 B.C. and include a variety of spear points, knives, pendants and ancient house floors. These early New England Indians were a primitive people, perhaps skilled in agricultural activities and pottery making, but hardly artistically or architecturally gifted. It is not clear whether these Indians survived as ancestors of the later Algonquians, or whether they slowly died out to extinction. Whatever their fate, their society was an unimposing one.

The Indians were on hand to witness the landing of the Vikings, who were the first documented European visitors to North America. In 1000 A.D., King Olaf of Norway commissioned a young Leif Ericsson to bring Christianity to the new Viking settlement in Greenland, founded only 15 years earlier by Eric the Red, Leif's father. Despite the ungodly winds that blew his *knarr* (Viking longboat) south of his appointed mission, Leif the Lucky lived up to his name and discovered for his sovereign a new land where grapes and wheat grew wild, Vinland the Good.

On hearing Leif's report of the new country, fellow thrill-seeker Thorfin Karlsefni set sail three or four years later with several families and a few cattle, intending to establish a permanent settlement in Vinland. At first, the new frontier treated these Vikings well. They were impressed by the fertile land, the fish-filled streams and the game-packed forests.

Round One to the 'Skrellings'

But the Indians proved too strong for the small band of Norse homesteaders. Initial relations between the two groups were good; although the Vikings thought their hosts deformed and repulsive in appearance, a cordial exchange system was established where Viking cloth was traded for local furs. All was well, says one saga, until the *skrell-*

Island, marks the southernmost extent of their explorations. Other evidence pointing to an 11th Century Norse visit to New England includes a Viking axe discovered at Rocky Nook, Massachusetts (only a few miles from Plymouth Rock); early English accounts of blue-eyed Indians; and reports that Karlsefni and his band wintered in a place without much snow. Dismissing such material as either circumstantial or forged, other historians refuse to believe that the Norse ventured anywhere south of Nova Scotia. Regardless, the debate is only of antiquarian interest: wherever Vinland may have been, it wasn't a lasting accomplishment.

Although the Norse visits would certainly have made suitable material for Indian

ings (Norse for dwarfs) were startled to martial frenzy by a bellowing Viking bull. A fierce battle ensued in which several Vikings fell (including Leif's brother Thorwald). Concluding that "although the country thereabouts was attractive, their life would be one of constant dread and turmoil" because of the natives, Karlsefni and his followers headed home to Greenland. The aborted expedition cured the Vikings of their wanderlust; they did not return.

The Vikings' visit to North America is clearly documented, but exactly where Vinland the Good lies on a contemporary map of North America is a matter of much debate. Some claim that the stump of a round stone tower found in Newport, Rhode

legend, no such oral record endured. No historical continuity has been established between Leif's *skrellings* and the tribes of the Algonquian language group.

The Algonquians

The Algonquians were the Indians of the real Age of Discovery and the Indians who were first befriended and then destroyed by European fortune hunters and refugees. Represented as far west as the Rockies and

According to legend, Vikings reached Cape Cod in craft like the longboat, left, about 1000 A.D. Right, a fanciful recreation of the Viking discovery of America.

as far south as the Carolinas, the Algonquian tribes were related to one another approximately as the French are to the Spanish. Although intertribal communication often demanded an interpretor, each language shared basic grammatical and phonetic constructions.

The Algonquians seeped into the New England forests probably sometime during the 14th or 15th centuries. They did not come in droves; by 1600, no more than 25,000 Indians populated New England, fewer than one for every two square miles (five square kilometers). Nor did this population comprise a unified culture: the Algonquians broke down into at least 10 tribal divisions. Tribes included the Narragansetts of present-day Rhode Island, the Abnaki of

and clothe themselves. With an excellent understanding of agricultural techniques, they grew crops such as beans, pumpkins and tobacco, but relied most heavily on maize, the Indian corn. Meat and fish sufficiently balanced the vegetable fare. Plentiful moose and beaver, turkey and goose, lobsters and clams, salmon and bass, along with other delectables, made for an enviably varied menu.

Everyone contributed to the efficient workings of the typical Algonquian community. While the men took care of the chase, the women sowed and harvested the fields, tended the children, and maintained the portable family wigwams. The Algonquians were, in fact, dumbfounded by the inequity of European sex roles. As one

Maine, the Pennacocks of New Hampshire and the Massachusetts of their namesake, as well as lesser groups such as the Nipmucs, Nausets, Pocumtucks and Niantics. Some tribes could boast no more than 200 or 300 members.

Far from being the crazed nomads of later characterizations, the Algonquians were agricultural and semi-sedentary, wandering little more than the fashionable Bostonians who summer on Cape Cod. Tribal communities moved with the seasons, following established routes restricted to particular tribal domains. In the winter they occupied the sheltered valleys of the interior, in the warmer months the fertile coastal areas. But the Indians had to toil year-round to feed

Englishman reported the Indians' reaction to the white female's social function: "They say *Englishman* much foole, for spoiling good working creature meaning women. And when they see any of our English women sewing with their needles, or working coifes, or such things, they will cry out Lazie *Squaes*!"

It was not all work, however; there was time for fun and games, including the still-popular lacrosse. In the Indian version of that sport, the goalposts were placed more than a mile apart.

Politics and state affairs were left in the charge of the *sachem*, a hereditary chief who commanded each tribe in much the same way that monarchs ruled medieval Europe.

Although men usually controlled the sachemships, there were many cases of women filling the top posts. Sub-*sachems* and war captains, the Indian equivalents of lords and knights, paid material tribute to these rulers and were nominally subject to their will. The *powwows*, or medicine men, gained considerable political might as the vicars of Indian religion. They combined healing with religion and enjoined their parishioners in intense mystical rites.

In no sense did the Algonquians comprise a nation in the modern European style. Unlike their Iroquois neighbors to the west, no council, senate or chief-of-chief disciplined the Algonquian tribes toward unified action. Divided into sachemships, New England's Indians were not simply dis-

The early European explorers of North America were not mere adventurers, but determined fortune hunters seeking an easier passage to the Orient and its treasures. When the Genoese sailor Cristoforo Colombo (better known by the Latinized Christopher Columbus) was trying to persuade a monarch to bankroll his expedition, he spoke of riches and trade and a new path to the wonders of India. So when he returned with a new continent, but with no gold or spices, he was ridiculed and disgraced.

Columbus' countryman Giovanni Caboto (John Cabot), searching for the Northwest Passage to the East, received slightly better treatment from his patron, Henry VII of England. The first European to visit Ameri-

united; they were constantly at each other's throats. "The savages ... for the most part," reported merchant-adventurer George Peckham, "are at continuall warres with their next adjoyning neighbor." These internecine conflicts could be extremely vicious, typified by the grotesque torture of prisoners and the proud parading of a slaughtered adversary's head and hands.

Path to Settlement

Tribal animosities so hardened by generations of battle would later contribute to the Algonquians' downfall by preventing the tribes from unifying against the advancing white settler, a formidable common enemy.

ca's northern shores (at Labrador, historians believe) since the Norse, Cabot was blessed with a whopping royal pension of £20 a year after his 1497 expedition. It was a good bargain for the Crown, considering that England put its claim to all America east of the Rockies and north of Florida, based on the extent of Cabot's exploration.

For the greater part of the 16th Century, Spanish *conquistadores* dominated the New World, where they profitably exploited resource-rich Central and South America.

Left, French explorer Jacques Cartier, who discovered the St.Lawrence River in 1534. Right, Giuseppe da Verrazano, an Italian who charted the New England coast in 1524.

After Cabot's venture, the less inviting and accessible north was largely neglected and the Northwest Passage remained no more than a merchant's dream. Sailing for the French king Francis I, Giovanni da Verrazano travelled the Atlantic seaboard in his *Dolphin* as far north as Narragansett Bay. Jacques Cartier laid the foundation for what would later become New France by navigating the St. Lawrence River. The Portuguese joined the French in fishing the teeming waters of the Grand Banks. But, as yet, there was little talk of settling the then-unchristened land of New England.

The English Take Over

In the closing decades of the 16th Century, Elizabeth I's England eclipsed Spain as master of the seas. Recognizing conquest and colonization as a path to power, the late-starting English were to take over from the *conquistadores* as pioneers of the New World. In 1583, equipped with a royal charter to discover "remote heathen and barbarious land not actually possessed by any Christian prince or people ... and to have, hold, occupy and enjoy" such territories, Sir Humphrey Gilbert was the first Englishman to attempt the settlement of North America. Sailing from Plymouth with his flagship *Delight* and three other vessels, Gilbert intended to establish a trading post at the mouth of the Penobscot River. But after reasserting English control of Newfoundland, he sailed south to disaster. The expedition never reached its goal: three out of the four ships sank and Gilbert himself lost his life.

The misfortune of Gilbert proved only a temporary inhibition to other pathmakers. The first years of the 17th Century saw a renewed interest in exploration. Between 1602 and 1606, expeditions led by Bartholomew Gosnold, Martin Pring and George Weymouth went smoothly and, although not ambitious enough to plant settlements, these voyages did discover a commercial lure to New England — plentiful sassafras bark, then considered a powerful cure-all. Weymouth brought back to England another er interesting cargo — five Indians abducted from the coast of Maine.

In 1606, James I granted charters for two new ventures, the Virginia Companies of London and Plymouth, giving the latter rights to found a colony somewhere between North Carolina and Nova Scotia. Directed by luminaries such as Sir Ferdinando Gorges, Raleigh Gilbert (son of Sir Humphrey) and the veteran Pring, 100 adventurers set out from Plymouth in early 1607. Loaded with the usual arms and foodstuffs, some livestock and trinkets to trade with the natives, the crew built Fort St. George on Parker's Island in Maine. There they wintered, but, finding no evidence of precious metals, and the weather "extreme unseasonable and frosty," the group abandoned its foothold the following spring.

Recognizing the need to plan more carefully, the Plymouth Company next commissioned the experienced surveyor John Smith to take a critical look at the region's potential for settlement and profit. Smith is credited as the first to give the region its name of "New England."

Although the early English pioneers had come no closer to establishing a permanent settlement in New England than had their Viking predecessors, their eyewitness descriptions — the guidebooks of other times — painted an attractive picture for those who would soon be seeking refuge from their mother country. John Smith wrote in his widely circulated *Description of New England:*

"And surely by reason of those sandy cliffes and cliffes of rocks, both which we saw so planted with Gardens and Corne fields, and so well inhabited with a goodly, strong and well proportioned people, besides the greatnesse of the Timber growing on Them, the greatnesse of the fish and moderate temper of the ayre ... who can but approve this a most excellent place, both for health & fertility? And of all the four parts of the world that I have seen not inhabited, could I have but means to transport a Colonie, I would rather live here than anywhere ..."

Smith's dreams would soon come true. Determination would triumph, the new land would be settled.

Answering a Higher Call

"What the Puritans gave the world was not thought, but action."
— *Horace Greeley*

The explorers of the 16th Century were driven by the profit motive. Since they discovered neither the coveted Northwest Passage nor gold and diamonds, they couldn't discern the promise of the New World. Decades of work produced no more than a few crude maps and travelogues. The Cabots and Gosnolds and Weymouths were not interested in settling New England; only à higher call would people the new land.

Renaissance Europe could not imagine religious tolerance. Dissent was treason, and heretics mounted the same scaffolds as did traitors. To the Puritans, who were devotees of more extreme Protestant beliefs, the symbols of papal domination — jeweled miters, elaborate rituals and power-hungry bishops — were the Devils' work. Satan himself was said to be a representative of the Apostolic See.

Perhaps even more disturbing to the Puritans was the persecution they suffered under Catholic sympathizer James I. The Puritans had enjoyed years of respectability during Elizabeth I's reign. Their followers included highly placed academics and public officials, many merchants and local clergymen. The

shock of disgrace under James I, therefore, was all the more frightful. The new king wasn't lopping off any heads, but harassment went beyond mere inconvenience. "Some were taken, & clapt up in prison, others had their houses besett & watcht night and day, & hardly escaped their lands," related Puritan leader William Bradford in his oft-quoted *History of Plimouth Plantation,* "and ye most were faine too flie & leave their houses & habitations; and the means of their livelihood."

Where to? In 1602, a group of several hundred Puritans from the county of Lincolnshire migrated to the quaint college town of Leyden, Holland, but they did not prosper. The exacting Puritans found their travel along the True Path hindered by the fact that "the morals of the people in the Low Countries were loose." And so, the Puritans struck a deal with the Plymouth Company to finance a settlement in the unpopulated north of America. In the early summer of 1620, 66 of the Leyden community sailed with the *Speedwill* from Delftshaven to Southampton to prepare for the trials that lay ahead. "They knew they were pilgrims," Bradford wrote upon their departure, and so they are remembered by history.

Leaving from Plymouth on the 180-ton *Mayflower*, the Pilgrims packed everything they needed to start and maintain a self-sufficient community. The trip itself was no luxury cruise and after more than two months at sea, the travelers "were not a little joyful" to sight Cape Cod on November 11. Deciding that the sandy cape was not the best place to till the land, the group dispatched Captain Miles Standish (nicknamed "Captain Shrimp" because of his height) to find a more fertile site. In mid December, the Pilgrims debarked at Plymouth Rock.

The first winter was a miserable ordeal, testing fully the hardened Puritan will. Scurvy, pneumonia and other infections killed more than half of the settlers, including Governor John Carver and the wives of Bradford and Standish. At any one time, no more than six or seven remained in good health. But with warmer weather came better times and the critical cooperation of the local Indians. As luck would have it, Squanto, one of those brought back to England by George Weymouth, had returned to his homeland and was there to greet the Pilgrims. Squanto persuaded Massasoit, the local *sachem,* to help the beleaguered English pioneers. A treaty of friendship was signed.

Heavenly Aspirations

Acknowledging the native contribution, the Pilgrims hosted a feast of celebratiion nearing the first anniversary of their arrival. In this first Thanksgiving, red man and white man together enjoyed a meal of roasted game (including turkey), eel, fruits, vegetables and cornbread. A few weeks later, 35 new freedom-seekers, packed with provisions joined the *Mayflower* survivors, and by the spring of 1624, Plymouth was a thriving village of more than 30 cottages.

Left, the seal of the Plymouth Colony. Right, a typical Pilgrim Thanksgiving reenacted at Plymouth. Over 4½ centuries later, New Englanders take great pride in their heritage.

With tracts such as Edward Winslow's *Good Newes From New England* making their way back to the mother country, more settlers overcame an understandable timidity to join the religious migration.

In 1628 another group of Puritans, led by Thomas Dudley, Thomas Leverett and John Winthrop, obtained a royal charter as the "Company of the Massachusetts Bay in New England." The next summer, 350 hopefuls arrived at Salem, followed by another 1,500 in 1630. Like the Pilgrims before them, these later settlers suffered many casualties during the early days. But they, too, were determined not only to establish themselves permanently in the New World but also to live fully their religious ideals, in order to become an example for the chosen.

settlement every year between 1630 and 1637, and, to accommodate these arrivals, new communities such as Ipswich, Dorchester, Concord (the first inland village), Dedham and Watertown, sprang up.

In 1636, the Puritan clergy established Harvard College to train future ministers. A General Court was formed to manage administrative and judicial affairs, a governor and deputy governor being indirectly chosen by the colony's freeholders (those who owned Bay Company stock). At lower levels of government, the founders of each town ordinarily convened to confront problems of general interest; this was an entirely practical mechanism of administration given that, even as late as 1700, the average town included no more than 200 or 300 families.

"For wee must consider that wee shall be as a Citty upon a hill," Governor Winthrop declared. "The eies of all people are upon us; so that if we shall deale falsely with our god in this worke…wee shall shame the faces of many of God's worthy servants, and cause theire prayers to be turned into Cursses upon us till wee be consumed out of the good land." Driven by such heavenly aspirations, these religious refugees fared well with their worldly pursuits. The founding of New England was a Puritan achievement.

As Charles I and his Archbishop William Laud tightened the screws of persecution back home, the Massachusetts Bay Colony grew quickly despite primitive conditions. An estimated 2,000 immigrants joined the

Growth was not limited to the immediate area of the first landings on the Massachusetts shore. The reverends Thomas Hooker and Samuel Stone, along with former Bay governor John Haynes, left Cambridge for Connecticut, where they settled the towns of Hartford, Wethersfield and Windsor. Londoners Theophilus Eaton and John Davenport soon after established themselves at New Haven. The Plymouth colony had been operating a trading post on Maine's Kennebec River since 1627, and New World magnates John Mason and Ferdinando Gorges tried to develop vast property grants in New Hampshire and Maine, but these ventures were humbled by the region's obvious inhospitality.

Elsewhere, groups of New Englanders helped pave the frontiers outside the region. Puritan communities transplanted to New York, North Carolina and Georgia maintained ties with their old homes. One such group, originally from Westmorland, Connecticut, continued to send representatives to the Connecticut Assembly long after moving to Pennsylvania.

The social satirist and Revolutionary War general Artemus Ward once observed: "The Puritans nobly fled from a land of despotism to a land of freedom, where they could not only enjoy their own religion, but could prevent everybody else from enjoying his." Dictating rules of conduct not just for the church but for all worldly pursuits (theater, for example, was banned until the late

from his pulpit in Salem that "forced worship stinks in God's nostrils." Williams' compatriots in the General Court banished him from the colony in 1636.

But Williams did not return to England. He turned instead to Canonicus and Miantonomi, the two Narragansett *sachems* whom he had befriended in the course of studying the native population. The chieftains saw fit to grant him, *gratis*, a large tract on the Pawtuxet River. Here, Williams founded the town of Providence. Fellow exiles joined him over the next few years — Anne Hutchinson (mother of 15) and William Coddington on nearby Rhode Island (so named after a fancied resemblance to the Greek isle of Rhodes), and Samuel Gorton in Warwick.

1700s) as ungodly, their rigorous Calvinistic standards made the Puritans far less tolerant of social or theological deviation than their oppressors back in England had been. Indeed, in 1661, the king himself intervened to protect Quakers in the Bay Colony after several were hanged publicly on the Boston Common. As has often been the case in American history, tragic deeds of injustice belied the ringing slogans of liberty.

Such intolerances did, however, bear an unwanted but ultimately productive child in the new colony of Rhode Island. In the early years of Massachusetts Bay, the Reverend Roger Williams, a graduate of Cambridge University, took it upon himself to protest the shackles of imposed religion, preaching

Though the new settlement grew slowly — from fewer than 20 families in 1638 to no more than 1,000 individuals three decades later — the Providence and Rhode Island plantations proved an unholy thorn in Massachusetts' underbelly. No kind words here: Hutchinson, with her "very voluble tongue," lambasted her former parish with "Call it whore and strumpet not a Church of Christ"; while back in Massachusetts, the ordinarily restrained Cotton Mather continually insulted the colony as the "fag end of

The Puritans exaggerated native Indian ferocity and persecuted settlers who held divergent religious views. Left, barricading a house against Indian attack. Right, a pillory.

creation," "the sewer of New England" and, ever so cleverly, "Rogue's Island." But Rhode Island lived up to its intent, and religious freedom was guaranteed by a 1663 royal charter. Aside from outcast Puritans, the new community welcomed New England's first Jewish Lémigrés in 1662, along with scores of Quakers and French Huguenots.

A much worse oppression than Williams had suffered was imposed upon the indigenous population. Although the Puritans owed much to the Algonquians for their co-operation in the early days of settlement, and although they were not racially prejudiced against the Indians (one contemporary theory held that they were descended from a lost tribe of Israel), the Puritans soon assumed the self-appointed task of converting their new found neighbors from their heathen ways.

Missionary efforts did show some initial promise. The Bible was translated into the Algonquian language. The Reverend John Eliot set up a string of "Praying Towns," along the Connecticut River and near Cape Cod, in which Christian Algonquians had their own preachers, teachers and magistrates. During the 1660s and early 1670s, these communities may have accounted for as many as one-fifth of all New England Indians. But the Puritans were looking for more than religious fellow-travelers; they sought nothing less than a breed of neo-Englishmen. As historian Alden T. Vaughan concluded, the Indians would have had to "forsake their theology, their language, their political and economic structures, their habitations and clothing, their social mores, their customs of work and play" — in short, commit cultural suicide — to sufficiently please the white New Englander.

Along these lines, several Algonquians were sent to Harvard for ministerial training, but only Caleb Cheeshahteaumuck, Class of 1665, graduated. Many natives took to drinking the "strong water" introduced by the English, and were chastised for their supposed indolence, a cardinal Puritan sin. A few Indians might have made the crossing to "civilization," but to expect all to do so was unreasonable and typical of a profound disrespect for a proud society. The frustrated evangelists could now justify more inhuman pursuits.

It was empire-building that provided the real motivation for bloodshed. At first, there was plenty of room for the Indians and settlers to coexist peacefully. About a third of the Algonquian inhabitants had fallen victim to a great plague in the early 1600s;

only about 16,000 populated New England at the time of the landing of the *Mayflower*. And as the English pushed south, the Indians realized that the white man intended to expand his holdings.

In 1636 war erupted with the Pequots (a fearsome tribe whose name means "destroyer" in Algonquian), and battles at Fort Mystic and Fairfield, Connecticut, saw several hundred lives lost on both sides. It was King Philip's War (1675-76), however, that marked the demise of Indian society in most of New England. The Nipmuck, Narragansett and Wampanoag forces, nominally led by Philip (whose real name was Metacom), suffered from chronic tribal disunity and were outnumbered by at least five to one. At the "Great Swamp Fight" near

present-day South Kingston, Rhode Island, 2,000 Narragansetts were slain (many of them women and children trapped in burning wigwams) in one of the fiercest battles ever fought on New England soil. The Indian will was broken; for them, the war had been a veritable holocaust.

With missionary targets gone and increasing numbers of non-Puritan immigrants diluting the ascetic zeal of the first settlers, the moral climate of New England degenerated considerably during the 18th Century. In the bustling port of Boston, prostitutes roamed the streets, and as many as half of all first children were born out of wedlock. Politics, not religion, would be the rallying call of a new era.

Painted by Chappel.

Engraved by Phillibrown.

BATTLE OF BUNKER'S HILL.

From the original painting in the possession of the Publishers.

Johnson, Fry & Co. Publishers, New York.

Entered according to Act of Congress A.D. 1859 by Johnson, Fry & Co. in the clerks office of the district court of the southern district of New York.

Q: ... were you not oppressed by the Stamp Act?

A: I never saw one of those stamps. I certainly never paid a penny for one of them.

Q: Well, then, what was the matter? And what did you mean in going in the fight?

A: Young man, what we meant in going for those Redcoats was this: we always had governed ourselves, and we always meant to. They didn't mean we should.

— Captain Preston, a veteran of the Revolutionary War, interviewed by Mallen Chamberlain in 1842.

Politics were not new to New England. But the northern colonies had, for the most part, been left to their own devices from the first landing at Plymouth up until the dramatic Stamp Act crisis of 1765. When the mother country attempted to leash in her distant child, the reaction had been quick and biting, a portent of the more drastic rebellion which lay ahead.

Suffering serious political turmoil in the early 17th Century, highlighted by the beheading of Charles I and the subsequent ascendancy of Great Protector Oliver Cromwell, England had little time to attend to the governing of dissident settlers 3,000 miles from London. The Puritans gladly filled the vacuum and took on the responsibilities of *de facto* autonomy. Even before reaching their destination, the Pilgrims signed the famous Mayflower Compact, creating a government "to enact, constitute, and frame such just and equal Laws, Ordinances, Acts, Constitutions, and Offices, from time to time, as shall be thought most meet and convenient for the general good." John Winthrop and his followers carried with them their royal charter when they sailed to Massachusetts, and in 1631 the freemen of the new colony gave an oath of fidelity not to the King but to the Bay Company and its officers. The settlers agreed that if England tried to impose its

own governor, "we ought not to accept him, but defend our lawful possessions."

Dominion Days

Fifty-five years later, they were given the chance. In 1686, James II unilaterally revoked the northern colonies' sacred charters and consolidated English holdings from Maine to New Jersey into a vast Dominion of New England in America. The monarch justified his decision as a security measure, a benevolent protection from the

French and Indians. The colonists knew better: who could presume that the Puritans would graciously kowtow to a royally appointed governor? The king's first envoy, Joseph Dudley, an avid Anglican, was scorned as having "as many virtues as can consist with so great a thirst for honor and power." His successor, Edmund Andros, was ridiculed as "the greatest tyrant who ever ruled in this country." When the new administration extorted taxes, "ill Methods of Raising money without a General Assembly," the disenfranchised populace grew further incensed.

A strong cue from England itself moved New England to action and revolt. At the "Glorious Revolution" of early 1689,

Preceding pages: a Revolutionary reenactment. Left, the Battle of Bunker's Hill, a turning point in the war. Right, General Thomas Gage, British colonial governor of Massachusetts.

William and Mary, in cahoots with Parliament, seized the throne from James II. New England spontaneously erupted; Andros and his cronies were dragged from statehouse to jail cell. The old powers of self-government were largely restored, along with a certain mutual respect between Crown and colonies. Though only three years long, the Dominion days had nonetheless decisively molded the New Englander's political instinct.

But Hanoverian monarch George III would have a prostrate America, or none at all. London's first *faux pas* on the road to losing her New World empire was the Revenue Act of 1764, which imposed duties on sugar, silk and certain wines. The tax was duly denounced and boycotts proclaimed.

Minister Charles Townshend boasting before the Commons, "I dare tax America," Parliament passed the Townsend Acts, imposing harsh duties on such imports as paper, glass and tea. Two regiments of British troops landed at Boston to put some muscle behind Governor Hutchinson's waning control.

A Massacre and a Tea Party

The Redcoats were not pleasantly received. On the night of March 5, 1770, a crowd of several hundred rowdy Bostonians gathered to taunt a lone "lobster-back" standing guard outside the customs house on King Street (present-day State Street). When shouts turned to stones and snow-

The infamous Stamp Act followed a year later, requiring that all commercial and legal documents, newspapers and playing cards be taxed. The measure was fiercely assailed. Stamp distributors were hanged in effigy and ridiculed at mock trials. Liberty was buried in symbolic funerals. Citizens of all stripes throughout New England, both of city and country, gathered to decry the new tax. Many of the demonstrations were peaceful but, in Boston, mobs ransacked the houses of stampman Andrew Oliver and Governor Thomas Hutchinson. Parliament, led by commoner William Pitt, took the hint and repealed the Stamp Act in March 1766.

But England had not learned a proper lesson. In the summer of 1767, with Prime

balls, seven Redcoats came to aid the sentry. One fired into the melee without orders, others followed, and after the smoke had cleared, three colonists lay dead (including a Black man named Crispus Attucks) and two were mortally wounded. The American revolt had its first martyrs, and the growing anti-British element in New England had a field day with the nocturnal showdown.

Tempers cooled after the Boston Massacre. In the early 1770s, economic prosperity returned to the colonies. A once-again pragmatic Parliament struck down the Town-

Left, "Retreat of the British from Concord." As the Redcoats fled from the colonies, enthusiastic citizens raised their "Liberty" flag over the land. It still waves in Deerfield, Massachusetts, right.

shend Acts — all except one, that is. Just to make sure nobody questioned who was still boss — or king — England maintained the tax on East Indian tea, a not-insignificant gesture given that tea was about as important as bread to the 18th Century diet. American addicts fled to smuggled Dutch blends or to "Liberty Tea," a nasty brew made from sage, currant or plantain leaves. The British responded by subsidizing their brand and, in September 1773, flooded the market with about half a million pounds of the "pestilential herb," with shipments to points all along the Eastern seaboard. It didn't work.

Boston emerged once again as the focus of resistance. The Massachusetts Committee of Correspondence, an unofficial legislature;

Most infamous, the Boston Port Act sealed off the city by naval blockade. The colonies wouldn't take any more. The First Continental Congress convened in Philadelphia on Sept. 5, 1774. Revolution was at hand.

A Shot Heard Round the World

An uneasy stalemate prevailed from the fall of 1774 to the spring of 1775. British garrisons controlled only the major towns. The countryside became virtually unpoliceable. New Englanders stockpiled arms and ammunition in farmhouses and barns to prepare for inevitable conflict.

The rebels didn't have to wait long for war. In early April 1775, London instructed Boston commander General Thomas Gage

and the local chapter of the Sons of Liberty, a fast-growing pseudo-secret society at the forefront of revolutionary activism; barred the piers and demanded that Governor Hutchinson send the tea-laden *Dartmouth* home. When he refused, the protesters' reaction was swift and theatrical. On December 16, 60 men (among them Sam Adams and John Hancock) disguised as Mohawk Indians and Blacks, descended on the *Dartmouth* and two sister ships. Boston Harbor became a giant teapot as 342 crates were dumped over the railings.

The Boston Tea Party, as it came to be called, was a display of profound disrespect to the Londoners. Parliament leveled the so-called Coercive Acts on an uppity America.

to quash seditious activities in rural Massachusetts, where a Provincial Congress had assumed *de facto* governmental control. Late on the night of April 18, Gage accordingly dispatched a contingent of 700 soldiers to destroy a makeshift arms depot in Concord, 20 miles (32 kilometers) west of Boston. At Lexington 70 ragtag colonial soldiers, the original Minutemen, lay in wait by dawn's light, having been forewarned by the daring early-morning rides of patriots Paul Revere and William Dawes.

The two forces met on the town common. A musket was fired. Minutes later, eight Americans lay dead. The unscathed Brits continued on to Concord where the colonial militia triggered, in Ralph Waldo Emerson's words, "the shot heard round the world." The Minutemen made up for what they lacked in numbers by employing unconventional guerrilla tactics, harassing their enemies with crack sniper fire. By nightfall they had knocked off 273 English soldiers.

Sensationalist accounts of these initial skirmishes sent settlers from Maine to Georgia reaching for their rifles. "The devastation committed by the British troops on their retreat," reported one, "is almost beyond description, such as plundering and burning of dwelling houses and other buildings, driving into the street women in child bed, killing old men in their houses unarmed. ..." Among the dead bodies, the card of compromise lay discarded.

The first major engagement of the war,

bravery, that Colonel William Prescott issued his famous command: "Don't fire until you see the whites of their eyes, men."

Bunker Hill was an expensive triumph for the Crown, which suffered more than 1,000 casualties. Optimism, seen in remarks like General John Burgoyne's "We'll soon find elbow room," was reduced to the doubting reflections of another British officer: "This victory has cost us very dear indeed. ...Nor do I see that we enjoy one solid benefit in return, or likely to reap from it any one advantage whatever." Less than a year later, an embattled General Gage evacuated his troops to Halifax.

A few months later, on July 4, 1776, the Declaration of Independence was adopted by the Continental Congress. Of the proud

the Battle of Bunker Hill, broke out in June on the Charlestown peninsula, across the Charles River from Boston. To consolidate control of overland access to the port city, Continental Army General Artemus Ward ordered the fortification of Bunker's Hill (as it was then known), although it was actually on adjoining Breed's Hill that the Americans dug in.

The British could not allow such a buildup if they were to entertain even the faintest hope of holding Boston. On June 17, Redcoats scaled Breed's slopes twice but were rebuffed. In a desperate third attempt they succeeded, but only because the colonial force had exhausted its supply of ammunition. It was for this reason, and not out of

signatories, 14 came from the charter states of Massachusetts, Connecticut, New Hampshire and Rhode Island. Except for Newport, Rhode Island, which was not taken from the British until October 1779, the rest of New England had won its independence.

Once the Revolutionary War was over in 1781, the magnates of New England's prosperous cities turned to protect their newly established interests as the 13 independent colonies hammered out an integrated union. Concerned that a centralized federal

One of the earliest sources of New England's wealth was whaling, left. The 19th Century saw many improvements in transportation, including the Fall River paddle steamer, right.

government would prove as insensitive to local sentiment as had the Crown, revolutionary heroes Sam Adams and John Hancock gave only grudging support to the Constitution. Rhode Island, in more than a dozen votes between 1787 and 1789, voted down the Constitution and only ratified it after the Bill of Rights was added.

The Industrial Age: Cash and Culture

New England's leaders became increasingly reactionary as they went about guarding their economic interests. In Massachusetts, poor farmers of the hill country rose up against the state government during Shays' Rebellion of 1786, demonstrating

there, the rum was transported to Africa where it was traded for slaves who were shipped to the West Indies and, in turn, traded for molasses. New England shipyards gained world fame for crafting swift, easily managed ocean-going vessels, a tradition launched even before Pilgrim settlement with the construction of the *Virginia* in the short-lived Popham, Maine, colony in 1607.

Disrupted by the Revolution, maritime trade bounced back quickly, mining the riches of China and India so coveted by the early American explorers. In 1792, Boston's *Columbia* threaded the Straits of Magellan en route Canton to trade for tea, spices, silk and opium. The magnates of rival Salem — Elias Haskett Derby, Joseph Peabody and Billy Gray — preferred to sail east, skirting

that genuine equality remained a far-off dream. And in 1812, fearing the loss of a thriving maritime trade, New England emerged firmly opposed to renewed conflict with Great Britain.

When not calling comrades to religious or political barricades, the colonial New Englander attended to the more practical pursuit of commerce: it was out of and on the seas that New England's money was made.

Codfish and whale products provided a lucrative export to Catholic Europe. New England was at the pivot of the profitable triangular trade: in harbors like Newport, a fleet of 350 ships unloaded West Indian molasses and reloaded it with rum. From

the southern tip of Africa on frequent and tremendously successful ventures to the Orient.

But, alas, the first two decades of the 19th Century demonstrated how vulnerable maritime trade was to the whims of international politics. The Napoleonic Wars, President Thomas Jefferson's Embargo Acts and the War of 1812 ("Mr. Madison's War") severely hampered New England's chase after an honest, apolitical dollar. Recognizing that it is not best to put all one's commercial eggs in one flimsy basket, her merchants turned to the herald of a new industrial age.

In the fall of 1789, a teenaged Samuel Slater sailed from England to New York disguised as a common laborer. Slater departed in defiance of British laws forbidding the emigration of skilled mechanics. For seven years Slater had apprenticed to Jedediah Strutt, a partner of famed industrial innovator Richard Arkwright, and had memorized the specifications of Arkwright's factory-sized cotton-spinning machine.

In America, the reduction of raw cotton was still being done by the notoriously inefficient "put-out" system, where laborers worked in their own homes on individual looms. An early attempt at consolidating the process, a mill at Beverly, Massachusetts, had been a miserable failure owing to the crudeness of its machinery. Arkwright's device, already proven across the Atlantic, was the answer. In December, Quaker financier Moses Brown engaged Slater to

he collected another $90,000 from the so-called "Boston Associates" — the families of Lawrence, Cabot, Eliot, Higginson and others — to establish a small mill (with a power loom and 1,700 spindles) at Waltham.

Lowell died in 1817, but his plans were realized by his associates under the aegis of the Merrimack Manufacturing Company. In 1820, the mill was moved to a tract on the Merrimack River, just above the tiny village of Chelmsford.

A 'Commercial Utopia'

Paying dividends as high as 28 percent, the operation was wildly profitable. Sales went from a respectable $3,000 in 1815 to an unprecedented $345,000 in 1822; 100,000

come to Providence and put his knowledge to use. Together, they built America's first successful cotton mill on the Blackstone River at Pawtucket.

Its underpaid workers kept at the grind 60 or 70 hours a week. Before long, Pawtucket became the site of the nation's first strike in 1800. It was left to Bostonian Francis Cabot Lowell (from the family that would later produce a Harvard president, a celebrated astronomer and a cigar-smoking poetess) to take a more enlightened approach.

During a two-year visit to England, Lowell became an avid industrial tourist, and on his return to Massachusetts, he was determined to duplicate British weaving feats. Putting up $10,000 of his own money,

spindles wove more than 30 miles (48 kilometers) of cloth daily. In 1826, the growing community was named after its founder.

The Merrimack Company took care of its people. Young lady workers "mill girls" were housed in comfortable dormitories where protection of their morals was attended to scrupulously. New England had its first company town which was, in the words of English novelist Anthony Trollope, "the realization of commercial utopia."

As had been the case with politics during

The late 19th Century saw new offices and factories erected throughout New England. Left, the U.S. Custom House and Post Office in Fall River, Massachusetts; right, a woolen mill in the same city.

the revolution, New England was the acknowledged center of industrial America. The region boasted two-thirds of the nation's cotton mills, half of them in Massachusetts; tiny Rhode island alone processed more than 20 percent of America's wool. In Connecticut, Sam Colt (of six-shooter fame) and Eli Whitney, better known for his invention of the cotton gin, manufactured the first firearms with interchangeable parts. Edward Howard applied the same concept with his Roxbury wristwatch business, using screws so minute that 2,000 of them weighed not a pound. In the paper, shoe and metalworking industries, New England also stood unchallenged. The Connecticut firm of Edward and William Pattison minted coins for South American governments. Indeed, even

pioneers set up small farms, built their own houses and barns, and raised wheat, corn, pigs and cattle to fill the dinner table. These rugged families were almost completely self-sufficient. In the Berkshires, a family might need only $10 a year to supplement their own labors. This was the frontier, New England's West.

But this frontier's potential was limited by nature. The climate was inhospitable: in 1816, for instance, a June snowfall resulted in total crop failure. Agricultural machinery could not plough the irregular farmland. Property consolidation was difficult as families jealously guarded original claims; small-scale production could not compete with more efficient new suppliers elsewhere in the United States and around the world.

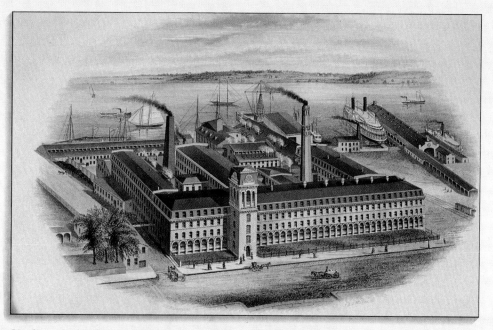

Yankee ingenuity stopped at nothing; Boston's Frederick Tudor made a fortune exporting thousands of tons of ice to places as far away as Calcutta.

Life on the Frontier

Not everybody shared in the boom. During the last half of the 18th Century, northern New England had enjoyed a dramatic infusion of people, as land grew scarce in the densely populated coastal areas. More than 100 new towns were established in New Hampshire in the 15 years preceding the Revolution; between 1790 and 1800, the populations of Vermont and Maine nearly doubled. On the craggy hillsides, the

Save for a few scattered industrial concentrations like Manchester, New Hampshire, northern New England had seen its zenith by 1850.

After that, a slow, sapping decline attacked upland vitality. By the turn of the century, population growth had leveled and agricultural production dived. More than half of New Hampshire's farmland lay abandoned. Cheese production in Maine, New Hampshire and Vermont fell by some 95 percent between 1849 and 1919. Young men went off on the more promising Western trials, girls to the Massachusetts mills.

The hill country's plight was much lamented in the national press, hardly a week passing without a painful description of a newly ghosted upland town. *The Nation*'s C.G. Nott asked, "What shall the New England farmer do?" He could do nothing but move.

Cultural Laurels

Long before the wheels of industry started to churn, New England minds had been hard at work thinking big thoughts, putting them on paper and canvas and, in the process, establishing a cultural life unparalleled in the New World. In education, the media, the arts and letters, America looked to New England for guidance and inspiration. New England ushered in the first great flowering of American culture with Boston — variously dubbed the Athens of America and the Hub — leading the way.

As one might expect, New England boasted the laurels of many cultural firsts. Ever mindful of the intellectual responsibilities of being God's chosen, the Puritans had hardly built their churches before they set about looking after the proper education of their future clergymen. The nation's first secondary school, Boston Latin, opened its doors in 1635, and Harvard College, destined to join Oxford and Cambridge among the world's finest academic institutions, was founded the next year. Comely New Haven's Yale followed in 1701, established by a cabal of young Harvard graduates.

During the 18th Century, New Englanders continued to establish colleges that today number among the finest in the country — Rhode Island College, founded in 1764 and later renamed Brown University; Dartmouth College, established in 1769; and Bowdoin College in Maine, which counts among its alumni, Nathaniel Hawthorne, Henry Wadsworth Longfellow, Admiral Robert Peary and President Franklin Pierce.

While colonial classes often had fewer than a dozen students, the early settlers attended to the education of those not able to beef up their résumés with college degrees. In 1639, a printing press was assembled in Cambridge. Its early releases included the *Bay Psalm Book*, the *New England Primer* and the freeman's oath of loyalty to Massachusetts. In 1690, the colonies' first newspaper, *Publick Occurrences Both Foreign and Domestick*, appeared in Boston but was succeeded by the more popular *Boston News-Letter* in 1704. Other memorable tabloids, including the *Rehearsal*, *The Massachusetts Spy* and the *Independent Advertiser*, kept New England informed, if not always accurately, as the country roared to revolution. By the 1850s, the region hosted no less than 424 periodical publications. "All these people busy themselves with politics," observed French maxim-writer Duc de la Rochefoucauld, "and from the landlord to the housemaid they all read two newspapers a day."

Libraries, meanwhile, gave the common man the chance to investigate the issues of his day, and of other days, in greater depth. The Wadsworth Atheneum in Hartford, founded in 1842, and the Providence Atheneum, a haunt of Edgar Allen Poe, provided members access to impressive collections and cultural events. By 1854, when the Boston Public Library became the world's first free municipal library, almost 750,000 volumes lined the shelves of hundreds of less ambitious local depositories.

Sophisticated Tastes

"High culture," traditionally a preserve of the privileged classes, was similarly opened up to broader audiences during the late 19th Century. In 1871 came the Museum of Fine Arts. The Boston Symphony Orchestra, established a decade later by Brahmin Henry Lee Higginson, took its place among the globe's foremost ensembles. The BSO's summer festival at Tanglewood in the Berkshires (inaugurated in 1936) today flourishes as a mecca for music lovers the world over. The Boston Pops conducted its first concert in 1885. Boasting the Long Wharf, Schubert and Yale Repertory theaters, the New Haven stage has become an influential force on the American cultural scene.

Such institutional achievements are impressive. But behind them lay great individual minds, the region's many intellectual and artistic giants. Numbered among these were transcendentalist philosher and essayist Henry David Thoreau (1817-1862), famed for his celebration of nature in *Walden*; painter Winslow Homer (1836-1910), whose powerful marine watercolors now hang in New England's finest art galleries; and poetess Emily Dickinson (1830-1886), whose solitary, unconventional work brought posthumous fame.

The cultural roster does not end here. The painting of John Singleton Copley, and the prose and poetry of Ralph Waldo Emerson, Henry Wadsworth Longfellow, John Greenleaf Whittier, Nathaniel Hawthorne, Herman Melville, Robert Lowell and Robert Frost, are acclaimed the world over. Each of their lives testifies to the spirit and lofty ideals of New England.

The faces that built New England: a composite of portraits of the leaders of 19th Century manufacturing and industry.

The prosperity of my native land, New England, which is sterile and unproductive, must depend hereafter on the moral qualities, and secondly, on the intelligence and information of the inhabitants.

John Lowell, Jr.

By the beginning of this century, New England had done all that it could. It had been America's leader in politics, in economics, in culture. In many ways, New England was America, epitomizing its ideals, drive, determination and success.

— New England suffered in Washington. The region no longer bounded a physical or psychological frontier; it was not here that battles had to be fought, decisions made, leaders trained and tested. The White House was no longer the domain of Harvard and the Adamses.

New England turned to the task of managing itself after two last gasps of political pre-eminence — the abolitionist crusade against slavery led by William Lloyd Garrison and his *Liberator* in the years before the Civil War; and the social-reform movements

Heliotype Print. HOTEL BRUNSWICK. TRINITY CHURCH.

HOTEL BRUNSWICK, BOYLSTON STREET, BOSTON.

Barnes & Dunklee, Proprietors.

The heights attained, however, New England could not help but falter and descend. Aging and tired, it did not adapt well; others more fresh took to the nation's command. Europe looks for guidance to Florence and Venice no longer. They are nice places to visit.

Political Decay

The symptoms of political decay emerged both at the national level, where New England's influence diminished, and locally, where corruption and social divisions humbled once proud democracy. If only by virtue of America's physical expansion — the great westward surge of the 19th Century

of the late 1800s, intent on correcting shocking conditions in the nation's prisons, mental institutions and public hospitals.

Difficulties on the homefront were formidable indeed. Most important, ethnic and religious homogeneity, so conducive to forging political consensus, eroded dramatically as migrating flocks of non-Anglo, non-Protestants hit the northern shores. Uprooted by the Great Potato Famine of 1840, the Irish packed their belongings and sailed with high hopes to the land of opportunity. Two

Left, one of the nation's first apartment houses was this 19th Century block in Back Bay, Boston. Right, a happy day at Orchard Beach, Maine, during the Gay Nineties.

centuries after the *Mayflower*, they arrived in Boston at a rate of more than 1,000 a month. Others, primarily Catholic, followed from Italy, French Canada, Portugal and Eastern Europe.

In Massachusets, immigration accounted for two-thirds of the total population growth during the 19th Century. By 1907, almost 70 percent of that state was of foreign stock (at least one parent born outside the United States), most of whom looked to Rome in spiritual matters. The influx touched every corner of New England; even in backwater

most successful of new arrivals, and their children and grandchildren. Politically, anti-immigration groups campaigned for tightened entry requirements. In the 1850s, the openly racist Know-Nothing party controlled governorships in Massachusetts, Rhode Island, Connecticut and New Hampshire. Later organizations, such as the American Protective Association and the Immigrant Restriction League, gathered substantial memberships in their efforts to contain the electoral power of their upstart neighbors.

OLD-ORCHARD BEACH.

New Hampshire, one out of every five residents had adopted, not inherited, the American flag.

Electoral Corruption

In the wake of this unprecedented human shock wave, an expected but decidedly undistinguished backlash erupted among the established citizenry, whose very fathers had fought so hard for democracy and equal rights. Yankees taunted the immigrants with such nasty quips as: "What is the greatest invention since the wheel? The wheelbarrow, because it taught the Irishman to walk on two legs."

The doors of society were shut to even the

It was all in vain. No matter how unfamiliar they were with the workings of democracy upon their arrival to America, the immigrants — the Irish in particular — did not take long to learn the power of votes well orchestrated. In 1881, John Breen of Tipperary became the first Irishman to take high office as mayor of Lawrence, Massachusetts. His triumph launched his ethnic brethren not only to political influence but political domination. Hugh O'Brien won the mayoral election in Boston only three years later, and Patrick Andrew Collin represented Suffolk County with a congressional seat in Washington. By the turn of the century, all levels of government, from the state house to city hall to milltown council, were being turned over to what was, after all, the majority. In 1900, an astounding 90 per cent of all legislators in some New England localities were Roman Catholic.

But with newfound responsibility also came vast and insidious corruption. Rhode Island, for one last time, was the object of biting criticism as "Boss" Charles Brayton and the *Providence Journal* ring bought their way to office. "The political condition of Rhode Island is notorious, acknowledged and it is shameful," deplored statesman Lincoln Steffens, "Rhode Island is a State for sale and cheap." Individual votes cost the machine between $2 and $5 in normal elections, as much as $30 in hotly contested ones. Sam Adams would have cringed at such perversions of the democratic process.

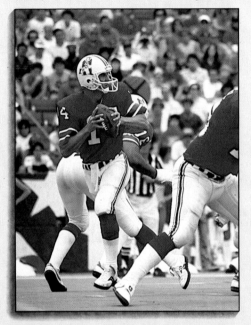

Many leaders, vividly embodied in the figure of James Michael Curley, abused the privileges of solid ethnic support. Curley displayed enormous political staying-power: he was elected mayor of Boston four times, once in each of the first four decades of this century; and governor of the state for one term, 1934-1938. The "Irish Mussolini," as his detractors tagged him, undoubtedly improved the economic welfare of his less privileged constituents. His imperious methods, however, left much to be desired. Inspired by New York's Tammany Hall, perhaps the most corrupt political machine of all American history, Curley doled out jobs and money to community leaders who in turn carefully steered their neighborhoods

in the appropriate direction when election day rolled around. There was some justice to the critics' call, "This is a Republic and not a Kingdom." When the mayor went to a ball game at Fenway Park, howitzers trumpeted his arrival.

Cultural Suppression

In Boston, cultural freedoms came under harsh attack. Led by Catholic leader William Cardinal O' Connell and the closely associated Watch and Ward Society, moralists lobbied successfully for prohibitions on such classics as Theodore Dreiser's *An American Tragedy* and Ernest Hemingway's *The Sun Also Rises*.

"Banned in Boston!," rang the crusaders and the phrase continues in the American idiom today. The Puritans, of course, probably would have burned at the stake the authors themselves. But one might have expected a little more progress in the course of 300 years.

Days of industrial glory passed. In much the same way that international competition now threatens America's economic might, other regions of the country challenged and overcame New England and her once-proud manufacturers. It was a question of costs, specifically labor costs, and the South underbid New England. Hourly wages in New England averaged 16 to 60 percent higher than those below the Mason-Dixon line. Owners gravitated to the cheaper work force, an industrial exodus dramatically illustrated by statistical indices. Up from a mere six percent 1880, the South wove almost half the nation's cotton goods by 1923. Industrial production in Massachusetts alone fell by 1 billion dollars during the 1920s. Unemployment in factory towns left idle a quarter of the total labor pool. Gone too were the days of Lowell's 28 percent dividends: expenditures in New England mills now surpassed earnings.

New England felt the brunt of the Great Depression. In Boston, the Depression cramped even Brahmin lifestyle; as one magazine noted, the old guard now dined only "annually upon champagne and terrapin in the memory of a crushed world." Hardships were, of course, far more shocking in already squalid working-class quarters. In 1930, only 81 out of 5,030 apartments in the North End had refrigerators, and only one in

The modern New Englander is often keenly interested in sports. Left, action in a New England Patriots professional football game in Foxboro, Massachusetts. Right, a college rowing regatta on the Charles River.

two had toilets. Here, wages plunged by half, and unemployment jumped to almost 40 percent in the months after the stock-market crash on Wall Street.

New England never really recovered from this economic displacement. Employment in textiles bottomed out at 75,000 in the early 1970s, a far cry from the hundreds of thousands who had once manned the power looms. Virtually bereft of natural resources, including oils, the region was hostage to Louisiana, Texas and the Middle East. Only 14 of America's largest 500 corporations are today headquartered in New England.

Political Revival

Despite the decline of New England's

efforts to strengthen anti-pollution laws, consumer rights, handgun control and civil rights. In 1970, the Massachusetts Supreme Court, heir to the oldest democratic tradition in the country, ruled that its citizens could not be forced to fight in an undeclared war — an outright condemnation of the tragic conflict in Vietnam. Today, New England plays a prominent role in grass-roots campaigns to control nuclear weapons.

The 1980s have seen a resurgence in its industrial base. Precision products — computers, electronic and biomedical machinery, special papers and plastics, and photographic hardware — have made State Highway 128, skirting Boston, a center of technological innovation equalled only by California's famed Silicon Valley. Boston itself has main-

political and economic fortunes during the 20th Century, the region looks forward to a new and useful role within the American colossus.

Political scandal has passed. The Irish have more than mastered the mechanisms of democracy; they have long since adopted its spirit, its essence. Irish leaders forged a partnership with the old establishment on equal terms, and it was from the ranks of "Green Brahmins" that John Fitzgerald Kennedy emerged to become one of the nation's greatest chief executives.

Having cleaned up its own political house, New England returned its attention to national politics with a thoughtful and progressive voice. New England leads

tained a prominence as the nation's mutual-fund capital. Hartford's insurance companies, capitalized at almost $50 billion, protect much of American business against damage and risk. Graced with a unique scenic beauty, New England counts tourism as its second largest industry. Fine institutions of culture and education not only endure, but blossom anew with each generation.

And so New England travels toward new goals, a new identity. But however easily man may forget those stone walls of history, New England's past remains the foundation on which she must build her future. New England has behind her the experience that brings wisdom, and with such wisdom comes hope.

THE PEOPLE OF NEW ENGLAND

What is a New Englander?

He is a taciturn Maine Yankee, answering "yup" or "nope" to almost anything he is asked; or a proud, independent Vermonter; or a patrician Boston Brahmin, the product of centuries of "plain living and high thinking." But he is also a roguish, wily Irishman, a master of politics, or a dynamic black leader.

New England has contributed more statesmen, writers, teachers and thinkers to the United States than has any other region of the nation. It's true that it got a head start on the rest of America. But even after the other states had caught up to New England, the flow of distinguished people produced by this unpromising land didn't cease.

New Englanders have always considered themselves the conscience of the nation. The Puritan heritage, and their region's harsh landscape and bad weather, have made them view life a little bit more seriously than the rest of the country does. But if the New Englander has never looked favorably on frivolity, he has tolerated quirky individualism for a long time. A New Englander will raise his eyebrows if this individualism means disturbing the peace of others, but he will approve if it means being self-reliant.

Most people think of this New England style as a Yankee style. But the genius of the New England style is that it has incorporated the styles of all the ethnic groups that have settled and lived here — Yankees, Irishmen, Blacks, Italians, French Canadians — and still remained distinctive. As confirmation, one need only remember President John F. Kennedy, a third-generation Irishman; or longtime Massachusetts Senator Edward Brooke, a Black American. Both of them are as characteristically "New England" as the most refined Boston Brahmin.

The Algonquian Indians:
Before the British

New England's oldest inhabitants, the Indians, have been in the area since 500 B.C. When the first English settlers arrived on the New England shore in the early 17th

Preceding pages: former Boston Red Sox stars gone fishing. Left, William Garrett poses with portrait of his Brahmin great-great grandfather, Ira Garrett. Right, Red Wing, a Mimac Indian in Chaplin, Connecticut.

Century, they found about 60,000 Indians, most of them concentrated in Rhode Island, Connecticut and Massachusetts. They were divided into tribes with well-established rivalries and territorial boundaries. All of Algonquian blood, the Indians shared a common tongue, although 13 different dialects have been identified.

These Algonquians were friendly to the first Englishmen, who seemed far too few in numbers to represent any threat. The Mohegans and Pequots of Connecticut, the Wampanoags of Massachusetts and the Narragan-

setts of Rhode Island imparted their age-old hunting, fishing, farming and canoe-making skills to the white man.

But this honeymoon was to last only about 15 years. In 1636, the English waged war against the Pequots in revenge for some real or imagined Indian outrage. The Narragansett Indians took the fatal step of allying themselves with the English, destroying the possibility of a united Indian front. When the war was over, the Pequots had been obliterated as a people. By 1670, there were 75,000 Englishmen in New England and only about 10,000 Indians. The Indians had sold much of their land, their settlements having been penetrated everywhere. Many had been converted to Christianity and lived in what were called "praying towns."

The wars of 1675-1676 marked the last desperate gasp of Indian resistance. In 1675, an alliance to fight the English — formed by Wampanoag *sachem* (chief) Philip with several of the smaller tribes — was crushed. Philip was beheaded, his body quartered, and the parts displayed in Plymouth for 24 years.

The English weren't content until the last trace of Indian independence had been wiped out. After the Wampanoags and the Pequots, it was the turn of the Narragansetts. And by the time the English were through with them at the end of 1676, less than 70 were left out of the original 4,000 or 5,000.

The Beginning of the End

Indian independence in New England was over. Many Algonquians fled west. Those who stayed entered the lowest levels of colonial society, working as indentured servants or as day laborers. Some Indian groups were granted reservations, like the Narragansett on Rhode Island and the Mashpee community on Cape Cod. These Indian territories steadily dwindled over the following two centuries and were sold off by the tribes or simply appropriated by the white man. Indian communities were given some self-government (they had, for example, their own magistrates or justices of the peace), but they were also given white overseers, who often administered to the Indians' detriment. In 1869 the Massachusetts legislature voted to end reservation status for those Indians still on reservations, and 11 years later the Rhode Island legislature abolished the Narragansett tribe as a legal entity. These Indians became citizens like everyone else.

Many, if not most, New England Indians did not live on reservations. They simply merged into the surrounding population. The 18th and 19th centuries saw a sad, slow decline of the old tribal associations, as the languages died out almost completely and the Indians came to the cities to take the most menial jobs. Indians who were lucky signed on board whaling ships and the Rhode Island Indians became famous as stone-wall builders. But the Indians who stayed on the reservations never adopted the farming methods of the white man. Instead, they rented out reservation lands to white farmers or eked out a meager existence from the manufacture of craft items.

For the most part, Indians in New England were so marginal a group that they faded out of public consciousness. A continual and drastic decline in population contributed to this. The white man's diseases finished what his guns had begun. In 1763, during one six-month period, 222 of the 358 Indians living in Nantucket died in an epidemic.

Although Indians fought bravely in both the Revolutionary War and the Civil War, few outstanding figures emerged from their own ranks to guide and lead them. An exception was the great Samson Occom, a Mohegan Indian born in 1723 in the town of Mohegan, Connecticut. Occom was a brilliant student at Eleazer Wheelock's school for Indians (which later became Dartmouth College); he learned Latin, Greek, some

Hebrew, and English. He became a vigorous Christian missionary among the Indians of the region and was probably the single most important factor in the large-scale conversion of the Mohegans and other tribes. Occom met with great success when he traveled to England to raise money for the movement to Christianize the Indians. He was bitterly disappointed when his old mentor, Eleazer Wheelock, decided to move his school from Connecticut to its present loca-

Left to right, gardening at the Fuller Gardens in North Hampton, New Hampshire; mixing a milkshake at the Common Ground Fair in Camden, Maine; and tending flowers along Main Street in Woodstock, Vermont.

tion in rural New Hampshire where, as Occom pointed out, there were very few Indians.

The Indians Today

Today, there are 21,000 Indians in New England, about a third on the nine existing reservations. Many are not the descendants of the Indians encountered by the Puritans in the 17th Century. Except for those in Maine, New England's present-day Indian population has a heavy concentration of Indians from other parts of the country. For most of this century, Indians in New England continued to live the unobtrusive, unnoticed life they had led for two centuries. But in recent years, there has been some-

tions. In 1977, a jury decided against the Indians on the grounds that they no longer constituted a tribe. An appeal is still pending.

The Narragansetts — 4,000 to 5,000 people of mixed Indian, White and African blood in southern Rhode Island — have filed a similar suit. Unlike the Wampanoags, the Narragansetts are completely assimilated. They haven't spoken Narragansett for over 100 years, and their tribal ceremonies probably bear little resemblance to those of their ancestors. In 1976, the Narragansetts sued the state for recovery of land taken away from them in 1881 when the state broke up their reservation. In an out-of-court settlement, the Narragansetts were awarded 1,900 acres (779 hectares).

thing of a renaissance.

A new consciousness of tribal identity has taken hold. It has found expression in cultural events and in attempts to right some of the wrongs perpetrated by the white man. Throughout the 1960s, the annual Powwow of the Wampanoag Indians of Massachusetts, which had been a modest affair, grew to include more dances, rituals, performances of music and meetings with other Indian tribes. In 1972, the Wampanoag communities in Mashpee and Gays Head, Martha's Vineyard, elected tribal councils. Four years later the councils moved into action. They brought suits against their respective towns contesting the 1869 law which, in effect, deprived Indians of their reserva-

The 700 Penobscot Indians of Maine, the only New England Indians who still speak their original tongue, sued the state in 1975 for recovery of 10 million acres. Lawyers for the Penobscots, the state of Maine, and the federal government negotiated a compromise settlement three years later. For the first time in almost 300 years, New England's Indians are holding their heads high.

The Proud Puritans

Never has there been a group of immigrants quite like the New England Puritans of the 17th Century. Fleeing religious persecution in England, they were fired by an extraordinary sense of mission. As the first immigrants to America, they would create a civilized society in the harsh, inhospitable New England wilderness, and they would set an example of purity to the rest of the world.

Because their motive for coming to New England was primarily religious and not economic, the Puritans were a socially diverse lot. Although most of these early comers were peasants and artisans, an unusually large number of educated men — ministers, theologians and teachers — were among them. These learned men set a tone for the Puritan community of strict disciplined piety, with religion pervading every aspect of life.

The religious organization of the Puritan church was congregational: that is, members of the community elected the governors of

the great bonds of society — language, religion, government, manners and interest." Having grown from a strictly controlled religious state to a cradle of revolutionary democratic ideas, this community was thought of as a distinctive nation-within-a-nation by other Americans at the end of the 18th Century. According to Dwight, New Englanders were distinguished by their "love of science and learning," their "love of liberty," their "morality," their "piety" and "unusual spirit of enquiry." Dwight, of course, was a New Englander himself and he naturally idealized his countrymen. For him, the typical New Englander was a combination of Ethan Allen, the Connecticut boy who led a daring guerrilla fight against the English in the hills of Vermont; fire-brea-

the church. Leaders of church, community and state were usually the same. From the earliest days of colonization, the Puritan leaders felt compelled to settle the rest of New England. There were two reasons: a high birth rate contributed to the rapid expansion of the Puritan community beyond the boundaries of Massachusetts; and the churchmen were evangelically eager to Christianize the Indians.

For 200 years, New England's population consisted of this tightly knit, homogeneous group. What Yale president Timothy Dwight said of Bostonians in 1796 could as well have been applied to all New Englanders: "They are all descendants of Englishmen and, of course, are united by all

thing Massachusetts preacher Cotton Mather; and learned statesman and patriot John Adams.

The rest of the country was more likely to characterize the Yankee, as he came to be called, as a speculator, an entrepreneur and an inventor. He was a man like early 19th Century Boston textile baron Francis Cabot Lowell, whose factory at Waltham was one of the first modern factories in America; or a member of one of the great Boston families

Left to right, a Russian Orthodox priest in Richmond, Maine; Nobel Prize-winning geneticist and cancer researcher Dr. George Snell in Bar Harbor, Maine; and tomorrow's Nobel Prize winner in a Boston high school science lab.

that made their fortunes in the China and East India trade.

The 'Exalted' Brahmins

New Englanders considered themselves the national elite. The self-proclaimed heads of this elite were the Boston Brahmins — rich Boston families like the Lowells, the Welds, the Cabots, the Lodges and the Saltonstalls, who made their money in the first half of the century in the railroad, banking, shipping and textile industries. The Welds, for example, who were in 17th Century Governor John Winthrop's entourage and had fallen into obscurity for six generations, made a fortune in shipping and railroads in the 19th Century. This elite group carefully

nurtured itself at a group of socially select schools and colleges, like Harvard. Boston Brahmin Edmund Quincy once said of the *Harvard Triennial Catalogue,* which contained a list of all Harvard University graduates: "If a man's in there, that's who he is. If he isn't, who is he?"

Despite this and the fact that today's Brahmins hold exalted notions of the ancientness of their ancestry, none descends from the *Mayflower* pilgrims and few from prominent Puritans of the 17th Century or from rich merchants of the 18th Century. For the Boston social system was not an aristocratic one; when a Brahmin lost his money, as happened to a good many of them in the 18th Century, he ceased to be a

Brahmin. The Brahmins may think of themselves as European-style aristo-crats (some have even adopted family coats-of-arms), but James Michael Curley, Irishman and a 20th Century mayor of Boston, was not far wrong when he remarked acidly that Boston's prominent Yankee families "got rich selling opium to the Chinese, rum to the Indians, or trading in slaves."

Although most Brahmins have long since deserted their traditional enclaves in Boston's Back Bay and Beacon Hill for suburbs like Lincoln, Bedford and Weston, they still consider Boston to be "the hub of the solar system."

Indomitable Yankees

Of course, other New England Yankees have disputed this belief. President Calvin Coolidge, a famous Vermonter, once declared at Vermont's Bennington College: "I love Vermont ... most of all because of her indomitable people. They are a race of pioneers who have almost beggared themselves to serve others. If the spirit of liberty should vanish in other parts of the Union and support for our institutions should languish, it could all be replenished from the generous store held by the people of this brave little state of Vermont."

The first inhabitants of the state were hardy trappers, not farmers; and this has contributed to the independent and self-reliant characteristics of the modern Vermonter. Freedom is a personal issue for the Vermonter, not just an abstract historical one, although Vermont has a long tradition of idealism. When neighboring states were laying claim to its territory during the Revolution, Vermont declared itself an independent republic. It maintained this status for 14 years, during which time it declared a complete prohibition of slavery and universal manhood suffrage. It was the first state to do so.

The New Hampshire Yankee is much like his cousin to the west, but has the reputation of being somewhat less tolerant than the Vermonter, and more frugal and stubborn. The Maine Yankee has been the most isolated inhabitant of the three northern New England states. In fact, until recently, a form of Elizabethan English was spoken in Washington County's Beals Islands (as well as parts of Appalachia and the Ozarks). Roads connecting Maine to the outside world have never been good. The "Downeaster," as he is called, has had to put up with bad weather, unyielding terrain and hostile Indians. This probably explains why he is crusty and quirky; hence, his down-to-earthness and his reputation for saying little except what counts.

A classic anecdote illustrates the Mainer's dislike for extraneous words. An out-of-state visitor asks a Maine fisherman, "Have you lived in your village all your life?" The Mainer replies, "Not yet." But if the Mainer tends to regard outsiders with a combination of bemusement and suspicion, he has a strong tradition of loyalty to fellow Mainers.

Rhode Island and Connecticut Yankees are perhaps less distinctive than other old New Englanders. The original populations of these states were the products of the first emigrations from Massachusetts, and today they have a reputation for being cautious and conservative.

Unlike those in Massachusetts, the Yankees here retained political control long after the 19th and 20th Century European immigration, which greatly reduced their proportion of the areas' total population.

After the Civil War, the New England Yankees knew their region was in decline and their numbers were fast dwindling. Nevertheless, they continue to think of themselves as the essential representatives of the nation's most cherished values and remain convinced that they symbolize all that is best about their country.

The First Blacks

The first Blacks in New England came to Boston in 1638 as "perpetual servants" from the West Indies. One hundred years later, slavery was well-implanted in the region. Although scattered episodes of violence against Whites were recorded, 17th and 18th Century New England Blacks were better off than their brothers in the South. They had more rights and legal protections than Southern plantation slaves, in the form of figurehead "governors" elected by the Blacks themselves.

Blacks were usually the slave servants of White merchant families, or were laborers in docks of port towns. Servants benefited from the paternalism of masters who, on the whole, were more humane than plantation owners in the South. And in further contrast, Blacks could be found in every industry. Half of the crews of whaling vessels were often Black, and Black labor was used extensively in the construction of Providence and New Haven.

Although some Blacks live in Connecticut and Rhode Island, it is in Boston that New England's Black population has always been concentrated. In 1752, there were about 5,000 Blacks (10 percent of the total population) in Boston. The percentage never reached this high again until around the middle of the 20th Century. In 1860, for example, only 1.3 percent of Boston's population was Black; today, the figure is 18 percent. The Revolution accounted for the sharp decline, as Black slaves fled with their Tory masters. By the end of the 18th Century, slavery had been abolished in Massachusetts.

Although Blacks lived a segregated existence in Boston between the Revolution and the Civil War, nowhere else in America had they been as free. Following the pre-Revolution pattern, they worked as domestics or unskilled laborers, although as many as half of the mulattoes were skilled.

Only about 2 percent of the Black population were doctors, ministers, teachers or lawyers. Most Blacks were very poor, but their community was an organized and vital one; many fraternal organizations served as a safety net for indigent members of the population. The most famous of these, the African Society, was founded in 1796 as a mutual-aid and charity organization which stressed temperance and, mirrored White Puritan morality. Black shops served as

Left to right, smiling faces of a pie-eating contestant, Grange Fair, Williamston, Massachusetts; a park ranger, Ferry Beach State Park, Maine; and an International Zucchini Festival goer in Harrisville, New Hampshire.

informal community centers, and Black churches helped bring the community together. Ministers were looked up to as leaders and towering above them were figures like anti-slavery activist Jehial C. Bemon.

Although Blacks in 19th-Century Boston rarely lived outside their quarter on the lower slopes of Beacon Hill, they mingled with the Whites. Black and White laborers drank together in North End taverns and, after 1855 when schools were desegregated, Black and White children studied together. There were Black students at Harvard before the Civil War. Until 1860, Massachusetts, Connecticut and Vermont were the only states to extend equal suffrage to Blacks.

As the vanguard of the abolitionist move-

ity increased fivefold.

Until around 1940, the social and economic position of the Blacks remained stagnant. They continued to work in the lowest rung of the occupational ladder as porters, laborers, janitors and domestics.

Civil Rights Leaders

An outsized number of Massachusetts Blacks became leaders of the national Black community. In fact, the Civil Rights movement of the 1960s would have been unthinkable without the ground-breaking work of W. E. B. DuBois, the impassioned chief spokesman for the NAACP and editor of its publications, who was born in the Housatonic Valley at Great Barrington in 1868; or

ment, Massachusetts was unique in allowing Blacks to stand for a political party (the Abolitionist Free-Soil Party in 1850) in elections to the state legislature. Yankees in the state never regarded the Blacks as inferior, partly because of the great prominence achieved by Massachusetts Blacks like John Swett Rock, as abolitionist doctor and lawyer; and Charles Remond, the first Black to argue a case before the Supreme Court. Many Blacks worked with William Lloyd Garrison, the abolitionist and founder of the New England Anti-Slavery Society.

After the Civil War, the size of Boston's Black population increased dramatically due to a heavy migration of freed slaves from the South. Between 1865 and 1900 the commun-

of Bostonian William Monroe Trotter, founder of the Black newspaper *The Guardian,* a militant defender of equal rights and an outspoken advocate of complete equality of opportunity for Blacks. But these were exceptions. Blacks did not start to improve their status until the 1950s. Between 1950 and 1970, the number of Blacks holding white-collar jobs in Boston nearly doubled, although the vast majority of Blacks remained poor and in the working class.

Today, the Black community in Boston is only just beginning to recover from ugly race riots touched off by a Federal judge's order in 1974 to desegregate schools through busing. The Irish of South Boston were infuriated by the order, and took out their rage in acts of violence against the Blacks, who reciprocated. Although the situation has calmed down considerably since then, Black are still afraid to go to events such as baseball games, and they will drive miles out of their way to avoid going through South Boston. As recently as 1979, a Black high-school football player was shot and paralyzed from the neck down by Irish teenagers in Charlestown.

Adding to the tense situation is the fierce competition between Blacks and Whites for the dwindling number of blue-collar jobs in a service-oriented city. But Black powerless-ness in Boston, which has persisted for years, seems to be on the verge of changing dramatically with the emergence of leaders such as Melvin King, a former state rep-

were shaken by riots. The picture is quieter today, although the problems persist. Hartford's recent election of a Black mayor may signal a brighter future for the Blacks in the state.

Irish Power

The Irish potato famine of 1845 killed 1 million people on the Emerald Isle in five years, and drove another million to seek bet-ter conditions elsewhere. Many came to Massachusetts. No precise figures are availa-ble, but one statistic claims that by 1860, 61 percent of Boston's population was foreign-born. Virtually all of these people would have been Irish, the only immigrant group to come in large numbers at that time.

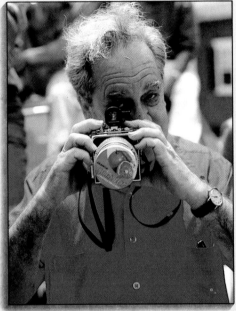

resentative and Democratic candidate in the 1984 mayoral election.

Connecticut is the only other New Eng-land state with a sizable Black population. The 217,000-plus Blacks here represent about 7 percent of the population. A small number of Blacks have been in the state since colonial days. But they first came in large numbers from the South after 1870 to work on the Connecticut Valley tobacco farms. The Black population grew at a low rate until the 1960s. Between 1960 and 1970, it grew from 111,000 to 196,000.

Connecticut cities have had their share of racial tensions. Busing failed in New Haven and Hartford, and in the summer of 1967, these towns and many others in the state

The Irish did not receive a warm welcome either from the entrenched Yankee aristo-cracy or the ordinary Yankee yeoman. The Yankee had great contempt for the Irishman's Catholic religion; it was an attitude not dissimilar to that of the British oppressors back home. The Irish had no sympathy for the idealism of the reform-minded Yankee. During the Civil War, Irish in Boston rioted when faced with a draft for the freeing of slaves, a cause in which they

Left to right, Ted Williams, former Boston Red Sox baseball superstar; photographer Aaron Siskind clowning in Rhode Island; and an ex-Marine whooping it up during summer holidays on Nantucket Island.

had no interest. For years, the Irishman had been confronted with a "no Irish need apply" sign wherever he went in search of a job. Bad feelings between the two communities escalated to the point that, after World War I, football games between the Irish of Boston College and the Yankees of Harvard had became so rough, that they had to be discontinued.

The Irish community in Massachusetts grew at an extremely rapid rate. Before long, the Irish went into politics and were very successful at it. The first Irish-born mayor of Boston was elected in 1885, and the first Irish Catholic governor took office in 1918. Between the world wars, the Irish controlled both Boston and state politics. But the Irish can't really be said to have

made it until Joe Kennedy, the father of the late President John F. Kennedy, became the first Irishman to penetrate the Yankee stronghold of finance and banking on Boston's State Street.

For a long time, middle-class Irishmen have integrated into the main-stream of Boston and Massachusetts life. Blue-collar Irish are a different story. Especially in Charlestown and South Boston, the Irish have fiercely maintained the separateness both of their communities and of their ethnic identity. The 22 percent of modern Bostonians who are of Irish descent tend to identify more with their communities than they do with the city as a whole. In South Boston pubs, Irish Americans sing a song called

"Southie is my Home Town." This "tribalism," as it has been called, erupted in 1974 when "Southie" rioted over busing. Irishmen felt their neighborhoods were gravely threaten-ed, that busing had been forced on them by upper-class Yankees, their traditional enemies. Eighteen months after busing began, public schools had lost one-third of their White enrollment. Melvin King, then a state representative, said in 1980 that racial hatred in Boston is a result of "the historical relationship between Irish Catholics and WASPS. The Irish still view themselves as a persecuted minority and therefore don't play the positive role in race relations that one would expect from people who experienced bigotry."

French Canadians

French Canadians have been emigrating to New England since the middle of the last century. Although there are more French Canadians in Massachusetts than in any other New England state, their influence is most evident in New Hampshire, where they make up as much as a quarter of the population; and in Maine, where 15 percent of the people are only one or two generations from Canadian birth.

The Canadians came to work in the textile mills, and (in Maine) as lumberjacks. More than any other group in New England, they have clung to their ethnic identity and maintained a remarkable degree of distinctiveness. They are strongly loyal to the Catholic church, moreso than the Irish or the Italians, and they still consider French their first language although more French Canadian teenagers are now going to English-speaking schools than in the past.

French Canadians in Maine live together in close-knit communities, have their own radio station, and go to Quebec frequently. Although French Canadians have been slower than other groups to move up the social and economic scale, they have a reputation for being hard-working and thrifty, and for keeping to their own.

Italian Subculture

Italians came to the United States in the first decades of the 20th Century, most of them as poor peasants from southern Italy and Sicily. Many of them settled in Massachusetts and Rhode Island. Italians and Irish have always been rivals in Massachusetts; the Italians have always been voted with the Yankee Republicans, the Irish with the Democratic party. Italians have managed to preserve a distinctive village subculture in neighborhoods. In recent years, areas like Boston's North End and East Boston have been threatened by gentrification and the expansion of Logan Airport. But the Italians — who comprise 11 percent of Boston's population — have successfully fought back with lawsuits and by lobbying.

In Rhode Island, the Italians are the wealthiest ethnic group in the state, having made their money in law, jewelry manufacturing, the real estate, construction and assorted other businesses. Italian success in Rhode Island is reflected in the careers of John O. Pastore, who in the 1940s was the first Italian-American to be elected governor in America and who later went on to the U.S. Senate.

Jews have been in New England since the 17th Century, but it wasn't until the great waves of emigration from Eastern Europe at the end of the last century that they established a significant presence in the area.

One of the oldest Jewish communities in the Western Hemisphere was established in Newport, Rhode Island, three centuries ago, thanks to the tolerance of the Puritan dissenter and freethinker Roger Williams. These first Jewish families came to Newport from Holland in 1658. They were Sephardics, descendants of Jews expelled from Spain at the end of the 15th Century. Nineteen years after they arrived in Newport, the Jews organized a congregation, the second to be established in North America (the first

was in New York). Not subject to any of the restrictions imposed on them in the Old World, the Jews flourished and prospered in Newport.

The Newport community began to dissolve around the beginning of the 19th Century as members emigrated to other parts of the country. For 100 years, Jews were scarce in New England. Jews didn't regard Boston as a favorable place to settle in, mostly because of the intolerance and rigidity of the Protestant Yankee establishment. But by the end of the century, Boston had become a much more ethnically and religiously diverse place, and so Jews from Eastern Europe began to settle there in large numbers.

By 1910, 42,000 East Europeans lived in the Boston area, almost all of them Jews. Ten years later 10 percent of Boston's population was Jewish. These Jews moved rapidly into the white-collar world, far more rapidly than any other cultural group. By 1950, more Jews in Boston held white-collar jobs than did old Yankees.

Jews have made their mark in Boston, notably in education, although they probably preserve less of their ethnic culture than New York Jews. In 1948, Brandeis University was established in Waltham, near Boston, thanks largely to the efforts of local Jewish businessmen. Brandeis, named after former Supreme Court Justice Louis Brandeis, was the first non-sectarian university sponsored by Jews in the West.

Arab Christians and Portuguese

New England boasts pockets of small ethnic groups which contribute greatly to the region's diversity. There are the 3,500 Syrian-Lebanese Arabic speakers of Rhode Island, who fled the religious persecution of the Turks at the beginning of this century. The Syrian-Lebanese are Christians, and they retain a strong loyalty to their churches, although some assimilation has taken place through intermarriage.

Several Portuguese communities exist in New Bedford and Fall River, Massachusetts. These Portuguese arrived in the mid 19th Century from the Azores, after coming into contact with American whaling ships that stopped at their islands. The Portuguese were originally hands on the whaling ships themselves, but toward the end of the last century shifted to the textile mills.

Left, a lovely summer resident of Martha's Vineyard. Right, Beany Kelley, who for 30 years has operated the ski tow at Black Mountain, New Hampshire.

PLACES

*Meanwhile it occurs to me that by a remote New England fireside
an unsophisticated young person of either sex is reading in an old
volume of travels...The young person gazes in the firelight at the
flickering chiaroscuro of the future, discerns at last the glowing
phantasm of opportunity, and determines with a wild heart-beat
to go and see it all—twenty years hence!*

—Henry James

There's no need to wait 20 years to see New England—no need
to delay at all, for New England is a polished place, ready to reward
the visitor with riches rarely equalled in America. New England is
six politically defined states and a thousand states of mind—Maine
and solitude and contemplation, Boston and bustle and culture,
Vermont and beauty and peace.

New England can mean running across a priceless antique in an
out-of-the-way backwoods store, or dining out in a sophisticated
Boston eatery. It can mean rafting down a New Hampshire river or
skiing down a Maine mountain, scrounging through a Berkshire flea
market or lounging on a Nantucket beach.

States—Massachusetts, Connecticut, Rhode Island, and
Maine—serve as convenient if somewhat artificial labels for New
England's varied regions. In the following pages, each state is
explored in depth and treated as a self-contained unit; but
Massachusetts, the most populous, has been divided into sub
sections on Boston, the North and South Shores, Cape Cod,
Martha's Vineyard and Nantucket, Central Massachusetts and the
Berkshires. Marginal maps help orient armchair travellers to
specific locations.

States of mind—calm, contentment, excitement, pride, surprise,
intrigue, enjoyment, pleasure—are to be found in all the places of
New England. From the scrub pines of East Chop on Martha's
Vineyard to the granite outcroppings of Vermont's Green Mountains, from the cobbled streets of restored Newburyport to the sleek
modernity of Boston's skyline, from Rhode Island's natural
wonderland, Block Island, to the manmade history that persists in
Lexington and Concord, this is New England, home of American
dreams.

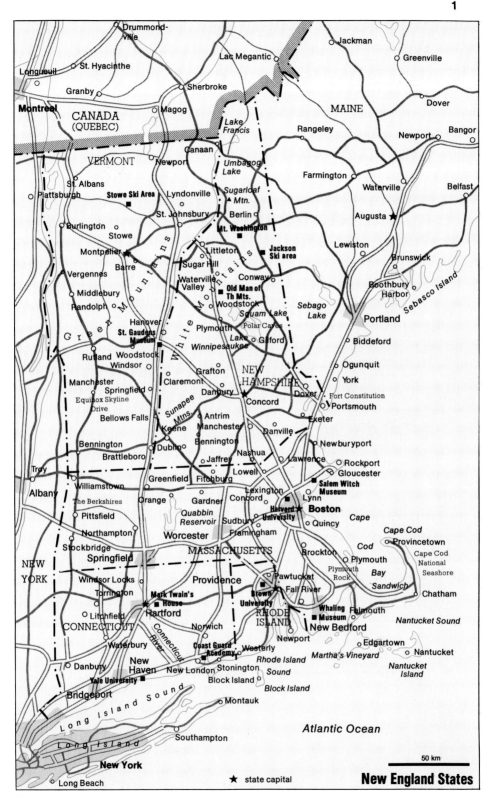

New England States

★ state capital

50 km

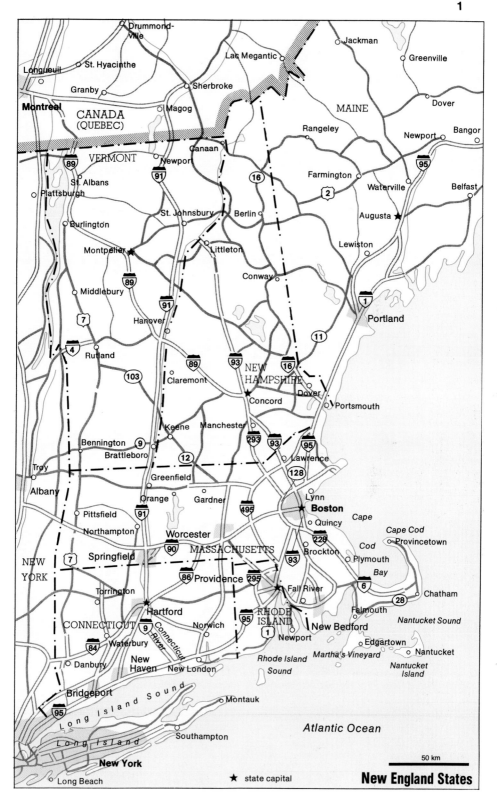

New England States

BOSTON

To visit Boston is to visit a city that Americans have looked at with mingled admiration, horror, love and annoyance for more than 350 years. Three and a half centuries is a long time in America, time enough to build a fine city, to join bricks and mortar, to raise townhouses and office towers, to construct docks and statues and bridges. And it's plenty of time to lay twisting cobblestone streets and concrete freeways, to decorate avenues and churches with lawns and trees, ponds, spires and fences. New York may be grander, Seattle more beautiful, but no city in America so nobly mingles its past with its present, tradition with innovation.

From 'Hell Upon Earth' To 'Hub of the Universe'

Not that everyone likes such a staunch attachment to the past. In large measure because of it, few cities have evoked so varied a response in their visitors.

There has been, for instance, revulsion: "I hate Boston," said the muckraker Lincoln Steffens. "I don't know why ... The general spirit is so far, far, far back that it gets on my nerves."

The fervid Reverend Cotton Mather was even less uncertain in one of his 17th Century jeremiads: "Boston is almost a hell upon earth, a city full of Lies and Murders and Blasphemies; a dismal Picture and an emblem of Hell."

There have been other expressions of displeasure. Author Raymond Chandler decided that "God made Boston on a wet Sunday," and Edgar Allan Poe remarked that "The Bostonians are very well bred — as very dull people generally are." Oliver Wendell Holmes even surmised that the citizen of Boston, through the blueness of his blood, remained unpleasantly English. "As the Englishman is the physical bully of the world," Holmes wrote, "so the Bostonian is the aesthetic and intellectual bully of America."

But then again, there has been veneration, and much of it. "This town of Boston has a history," wrote Ralph Waldo Emerson. "It is not an accident, not a windmill, or a railroad station, or a crossroads town, but a seat of humanity, of men of principle, obeying sentiment and marching to it..."

Holmes, in a better mood, was even more extravagant: "All I claim for Boston is that it is the thinking center of the Continent, and therefore of the Planet." He went on to christen his city "The Hub of the Universe," a nickname taken with surprising seriousness in these parts, though most Bostonians will settle more modestly for "The Hub of the Solar System."

Short Story of a Long History

Founded in 1630 when a band of Puritans who had landed in Salem (north of Boston) went searching for drinking water. Boston early on felt that "the eies of all people vpon vs," as their first leader, John Winthrop said. "Driven by this relentless self-consciousness and the certainty that God, too, was watching, the little "Bible Commonwealth" quickly made something of itself.

Prosperity came from the sea. By 1700, thanks to cod fishing and the maritime trade made possible by Boston's excellent natural harbor, the

colony was booming: its fleet was the third largest in the English-speaking world, its population the largest in North America.

Success, however, brought attention from home, and in the mid 18th Century, the English Crown began to tighten its hold on its precocious offspring, imposing a series of tough, new revenue measures that cooled relations between the colonies and the motherland. Finally, on the night of March 5, 1770, long-harassed British troops fired into a rioting crowd and killed five people, including a black man named Crispus Attucks. The funeral for the victims of this Boston Massacre was the first occasion for great patriotic demonstrations.

Relations deteriorated further in 1773 when a heavily taxed shipment of British tea arrived in Boston Habor. Not only did the town refuse to unload the crates of "East India Bohea," but on the evening of December 16, some 60 patriots disguised as Mohawk Indians hurled 342 of the crates from the ship into the Harbor, thus celebrating the Boston Tea Party. The port was closed immediately and a sort of martial law was declared. It soon flared into a brief, but famcus war — the American Revolution. Boston's great moments in those events shine in the mind of every schoolchild from Maine to Alaska. Paul Revere's Midnight Ride, "The Shot Heard 'Round the World" and the Battle of Bunker Hill are the exploits of American myth.

'The Athens of America'

But despite such vivid colonial and Revolutionary doings, it was during the high noon of the 19th Century that Boston took its present-day form. During that period, the merchant princes created a great city that would become known not only as "The Hub," but as "The Athens of America."

Slowed by the Revolution, Boston's maritime industries surged again with the coming of peace. Piloting swift clipper ships, indefatigable sea captains traded in ports farther abroad — Java, the West Coast and newly opened China. The Boston fishing fleet increased tenfold between 1789 and 1810 and created a "codfish aristocracy" of fortunes netted from the sea. A seemingly unending flow of gold made Boston

"Landing of the Pilgrims."

— or at least those Bostonians with names like Cabot, Lowell, Otis and Hancock — incredibly rich. These wealthy mercantilists, adopting the name of the priestly class of the Hindus who performed sacred rituals and set moral standards, emerged as the self-styled "Brahmins" of a modern caste system.

Growth accelerated through the century as Yankee ingenuity triumphed again and again and helped Boston lead America into a prosperous Industrial Age. A Boston traveling salesman named Gillette dreamed up the safety razor, while Alexander Graham Bell invented the telegraph in his attic at 109 Court St. Even more important, the Boston-designed sewing machine and the power loom, imported from England, inaugurated an era of heavy textile and shoe manufacturing.

To accommodate itself, Boston began to manhandle its land. The city's humble hills were shoveled into the surrounding marshes and coves to make new land for residence and industry. By century's end, in one of the great testimonies to that quintessentially American knack for making something from nothing,

Boston had tripled its size with landfill.

Growth was more than physical; Boston was also expanding its mind. With its legacy of Puritan high-mindedness, its publishing houses and its fashionable literary salons run by earnest first citizens, Boston suddenly found itself at the radiant center of intellectual America. Longfellow, Lowell, Whittier, Emerson, Thoreau, Holmes, Parkman, Alcott, Hawthorne: all were at one time or another citizens of the New England Parnassus: all could be found browsing at the Old Corner Book Store or dictating standards for civilization over seven-course meals at the Parker House, where Emerson convened his luminous Saturday Club. Magazines like the *North American Review* and *The Atlantic Monthly* were founded to spread the word, while a whole slew of cultural institutions celebrated and embodied it. Among these were the Boston Public Library, the Boston Symphony Orchestra, the Massachusetts Institute of Technology (M.I.T.) and Boston University, the first American university to admit women on an equal basis with men. Harvard, of course, had already ascended from its status as "that country

Harvard Yard
at the turn of
the 20th
Century.

120

BOSTON ILLUSTRATED.

VIEW OF HARVARD COLLEGE: THE QUADRANGLE

college in Cambridge" to its place among the world's great universities.

The Great Immigration

But while the Boston of privileged thought and power was progressing so mightily, a catastrophe occurred in Europe that was to affect the city more seriously than any other single event. The Irish potato famine was to change the city forever. When it began in 1845, Boston was at the apogee of its gleaming social and cultural preeminence. Suddenly, thousands of impoverished Irish immigrants arrived, promptly constituting a new underclass. Unlike the generally well-educated religious dissenters, adventurers and traders who had preceded them, the Irish were an uprooted peasantry from Europe's poorhouse. Arriving to settle in what is now East Boston and the North End, the Irish debarked in America almost totally bereft of advantages.

As the population exploded – swelled further by additional waves of Italians, Poles and Russians in the 1880s — census figures multiplied thirtyfold during the 19th Century to about 560,000 people in 1900. Newcomers and incumbents clashed, and Boston was divided into two distinct cultures with no more intercourse than if 3,000 miles of ocean still separated them. While the ethnics became a clannish foreign element, established Bostonians withdrew into their own carefully defended elite of geneology and crypto-Puritanism.

Yet if the new citizens became virtual slaves as they sweated in factories and did handwork, they remade Boston in their own image. Once dominated by fastidious English names, the Puritan "City upon a Hill" became a Catholic megalopolis of Irish and Italian names: numbers prevailed, most dramatically in the arena of city politics. Having groped steadily upward through 1870s and 1880s, the Irish masses finally elected Hugh O'Brien in 1884, the city's first foreign-born mayor. Successes were quickly consolidated as men like Martin Lomasney, the greatest of Boston's bosses, built political fiefdoms by allocating "favors" in exchange for instructions to vote Democratic. Ever since, the Irish have kept the mayor's office and the civil service occupied almost exclusively by Irishmen while also giving the nation

such leaders as John W. McCormack, former Speaker of the House of Representatives; Thomas P. "Tip" O'Neill, another Speaker; and, of course, the Kennedy clan. If the Brahmins have owned Boston, the Irish have run it.

Yet for all Boston's glory and growth during the 1800s, the century's end brought decline, a decline that would continue until the 1960s. While the Irish grew complacent and fat with pork-barreling, the Brahmins retreated behind the double-locked doors of Beacon Hill and Back Bay to purse their lips, collect Chinese porcelain, and stare at musty family portraits. As a result, while the skyscrapers of frenzied Manhattan and industrious Chicago shot up with rude confidence, Boston hugged the ground, prating primly about height-limits and preserving the past. New York superseded her as a port; the textile mills and shoe factories headed South for cheaper labor and lower taxes. Lacking vitality, conscience hardened into prudery, and culture softened into effeteness. By the 1940s and 1950s, Boston was literally shrinking, the only large city to lose population during the post-World War II Baby Boom.

But then, just as suddenly as the city had lapsed into torpor, it woke up. For the first time, Boston's Protestant elite, representing wealth, and its Irish Catholics, representing political power, cooperated in the management of city affairs and began a success story of rejuvenation that has been nothing less than astounding. Prudential Center, including what was then the tallest skyscraper outside New York, materialized. Government Center rose on the ruins of Scollay Square. The silk purse of Faneuil Hall Marketplace was created from the sow's ear of some wholesale meat warehouses. The waterfront was revived. Suddenly, amazingly, Boston was different and altogether exciting. Such large accomplishment in a Sun-Belt city would be impressive, but in an eccentric antique like Boston, it is unprecedented.

The city further benefited as the Baby Boom grew up, went to college, then looked for jobs and apartments. Millions of young people have attended one of the three score colleges in Boston. Many, having graduated from schools like M.I.T., have set up shop and transformed the Boston area into one of the centers of the Technology Revolution. With the transfusion of new, young

Acorn Street in Beacon Hill is a perfectly preserved glimpse of old Boston.

blood, the Boston of today is hip, 40 percent under the age of 25, 60 percent unmarried. It's also well-educated and energetic.

But more than anything, Boston remains what it's been for a long, long time — streets and the art of walking them, exploring their beguiling turns and primitive angles, getting lost in them. Boston is charmingly, perversely bereft of a main drag, and her streets practice the old European vices of waywardness and digression. The visitor should, too. There's no telling what he'll find.

The Hub of History

Ask any Bostonian which is the city's oldest neighborhood and no doubt he'll reply, "Back Bay." He'll be wrong. The answer is the **North End,** a busy little neighborhood north of the waterfront and northeast of the downtown business core. This picturesque old jumble is Boston's true heart, and to walk these streets is to walk among legends. Indeed, many of the attractions along Boston's official **Freedom Trail,** a tour of the historical sites of the Revolution, are found here in the North End.

But the North End does more than serve tourists as a sort of Early America theme park. This neighborhood is the ethnic heart of Boston: once Irish, then Jewish, now Italian, the North End is a place where laundry hangs from clotheslines stretched from tenement to tenement and where freshly ground sausages are displayed in storefront windows.

A stroll through the North End should start at **Paul Revere's House** in North Square. Built around 1680, it is the oldest building standing in the city, and the period furnishings on display include some items owned by the Reveres. From here, head toward Hanover Street and the Old North Church, but walk at a leisurely pace and take in the sights — and smells — of Old World Italy.

Here is a paradise of fresh-baked bread, dried squid, pastries, provolone and garlic strings. The fortunate visitor will witness one of the saint's festivals, when the streets are spanned by arcs of colored lights and jammed with people surrounding madonnas dressed in dollar bills. But at any time, strolling the narrow streets is a delight — particularly around dinnertime. Within a few blocks of Hanover Street are perhaps dozens of

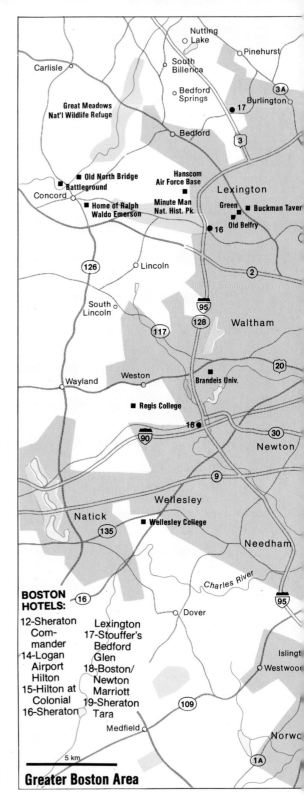

BOSTON HOTELS:

12-Sheraton Commander
14-Logan Airport Hilton
15-Hilton at Colonial
16-Sheraton Lexington
17-Stouffer's Bedford Glen
18-Boston/Newton Marriott
19-Sheraton Tara

Greater Boston Area

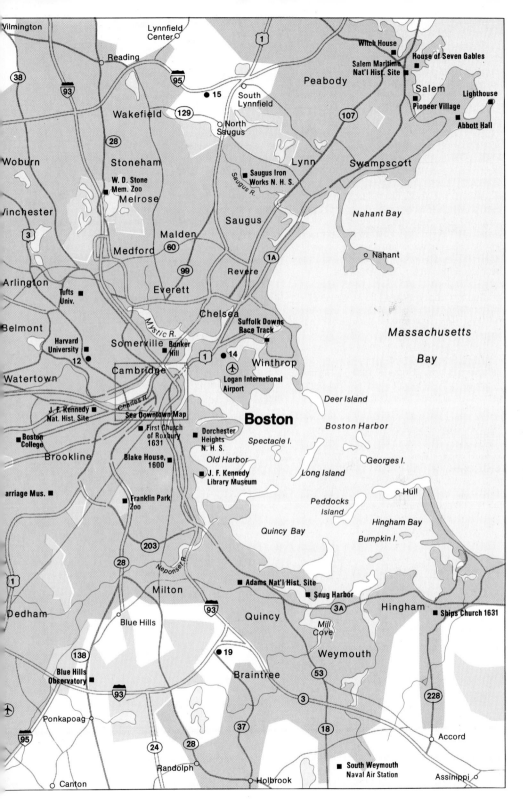

first-class Italian restaurants.

At the end of Hanover Street stands the **Paul Revere Mall** with its rather comic equestrian statue of Revere looking a tad drunk. At the end of the tranquil, tree-shaded mall, also occupied by a fountain and old Italian men playing checkers, stands Boston's oldest church, Christ Church of the **Old North Church** of Paul Revere's lanterns and Longfellow's poem. The graceful spire of Old North stands as a beacon to hundreds of tourists. Inside, the stately pulpit presides, and the soft glow of light that filters through the surrounding treetops gives the lofty sanctuary a gentle aura of serenity. The beauty of this space finds lovely accompaniment in the "royal peal" of its eight bells, considered the best and sweetest in America. The largest weighs 1,545 pounds (695 kilograms) and the smallest 620 pounds (279 kilograms). One is inscribed, "We are the first ring of bells cast for the British Empire in North America, Anno 1774."

Behind Old North, between Hull and Charter streets, stand the weathered headstones of **Copp's Hill Burying Ground**, where many early Bostonians, including Cotton Mather, are buried.

The terrace commands a fine view of the *USS Constitution* at berth, a sight to remind the visitor that Boston is very much a port city.

Perhaps the most surprising sight, even to the native Bostonian, is the waterfront, which starts here at the edge of the North End. Although water almost completely surrounds the city, the modern Bostonian can go months without so much as a fleeting glimpse of the waterfront. Sure, he knows the water's there; he finds its imprint on his menus and he even smells its fishy tang when the wind blows in from the east. Yet so blocked from his vision is the harbor, so lacking is his city in hilltop views like those of San Francisco or Seattle, that he needs a map to remember Boston's 40 miles (64 kilometers) of waterfront and 75 square miles (184 square kilometers) of island-jammed harbor.

Military Memorabilia

Whichever direction is taken in the North End will sooner or later lead to water. Across **Charleston Bridge** to the north a famous bit of history lies at anchor: the **USS Constitution,** the ven-

1-Back Bay Hilton
2-Bostonian
3-Marriott-Long Wharf
4-Park Plaza
5-Colonnade
6-Copley Plaza
7-Hyatt Regency
9-Parker House
10-Ritz-Carlton
11-Sheraton-Boston

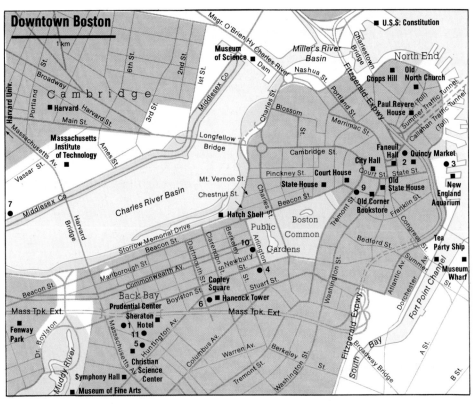

erable frigate built in 1797 but still commissioned in the United States Navy. Her majestic masts make an inspiring sign of Boston's past as they soar above the **Boston Naval Shipyard.** For the record, the Constitution fought 40 battles during her career and never lost one.

It's not far from there to the **Bunker Hill Pavilion**, where a multimedia extravaganza depicts the Patriots' heroic loss to the Redcoats in the second battle of the Revolution. Nearby rises the outsized obelisk of the **Bunker Hill Monument** itself, a needle of granite 221 feet (67 meters) high.

Climb this — there are 294 steps for those who want to know — and contemplate the bewildering, immense complexity of the Harbor, in which float more than 100 islands that range in size from a few square feet at low tide to many acres with stands of trees. Many of these islands have queer little histories; some have to do with Indians, some with industry, some — as in the case of Nix's Mate Island — with the visits of pirates like Captain Kidd. Two islands have supported hospitals, another a prison, and several others have been fortified. During the Civil War, hundreds of soldiers were trained for the Union Army at Fort Warren on **George's Island,** and more than 1,000 Confederated imprisoned.

To make things even more intriguing, the Metropolitan District Commission and the Department of Environmental Management have, since the mid 1970s, opened five of the islands to camping. Four of them are accessible by free water taxis from George's Island, the terminus of several commercial ferry lines. **Bumpkin Island** offers trimmed, grassy trails walled with raspberry bushes in which rabbits and pheasants hide, while **Peddock's Island,** once known for its harvest of turkeys, presents giant buildings, brick ghosts that look more like Southern mansions than the Army Barracks of **Fort Andrews.** These were last used to house Italian prisoners during World War II. To the north, **Great Brewster,** the most rugged island of the family, boasts high bluffs that on a clear day offer sweeping views from Plymouth to Cape Ann. If the hazy prospect of the Harbor sounds beguiling, contact one of the harbor cruise companies located on Long Wharf near the Aquarium. They'll take visitors out among the islands and the sailboats scudding on the water.

Downtown Boston from the John Hancock observatory.

Back on the mainland, on the eastern boundary of the North End is the **Waterfront** district, a fine place of leisure for citizens, suburbanites and tourists alike. If the tall ships have left, the great wharves remain, many now recycled as apartments, shopping arcades and swinging and non-swinging restaurants. At the center of it all is the **Christopher Columbus Waterfront Park,** a pleasant stretch of spacious lawns, trees and intriguing trellises.

The Waterfront District

And there are museums. For example, the fine **New England Aquarium,** on Central Wharf at the harbor end of Milk Street, boasts what is reputed to be the largest seawater fish tank in the world, a gargantuan three-story, 180,000-gallon (819,000-liter) ocean in which sharks, four-eye butterfly fish and noble salmon cruise, dart and glide.

Farther south, along Fort Point Channel, is the **Boston Tea Party Ship and Museum,** which offers an instructive lesson in American mythology for schoolchildren of all ages. For added fun, the museum dispenses tea chests for visitors to hurl defiantly into the Harbor from the deck of the *Beaver II,* a full-size replica of one of the three tea ships whose cargo, on that chilly night in 1773, helped make the Harbor into a rather large pitcher of iced tea.

Next door is the Museum Wharf, home of the **Children's Museum.** Housed in a nicely renovated warehouse, this museum comes highly recommended. Here children clamber across a gigantic desk top littered with five-foot pencils and two-foot paperclips, anchor a television news broadcast, and take their shoes off to enter an authentic Japanese house transplanted piece by piece from Boston's sister city, Kyoto. Pre-teens accustomed to constant warnings of "Don't touch!" and "Be careful!" will find a paradise of things to squeeze, crank, push, pull and explore. In summer, the wharf in front becomes a lovely place to waste any number of hours. The scene is made pleasantly surreal by the presence of an immense milk bottle which dispenses ice cream, yogurt and popcorn.

Returning north to Christopher Columbus Park, turn a few hundred yards inland to **Faneuil Hall** and its markets,

Paul Revere's house.

lodestone of the tourist trade and a famed experiment in urban redesign. Everyone goes here, and almost everyone has a great time.

Faneuil Hall, the fulcrum of the place, was given to Boston by Peter Faneuil, a French Huguenot merchant who traded in slaves. This "Cradle of Liberty" was first incarnated in 1742 on a site that was, remarkably enough, Boston's Town Dock. In 1976, after 150 sometimes glorious, sometimes scruffy years of service, **Quincy Market** and Faneuil Hall opened again, this time rising phoenix-like from a massive renovation that converted her boisterous, rugged markets into a chic, cleverly remodeled and wildly successful array of fern bars, jewelry emporia and designer-clothing outfits. In addition, several score food stands that line the long hall of the central building make it hard to walk its length without stuffing oneself with burgers, pizza, candy, ice cream, egg rolls and croissants. Faneuil Hall/Quincy Market is elegant, clean and wholesome — as well as mobbed — yet it is also polished, sanitized and cellophane-wrapped. Some miss the exuberant grunginess of bygone days. But why

carp? This thriving center of the knick-knack trade remains one of the principal ornaments of Boston, and perhaps the finest architectural example of its period in America.

For those who may wonder why all the shopping bags and restaurant menus bear an image of a cricket: when Faneuil gave Boston the hall, he had a large cricket weathervane placed atop its cupola. During the war of 1812, "cricket" became a password and patriot rallying cry of the Boston port. Strangers who could not identify the cricket as the image of Boston met uncertain fates as spies.

Government Center

Looming just inland from the Hall across Congress Street is **Government Center.** Here, it seems, Boston Redevelopment Authority director Edward Logue, Mayor Collins and the great urban designer I.M. Pei constructed a radically new city of their own in Boston's middle. Indeed, Government Center represents building on a grand scale. And depending on the temperament of the beholder, it's either inspir-

A visitor stops to sit with a very permanent Boston resident.

ing or forbidding.

At any rate, it's big. Taking what was Scollay Square, a sleazy confusion of shooting galleries, tattoo parlors and burlesque houses, the designers razed building and removed streets until they'd cleared a huge open space. On this plaza, they arranged several buildings of imposing scale and abstract design.

A massive new **City Hall** by Kallman, McKinnel, and Knowles dominates. Described as an "Aztec temple on a brick desert," this huge affair of concrete provides a fitting, though rather inhospitable, monument to the nearly religious role politics plays in Boston. Arranged neatly around City Hall are additional government buildings, all in the modernist style. For a little comic relief, the quirky little **Sears Crescent** has been allowed to remain from pre-Pei days. A 227-gallon (1,033-liter) teapot, steaming happily, hangs from this 19th Century office building. It's ridiculous, but it's a charming totem for another government institution, the bureaucrat's breakfast.

To the southeast rises the tall confusion of pin-striped Boston, the banks and office towers along Franklin, Congress, Federal, State and Broad streets. Big and confident as they rise from their primitive warren of jumbled byways, these well-tailored behemoths constitute the Hub of Business, the Boston that still regards (as it did in the 17th Century) money as holy, a sign of election.

Historic Downtown

To the southwest beats the throbbing heart of downtown, as well as some buildings illuminated brightly in history. At Washington Street's intersection with Court and State streets stands the **Old State House,** a glorious center of 18th Century public life that today exhibits its heritage of survival by the stubbornness with which it holds the city's predatory skyscrapers at bay. It was here, in 1761, that James Otis first fulminated against the British Writs of Assistance in a spellbinding speech that prompted John Adams to write that "then and there the child Independence was born." In 1770, the infamous Boston Massacre took place just outside the State House. Some years later, after the end of the Revolution, the building served as the meeting place for the Commonwealth Government until the present State House was built. Now, having survived use as a commercial building and demolition plans that were halted only when the city of Chicago offered to buy and relocate it in 1882, the Old State House stands still, a lively little museum inside and a subway stop directly below.

The Old Corner Bookstore, at the corner of Washington and School streets, was once a sort of clubhouse for the likes of Hawthorne, Emerson and Thoreau. Later home of the *Atlantic Monthly* when it was launched in 1857, it is now a prettified bookstore and office for the *Boston Globe,* Boston's journal of record.

Turning right at School Street, wander past the **Old City Hall,** a grand affair that out-Second Empires the French Second Empire, and then **King's Chapel** (1750), one of this Puritan town's first attempts at real architectural class. Turn left at Tremont Street and stroll through the **Granary Burial Ground,** a pleasant glade where generations of tourists have contemplated their mortality among the graves of Peter Faneuil, John Hancock, Samuel Adams, Paul Revere, six Massachusetts

Waterfront attractions: Left, the Boston Tea Party ship; and right, the New England Aquarium.

governors and the victims of the Boston Massacre. A few more paces down Tremont lead to Peter Banner's elegant **Park Street Church** (1809), which Henry James decided was "perfectly felicitous" and "the most interesting mass of brick and mortar in America." On July 4, 1829, William Lloyd Garrison made his first anti-slavery speech here and so launched his emancipation campaign.

An alternate route, continuing down Washington Street from The Old Corner Bookstore, leads to the **Old South Meeting House,** from which 60 whooping "Mohawk Indians" set off for Griffin's Wharf and a Tea Party. After the Meeting House come the **Four Corners,** where hordes of wild suburban shoppers stampede the city's major department stores. Probably the busiest intersection in Boston, it is the location of the phenomenal **Filene's Basement,** perhaps the world's most celebrated bargain store. On weekends, hundreds of thousands of prim professionals, blue-headed matrons, poor Hispanics and blown-dry teen angels can be seen shoving and elbowing each other as they rummage through this cut-rate El Dorado for slippers, belts and forest-green Charles Jourdan pumps.

An Uncommon Place

Government Center is grand and the Old State House is conducive to patriotism, but allowed only one Polaroid memory of Boston, most visitors would save it for America's oldest park, the **Boston Common.** Every metropolis has a great park somewhere in its outline, but no American city boasts as magical a swath of lawn and trees and benches as the area bounded by Tremont, Park, Beacon, Charles and Boylston streets. Sitting in the sun-mottled shade of some May or September watching the pigeons and the Frog Pond, the out-of-towner can understand how Bostonians might mistake this spot for the center of the world.

The land that was to become the Common originally belonged to Boston's first English settler, one Reverend William Blaxton. Having fled first England and then an aborted colonial attempt farther south, Blaxton settled in 1625 on the western slope of what is now called Beacon Hill. There, he tended his orchard and read in peaceful solitude until his serenity was rudely interrupted in 1631 by the arrival of a band of new settlers led by Governor John Winthrop of the Massachusetts Bay Company. The new Bostonians were nobly determined, as Winthrop had written on the ship, to "be as a Citty vpon a Hill," and their presence did not please Blaxton. In 1634, he sold his land to the town for about $150 and fled farther into the wilderness.

The 45 acres (19 hectares) he left behind quickly became a versatile community utility. During the next 150 years, it was used as a cattle and sheep pasture and as a drilling ground. And although, as an account written in 1663 says, "the Common was the beauty and pride of the Town, ever suggesting the lighter side of life," it also proved useful as a place to hang people — for stealing, for piracy, for being a Quaker, for being an Indian, for being a woman who snatched a bonnet worth 75 cents from another woman. There were the whipping post and the pillory, and there was dueling. As a military post, the Common put up the Redcoats all through the Revolution, and during the Civil War provided a backdrop for the tears

Shoppers' paradise: Faneuil Hall.

86

of recruiting and departures.

Now the Common is sweetness and light, a park and nothing else. Climb the little knolls and walk the meandering paths past bronze statues and dignified fountains. Up at the Park Street subway, which as the main crossing of the country's oldest subway has disgorged passengers since 1897, there will be a street musician playing saxophone or mellow guitar. When it's at its best, when the magnolias bloom or the breeze of Indian summer blows the newspaper of the man sitting on that bench, the Common really might be the world's center.

West from the Common and across Charles Street, the elegant **Public Garden** beckons and though it continues the pleasant green of the Common, it has quite a separate past. Indeed, these willows, meandering paths and beds of tulips were mere marsh when the Common was well into its second century of tempestuous history. First deeded at the end of the 18th Century as a riverside ropewalk — the Charles had not yet been filled here — these 24 acres (10 hectares) at the Common's foot were bought back by the city in 1825 for

The modernistic stillness of Boston's Government Center.

$55,000. In a series of disputes during the first half of the 19th Century, some argued that the valuable land would be best sold. But the park soon began to be laid out, though the destruction by fire of an early conservatory for birds and camellias slowed development. By 1867, the Garden had taken its present graceful shape, complete with weeping willows, a bridge for daydreamers and a sleepy four-acre pond. And one can't forget the Swan Boats, those fabled gondolas that carry happy tourists across the placid waters of the pond. At the Commonwealth Avenue entrance, an equestrian George Washington bronze by Thomas Ball presides.

Beacon Hill

Back up at the east end of the Common rises the gold dome of the **State House,** gleaming atop Beacon Hill. Completed in 1798 when the Old State House became too small, this design by Charles Bulfinch, with additions by several others, symbolizes the eminence of politics in Boston. It is less awesome than City Hall at Government Center, but more serenely elegant. A visit to the

grand legislative chambers shouldn't be omitted from any tour. The walk to the chambers passes through a series of splendid halls, beginning with the Doric Hall of the Bulfinch era and leading to the Senate Staircase Hall and the Hall of Flags, both symphonies of *fin de siecle* marble opulence supplied plentifully with statues, busts, flags and patriotic mottos. But none of this dulls the eye to the House Chamber in the Brigham extension, a paneled hall under a two-stage dome. The decorations are inspirational to the point of absurdity: great moments of Massachusetts' freedom march the walls in a series of Albert Herter paintings, while above circles a frieze carved with a roll call of the state's super-achievers. The portentous codfish, a sleek, stiff carving in pine that commemorates Boston's great Federal-era fishing industry, was first hung in the Old State House. Without this odd mascot, the House refuses to meet.

The State House, now hemmed in by Beacon Hill residences, seems about as centally located as a building can be, but it wasn't always that way. In 1797, residents of Boston thought that the Wild West itself began on the far side of the Common, hardly a quarter-mile from the State House. Cows still grazed there, and much of the surrounding land had the bucolic air of pastures trailing off into forest. Even Beacon Hill rose, not as a polite demi-hill, but as a rugged mass of wilderness, then called the Trimount because of its triple-peaked summit. The westernmost of these peaks was isolated enough from the Puritan stronghold of town that it could be put to the purposes suggested by the name Mount Whoredom.

Predictably enough, moving the State House into this setting brought the area to the city's focus and changed things for good. While the Common became a true park, the Trimount became the subject of land speculation. It was quite ingeniously leveled and quickly became the compressed but still idyllic neighborhood of bow-fronted townhouses known now as "The Hill." At first, everyone expected that the new residences of Beacon Hill would be urban estates along the lines of Bulfinch's **No. 85 Mount Vernon Street,** which is to this day one of Boston's most majestic houses. But the mansion plans were quickly scaled down to the smaller blocks one sees today. At No. 55 Mount Vernon, the **Nichols House** offers a more typical example of Beacon Hill building. Also a Charles Bulfinch project, the house is now a small museum

To get a sense of The Hill, walk west down Beacon Street from the State House. At numbers 39 and 40 Beacon stand the twin mansions that now house the **Woman's City Club of Boston,** open for tours one day each week. At numbers 42 and 43, the **Somerset Club,** built in 1819 as a mansion for David Sears, was acquired by the most exclusive of Boston social clubs in 1872. At number 45 Beacon stands the third of Harrison Gray Otis' houses, built in 1805.

Charming Charles Street

At the foot of the hill, a right turn leads to **Charles Street,** at once among the city's most charming and most sophisticated places to stroll, shop and snack. Here is Boston's leading concentration of antique stores — **A. Kim Oriental Antiques, George Gravert Antiques** and **Marika's** are especially worth investigating — as well as a di-

A lively greengrocer in Boston's Haymarket.

verse collection of coffeehouses, bakeries, florists, cafes and boutiques. **DeLucca's Market** is wonderful with the smells of well-ripened melons, fresh sausage and coffee beans, while across the street **Il Dolce Momento** serves noble cakes, exquisite *sorbettos* and rich Florentine ice creams.

The street's principal landmark is the **Charles Street Meeting House** at the corner of Charles and Mount Vernon streets. Built first for the Third Baptist Church in 1807, it served as the home of the African Methodist Episcopal Church and later the Unitarian-Universalist Church. This simple, blocky and unpretentious building now houses several antique stores, a flower shop and a designer ice-cream place.

Wander off Charles onto the shady, peaceful streets that parallel it and lead back up the hill. Many of the houses here are noteworthy either for the talent of their architects or the luminous names of their former occupants. Admiral Richard E. Byrd, the first man to fly over both the North and South poles, lived in No. 7-9 Brimmer St., and No. 44 Brimmer was the lifelong home of the great historian, Samuel Eliot Morison. The Victorian clergyman and philospher William Ellery Channing lived at No. 83 Mount Vernon St., next door to the Otis mansion.

Louisburg Square, developed between Pinckney and Mount Vernon streets around 1840, epitomizes the Beacon-Hill style and its urban delicacy. The Square may well stand at the summit of Boston society. William Dean Howells, the novelist and *Atlantic Monthly* editor; Louisa May Alcott, author of *Little Women*; and Jenny Lind, the "Swedish Nightingale," all lived at one time or another in the houses surrounding the Square's elegant green. Lind married her accompanist Otto Goldschmidt at No. 20 during an America tour in 1852.

Another charming example of Beacon Hill's spirit can be found at numbers 13, 15 and 17 Chestnut Street, where Bulfinch built for the daughters of his client Hepzibah Swan three exquisite townhouses in a prim little row. Chestnut Street, incidentally, might be the prettiest street on the hill, so fetching is the gently animated conversation of its porches and windows, flower-box geraniums and romantic gaslights.

A vision in the middle of the city: the Boston Public Gardens.

But to enjoy the happy rectitude of Beacon Hill, don't plan ahead. Just walk. Know that if the sidewalks are bumpy and steep, few urban settings remain so picturesque.

Elegance Made From Mud

From Beacon Hill, it's an easy transition both in distance and architectural feeling to the handsome streets of **Back Bay,** the area that has come in recent years to epitomize "Old Boston." But for all the suggested venerableness, don't be fooled: Back Bay literally crawled from the mud into prominence. The massive program of filling by which the Back Bay came into being epitomizes the practical stubborness that is altogether Bostonian. In defying topography, in ignoring what previously existed, Back Bay proclaims the triumph of Puritan doggedness over adversity, in this case a festering swampland that, in 1849, was declared "offensive and injurious" by the Board of Health.

The heroic story begins in 1857 when the legislature adopted a grand plan for the Back Bay: there would be long vistas down dignified blocks, and a wide boulevard with a French-style park down the middle. There would be nothing better. In 1858 the first load of fill, which had been loaded by an innovation called the steam shovels, arrived by train from Needham, about 10 miles to the south-west. During the next 20 years, some 600 acres (246 hectares) of dry land emerged from the muck of Back Bay.

And sure enough, as houses began to appear, they were dignified. Despite the vagaries of individual taste and the piecemeal selling of lots, the new blocks went up with a harmoniousness that from the beginning gave Back Bay the stately unity it still possesses. One young man who planned to build his bride a house in Back Bay was icily informed by his prospective father-in-law that he would never allow a daughter of his to live on "made ground." But such qualms were rare, and the new streets quickly became fashionable.

Today, the area is as elegant as ever, and its streets offer a truly civilized display of urban living. Indeed, Back Bay presents as great a showing of the Boston domestic architecture of the second half of the 19th Century as Beacon Hill does of the first. The verdant mall of **Commonwealth Avenue** centers things, and the houses that line it as well as the residential streets of Marlborough and Beacon reveal their beauty in the subtle detailing of their architecture.

Starting at the Arlington Street entrance to the Public Gardens, the visitor may want to stop at the **Ritz-Carlton Hotel,** down one block on the corner of Newbury Street. The Ritz-Carlton is the perfect place to fortify oneself with a cocktail or a cup of tea and to watch the prim Brahmin ladies. From there, head north to No. 137 Beacon Street, between Arlington and Berkeley (the streets here ascend in alphabetical order). Built in 1860 during the earliest days of Back Bay building, the **Gibson House** has been left substantially as it was; it now houses a museum that recreates the feel of Back Bay living in its heyday. Continue to the corner of Commonwealth and Clarendon for a look at the **First Baptist Church,** a virile design by H.H. Richardson. Its tower is graced with figures modeled after celebrities of the day — Emerson, Hawthorne and Longfellow.

Runners jockey for position near the start of the Boston Marathon.

In the block between Clarendon and Dartmouth, Commonwealth Avenue (known as "Comm Ave" to the locals) displays its most memorable structures. The romantic houses that march down this stretch perfectly justify the avenue's reputation as America's Champs-Elysées.

Paralleling Commonwealth on the south are Newbury and Boylston streets, the Back Bay that has been taken over by commerce and the rarefied air of uptown chic. On Newbury Street, the hairstyles are elaborate and the clothes are designer. Pricey restaurants, sidewalk cafes and seductive storefronts abound, and a number of fine galleries operate in sleekly converted townhouses. Prominent among these are the **Impressions Gallery** at Newbury and Dartmouth, **Child's Gallery** at No. 169 Newbury, and **Vose's Gallery** at No. 238 Newbury. Specializing in American painting, 1669 to 1940, Vose's has been in Boston since 1897 and is the oldest private gallery in the United States. Five generations of the same family have faithfully maintained the tradition.

A chorus of voices backs the Greater Boston Youth Symphony Orchestra.

Classical Copley Square

Follow Dartmouth Street to Bolyston for one of the most exciting display of architecture in the city — **Copley Square.** First, H.H. Richardson's wonderful **Trinity Church** (1877), a *tour de force* in Romanesque inventiveness, somehow fuses almost brutal power with an endless array of delicate details. Inside, the first-time visitor will be amazed by the sheer size of the place and the fabulous wealth of murals, mosaics, carvings and stained glass.

Across the square stands Charles McKim's **Boston Public Library** (1895), a classical contrast to Trinity's medievalism. This simple, serene and high-minded Parnassus might well be the center of the Boston that claims to be the "Athens of America." What better monument to a literary legacy populated by the likes of Emerson, Hawthorne, Thoreau and Alcott? (Bret Hart once observed that in these parts it was impossible to fire a pistol without bringing down the author of a two-volume works.) With some 5 million volumes, this is one of the great libraries in the world. But it's more than a building of

books. There's art everywhere — murals by Sargent, statues by St. Gaudens and Daniel Chester French — and, at the center of a maze of stairs and passages, a beautiful inner courtyard features a fountain and trees. Philip Johnson's massive but unobstrusive 1972 addition completes the place.

Above everything looms I.M. Pei's magnificent blue-green mirror, the **John Hancock Mutual Life Insurance Tower.** Proud to be a building, proud to be in Boston, it has the look of a shimmering prism breaking free of the city's prim lowness and singing of stratospheric freedom. It has an excellent observatory on the 60th floor where visitors can speculate madly on everything below as well as attend to informative multimedia exhibits about Boston. The only thing wrong with this gargantuan prism has been its propensity to lose the huge sheets of glass that cover it, especially when the wind blows. The problem was controlled, but not eliminated, in 1974 and 1975 when all 10,344 panes — some 18½ acres' (7½ hectares) worth — were replaced at a cost of $8.5 million. To this day, sheets of glass occasionally plummet to the ground.

Miraculously, no one has been hurt, so Bostonians can laugh at the Tower's fickle ways and dangerous beauty.

West from Copley, **Boylston Street** makes an exciting place to walk, especially when the mad-dog creatures of the Boston night give it the voltage otherwise available only in Manhattan and darkest Los Angeles. Everyone along here seems to be looking for something — a movie, a bar, a restaurant. Although it's not always clear whether they find what they're looking for, it's fun to watch the search.

On the south side of Boylston, no one can miss (though he may want to) the **Prudential Center.** Intended as the new focus of the city, "The Pru" is, in fact, a rather graceless development of the sort favored by the builders of the Soviet Utopia. Developed out of an old railroad yard, the complex includes a major auditorium and convention center, a 29-story Sheraton Hotel, a Saks Fifth Avenue, a Lord and Taylor and a miscellany of additional shops. Above these rises the 52-story Prudential Insurance Tower. It's not beautiful, but there is a nice bar at the top that offers a view of sparkling lights and

The Christian Science Mother Church.

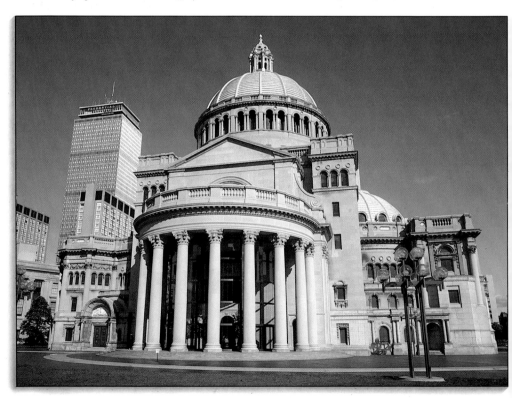

sunsets with the gin. Every Patriots Day, the Prudential becomes the destination of the thousands who enter the world-famous Boston Marathon, perhaps the most celebrated running event on the planet.

The Story of Christian Science

The **Christian Science Church Center** occupies the 22 acres (nine hectares) immediately south of the Prudential Center. The complex includes three older buildings — the Romanesque **Mother Church** (1894), the Italianate **Mother Church Extension** (1904) and the **Publishing Society** (1933) — as well as I.M. Pei's recent additions. The expanded center, a happy marriage of old and new architectural styles, makes an impressive Vatican for a religious denomination scarcely a century old.

The founding of Christian Science dates to 1866 when a frail, impoverished 45-year-old woman named Mary Baker Patterson took a severe tumble on the ice as she was walking home from a temperance meeting in Lynn, north of Boston. Several days later, after turning to the New Testament for strength and

inspiration, Mrs. Patterson was suddenly healed, not only of the injuries she'd suffered in the fall, but of the chronic illness that had plagued much of her younger womanhood.

After several years of Bible study, she began to heal others. In 1875, she posted a notice on her Lynn house designating it as a "Christian Science Home." She was on her way to establishing a major American religious movement at an age when she might have been expected, in her own ironic words, to be a little old lady in a lace cap. Though local gossip assumed the occupant of the Lynn house was either a spiritualist, a hypnotist or an advocate of free love, the next decades saw Mrs. Patterson's tiny band grow from a national to an international movement.

After marrying a follower named Asa Eddy, she moved to Boston where she continued teaching, writing and guiding the establishment of her church. In 1908, at the age of 87, she founded the *Christian Science Monitor,* a respected worldwide daily newspaper which today boasts some 200,000 readers. There are more than 3,000 Christian Science societies in some 50 countries. Though Boston seems full of all manner of cults and sects — the Hare Krishnas and the Scientologists each has a major headquarters in the city — none has made as much of a mark here as the city's own Christian Science Church.

To the south and east of the Christian Science Center sprawls the **South End.** Once prosperous, the South End saw a 100-year decline. Now thanks to the intercession of both gentrification and community development programs, the neighborhood is pleasant and fashionable once again. For the casual stroller the striking, brooding residential areas around **Worcester Square, Rutland** and leafy **Union Park Square** form a very satisfactory itinerary indeed.

The Hub of the Arts

From the South End and the Christian Science complex the demi-urban thoroughfare of **Huntington Avenue** leads southwest past several of Boston's greatest institutions.

At the northwest corner of Huntington and Massachusetts avenues stands the majestic gable-roofed volume of **Symphony Hall,** the acoustical heaven in which the renowned Boston

The Museum of Fine Arts.

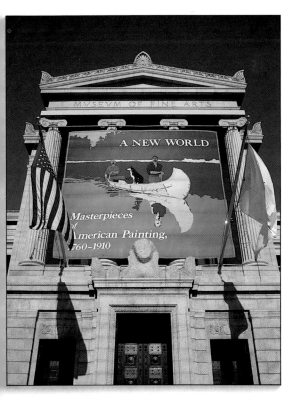

Symphony toils gloriously under the baton of music director Seiji Ozawa. Tickets can be hard to come by, but any amount of exertion toward admission will be well worth it, especially if Beethoven or Brahms grace the program. The accommodations are shared by the Boston Pops Orchestra, whose concerts are to those of the Symphony as Norman Rockwell is to Monet. Long conducted by Boston's "Music Man" Arthur Fiedler, after whom a bridge is now named, the Pops currently play their happy, family-style repertoire under the direction John Williams. Williams, by the way, is a very rich man: he composed the scores for such Steven Spielberg movies as *Jaws, Star Wars* and *The Empire Strikes Back.*

Continuing down Huntington Avenue, one arrives at the spectacular **Museum of Fine Arts.** Built in 1909 to house holdings that were bursting the joints of an earlier building situated in Copley Square, Guy Lowell's imposing design affords space for plenty of Impressionists — including the largest number of Monets outside France. This incredible museum boasts the most complete assemblage of Asian art under one roof anywhere; the world's best collection of 19th Century American art; and the finest collection of Egyptian Old Kingdom objects outside Cairo. The latter includes what some consider one of the greatest portraits ever executed by the human hand — a limestone bust of Prince Ankh-haf (2520 B.C.) that is wholly unearthly in its magnificence. I.M. Pei has added a stone-clad, glass-topped new wing that perfectly complements the original building and creates an inspiring, expansive space of light. This is a superb place to contract what Robert Benchly called "museum feet."

Within sight of the Museum of Fine Arts stands the **Isabella Stewart Gardner Museum,** the personal fantasy palace of a brilliant, unabashedly eccentric millionairess. A perfect antidote to the Fine Arts' monumental excellence, it's one of the great small museums in the world as well as being one of the most eclectic and fun.

Ms. Gardner began collecting art in 1888, filling her two Beacon Hill brownstones with hundreds of works collected on trips to Europe and Asia with her merchant millionaire husband. During the 1890s, with the aid of the young art critic Bernard Berenson and the inheritance first of $2,750,000 from her father and then another $3 million from her husband, she raised her sights to such masterpieces as Titian's "Rape of Europa," Rembrandt's "Storm on the Sea of Galilee" and Vermeer's "The Concert." In 1869, work on Fenway Court began. This stately pleasure dome that rises in the manner of a Venetian *palazzo* from the marshes of the Fens enjoyed a gala opening on New Year's Night 1903. The galleries that frame its four-story glass-roofed courtyard have remained, by order, unchanged and therefore extraordinary.

North of the museums broods another of Boston's great shrines, **Fenway Park,** on whose bright-lit green baseball diamond the Boston Red Sox do heroic, usually tragic, battle for the pennant of the American League East. Here, as the world turns slowly on a muggy twi-night doubleheader, the out-of-towner experiences firsthand how Boston turns sport into religion. Indeed, such past stars as Ted Williams and Carl Yastrzemski have been almost deified.

The River Charles

Great cities — Paris, London and Rome come to mind — embrace great rivers from which they are inseparable. The same is true of Boston, for to the north and west the river Charles makes her grand exhibition. Here, before the townhouses of Back Bay, it widens into a great basin the image of which is integral to anyone's memories of Boston. What a beautiful image it is; what a noble finale for an altogether pathetic, unambitious river. To the west and southwest, the Charles twists and turns for 40 miles (64 km) as it makes its vague and indecisive effort to find the sea. When it nears Boston, it seems not to flow at all but to open into a great, wide mirror held up to the city's most favoring profile.

How glorious it is! What flattery for a deserving city. And it's more, for since the construction of the **Esplanade,** a winding park of lagoons, trees and walks, the river's edge has become one of the city's favorite places to get a little air and stretch its legs. Roller skaters wired for sound, joggers, bike riders and sunbathers all migrate here. So do

Bill Evans, Boston Red Sox baseball scout, studies a prospect at Fenway Park.

the great crowds that turn out to hear the Pops play under open summer skies at the **Hatch Shell.** To everyone, this river is beautiful, whether at night when a thousand orange and white lights dance on its black surface, or on a fall afternoon when the sailboats are out, their sails snapping at the wind.

What's more, the Charles gives a home to another great Boston institution — Boston's **Museum of Science,** built on a dam across the river. Here, visitors watch live chicks hatch, climb into a model of the Apollo lunar module, cower under a plastic Tyrannosaurus Rex, and witness leaf-cutting ants build their empire.

The Hallowed Halls of Cambridge

Elizabeth Hardwick once described Boston and **Cambridge** as two ends of the same mustache. Indeed, across the Charles lies a separate city that is absolutely inseparable from its companion metropolis. Neither suburb nor next town down the pike, Cambridge is the brains of the act, the nerve center of the body.

Crossing **Harvard Bridge,** which is exactly 394.4 smoots and one ear in length according to the fraternity that annually measures the span in units derived from the height of a 1959 pledge named Oliver Reed Smoot, one first comes to the **Massachusetts Institute of Technology** (MIT). Housed in the solid, geometrical buildings, impersonal and mysterious as natural laws, MIT produces Nobel laureates, new scientific advances and White House science advisors with absolute reliability. In addition, some 9,500 students from 96 countries, heavily armed with calculators, learn the ways of the quark and the analog, as well as express themselves with a truly weird sense of humor that each year leads to tiddlywinks competitions, unicycling clubs and unspeakably bizarre pranks. MIT has a strange subterranean feel, possibly caused by the introversion of great tinkerings and the solution of many equations in many unknowns. At any rate, the visitor will quickly get a sense of the intellectual intensity that makes Cambridge the ultimate mecca in academe.

Yet the true *raison d'être* of Cambridge lies another mile or so to the north up Massachusetts Avenue. There,

Renaissance Italy finds a home in Boston at the Isabella Stewart Gardner Museum.

standing proudly above the red brick and green ivy, are the spires and towers of **Harvard University,** America's oldest institution of higher learning. Like Disneyland and Mickey Mouse, Chartres and its cathedral, Cambridge without Harvard would be pointless, one more lost town in the provinces. Self-confident and backed by enormous wealth, Harvard has been a world index of intellectual accomplishment almost since that day in 1638 when the first 12 freshmen convened in a single frame house bordered by cow pastures. *Alma mater* of six American presidents, Harvard remains — great, a little stuffy, unavoidable.

The heart of the place is the **Old College,** the fabulous, ancient Yard, withdrawn tranquilly behind the walls that separate it from the maniacal whirl of human and automotive madness in Harvard Square outside. Passing through the gate which proclaims "Enter to Grow in Wisdom," the visitor finds a half-believable fairyland of grass and trees, ghosts and venerable brick. These buildings, and those in surrounding blocks, provide a living, entirely walkable museum of American architecture

Harvard
Square,
mecca of
students.

from colonial times to the present.

Massachusetts Hall (1720), Harvard's oldest standing building, shows the beautiful simplicity of its period, but its history is complex. While it has always provided students with rooms, the Hall has also quartered American Revolutionary troops, as well as housed a lecture hall, a famous drama workshop and, since 1939, the offices of the University president. Nearby, set among the cluster of the Old Yard, stands little **Holden Chapel** (1744), once described as "a solitary English daisy in a field of Yankee dandelions." At the Yard's center stands Charles Bulfinch's **University Hall,** built of white granite in 1815. In front of it stands Daniel Chester French's statue of John Harvard (1884), the young Puritan minister for whom the college was named after he left it half his estate and all his books. Since no likeness of Harvard existed, French wrought an idealized figure for his statue. using a student as his model.

East of University Hall, three great buildings set off the central green on which commencement is celebrated each June. These are H.H. Richardson's 1880 masterwork **Sever Hall,** with

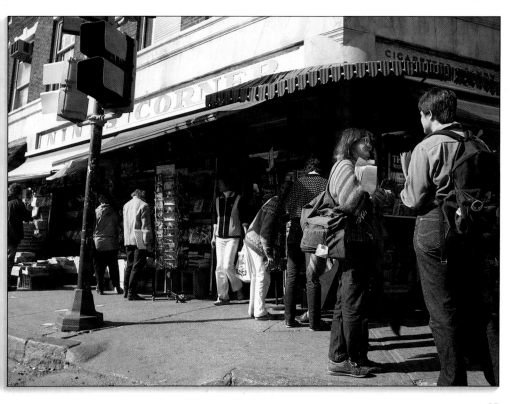

its subtle brick decorations; **Memorial Church** (1932), with its Doric columns; and the monumental **Widener Library,** fronted by a broad flight of steps and 12 stone columns. Given by the mother of one Harry Elkins Widener, '07, who died on the *Titanic,* the library centers Harvard's network of 92 libraries. Together, these house 10 million volumes, the second largest collection of books in America.

Around this historic core, the university sprawls throughout central Cambridge. The **Harvard Houses** (1930), between the Yard and the Charles, represent a return to the Georgian traditions of the 19th Century. These are the residences of sophomores, juniors and seniors. To the east of the Yard stands the **Carpenter Center for the Visual Arts** (1963), a cubist, machine-like design that represents the only American work of the great French architect Le Corbusier. To the north lies Walter Gropius' Bauhaus **Harkness Commons** and **Graduate Center.** And Harvard extends even beyond Cambridge. The Business School ranges across the Charles' Brighton banks, while the Medical School is in Boston, near the Museum of Fine Arts.

Of special interest to visitors are the university's museums. Just outside the Yard to the east is the **Fogg Art Museum.** The Fogg's massive holdings include such masterpieces as Van Gogh's "Self Portrait," Renoir's "Seated Bather," Fra Angelico's "Crucifixion," and several early Picassos. It also owns one of the finest collections of Chinese cave paintings and archaic Chinese jades in the world. In 1985, the **Arthur Sackler Museum** will open next door to the Fogg and provide a home for the Fogg's Ancient, Islamic and Oriental collections.

Several blocks north on Quincy Street stands a huge complex housing five more great museums. The **Busch-Reisinger** is Harvard's museum of central and northern European art, one of the premier collections of 20th Century prints and German expressionist painting outside Germany, including masterworks by Beckmann, Klee and Kandinsky. At the **Botanical Museum,** visitors may behold one of the more unlikely achievements of the human mind — the "Glass Flowers," a collection of true-to-life models of more than 700 different plant species excuted by Leopold

Blaschka and his son Rudolph in 19th Century Dresden.

In the same building, the **Museum of Comparative Zoology** houses, among other things, a whale skelton, the largest turtle shell ever found, the Harvard mastodon, the lobe-finned coelacanth "living fossil," the giant sea serpent *kronosaurus,* George Washington's pheasants (stuffed), the world's oldest reptile eggs and an insect collection containing more than 4 million specimens. If these aren't enough, gems, minerals and meteorites are on display at the **Minerological Museum,** and ancient baskets and masks are at the **Peabody Museum of Archaeology and Ethnology.**

A fine, exuberant end to the tour lies right in Harvard's midst, at **Harvard Square,** the frenetic playground of bookstores, coffeehouses, boutiques and tweedy clothing stores to the east and north of the Old Yard. At its center, terminus to all wanderings in the vicinity, stands the **Harvard Cooperative Society** — "Coop" for short — a century-old Harvard institution which has taken the idea of a college bookstore and expanded it into an all-around department store.

But again, wander the streets. Every block presents some window or door to investigate. Browse the fine bookstores like **Wordsworth** and the **Harvard Book Store,** check the movie schedules at the **Harvard Square, Orson Welles** and **Brattle** theaters. There's even a great old tobacco store, a dark cave called **Leavitt and Pierce** that will start nicotine addicts of discretion nodding in satisfaction and remembering the grand old days. And most emphatically, try the ice cream, which is in great abundance since the Square has, of late, gone absolutely bananas over sundaes, cones and frappes.

But enough said. Just disappear into Harvard Square's incredible menagerie of horn-rimmed professors, head-shaved punks, waitresses, wanderers, *New Republic* readers, stray dogs, Irish cops, Italian grocers, bluebloods, car salesmen, authors of Great American Novels, remnants of the Sixties, students of the law, Krishnas, poets, mutual-fund handlers, fresh-looking undergraduates, tourists from Dallas, corn farmers from Iowa, Saudi oil shieks and assorted good souls. And accept that this is Boston of the 1980s.

Harvard students surround the statue of their benefactor, John Harvard, in the Old Yard.

99

GREATER BOSTON

The myth that New Englanders are the staid products of the Puritan tradition, unaffected by ethnic changes, dies hard, perhaps because the natives work so hard at perpetuating it while privately chuckling over a draught beer and a platter of cherrystone clams. In fact, both Boston's North and South shores feature diverse and vibrant populaces enjoying an environment rich in beauty and tradition.

But the secret pleasures of this suburban stretch of Massachusetts are revealed only grudgingly to the outsider. The wily resident is likely to hand a prepackaged dose of Puritan homesteads and Revolutionary battle sites to the naive visitor simply to steer traffic away from the quiet splendor of hidden beaches and the gastronomic ecstasy of low-key seafood restaurants. Visitors with the initiative to pursue the truth will discover what residents already know — that puncturing myths can be great fun, especially when the beer is cold and the cherrystones shucked.

A few earnest South Shore chamber of commerce types, pointing to the recent population growth of their area, gamely insist that it offers everything to a visitor that the North Shore does. This claim draws a chuckle, a knowing smile and a thorough rebuttal from North Shore wags. They point out that the South Shore's major claim to historical fame, the Plymouth site of the Pilgrims' "first landing," is pure hyperbole, since the *Mayflower* spent five weeks docked at Provincetown before venturing up the coast. To add insult to injury, the North Shore history buff will suggest that the 1620 Plymouth colony was a social and economic disaster compared to the industrious fishermen who settled at Cape Ann in 1630. "It was fish that brought the first Englishmen to America," wrote Herbert A. Kenny in his 1971 book *Cape Ann: Cape America*, "and it was a profound understanding of the meaning of America that led the State House of Representatives to mount in its sacred chamber a replica of the codfish and not a replica of Plymouth Rock." So much for the South Shore's claim to primacy.

18th Century graphic of Newburyport.

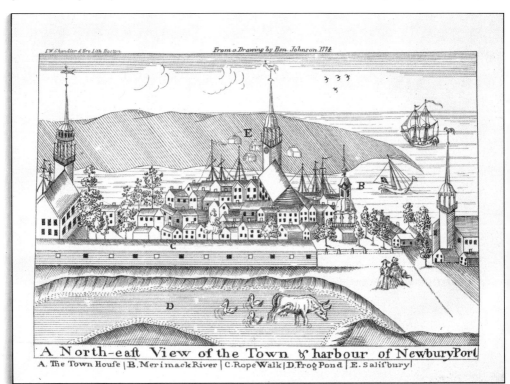

S.W. Chandler & Bro Lith Boston.   From a Drawing by Ben. Johnson 1774

A North-east View of the Town & harbour of NewburyPort

A. The Town Houfe | B. Merimack River | C. Rope Walk | D. Frog Pond | E. Salifbury

The North Shore

Although the southern reaches of Massachusetts Bay do offer an abundance of beautiful beaches and striking architecture, the North Shore is first stop for the wise traveler. A thorough tour should begin in **Newburyport,** 35 miles (56 km) north of Boston, the smallest city in Massachusetts with only 16,000 residents. Careful preservation and loving restoration have retained the flavor of a port that once housed a magnificent merchant fleet and a thriving shipbuilding industry.

Drivers approaching the old port via U.S. Highway 1 will pass through miles of sleepy farmland in Rowley, Newbury and **Topsfield.** (The latter is the site of the nation's oldest country fair; it is held every October complete with prize cattle and petting zoo.) In fact, it was farming interests that settled the banks of the Merrimack River in 1635. The visitor who registers culture shock upon emerging from the hinterlands into the European-style harbor is on the way to debunking his first myth — that all colonists shared common interests. History tells of escalating tension between the incumbent farmers and the emerging mercantile class who drew their living from the sea, tension that intensified with the incorporation of the harbor into the independent city of Newburyport in 1764. (A decade later, the colonists did manage to cease internal bickering to unit — temporarily — in opposition to the British.)

The onset of freighters turned "the Clipper City" into an aging relic by the early 20th Century. But a model renewal program begun in the Sixties has brought new popularity to Newburyport. The newly renovated Market Square district is a symphony of brick and bustle, with dozens of fine shops and restaurants plus live outdoor entertainment in good weather. High Street is where the more successful sea captains built their Greek Revival and late Georgian palaces, some with the symbolic "widows' walks" atop the roofs, where anxious wives strained for a glimpse of their husbands' return to port. The Cushing House, a three-story brick mansion at No. 98 High St., belonged to Caleb Cushing, first U.S. Ambassador to China; visitors can view the exotic booty of rugs and furnishings

20th Century Newburyport street, meticulously restored.

he brought home. Fartner up the street, the Court House, designed by Charles Bulfinch, perches at the edge of Bartlett Mall.

While natives of the North Shore's historic cities are proud of their reconstructed heritage, they especially savor the easy proximity to the immutable pleasures of sea and sand. Newburyport is blessed with the **Parker River National Wildlife Refuge,** just three miles (five km) away via Water Street and known to all simply as **Plum Island.** The six miles of sand dunes and ocean beach are among the last natural sea barriers left in the Eastern United States. Depending on the season, Plum Island yields a riot of false heather, dune grass, scrub pine and delicious wild beach plums and cranberries that are harvested by visitors in the fall (three quarts per person, no rakes allowed). Geese, pheasants, rabbits, deer, woodchucks, turtles and toads roam freely over the preserve. Fishing, hiking and bird-watching are encouraged, but in typical New England fashion appreciation of nature goes only so far — nudism is prohibited, much to the dismay of the assorted flying insects that feast on exposed flesh during midsummer. Only a limited number of visitors (350 cars) are allowed into the refuge at one time.

The Road to Ipswich

State Highway 1-A leads out of Newburyport toward Ipswich along a lazy, tree-lined road, where hand-built stone walls (too low to keep people out but high enough to keep sheep in) give way to quaint roadside stands. Here dies another myth, that of the aloof New Englander indifferent to the passing parade. God hath created no friendlier being than a North Shore wayside entrepreneur intent on selling something; and while eggs and fish advertised as fresh are likely to be just that, beware of "fresh" corn offered in months other than August, or "antiques" displayed in homes far older than anything for sale within.

This is not to belittle the role of the entrepreneur in North Shore history. Indeed, the coastal city of Revere, just north of Boston, was the birthplace of Horatio Alger, Jr., the most legendary of American rags-to-riches stories. A

The Clam Box in Ipswich home of the classic fried clam.

look at the treacherous currents off the rocky coastline and a glance at the thin topsoil that yielded material for endless stone walls will explain why neither fishing nor farming alone has ever provided sustenance for all who live here.

The old streets of the town of **Ipswich** are lined with restored 17th and 18th Century houses. On Main Street, the Whipple House is furnished in period style, and the John Heard House displays Chinese and American artifacts. Six miles (10 km) outside of town, Richard T. Crane's Beach Reservation presents a wild contrast to the gracious old houses in town. Dozens of artists can be seen toting their easels and oils around.

But despite the local color, Ipswich is best known for its beloved clams, appropriated as the town's symbol. In fact, the region's best — and certainly first — fried-clam restaurant is not in Ipswich at all, but a few miles down State 133 in **Essex.** Raw clams have been a staple of the New England diet since Indians thrived here undisturbed, but the clam only became a regional obsession when it was dipped in batter and fried in oil, and that's where Wood-

man's restaurant comes in. The story goes that on a hot July day in 1916, local restauranteur Lawrence Woodman was frying potato chips and complaining to a fisherman friend that business was slow. "Why not toss some clams in with those chips?" suggested the unsympathetic friend. "That ought to bring in some traffic." Woodman did, thus creating not only the first fried clam but the first fried-clam platter, for which hordes of hungry visitors now wait in line to devour. Happy diners in Woodman's wooden booths (or the spillover crowd enjoying similar delights at Farnham's a bit further down State 133) often toast the day that the creative clam juices flowed in Lawrence Woodman's veins.

Proud Cape Ann

From Essex, follow State 1-A to State 128, and at Riverdale, take State 127, the scenic drive along the coast of **Cape Ann.** Visitors to Cape Ann (named for the mother of England's King Charles I) should take special care not to confuse it with Cape Cod, lest they infuriate the locals, who consider the better known and more commer-

The rocky north shore.

cialized cape to be an elongated slum compared with their regal turf. Partisans are quick to point out that it was Cape Ann fishermen who kept other Massachusetts Bay colonists alive with the catch they shipped down to Boston.

From **Annisquam,** at the mouth of Ipswich Bay, to **Pigeon Cove,** the landscape along this drive looks like old New England — quaint fishing villages and rockbound coast. Despite the benign appearance of the towns and harbors here, they have witnessed some violent behavior. A gang of pirates headed by one John Phillips terrorized Gloucester during the 1720s, until one day a captive fishing crew gained the upper hand and sailed into Lobster Cove, near Annisquam, with Phillips' head hanging from the mast. In Ipswich Bay, a towering rock, now known as **Squam Rock,** was originally called Squaw Rock to commemorate the Indian girl who threw herself to her death there, motive unknown. Today, the populace lead somewhat more sedate lives, and visitors can enjoy the vistas of sea, shanty and rugged landscape that have lured artists like the great American painter Winslow Homer to this lovely peninsula.

Bustling **Rockport,** a former fishing village-turned-artists' colony and tourist attraction, may come as a surprise after the succession of quiet villages to the north. In the early 18th Century, the Cape Ann fleet roamed as far south as Havana and New Orleans, as far east as Glasgow and London, and the riches with which they returned stocked the rows of shops that still line Bearskin Neck. Today, the old shops are art galleries and souvenir stores.

In the 19th Century, a new twist was added to Rockport's maritime trade. Granite, quarried nearby, was shipped to ports around the world. Today, locals swim in the freshwater pool of the Lainesville Quarries, which provided granite for Boston's buildings.

The sea and fishing dominate **Gloucester,** the oldest seaport in the United States. It still boasts an active fishing fleet that scours Georges Bank, and the catch is processed in the plants near the waterfront. Every year, the fishermen, who are of predominantly Portuguese and Italian ancestry, participate in the Blessing of the Fleet. Landlubbers get into the act as well: visitors

Fishing boats in Gloucester Harbor.

104

can take one of the whale-watching cruises that leave daily from the Cape Ann Marina. And the old salts who died at sea haven't been forgotten: Leonard Craske's famous statue of the Gloucester Fisherman memorializes "they that go down to the sea in ships."

Something Fishy

Even controversy in Gloucester has a fishy smell. Recently, the Reverend Sun Myung Moon's Unification Church has outraged many residents by buying up restaurants and tuna boats as well as the magnificent estate of the late Cardinal Cushing, Archbishop of the Roman Catholic Archdiocese and a close friend of the Kennedy family. Gloucester's fishermen, worried about Moon's interest in the fleet, boycott the annual tuna-fishing contest he sponsors.

Just south of Gloucester, off State 127 on Hesperus Avenue, stands **Hammond Castle.** At dusk, when the ocean breezes carry a faint scent of cod and kick up whitecaps around the boats in Gloucester Harbor, a visitor enjoying the view from the castle can easily understand the pride of the Cape Ann

native. The view so inspired inventor John Hays Hammond, Jr., that in the late 1920s he built his mock-European castle here. To express his deep satisfaction in music, he installed an 8,600-pipe organ that stands eight stories high.

Although some North Shore natives will gladly don a Pilgrim's outfit to satisfy a tourist's need for authenticity, the ethnic makeup of the area has long since been changed. Irish, Portuguese and Italian surnames are far more common than ones like Alden or Standish, but the legacy of earlier lifestyles does live on in portions of Magnolia, Manchester and Beverly, abutting State 127 south of Gloucester. Named after the local abundance of swamp flowers, **Magnolia** was once the site of luxury hotels drawing summer visitors from as far away as New York, Cincinnati and St. Louis, then later the scene of extravagant summer living by an elite that built palatial mansions and moored their yachts in the harbor. Outsiders referred to Main Street's expensive shops as "Robbers Alley," but after World War I, the clientele spent less freely and the stores became less swank. Most of the huge vacation homes are now

Gloucester's most famous fisherman.

divided into guest housing or smaller apartments. Ravenswood Park, off Western Avenue, contains the homesite of one of Magnolia's more eccentric citizens, a hermit named Walton. In 1884, his doctor advised him to go live in the wood, and Walton liked it so well he returned every spring for 14 years.

A bit farther along State 127 is **Manchester,** a lovely resort town that some still insist on calling Manchester-by-the-Sea. This pure upper-class New England affectation, the artifice of James T. Fields, a wealthy summer resident of the late 18th Century, whose vanity prompted local wits to start referring to "Beverly-by-the-Depot" and "Gloucester-by-the-Smell." Manchester by any name features stately mansions and Singing Beach, where a bare foot scraped across the hard-packed white sand produces a musical tone that mingles sweetly with the gentle splash of ice-cold surf.

Bewitching Salem

Although myth-lovers will undoubtedly wish to tread the well-worn trail of **Salem's** witch hysteria, the area has much else to recommend it. Salem (on State 1-A south of State 128) owes its grandeur, now carefully restored, to its former prominence as a seaport. The Salem Maritime National Historic Site offers a glimpse into the city's maritime past. Visitors may tour the Derby Wharf and a replica of a 19th Century brigantine, the *Republic*; the Custom House, where Nathaniel Hawthorne once worked; and Derby House, a merchant's mansion built in 1761. Nearby on Turner Street is the House of the Seven Gables, which inspired Hawthorne's novel of the same name.

On Essex Street, the Essex Institute preserves six houses that span two centuries of New England architecture, from the Colonial through the Georgian and Federal styles. Also on the grounds of the institute is a museum displaying exhibits of period furniture.

No visit to Salem should skip the Peabody Museum, which features excellent displays related to the maritime trade and a superb collection of artifacts brought back from the Far East.

Salem's maritime glory notwithstanding, myth will have its day, and most visitors will want to tour the scenes of

Salem today and yesterday: left, an artisan carefully restores an old house; and right, "The Trial of Mrs. Hutchinson, an Example of Puritan Hysteria."

the infamous witchcraft trials. Today, Salem's spasm of fear and hatred is portrayed as an aberration of a democratic colony, but this is yet another misleading myth. This witch trials of 1692 came at the peak of a raging political battle between the conservative established gentry and an individualist faction. The gentry, in the person of the convicting judges, fell back on the time-honored method of attacking political and social upstarts as moral deviants.

Several reminders of the witch hunts remain in Sales today: the Witch Museum displays scenes that describe the events of the hysteria; the Witch House, the home of one of the judges, was the site of the preliminary hearings; and (four miles northwest in **Danvers**) the Rebecca Nurse House preserves the old saltbox where one of the convicted lived.

A short side trip from Salem to **Marblehead,** formerly a bustling port and now a resort and boating center, should include a visit to Hood Sailmakers. Hood's is a tribute to living Yankee ingenuity. Federick E. (Ted) Hood, who came from a yachting family, head a boyhood hobby of tinkering with sails in the family living room. In 1951, his father helped him buy two looms to make his own sailcloth. With his custom-made sails as his trademark, Ted Hood went on to become a world-famous yachtsman, successful defender of the America's Cup for 19 years and founder of Hood Enterprises, world's most successful sailmakers.

Home of the Minutemen

From Salem, State 114 leads to State 128, which wanders west toward the historic sites at Lexington and Concord. Americans tend to forget that the colonists' uprising was a truly conservative revolution, fought largely by well-to-do landowners concerned with a growing British bite out of their profit margins as well as with theories of liberty and participatory democracy. But a visit to **Lexington** Green reveals spacious 18th Century homes, and the largely overpriced shops and restaurants that lie a musket shot away from Henry Kitson's Minuteman statue reflect the town's well-heeled past and present. A further sense of that not-so-distant time and place is provided by a tour of Buckman

Sport fishermen take to the sea.

Tavern, now restored to its original appearance. Here, Captain Parker and his 77 Minutemen sipped beer in stately surroundings (including a complete ballroom) while awaiting Paul Revere's warning.

After the brief skirmish at Lexington, where the greatly outnumbered Minutemen lost eight of their troops, the colonial forces beat a hasty retreat to their arms cache at **Concord.** Modern-day visitors should do the same, for Concord offers unmatched classical New England beauty and atmosphere.

For true historical contrast, travel State 128 ("America's Technology Highway") past the familiar names of the contemporary high-tech revolution such as Raytheon and Digital, and enter Concord via State 2. Stop at any of the farm stands that border the road and buy a picnic lunch of fresh local fruit and apple cider in season. Then proceed to the Lowell Road bridge over the Concord River and rent a canoe for an approach to the Old North Bridge that few tourists experience. Paddling slowly along the winding river, with the branches of stately trees providing shade as they have for more than two centuries, one can understand why men were willing to spill blood to defend this land and preserve its contemplative wonders as their own. At the replica of the Old North Bridge, dock and walk the road and bridge where General Gage's British troops, crowded into the narrow pathway, were easily routed by the ragtag Americans. (Here, too, nature has shaped New England history: annual spring floods that left much of the hill under water had forced the road to be built unusually small, the better to ambush British soldiers.

Although the Minutemen probably had other motives, it's nice to think they fought in part to preserve the freedom of thought and lifestyle that later Concordians explored to fruitfully. Spend a half-day visiting the Ralph Waldo Emerson House off State 2-A; the Wayside, on Lexington Road, where Hawthorne lived; the Orchard House next door, where Louisa May Alcott wrote *Little Women*; and Henry David Thoreau's famous cabin site in the peaceful woods at Walden Pond. To tour Concord is to comprehend why these transcendentalists came to believe in the mystical unity between man and

Lighthouse off the north shore.

108

nature.

Continuing on the State 128 belt that circles Boston en route to the South Shore, there are several worthwhile detours. The Cardinal Spellman Philatelic Museum on the campus of Regis College in **Weston** contains one of the world's largest international stamp inventories, including the prodigious personal collection of President Dwight David Eisenhower, among others. The campus of Brandeis University in **Waltham** has some impressive examples of modern institutional architecture as well as the Rose Art Museum, which frequently houses rare exhibits reflecting the school's singular place in Jewish history and culture. On Wells Avenue in **Newton,** Kenneth W. Rendell operates an internationally known rare book and autograph house. Rendell is the man who, while others were in an uproar over the alleged discovery of Adolf Hitler's personal diaries, calmly examined the documents and definitively proved them fakes.

The South Shore

"The Battle of Lexington."

The stretch of picturesque coastal towns and hard-working inland communities loosely known as the South Shore may lack some of the charms and legends of the North Shore. Indeed, most of the South Shore has held little appeal as a place to settle until the last 20 years or so, and housing prices remain lower here than in any other part of the Boston metropolitan area. Outside of scattered pockets of wealth in shore towns like Cohasset and Hingham, the South Shore is primarily inhabited by God-fearing, lower and middle-income, ethnically diverse residents who have little in common with North Shore-ites and nothing at all in common with the Pilgrims. And from Quincy to Brockton to Plymouth, the people know who and where they are and like it just fine, thank you. "We think of the area as the Sun Belt of New England," says the publisher of the area's largest newspaper, the *Patriot Ledger* of Quincy.

A trip down State 24 off State 128 takes travelers into the heartland of the region, physically not unlike the suburban sprawl that emanates from most American cities, but distinguished by a contentious spirit that stems as much

from the frigid winters and sweltering summers as anything else. The town of **Stoughton** is noteworthy for two things — the Stoughton Diner, where incredibly cheap and delicious home-cooked breakfasts and lunches are served up by sharp-talking, fast-moving waitresses; and a prolonged battle by townspeople against a pornographic bookstore that opened in the town in 1982 and closed in 1983 after daily picketing and nationwide publicity.

A few miles along State 27, off State 24, is **Brockton,** an international center for shoe manufacturing at the turn of the 20th Century. Unable to withstand the competition of foreign imports, the industry collapsed, and Brockton started a downward slide. Today, the city is undergoing urban renewal. The great world heavyweight boxing champion Rocky Marciano was a Brockton native. Now visitors to the Petronelli Brothers Gym over Brockton Hardware on Centre Street might catch a workout by a modern-day Brocktonian who threatens to eclipse Marciano's legend. He is "Marvelous Marvin" Hagler, undisputed middleweight champion of the world, whose motto is "destruction and destroy." He has lived up to his motto with 47 knockouts in his career.

While Hagler symbolizes the street-tough side of blue-collar Brockton, the sweeter side of the city is represented by Gowell's Chocolates on North Main Street, a tiny storefront operation founded in 1959. The original Mr. Gowell died a few years back, so his son Richard runs the kitchen while Mrs. Gowell holds forth in the store. When the late actor John Wayne was hospitalized in Boston in mid 1970s, he sent two nurses down to pick up boxes of Gowell's chocolates, which are made without preservatives. Orders flow into Gowell's from as far away as Europe and the Far East, with dark chocolate bark, chocolate letters and chocolate lollipops especially popular.

Plymouth and Îts Rock

State 27 continues along to **Plymouth.** Sitting on the town wharf, those who insist on mythologizing the *Mayflower* can comfortably picture its entry into Plymouth Harbor. Or they can wander over to the Plymouth rock, reputedly the landing spot of the Pil-

Reenactment of a true Pilgrim thanksgiving in Plymouth.

grims. A stone's throw away; *Mayflower II* is a full-scale replica that was built in England and sailed to Plymouth in 1957. About three miles south of town, on State 3, the Plimouth Plantation is a reconstruction of the 17th Century Pilgrim village. Modern-day New Englanders portray the early settlers and their Indian neighbors; the cottages are furnished in period style.

From Plymouth, State 3-A skirts the coast north to **Duxbury,** where the 130-foot (40-meter) high Miles Standish Monument celebrates the spectacular ocean view as much as it does New England's first commissioned military officer, whose name it bears. Lovers of architecture will enjoy seeing the "King" Caesar House on Powder Point; it was built in 1798 and is as elegant and evocative of a bygone lifestyle as anything north or west of Boston.

Farther north on State 3-A is **Hingham,** replete with 18th Century homes and streets shaded by ancient elm and maple trees. The Old Ship Church on Main Street, the last intact Puritan meetinghouse remaining, was built by ship's carpenters in 1681, and the inside resembles a giant hull turned upside

A roving photographer captures his subjects at a country fair.

down. How the Puritans would have flipped their wigs if they could have foreseen that one day their district's Congressman, Gerry Studds, would be censured by Congress for a homosexual affair with a Congressional page, then win his constituency's 2-to-1 support against his resignation. Yet many of these same citizens who stood behind Studds raised such a hue and cry against the proliferation of video games in the town of **Marshfield** that the selectmen went to court to ban the machines. Mark Twain was referring to New England weather when he suggested that "if you don't like it, just wait a minute," but he might as well have been alluding to the unpredictable social milieu that characterizes the South Shore.

Traditionally the South Shore has seen dramatic ups and downs, and perhaps this explains why the natives are so volatile. In 1750, the first attempt at localized manufacturing in the colonies took place on Shed's Neck in **Quincy,** just north of Hingham on State 3-A. In order to man a proposed glass-manufacturing company, hundreds of German laborers were imported with the promise of inexpensive living and civil and religious freedom. Marketing problems and the destruction of much of so-called "Germantown" by fire doomed the project to failure, but many of the settlers' descendants remain, and their neighborhood is still known by its ethnic nickname. Some of them work at the massive and impressive General Dynamics shipyard on East Howard Street, itself a stoic survivor through alternately fat and lean economic times.

Despite its second-class status next to the elegant time warps of Gloucester or Concord, the South Shore stands without apology as a vibrant, often beautiful slice of New England. This fact is affirmed by a strange ritual that takes place every spring in the remotest corner of the South Shore, the town of **Attleboro** near the Rhode Island border. There, at the LaSallette Shrine, founded by Catholic priests in 1952, the annual Blessing of the Cycles ceremony takes place. One by one, motorcyclists from throughout New England ride up to the church parking lot to receive a personal blessing from the priests. Truly, all New Englanders are blessed by their secret pleasures of sea and sand, legend and heritage, and their distinctive way of living.

CAPE COD

Like a muscular arm beckoning Pilgrims from Europe, Cape Cod extends deep into the Atlantic Ocean. Thirty-one miles (50 km) eastward, then another 31 miles to the north, this sandy peninsula is dotted with a few low hills and lined with more than 310 miles (500 km) of beaches. The crook of the arm forms Cape Cod Bay and keeps its waters warm and free of dangerous ocean surf. Its lighthouses and harbors provide guidance and refuge for mariners plying the cold Atlantic waters.

Cape Cod's fame as a holiday resort has spread, bringing visitors from the 50 states, Canada and overseas. In the high season of July and August, lodgings are filled to capacity, traffic on the Cape's few highways is heavy, and local merchants work hard to make the profits which, in many cases, must carry them through the winter until the next season. Despite the crowds of visitors, the rows of shops, the lines of cars and the various amusements, Cape Cod preserves its wild charm and dramatic beauty.

Much of this charm and beauty is protected within the boundaries of the Cape Cod National Seashore, a vast 27,000-acre (11,070-hectare) nature reserve established by foresighted legislators in 1961. The natural beauty of the Seashore, which resulted from its unique geologic history, is now one of the prime attractions of the Cape.

Formed during the Ice Age, which began about 1 million years ago, Cape Cod is a recent feature in geologic history. An enormous ice sheet, several miles in thickness, moved southward out of Hudson Bay, covering the northeastern United States all the way to Long Island, Nantucket and Martha's Vineyard. There, the slow-moving river of ice, laden with glacial debris, met warmer air and water which melted the leading edge of the ice and freed the soil and rock to sink in the ocean. For hundreds of thousands of years, this leading edge was poised where Nantucket and Martha's Vineyard are today, and the soil and rock dumped during that long period of treadmill activity formed glacial moraine. The air and water grew even warmer, and the glacier retreated

25 or 30 miles (40 or 50 km) to the area known now as Cape Cod. The wall of ice melted away at this point, laying down another moraine, the foundation of the Cape.

When the glacier retreated to the polar ice cap, the ice turned to water and filled the oceans. But the earth, long compressed under the weight of ice, rebounded and thrust the moraines above the surface of the sea. Wind and water erosion, acting during the last few tens of thousands of years, finished the sculpting of Cape Cod.

Simple Pleasures

A stroll through a neighborhood in elegant Chatham, past enormous cedar-shingled "summer cottages," or an evening out in Provincetown's honky-tonk maze of sidewalk amusement stands might lead one to think of Cape Cod as the eternal summer resort. Not so. It was the steamship, railroad and automobile which first brought the hordes of summer visitors here less than a century ago. Escaping the heat of the cities (Boston, Providence and New York) for the cool sea breezes on the

Preceding pages: lobstering gear on Cape Cod fisherman's hut. Left, a salty angler. Right, antique glass in a Sandwich museum.

shore, early visitors found low prices, inexpensive real estate and the simple pleasures in abundance.

Cape Cod, prior to modern transport, was a poor and backward area peopled by Wampanoag Indians, hardy Yankees and tough immigrants from the coasts and islands of Portugal. Since the land was too poor to farm for more than local consumption, they made their living from the sea. Fishing, saltmaking, whaling and "wrecking" — scavenging the beaches for the flotsam and jetsam of ships lost at sea — provided the local people with a livelihood, however uncertain. One year might bring a small fortune in whale oil, or a windfall of English cloth washed ashore from an unfortunate wreck, or a hoard of doubloons dumped on the sand at whim by the sea; the next might bring little income, more death at sea, and much destruction from drought and storm.

In 1602, a mariner named Bartholomew Gosnold sailed by this long arm of sand, noted a great many codfish in the waters and added the name "Cape Cod" to his map. In 1620, the Pilgrims arrived in the *Mayflower* from England, stopping at what is now Provincetown to draw up the *Mayflower* Compact. They constituted themselves as a "civil Body Politick," and vowed to work together under just laws for the good of all. This early "constitution" was the seed that grew into the government of the Commonwealth of Massachusetts.

Across the Cape Cod Canal

Purists could actually call Cape Cod an island, for in 1914, after five years of work, the cape was effectively severed from the mainland by the **Cape Cod Canal.** Improved and widened in 1927, the canal is a boon to north-south ships, which no longer have to venture out into the stormy Atlantic in order to get around Cape Cod.

Visitors come to Cape Cod by air, by sea and by road. The Cape towns of Hyannis and Provincetown have scheduled air service to and from Boston; there are New York-Hyannis flights as well. Small planes shuttle passengers from Hyannis across the water to the islands of Nantucket and Martha's Vineyard. During the busy summer months, daily excursion boats

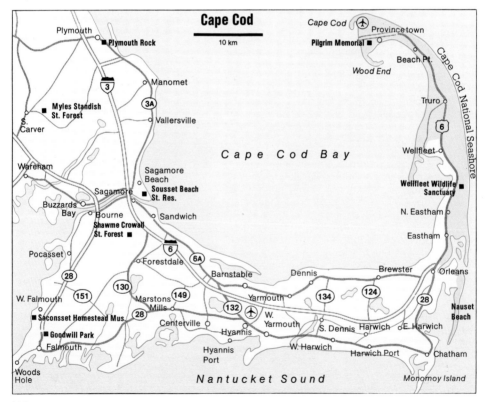

leave Boston Harbor each morning for Provincetown, three hours away. The return trip can bring day-trippers back to Boston that same afternoon.

In earlier times, the railroad brought vacationers to the Cape. Visitors can get a sample of what early Cape rail travel was like by booking a seat on **The Cape Cod & Hyannis Railroad.** These scenic runs are more for fun than for transportation. The tracks run from Falmouth north to Buzzards Bay, then to Sandwich, then east and south by Hyannis. A loop journey can be made in connection with the passenger ferries to Martha's Vineyard and then to Falmouth again. As for the rest of the Cape's network of track, it has largely been removed. One long section of roadbed has been put to an energy-saving, pleasure-making use, however. The **Cape Cod Rail Trail** is a 14-mile (22½-km) paved stretch of railroad bed which runs from State Highway 134 in Dennis through Nickerson State Park to Locust Road in Eastham. The trail has turned the old railroad right-of-way into a fine path for bicycling, hiking, jogging and horseback-riding.

But by far the most popular way of

Wellfleet Bay
Wildlife
Sanctuary

getting to Cape Cod is by bus or car. Expressways bring traffic right to the very edge of the Cape, and two highway bridges tie the Cape to the mainland. To the north is the **Sagamore Bridge,** a graceful arched structure with one foot in the Cape town of Sagamore. State 3 comes south from Boston and goes right across the Sagamore Bridge to join U.S. Highway 6, the Mid-Cape Highway. Near the southwestern end of the canal is the **Bourne Bridge,** leading to State 28 headed for Falmouth and Woods Hole. Near the mainland foot of each bridge is an Information Booth. Here travelers can get help finding accommodations during the busy months of July and August.

Before venturing too far "down-cape," the visitor must learn the nomenclature. "Upper Cape" refers to the east-west portion nearest the mainland; "Mid-Cape" is roughly from Hyannis to Chatham and Orleans, where the "arm" bends; "Lower Cape" is the "forearm" jutting northward to Eastham, Truro and Provincetown.

Once the traveler is on the Cape, the question arises of which route he should take. Those in a hurry to reach their

destination invariably opt for U.S. 6, the four-lane, limited-access Mid-Cape Highway; or, if headed for Falmouth and Woods Hole, for the equally speedy State 28. But the true flavor of the Cape is not found by avoiding the towns. The scenic alternative is State 6A, starting in Sagamore and running eastward, roughly parallel to the Mid-Cape Highway. This excellent two-lane road, lined with graceful old houses, antique shops, restaurants and lodgings, meanders through dunes and marshes, and past cranberry bogs and charming towns. Follow State 6A at least as far as Orleans, then U.S. 6 or State 6A all the way to Provincetown. On the return trip, leave U.S. 6 at Orleans and head south to Chatham along State 28. This same highway travels westward along the southern coast all the way to Falmouth and then north to the Bourne Bridge.

Glass With Class

From the motels, gas stations and businesses at the southern end of the Sagamore Bridge, the road loops around and follows the southern bank of Cape Cod Canal. Before leaving **Sagamore,** watch on the left side of the road for the **Pairpoint Glass Works,** a small building in which master glassblowers still practice the art of making fine crystal by hand. Cape Cod is a natural place to make glass, since the raw material — sand — is available in such abundance.

The next town down the line, **Sandwich,** is particularly famous for its glassware. Lucky browsers in the Cape's many antique shops may come upon objects of cut glass, some in delicate lace-like shapes, which were made in the workshops of the Boston and Sandwich Glass Company. Taking advantage of Sandwich's abundance of sand and of its timber to stoke the glassmakers' fires, the company produced pleasing cut glassware at popular prices in the years between 1825 and 1888. Those who haven't been lucky enough to pick up a piece of Sandwich glass should nonetheless drop in at the **Sandwich Glass Museum,** where they can study the history, and the artistry, of this famous local industry.

The comely town of Sandwich was founded in 1637, and today preserves as

Cape Cod escarpment.

118

much grace and charm as any town on the Cape. In the center stands the **Dexter Mill** and the **Hoxie House,** dating from colonial times. For more glimpses into the American past, follow the signs to **Heritage Plantation.** Fanciers of antique cars will head first for the plantation's Automobile Museum. The cars here date from the great early years of the automobile, up to the start of World War II, and include Gary Cooper's beautiful 1931 Deusenberg. The museum building itself is of great interest; it's a replica of the famous Round Stone Barn built by the Shaker community in Hancock, Massachusetts. Early American arts and crafts as well as artifacts from America's early military history are on display in other buildings.

Barnstable (pronounced "BARN-stuh-bull") includes the settlements of Barnstable, Hyannis and Cummaquid. Barnstable Harbor is sheltered by the long sand spit called **Sandy Neck,** which also serves as a fine swimming beach. Though fishing, lobstering and scallop-gathering still flourish at other ports on the Cape, Barnstable Harbor shelters mostly sleek yachts and motorboats

today. For a look at the harbor's maritime past, drop in at the **Donald G. Trayser Museum,** once Barnstable's Custom House.

Some miles east of Barnstable, **Yarmouth Port** is a delightful village with fine old houses and a big stagecoach inn, still in operation, though the stagecoaches have been replaced by tour buses. The Historical Society of Old Yarmouth has set up several botanic trails near the **Baggs Hallett House,** once owned by a sea captain in the China trade. Other houses to tour are the **Colonel John Thatcher House** and the **Winslow-Crocker House.** Ready for a swim? **Grey's Beach** at the end of Centre Street in Yarmouth is free and open to the public — perhaps the only beach on the Cape without a municipal use fee.

Entering the town of **Dennis,** look for a cemetery on the right (south) side of the road. Just after, turn right onto Old Bass River Road, and then onto Scargo Hill Road, to reach **Scargo Hill Tower.** From this observation point, on a clear day, Cape Cod is laid out like a map, with Provincetown easily visible at the northern tip.

Windsurfing off Truro.

Besides its fine old houses and inns, **Brewster** has a variety of attractions. Right on State 6A is **Sealand of Cape Cod,** with a fine aquarium, plus shows of performing seals and dolphins — favorites with children. The **Drummer Boy Museum** concentrates on a historical panorama of the American Revolution, while the **New England Fire and History Museum** has large collections of fire-fighting equipment and memorabilia. The small **Sydenstricker Glass Factory** is on the right-hand (southern) side of the road. After watching glassware being formed by an original method, visitors can buy items produced in the factory.

For the **Stony Brook Mill,** follow Main Street and Stony Brook Road southwest off State 6A. One of the most picturesque sights on Cape Cod, this old mill still grinds kernels of corn into cornmeal several days a week. Upstairs in the mill building is a small museum, and behind the mill, the pond is a fine place for a stroll and a few minutes' rest. The mill hosts an eye-catching event each spring from mid-April to early May. Making their way from the Atlantic, schools of *alewives* (herring) leap up a system of fish ladders to spawn in the freshwater pond behind the mill, in a timeless ceremony similar to a salmon run.

Railroad magnate Roland Nickerson once owned vast tracts of open land in Brewster and held them as his personal hunting and fishing preserve. After his death, the land became **Nickerson State Park,** open to all. Swimming, picnicking and nature walks are offered; in July and August, there may be a one or two-day waiting line for camping. No reservations are accepted.

The National Seashore

A popular base for touring the Cape, Orleans also offers the first sight of **Cape Cod National Seashore** in the form of Nauset Beach, one of the Cape's finest. The settlement's name was Nauset, the Indian name, until its incorporation in 1797, when it was renamed for the Duke of Orleans, who had once visited the Cape. Orleans has another "French connection": it was the stateside terminus for a transatlantic telegraph cable to the town of Brest in France. Hooked up in 1879, the cable

Waterfront scene, Province-town.

performed well for years, and today is commemorated in the **French Cable Museum** on State 28.

The big attraction in **Eastham** is the **Salt Pond Visitor Center** of the Cape Cod National Seashore. Interpretive films and exhibits explain the ecology of the Cape, a shuttle bus takes swimmers down to the **Coast Guard Beach,** and a bicycle trail winds through the pine forests and over the marshes to end at the same beach. Bikes can be rented, for those who didn't bring their own, and there are two nature trails.

Just across the road from the entrance to Salt Pond Visitor Center, the **Eastham Historical Society Museum** has a unique gateway: the jawbones of a great whale. The museum itself was once a schoolhouse, built in 1869. A short distance south of Salt Pond Visitor Center on U.S. 6 is Eastham's windmill, the oldest on Cape Cod (1793). For a deeper side trip into Cape Cod's history, head west from the windmill to **First Encounter Beach.** Here, the Pilgrims first encountered the original Wampanoag Indian inhabitants of Cape Cod. A plaque set in a glacial boulder on the hill just north of the parking lot commemorates the uneasy meeting. The town charges a fee of several dollars to park and swim here. Following the procedure used on most of the Cape's town-owned beaches, a clerk seated at the entrance to the parking area collects money and issues receipts.

Nauset Light Beach is just north of Coast Guard Beach on the National Seashore. Even those who don't intend to swim should take the detour for a look at Nauset Light, one of the Cape's many picturesque lighthouses.

Famous for its oysters, **Wellfleet** is one of Cape Cod's most pleasant towns. Oyster and fishing boats tie up in Wellfleet Harbor, bringing in the daily catch for the town's several seafood restaurants and for others far and wide. The Congregational Church downtown has a clock which chimes "ship's bells" rather than the hours. Gallery-browsers will love Wellfleet, where a dozen galleries welcome potential customers.

Part of Wellfleet's charm is its wildlife areas. To the east is the **Marconi Area** of the National Seashore. Named for radio pioneer Guglielmo Marconi, the area's center of attraction is the site of the first wireless station in the United States. Marconi set up the

station and transmitted the very first wireless message across the Atlantic Ocean to Europe in 1903. The beach here has lifeguards. **Atlantic White Cedar Swamp Trail,** beginning from the Marconi site, is among the Seashore's finest.

The **Wellfleet Bay Wildlife Sanctuary,** administered by the Audubon Society, lies south of town on the west side of U.S. 6. Visitors can observe nature here in the sancturary's 700 acres (284 hectares). Follow signs, around to the north and west of Wellfleet, that lead to **Great Island,** also part of Cape Cod National Seashore. Next to the parking lot is a picnic area. Great Island Trail leads all the way to the southern tip of the long peninsula that reaches into Cape Cod Bay.

Farther north, the landscape becomes ever more wild and barren. Scrubby vegetation gives way to desert-like sand dunes. East of **Truro, Cranberry Bog Trail** in the National Seashore offers a look at the natural habitat of the tiny red fruit which has such an important place in American history and in the modern economy of Cape Cod. Another road east leads to

The Pilgrim Monument, Province-town.

Highland Light, which looms above **Head of the Meadow Beach.**

Portrait of Provincetown

The very tip of Cape Cod is among its most beautiful and interesting areas. Besides the fascinating, colorful, circus-like atmosphere of "P-Town" itself, the tip holds some of the National Seashore's prettiest landscapes. An interpretive shelter in the **Pilgrim Heights** area will divulge the secrets of the landscape's beauty. Turn off U.S. 6 at the sign for "Dune Parking" from the parking lot, climb the sand dunes which look as though they came straight out of an Arabian vision.

The tip of the Cape is almost entirely within the boundaries of the National Seashore. Three lighthouses and two vast beaches **(Race Point Beach** and **Herring Cove Beach)** are perfect for exploring. For an overview, drop in at the **Province Lands Visitor Center.** Bicycle and hiking trails, bridle paths and tours of the dunescape by off-road vehicles are available.

Contrast the subtle beauties and serenity of the National Seashore lands with the raucous and sometimes tawdry atmosphere along Commerical Street in **Provincetown.** Sidewalk artists will do a pastel portrait, or perhaps a cartoon caricature, in a flash. Shops emblazoned with advertisements sell fine works of art, bad works of art, kitsch souvenirs, hundreds of things to munch and nibble and drink on the street. There are good restaurants and bad restaurants, beautiful old inns and inexpensive guest houses, tacky shacks and graceful mansions.

The year-round population of Provincetown, about 5,000 souls, increases elevenfold in the summertime. Motels, inns and guest houses may be filled to capacity. Visitors should have a reservation before they arrive, or they may not find the sort of accommodation they want.

With its well-protected harbor, Provincetown began as a natural fishing port. So it remains today. Portuguese fishermen, many from the Azores, came here a century ago by following the good fishing. Their descendants still make up a sizable proportion of the town's year-round residents, and also of its fishermen. Other townfolk are artists

Sal's Place: Salvatore Del Deo's landmark restaurant in Provincetown.

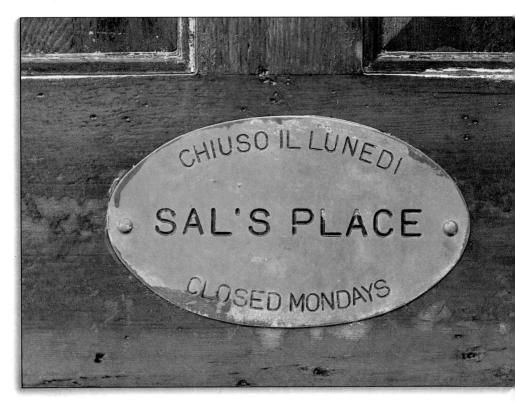

122

and writers, keeping alive the tradition started in 1901 with the founding of the Cape Cod School of Art. Famous dramatists such as Eugene O'Neill and Tennessee Williams, and writers such as Sinclair Lewis and John Dos Passos, began their careers here, far from city distractions.

In the summer, however, the city comes to Provincetown. Direct buses, flights and voyages link P-Town and Boston; crowds make their way here from the rest of New England, from New York and from Montreal. A significant proportion of vacationers are gay. Like San Francisco, Provincetown prides itself on its fairness and open-mindedness.

Though the flow of the crowd on Commercial Street is the first thing that impresses visitors, there is a lot more to see here. The lofty Italianate tower looming above the town is the **Pilgrim Memorial,** open to visitors. (Yes, it has an elevator!) Besides the panoramic view of the town and the entire Cape, the Memorial has **Provincetown Museum,** stocked with local memorabilia. Along Commercial Street are the **Aquarium** and several smaller

museums. The streets of the West End are lined with fine old houses from the 18th and 19th centuries. Many have now been converted to inns.

The Southern Shore

Cape Cod's southern shore from Chatham to Falmouth holds a never-ending array of contrasts. State 28 starts from Orleans and goes all the way to Boston and beyond. Therefore, even though the route leaving Orleans heads due south, it's marked "Route 28 North." Chatham, Hyannis and Falmouth are all on State 28.

The aristocrat of Cape Cod, **Chatham** has something of the feeling of Newport, Rhode Island, about it. Though Chatham's huge cedar-shingled "summer cottages" are hardly as large as Newport's mansions, they exude a similar feeling of wealth and gentility.

The famous old **Chatham Bars Inn** was a watering place for the upper classes for the better part of this century. The **Chatham Railroad Museum** is housed in the town's Victorian railroad station, out of use for many years now. **Chatham Light,** yet another picturesque

Coast Guard lighthouse, is just behind a town beach noted for its warm waters. At the **Fish Pier,** an observation deck is the perfect spot to watch the fishing fleet bring in the daily catch between 2 and 4 o'clock each afternoon.

Bird fanciers will want to make a point of visiting **Monomoy Island,** an important stopping point for hundreds of species of birds traveling the Atlantic Flyway. Now protected as the Monomoy National Wildlife Refuge, it is accessible only by boat, as authorized by the refuge administration.

Picturesque **Harwich** and **Harwich Port** are the last peaceful settlements before the Cape's commercial belt. From **West Harwich** to Hyannis, State 28 is lined with motels, restaurants, businesses and amusements. It's a lively, tawdry stretch always full of life and bustle. In high summer, the traffic forms long lines and moves very slowly.

The commercial center of Cape Cod, **Hyannis** is the place to go for automobile repairs and department-store shopping or for a flight to Boston, New York or beyond. Interstate bus lines connect with local lines here. From the town's docks, ferryboats crisscross Nantucket Sound to the islands of Nantucket and Martha's Vineyard.

The commercial atmosphere of Hyannis doesn't extend to the posh estates of **Hyannis Port,** famed as the summer home of John F. Kennedy. A monument to the late President is set in a wall on Ocean Street, but the Kennedy Compound is not open to visitors.

West of Hyannis, the sea of commerciality gives way to more of Cape Cod's natural beauty. Heading southwest toward Falmouth, keep an eye out for the town of **Mashpee,** which is actually a sort of reservation for the Massipee Indians. Losing ground before the influx of colonial settlers, the Massipees were granted a large "plantation" as their homeland. Mashpee Plantation was later incorporated as the town of Mashpee. Those not lucky enough to arrive during the town's annual Pow-wow should at least have a look at the **Gld Indian Meetinghouse,** oldest church building on the Cape. It was built in 1684 to house the Christian Indian congregation of the Reverend Richard Bourne, and counted among its Indian preachers several descendants of the great chief Massasoit, friend and benefactor of the Pilgrims at Plymouth.

If one phrase could describe **Falmouth,** it would be "a microcosm of Cape Cod life." The town green, surrounded by fine old houses, a museum and a monument to Katherine Lee Bates, composer of *America the Beautiful,* is one of the prettiest on the Cape. The downtown commercial district has enough shops and stores of all varieties to answer any need. Falmouth Harbor is lined with motels and filled with pleasure craft, while surfers and windsurfers favor the beaches and guest houses of Falmouth Heights.

One of the nicest activities in Falmouth is to rent a bicycle and follow the old railroad bed, now a bike path, down to **Woods Hole.** This small town is devoted exclusively to maritime activities. Most people come here to board the car ferries for Martha's Vineyard, a 45-minute voyage away. But Woods Hole is the home of the world-famous **Woods Hole Oceanographic Institute,** the Marine Biological Laboratory and the National Marine Fisheries Service. For the summer visitor, the Fisheries Service is of special interest because of its **aquarium,** open to view.

Left, venue of Chatham chocolate lovers. Right, a day's catch from Nantucket Sound.

124

MARTHA'S VINEYARD

A full-page advertisement in the *Vineyard Gazette* announces "Stop the Invasion of Off Island Real Estate Speculators." It goes on to appeal readers to join the fight to save Lake Tashmoo from death by development. It is the height of the summer, and the most burning concern on Martha's Vineyard could just as easily be the quality of the tomato and corn crops.

But on an island where few residents are indifferent to outside assaults, there is never a season to let down their guard. Such activism and concern for the Vineyard can go unnoticed amidst its diverse and diverting sights, but they sum up the passionate feelings which Vineyard residents have about threats to a way of life they have long struggled to preserve.

Martha's Vineyard, like Cape Cod and Nantucket, is a geological remnant from the last Ice Age. Two advancing lobes of a glacier molded the triangular northern shoreline of the island, then retreated, leaving the hilly moraines, low plains and many-fingered ponds that characterize the island terrain.

The variety of landscapes is echoed in the varying personalities of the six independent island towns, whose separate histories form a composite tale of the island's past. The towns divide themselves evenly between the territories known locally as "down-island" — the busy, fashionable eastern half of the Vineyard where Oak Bluffs, Edgartown and Vineyard Haven have lured the rich and famous — and "up-island" — the sparsely populated and sleepy towns to the west. The distinction between the two cannot be overstated, for their atmospheres are as different as night and day.

It is paradoxical that virtually all of the spectacular up-island beachfront is off-limits to the public or restricted to residents. While up-island is home to to many year-round residents who cannot afford down-island prices, substantial amounts of land and beachfront belong to some of the wealthiest people in America. In recent years, a few publicized clashes between these different up-island inhabitants over use of the beaches have highlighted how strongly

The cocktail crowd in Edgartown.

people feel about *their* island!

Long before the Cape Cod Canal provided a shortcut between Boston and ports south, boats had to travel around Cape Cod to make a coastal journey. As traffic on this route and those striking out to the West Indies increased, the harbor at the tip of the Vineyard grew in importance as a shelter and a source of supplies. Known until 1870 as Holmes Hole, **Vineyard Haven** blossomed into a busy port during the 18th and 19th centuries, with both maritime businesses and farmers profiting from the constant movement of ships in and out of the port. Today, the ferry that plies between Woods Hole and Vineyard Haven brings vacationers to the island. (Vineyard Haven is something of a misnomer; the name of the town is officially Tisbury, but everyone calls it by the name of its primary village.)

Vineyard Haven has a no-nonsense, matter-of-fact quality about it, with little of the preciousness of Edgartown or the cuteness of Oak Bluffs. Handsome houses dating from the years before the great fire of 1883 can be found on Williams Avenue, a block off Main Street. On Beach Street, near the water, is the **Ritter House** (1796) containing a town museum run by the Martha's Vineyard Historic Preservation Society. The **Liberty Pole Museum,** located at Colonial Lane and Main Street, is named after the flagpole that was destroyed by three village girls in 1776 to prevent its being captured and used by the British as a spar for one of their warships. The Daughters of the American Revolution run a museum here that exhibits Vineyard crafts and items brought back to the island by world-touring whaling ships. Another museum is the **Seamen's Bethel,** formerly a refuge for sailors in distress or simply in need of a brief shore leave. It is one of the few original waterfront buildings from the height of the shipping era.

On the outskirts of Vineyard Haven, but within the limits of Tisbury, is beautiful **Lake Tashmoo,** whose flowing spring waters were once pumped to the nearby neighborhood of West Chop to make possible its development by wealthy Bostonians. The lands around the lake are very private, and the beach where the lake and Vineyard Sound meet is available for use only by town residents. The old **Tashmoo Farm** nearby is surrounded by the stone walls that are a familiar sight up-island, a practical use of the glacial rubble left thousands of years ago.

The entry to Vineyard Haven Harbor is signaled by two lighthouses which stand on the cliffs overlooking Nantucket Sound. These landmarks, known as **East and West Chop,** are visible from far off at sea. They are also quiet, attractive neighborhoods for landlubbers. West Chop is in Tisbury, and is the home of many well-known writers and theater and television personalities who summer on Martha's Vineyard. East Chop stands just north of the town center of Oak Bluffs.

Oak Bluffs Whimsy

Oak Bluffs is a place where the unlikely combination of tourism and religion has produced a unique and lively community. The town is renowned for its "carpenter gothic" cottages, which impart an engaging gaiety that seems to possess all who visit.

In 1835, Methodists took to the backwoods out of Edgartown in search of a suitable site for a camp meeting, a place where the faithful could come for a short period of spiritual replenishment. They found a secluded circle of oak trees, named it Wesleyan Grove, and conducted the first summer camp meeting on the site. Twenty years later, there were more than 320 tents and thousands of people. Small houses soon replaced the tents, laid out along circular drives that rimmed the large central "tabernacle" where the congregation assembled.

Today this camp meeting site is known as **Trinity Park.** Tiny gingerbread cottages are a riot of color and jigsaw carvery, with all manner of turrets, spires, gables and eaves. Yet the park remains remarkably serene and intimate. The huge cast iron-and-wood amphitheater in the center of the campground, built in 1870, still hosts community gatherings. The traditional closing-night ceremony, when colorful glowing lanterns were strung up all over the camp, is still honored; a similar event known as Illumination Night is held in town every August.

Circuit and Lake streets mark the hub of town and the site of the **Flying Horses,** one of the oldest merry-go-

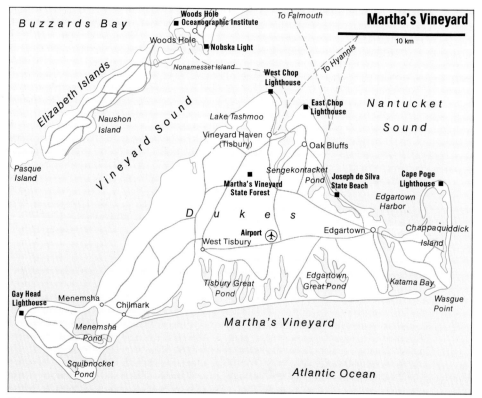

rounds in America. The name Oak Bluffs was coined, incidentally, by a development company that thrived on the tourist business unintentionally spawned by the camp meeting.

Edgartown Elegance

South of Oak Bluffs on the Beach Road, **Edgartown** is the oldest settlement on Martha's Vineyard. In 1642, missionaries arrived at Great Harbour, now Edgartown, from Watertown, Massachusetts, and set to work to convert the island's Indians to Christianity. The town grew at a slow pace until the 18th Century, making its living from fishing and farming. Then offshore whaling moved Edgartown into the ranks of the world's great whaling centers.

A rivalry has always existed between Martha's Vineyard and nearby Nantucket, and on the subject of whaling, Edgartown is adamant. Its fleet may never have approached the size of Nantucket's, but it claims to have sent more of its sons out to sea as captains on the ships of New Bedford, Fairhaven and, yes, Nantucket. As whaling ships grew larger, Edgartown became the port of departure for Nantucket's ships, which fully outfitted could not make their way over the sandbars surrounding Nantucket Harbor.

Today no ferries from the mainland serve Edgartown, so the hustle and bustle of a harbor town is absent. The main attractions in elegant Edgartown — which acquired its tidy appearance upon discovery by refined New Yorkers like Emily Post in the late 19th and early 20th centuries — are its beautiful buildings. Their shining white facades give the town its pristine and polished air. On North and South Water streets, many architectural styles converge, from the traditional saltbox to the grand Federal and Greek Revival styles of the captains' houses.

The most regal Edgartown residence is that built in 1840 by whale-oil magnate Dr. Daniel Fisher, who once supplied all U.S. lighthouses with Edgartown oil. His house sits on upper Main Street, next to the imposing Greek Revival **Methodist church** of 1843, whose enormous pillars and soaring tower are a rare instance of monumental scale in Edgartown. Tucked behind is the **Vincent House** (1675), an

Umbrellas in the sand at Lucy Vincent Beach.

example of the popular 17th Century Cape design. At the corner of Cooke and School streets is the **Dukes County Historical Society Museum,** whose collection includes whaling items, artifacts from daily Vineyard life and the famous French-made Fresnel lens which until 1952 cast the warning beam from Gay Head Lighthouse.

The 'Separated Island'

A stone's throw away from Edgartown, across a narrow neck of the harbor, is **Chappaquiddick Island.** Its name, an Indian word meaning "The Separated Island," is a clue to the psychological effect that 200 yards (183 meters) of water had on its residents before the days of modern transportation. Today the not-too-modern ferry *On-Time,* humorously named for its non-schedule, shuttles people and up to three cars at a time across to "Chappy" from Edgartown.

Two popular beaches and four wildlife refuges are the main points of interest for island visitors. South Beach (also known as Katama Beach) has a lifeguard; Joseph Silva State Beach does not, but it does abut the Felix Neck Wildlife Sanctuary, 250 acres (103 hectares) of beach, marsh, field and woodland jutting into Sengekontacket Pond. Mashackett Neck Wildlife Area is on Edgartown Great Pond near South Beach; Wasque Point Wildlife Refuge is at the island's southeasternmost corner; and Cape Pogue Wildlife Refuge, a lovely spot for swimming, fishing and picnicking, is to the north, three miles (five km) straight from the Chappaquiddick ferry landing.

Up-Island Escape

When the down-island scene has run the visitor ragged, it's time to retreat to the tranquility of up-island life. The drive west from Edgartown, leading through forests of pine and oak, starts the transition to a Vineyard where nature, rather than man, has the upper hand.

The town line of **West Tisbury,** a large, centrally located community, has the benefit of both Atlantic Ocean and Vineyard Sound beachfront. Yet it is the most private and reserved of all the

The *On-Time* Ferry connects Edgartown and Chappaquiddick.

island towns. The area is heavily wooded, and most sights are tucked away, out of view from the road.

Christiantown, on Indian Hill Road, was founded in 1659 as a home for the few "praying Indians" who had been converted to Christianity. Thomas Mayhew worked tirelessly to spread his religion among the native Algonquians; he is remembered by a plaque fixed to a boulder on the site. Together with a graveyard and a little meeting house, this is a touching and solemn memorial to the Vineyard's missionary era.

At the other end of Indian Hill Road, **Cedar Tree Neck Wildlife Sanctuary** provides a lovely spot for strolling and contemplating nature and the Vineyard Sound, of which there is a commanding view. The 4,000-acre (1,640-hectare) **Martha's Vineyard State Forest** — laced with walking and bridle paths and containing the island's only youth hostel — brings the scent of pines to the outskirts of West Tisbury Center. This modest and unassuming village traditionally has been a center of small industry (including woolen and flour mills) and farming. The town's Agricultural Hall still hosts Martha's Vineyard's annual county fair.

Camp-
ground
House in
Oak Bluffs.

The Far Southwest

Chilmark continues the rural up-island atmosphere. Three parallel roads travel from West Tisbury into this township; Middle Road traverses the most rugged, interesting glacial terrain. Chilmark Center is an off-beat, bohemian Vineyard village. Socialist Norman Thomas and journalist Walter Lippman were once among the writers and political activists who retreated to this community. Probably the town's leading attraction is Beetlebung Corner, a stand of tupelo trees from which "beetles" (mallets) and "bungs" (wooden stoppers) were once made. Nearby **Menemsha** is a tiny fishing village on Vineyard Sound that might be the most picturesque of all the island's harbor towns with its salty Scottish Highlands atmosphere.

It is extraordinary but fitting that the most spectacular natural sight on Martha's Vineyard should be situated at its westernmost tip, looking away from the commotion of the domesticated island and out to the untamed sea. From Chilmark, follow the single hilly road that at several points offers breathtaking views of Menemsha Pond northward and Squibnocket Pond to the south. At the end, a lighthouse marks the western terminus of the island and the location of the stunning, ancient geologic guides that are the **Gay Head** cliffs.

Photographers have recorded the many moods of the cliffs, from white stillness to excitable sunset red or reflective sea green. But geologists have found the most reward scavenging on the ever-changing contours of this 150-foot (46-meter) promontory. Fossils visible in the strata of clay, sand and gravel matter are millions of years old.

The crimson figure atop the cliffs is Gay Head Light, built in 1855. Large boulders strewn about the waters below were a serious hazard until President John Adams authorized construction of the first lighthouse here in 1798.

The community at Gay Head is one of only two Indian towns in the state of Massachusetts. In the faces of its people, and in the tenor of this soft-spoken town, are the traces of nobility that so often characterize the native American culture. This outpost of proud Wampanoag people is a fitting finale to a many-rhythmed tour of the island.

NANTUCKET

In 1830 the whaling ship *Suruh* returned home to Nantucket Island, carrying 3,500 barrels of valuable whale oil after a voyage of nearly three years. On the island, stately mansions, decorated with silks and china from faraway lands, awaited the returning captains. Schools, hotels, a library and the commercial activity on Main Street were indications of a prosperous people.

These were the halcyon days of little Nantucket Island, the shining moment in its turbulent past. Although its fortunes soon declined, time has stood still on Nantucket, and the intimate scale and refined taste of its heyday have survived to the present day to endow the island with its charm, beauty and magnetic appeal.

Nantucket may never again know the excitement and adventure of the whaling trade, but its new industry — tourism — has brought an equal amount of fame and fortune. Like the earliest settlers, who came to escape the Puritan lifestyle on the mainland, people today find a haven on Nantucket, a respite from the pressures of modern living.

Since its earliest days, Nantucket has been populated by determined and spirited people. The first white settlers, who arrived from Massachusetts in 1659, were taught "onshore" whaling by the native Algonquian Indians; they traveled out in open boats to chase and harpoon whales sighted from land. By the beginning of the 1700s, offshore whaling had begun, and with each generation of larger, more seaworthy craft, the whaling industry grew.

But the Indians lost out. Although they sailed on whaling boats, their way of life on the island was irreversibly changed by the white settlers. By 1855, disease and alcohol had taken the last of the Indians from Nantucket.

By the time of the Revolutionary War, Nantucket had a fleet of 150 whaling ships. But Quaker pacifism and Nantucket's interest in London markets for whale oil divided islanders' loyalties, and their ships suffered greatly at the hands of the Tories and Revolutionaries alike. No sooner had they rebuilt their fleet than the War of 1812 erupted; by

Nantucket Town, once the whaling capital of the world.

the conflict's end, their whaling empire had once again been left battered and exhausted.

Tenacity brought Nantucket back to life with a bang. Nantucket ships again sailed throughout the world and brought back record quantities of oil from their catches. It was during this period that Nantucket Town acquired much of its urbanity, but it was a period destined to be short-lived. Nantucket was too dependent on whaling, and when events conspired to make that industry suddenly obsolete, islanders were high and dry.

From a peak of around 10,000, Nantucket's population dropped to 3,200 in 1875. Those who remained applied their ingenuity to a new venture, one that thrives today and continues to capitalize on the gifts of the sea. Tourism took off toward the end of the 19th Century, as the arrival of the steamboat made the island more readily accessible from the mainland. Land speculators built hotels and vacation homes, especially in Surfside and Siasconset, once linked to Nantucket Town by a 19th Century railway. The rail is gone now, but tourism lives on.

An Indian word meaning "that faraway island," Nantucket is not too far away for the thousands of people who visit each year by ferry and airplane. The winter population of 5,600 — only half of what was recorded for the peak of the whaling era — increases fivefold when the "summer people" take over the sidewalks of **Nantucket Town** and give it its cheery aspect.

Nantucket Town

In sharp contrast to Martha's Vineyard, Nantucket's towns, mid-island moors and beaches are utterly open to visitors. Nantucket Town is unquestionably the focal point of the island, a full-service resort area centrally located on the north shore. Smaller residential neighborhoods dot the island's coast, but most of the shore is made up of beautiful, unspoiled beach.

A visitor can spend days walking in Nantucket Town and always see something new. The community is a gem of 18th and 19th-Century architecture, from the dominant clapboard-and-shingle Quaker homes to the grandeur of the buildings lining Main Street. And

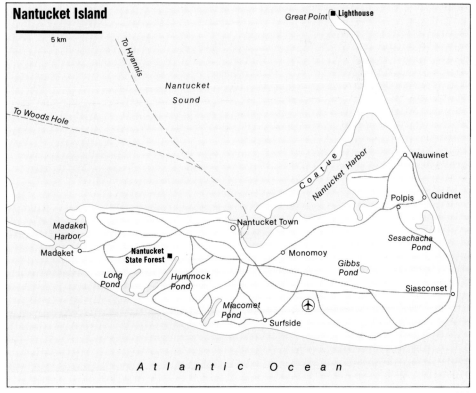

133

while the town may seem a maze of narrow streets, it is actually very ordered in its own cluttered way; early in the 18th Century, its center was laid out in lots that ran roughly east-west from the harbor. Nevertheless, it is best to tour Nantucket Town with a street map, for the density might otherwise cause disorientation and frustration.

The waterfront is certainly the spiritual center of Nantucket Town. Five wharfs extend into the harbor, the most central of which — **Straight Wharf** — is an extension of Main Street. First built in 1723, it has been restored to accommodate the yachts that frequently are docked in its slips. Straight Wharf is also the location of the **Nantucket Lightship** that floated offshore from 1936 to 1975 to guide ships around the treacherous shoals of the island; today, the public is welcome to climb aboard and inspect the spartan interior that was home to the ship's crew for weeks on end.

North, South and Commercial (the most southerly) wharves have been spruced up in recent years and sport imaginative boutiques, restaurants and tour and rental-car services. Small cottages can be rented on Old North (the most northerly) and South wharves.

Looking up Main Street from Straight Wharf, a picturesque shopping district lines the gently rising cobblestone road. Earlier wooden buildings on this street burned to the ground in 1846; the red-brick facades of today's shops date to the years immediately following that disaster. Main Street is always a hub of activity in the summer months, with its tree-lined, bricked-paved sidewalks offering every kind of distraction from art galleries to ice-cream parlors.

Nantucket is justly proud of its history, especially its grand old homes and museums. The **Nantucket Historical Society,** with headquarters at the corner of Union and Main streets, is anxious to assist visitors with maps and complete listings of notable buildings.

An Eye on the Past

A walk down South Water Street to Broad Street leads past two important museums. The **Whaling Museum** commemorates the story of Nantucket's seafaring era, with replicas of all the hardware that made snaring a great whale possible. The **Peter Foulger**

The Sankaty Head Lighthouse, Siasconset.

Museum offers a broader look into the island's history, reminding visitors that there were farmers and artisans on the island as well as whalers. This museum has an extensive library.

A short walk out of town, to the corner of South Mill and Prospect streets, leads to the **Old Mill** (1746), another lesson in the agricultural resourcefulness of the early islanders. On a windy day, the four whirling wings set in motion a clever series of gears and stones that work corn kernels into a fine powder. Visitors are allowed inside to watch the intricacies of this muscular machine at work. Ground cornmeal is bagged and sold on the site.

Two sedate Nantucket institutions are on Vestal Street, off Main Street near the Civil War Monument. The iron bars of the **Old Gaol** suggest that although Nantucket has never had much of a crime problem, it took seriously the business of incarcerating its few miscreants. Nearby is the **Maria Mitchell Association,** comprising a small observatory, lending library and the childhood house of Ms. Mitchell, who discovered a comet while gazing through her father's telescope and went on to become a leading professor of astronomy at Vassar College. The association runs a natural science museum at No. 7 Milk St., sponsors lectures and nature walks, and operates the larger **Loines Observatory** farther out on Milk Street.

The oldest house on Nantucket is the **Jethro Coffin House** (1686) on the northwest edge of town on Sunset Hill Lane. This plain saltbox design reflects the austere lifestyle led by the island's earliest settlers. The red-brick **Jared Coffin House** commands the corner of Broad and Centre streets and is one of the most popular inns on the island. Two more Coffin residences (the family was prolific) stand at **No. 75 and No. 78 Main Street,** rare examples of the brick Federal style of architecture. Farther up Main Street are the **"Three Bricks,"** architectural triplets built by wealthy whaler Joseph Starbuck for his three sons. Across the street, and worlds apart in style, stand the imposing **Hawden Houses,** shining white monuments to the Greek Revival style. **No. 99 Main Street,** with its detailed and finely proportioned facade, is one of the most handsome wooden Federal style buildings on Nantucket; it was built by the Macy family of merchandising fame.

Spits and Moors

"Nantucket! Take out your map and look at it," urged Herman Melville in his whaling adventure classic *Moby Dick.* An inspection of the map reveals an island with hamlets and hideaways sprinkled across its 15-mile (24-km) length. Despite what some might term rampant development, approximately one-eighth of the island and owned and protected by the Nantucket Conservation Foundation; and depending upon one's transportation, no corner of the island is off-limits to exploration, though many environmental restrictions control activity on dunes, moors and other fragile natural areas.

Nantucket Town is tucked into a corner near the mouth of Nantucket Harbor. Stretching to the northeast from this point is the six-mile (10-km) inner harbor, formed on the north by a thin spit of land called **Coatue** that acts as a barrier between the harbor and Nantucket Sound. Only by boat or four-wheel-drive vehicles (driven around the head of the harbor) can Coatue and its

Best friends on the beach near Surfside.

flat, white beach be reached. The spit extends north to **Great Point,** where a solitary lighthouse, built in 1818, still warns boats away from the infamous sandbars of Nantucket Sound.

Residential neighborhoods extend along the south side of the harbor. **Monomoy,** the nearest to Nantucket Town and the most developed settlement, affords spectacular views from its bluffs. From here, the Polpis Road Leads east to the more sparsely developed neighborhoods of **Shimmo, Quaise, Polpis** and **Pocomo.**

The rolling hills and low, somewhat scruffy vegetation over which this road travels are the **Nantucket Moors,** one of the island's most delicate and prized gifts of nature. Bayberry, beach plum, heather and other vegetation is lush — a lovely green and flowering pink in summer, brilliant red and gold in autumn. But the ecology of the moors is fragile, and although vehicles can travel the sandy paths that crisscross the terrain between the Polpis and Milestone roads, driving or walking over the moors is prohibited.

Wauwinet, at the head of the harbor, is a tiny community where cottages and

the Wauwinet House, a dozy inn right on the inner harbor, are tucked away amid the beach grass. South of Wauwinet, next to Sesachacha Pond, is the former fishing colony of **Quidnet,** now a quiet cluster of beachside homes.

Tourists discovered **Siasconset** (pronounced "Sconset"), the easternmost and second-largest town on Nantucket, in the 1880s. The railroad traveled between Siasconset and Nantucket Town long after it ceased operating along the island's south shore. Theater people from the mainland mingled with local fishermen; the resulting architecture ranges from clustered Lilliputian fishing cottages to the large rambling shingle-style houses situated along the bluffs outside the town's center.

Nantucket's most popular beaches are located on the flat, windswept south shore and washed by the cold, active waters of the Atlantic Ocean. **Surfside** is a small community of summer homes, a modest realization of the ambitious 19th Century resort development schemes that died with the railroad. The former Life Saving Station, established in 1873 by the Coast Guard, is now the island's only youth hostel. Surfers prefer the beach at **Cisco,** where there is a lifeguard, bathhouse and snack bar. **Madaket Beach,** at the southwestern tip of Nantucket, is popular for fishing as well as swimming; offshore **Esther Island** was part of the main island until it was cast off when Hurricane Esther stirred up the seas in 1971. Beyond Esther Island are **Tuckernuck** and **Muskeget,** privately owned and sparsely populated islands.

Along the north (Nantucket Sound) shore between Madaket and Nantucket Town are the gentle surf of **Dionis** and **Jetties** beaches. The latter gets its name from its proximity to the West Jetty, which protects the channel leading into Nantucket Harbor. **Children's Beach** is well inside the West Jetty, near Steamship Wharf, and (as its name suggests) it is a popular spot with the little swimmers of Nantucket.

Right inside the West Jetty are some of the older and finer beach houses of Nantucket Town. Overlooking the harbor from **Brant Point** is the second oldest lighthouse in the United States. It is a longstanding island tradition that those departing by sea who throw a penny at Brant Point are sure to return to the shores of Nantucket.

Summer in the sand dunes: left, Preppie Love; and right, leaping into action.

CENTRAL MASSACHUSETTS

New England's unique social and artistic bloodlines thrive in Central Massachusetts. Boston belongs to European ethnicity and contemporary gentrification; western Massachusetts seems more a part of New York State. Only in the Commonwealth's midsection are the heart and soul of the New England heritage so readily evident.

The vigor and sincerity of early Americans' social vision is on display from June through September at **Fruitlands Museums** in the little town of Harvard, an hour or so west of Boston via scenic State Highway 2. In the mid 19th Century, transcendentalist Amos Bronson Alcott, father of Louisa May Alcott (author of *Little Women*), left his Concord home with political activist Charles Lane and a group of followers to found an anti-materialist utopian community on the 18th Century Fruitlands farm. Vegetarianism, asceticism and a philosophical return to nature were their mandates, and despite their inspiring view of the beautiful Nashua River Valley, the commune soon dispersed. Today, however, the 'farmhouse has been transformed into a transcendentalist museum with presentations on Alcott, Emerson, Thoreau and others; its restaurant offers the same view of the Nashua Valley, and it is surrounded by several other museums.

Some 19th Century utopian experiments had greater longevity than that of Fruitlands. Most notable was that of the chaste and fervent Shakers, who persisted in Harvard town until 1919. Fruitlands' 1794 **Shaker House,** moved from that Harvard settlement, contains Shaker products and furnishings which tell of a lifestyle far different from that of today. The Shaker faith owed its naturalism and simplicity more to the pre-European Indian culture of the New World than to the European cultures which the colonists left behind.

Also at Fruitlands, an **American Indian Museum** has a fine collection of artifacts. The **Picture Gallery** displays the paintings of such Hudson River School disciples as Asher Durand and Frederick Church, whose work reflects the influence of New England's landscape and weather on its culture.

Continuing west on State 2 through the hills of north central Massachusetts, it is easy to see why the intimate relationship between man and nature has so long obsessed the New Englander. The countryside between Harvard and the Connecticut River Valley is spectacular in spring, summer and especially fall, when breathtaking woods give way to verdant valleys that explode with color when the leaves turn.

Near Athol, U.S. Highway 202 branches south to skirt the 412-billion-gallon **Quabbin Reservoir,** 128 square miles (331 square kilometers) of flooded valley that supplies the drinking water to Greater Boston. Area residents frequent Quabbin to fish, hike and admire the rare bald eagles that breed by the reservoir.

The Pioneer Heritage

Tiny **Deerfield** (population about 5,000) has a fascinating history dating from the 1660s, when it was settled as a frontier outpost against French and Indian attacks. The town was massacred in 1675 and set aflame in 1704, but sur-

Preceding pages: a western Massachusetts road in fall. Left, the juicy bounty of an apple orchard. Right, 20th Century lady and 19th Century house.

vived to become a prosperous agricultural center in the early 19th Century.

Deerfield's mile-long Main Street represents the first architectural restoration project ever undertaken in the United States. The colonial and Federal style structures first underwent renovation late in the last century. Among the more interesting of the 12 buildings open to the public are the **Ashley House** (1730), a former parson's home with intricately carved woodwork and antique furnishings; the **Asa Stebbins House** (1810), notable for its unusual wall decorations; the **Wright House** (1824) with early paintings, Chinese porcelains and Federal and Chippendale furniture; the **Dwight Barnard House** (1725), immediately recognizable by its handsome carved door, behind which is an 18th Century doctor's office; and the **Hall Tavern** (1760), where Historic Deerfield Inc. maintains its information center.

South of Deerfield, the highway descends into the **Pioneer Valley.** More than 100 species of dinosaurs once lived in the area, many of them man-sized precursors to the giant specimens of later ages. A proliferation of dinosaur tracks have been found in the rocks of the region; many are displayed (from March through December) at the **Granby Dinosaur Museum** on U.S. 202.

Now, the only dinosaurs are the archaic high-rise dormitories at the 24,000-student **University of Massachusetts** at **Amherst.** These dorms are so inhospitable that in 1983, small fires routinely forced dozens of student evacuations. The university itself, awkwardly protruding from rolling cornfields, suffers by comparison with nearby **Amherst College,** where state fraternity houses flank a campus quadrangle that is a classic of early 19th Century institutional architecture.

The town of Amherst is a hotbed of intellectual vigor and social independence. Noah Webster, father of the American dictionary, lived here; so did a reclusive master of the English language, poet Emily Dickinson. Visitors to her homestead in Amherst can experience the spartan environment that housed a sensitive, self-confined soul, whose emotions were vented solely in her lyrical writing.

Down State Highway 9 and across the Connecticut River is **Northampton,**

View of Northampton in 1839.

142

which also boasts a taciturn historical celebrity in 30th U.S. President Calvin Coolidge. Coolidge began his law practice in Northampton and later died there. His reputation as a man of almost no words once prompted a matron at a society banquet to coax him: "Mr. President, I have a wager with a friend that I can persuade you to say more than two words." Coolidge's reply: "You lose."

Modern-day Northampton has plenty to talk about. Through the loving restoration of many downtown buildings, it has been rejuvenated from an aging frontier outpost to a lively shopping area. A focal point for visitors is **Smith College,** founded in 1875 by Sophia Smith of nearby Hatfield with the goal of producing "the intelligent gentlewoman." When the school day is over at Smith and nearby **Mount Holyoke College** — which holds honors as the nation's first women's college — many of the gentlewomen and their dates can be found enjoying the huge bloody marys at **Fitzwilly's,** handsomely refurbished storefront on State 9.

The main business of Northampton and the Pioneer Valley is the exploration and enjoyment of freedom of thought and lifestyle, a pleasure they shared with their forefathers. Many of the stores in the valley feature locally handcrafted goods, just as they once bulged with Shaker products. In the food co-ops that thrive here, in the consortium that allows free student flow between five area colleges, and in the experimental co-ed "pods" that house students at **Hampshire College** near Amherst, the legacy of the early settlers still thrives. First-hand local testimony to the value of this heritage is given by independent moviemakers Amy Stechler and Ken Burns, former Hampshire College roommates. The founders of Florentine films (based in North-ampton), they won an Academy Award nomination for their documentary on the Brooklyn Bridge, and they are now hard at work on a movie about the Shakers.

Springfield: 'No Respect'

Springfield is one of those American cities with plenty of resources and history that, perhaps unfairly, can't shake the label of being (as one snooty Amherst student put it) "Nowheres-

The 17th Century Longfellow's Wayside Inn, South Sudbury.

ville." An industrial center located at the intersection of two major interstate highways (I-91 and I-90, the Massachusetts Turnpike), and just a short drive from Hartford, Connecticut, Springfield endures jokes like the one used by comedian Steve Martin to open a performance at the gleaming new **Springfield Civic Center:** "Gee, it's just great to be back here in Hartford."

Although it was the first major settlement west of the Boston area, Springfield has never been accorded much respect. Of the eight men who founded the city in 1636, none stayed more than a few months. In 1876, roadway construction near their nesting ground convinced thousands of frogs that Springfield was an undesirable hometown; they migrated so profusely down Walnut Street that one James W. Crook was prompted to write: "One could not step without lengthening the mortality list of the frog army."

Still, Springfield (population 160,000) deserves its due for contributions to American history and culture. The former **Springfield Armory,** once the nation's largest arsenal and home of the first American musket, now houses the

Benton Small Arms Museum, with an impressive display of weapons spanning five centuries. Also worth seeing are the four museums housed in **Museum Center** on State Street, particularly the Smith Art Museum, a lavish collection of Oriental art in an Italian-style villa, and the Connecticut Valley Historical Society Museum, with exhibits tracing the area's social growth. There are also a science museum and Museum of Fine Arts.

One of America's greatest contributions to world culture came out of **Springfield College** in 1891, when Dr. James Naismith hung peach baskets at either end of a YMCA hall and convinced his skeptical students to shoot a ball into them. The **Basketball Hall of Fame** on Alden Street memorializes that bit of inspiration (although it took a while for Naismith to realize that the game would flow more quickly if the bottoms of the baskets were removed),

West Springfield is the site of the **Eastern States Exposition,** New England's major annual fair. Every September, the 175-acre (71-hectare) fairgrounds are packed with shows and exhibits,

Some 30 miles (48 km) east of Springfield off U.S. 20, **Old Sturbridge Village** looms as a sort of Disneyland of early 19th Century rural life. Its authentic homes and original customs are scrupulously reproduced. Old Sturbridge is best seen in winter, when crowds are smaller and the harshness of New England weather that so shaped the early settlers' moral and physical toughness can be exprienced first-hand. Of special interest is the **Pliny Freeman Farm,** where visitors can watch workers in period dress engage in making maple sugar, shearing sheep, and laboriously building stone fences from the yield of the often-rocky soil. Concepts of political freedom and discourse grew, in part, from the emergence of a free and vibrant press, and the activities of the **Isaiah Thomas Printing Office** (including production of broadsides and tax forms) show how printed communication became an integral part of the new nation's growth.

Wonders of Worcester

A short drive past Sturbridge toward Boston is **Worcester,** the state's second largest city. Where would America be

A quiet evening in a Connecticut Valley home.

without Worcester? The city has spawned the country's first park, first wire-making company, first steam calliope, first carpet loom and (yes) first birth-control pill, not to mention the beginnings of liquid-fuel rocketry, female suffrage and the Free Soil Party, now known as the Republican Party.

Humorist Robert Benchley grew up in Worcester, and no doubt owed much of his unfettered freedom of speech to publisher Thomas, a Son of Liberty who fled Boston in advance of the British Army in 1770 and continued to publish his rabble-rousing revolutionary newspaper, *The Massachusetts Spy,* from Worcester. Thomas went on to become one of the wealthiest men in America, establishing the American Antiquarian Society on New York's Park Avenue in 1818. Today his legacy lives on most enjoyably at the **Isaiah Thomas Book and Print Store** on Main Street in Worcester, where the first floor and basement of a two-story wooden house are given over to an extraordinary assortment of books and original art.

Worcester is a thriving manufacturing center with a diverse populace of 165,000. Residents have included such

notables as rocketry pioneer Robert Goddard, abolitionist-composer Stephen Foster, socialist leader Emma Goldman and Yippie activist Abbie Hoffman; Sigmund Freud gave his only U.S. lecture at Clark University. Yet the city boasts little of the opulence and self-importance of Boston. Renovated townhouses line Court Hill and other areas, but Worcester's most significant attributes are clustered near the downtown shopping area.

The **Worcester Art Museum** is the second largest in New England and perhaps the most adventurous: their sponsorship of excavations at Antioch, Syria, in 1930s yielded a stunning collection of 2nd Century A.D. Roman mosaics. The museum has other antiquities along with fine collections of European and Eastern art. But perhaps most illuminating for the visitor is the extensive gallery of 17th, 18th and 19th Century American art, including paintings by Winslow Homer, John Singer Sargent and John Singleton Copley. In their portraits and landscapes, one can trace the emergence of a distinctly American culture, simple in fact but sophisticated in aspiration.

Kicking up the turf at a central Massachusetts racetrack.

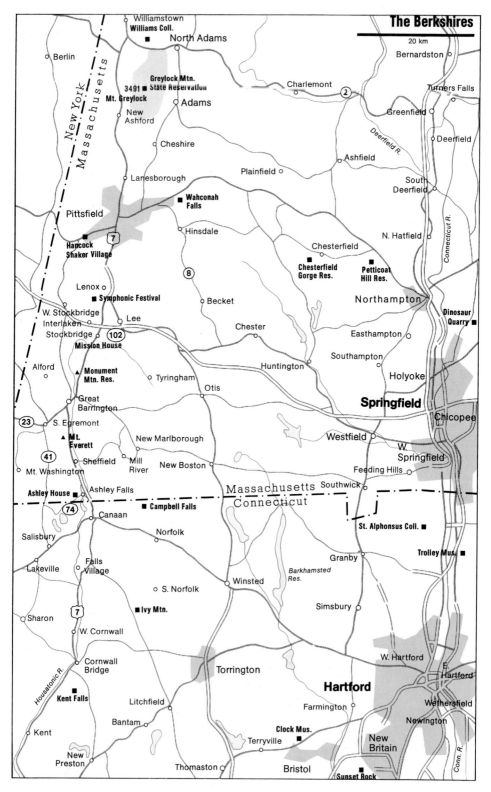

The Berkshires

20 km

THE BERKSHIRES

Berkshire County, frequently called "the American Lake District," encompasses a landscape that provides almost every variety of beauty — valleys dotted with shimmering lakes, rolling farmlands punctuated by orchards and wheat-fields, deep forests abundant with deer, and powerful rivers that cascade into waterfalls under the bluest of New England skies.

Everywhere one turns in this westernmost county of Massachusetts, the horizon is piled and terraced with mountains. Though less dramatic than the White Mountains of New Hampshire or the Green Mountains of Vermont, these gentle ranges have nonetheless provided the Berkshire Hills with an insularity that has historically set them apart from the rest of the state.

The Dutch, who settled New York in 1626 and moved north into the Hudson Valley, were prevented from further advancement by the stony resistance of the Taconic Range. Similar difficulties were met by the English, who found their progress west from the Connecticut River Valley blocked by the Hoosac Mountains — a wall of granite later dubbed the Berkshire Barrier.

Contained within this natural barricade, the Berkshires remained a wilderness until 1725, when Matthew Noble traveled through its dense forests to build a cabin in what is now the town of Sheffield. In the years that followed, farmland was cleared and towns were established along the Housatonic River and its tributaries. During the 19th Century, the Industrial Revolution brought prosperity to the Berkshires: its iron foundries melted ore for the country's first railroads, while marble quarried from its hills graced the dome of the Capitol in Washington, D.C.

As big business lured succeeding generations to the cities and better land beckoned farmers further west, the Berkshires receded into a sleepy silence. But city dwellers seeking pretty scenery and respite from summer heat have periodically rediscovered the Berkshires. During the 1890s, for example, the county became a playground for such wealthy families as the Carnegies and Vanderbilts, who built their man-

sions in the hills surrounding Stockbridge and Lenox. More recently, visitors have come for the summer music festivals, the splendor of fall foliage, or the challenge of winter skiing. Whatever the season, a timeless grace continues to lure the traveler to these hills.

The first settlers reached the Berkshires through the Housatonic Valley from Connecticut. The modern traveler can do the same, following U.S. Highway 7 north along the Housatonic. Many of Berkshire County's best-known attractions are located along U.S. 7 (or just a short distance from it).

Colonel Ashley and the Cobble

Just inside the Connecticut border on Route 7A is **Ashley Falls**, a village surrounded by hayfields and dairy farms, its landscape reminiscent of a Constable painting. The village was named for Colonel John Ashley, a prominent lawyer and major-general of the Massachusetts militia during the Revolutionary War. The **Ashley House**, built in 1735, is the oldest structure standing in Berkshire County. It has been restored

Colonial maids are living history at the Colonel Ashley House.

as a colonial museum, open from late May through Columbus Day.

Also located in Ashley Falls is **Bartholomew's Cobble.** This natural rock garden, with the hiking trails that meander along the banks of the Housatonic, is a bird-watcher's paradise and an excellent place to search for the trilliums and trout lilies of early spring. Botanists know the Cobble well: it contains more species of fern than any other area in the continental United States.

Sheffield, established in 1733, is the oldest town in Berkshire County and boasts two of the best-preserved covered bridges in Massachusetts. Traffic still travels over the larger, a narrow, barn-red structure that spans the Housatonic just east of town, on the road to **New Marlborough.**

The Berkshires' true beauty lies in the backroads and small villages that are so much a part of its charm. New Marlborough and nearby **Mill River,** small communities that prospered in the heyday of the Industrial Revolution, are gems. The Inn at New Marlborough, once a stagecoach stop en route from New York to Boston, has recently been restored. Visitors can dine on fresh lamb or breakfast on blueberry muffins. Creameries and sawmills once lined the banks of the Konkopot River in Mill River. Today the town is quiet, but trout still swim in the stream and a stroll through the local cemetery stirs memories of the past.

The Great Wigwam

Great Barrington offers an excellent base from which to explore the towns and villages of the southern Berkshires. While it does not have the architectural charm of towns farther north like Stockbridge and Lenox, great Barrington does have a certain homey quality that many people find inviting.

The Housatonic River courses through the center of town, and it was here, at a natural ford in the river, that the Mohican Indians built their Great Wigwam. It was also in Great Barrington that William Stanley (later to found the General Electric Company) first successfully demonstrated the use of alternating current; in 1886, the town became one of the first communities ever to be lit by electricity.

Eastover Resort near Lenox.

There has been a large Black community in Great Barrington since before the Civil War, when fugitive slaves journeyed to Massachusetts on the Underground Railroad. Black socialist and scholar W.E.B. DuBois was born here in 1868.

At the far corner of the county, 2,000 feet (610 meters) up and teetering on the edge of New York State, is the tiny hill hamlet of **Mount Washington.** The smallest town in the Berkshires, Mount Washington offers some of the finest blueberry picking and fall-foliage viewing in New England.

Continuing along the Mount Washington road, the traveler arrives at **Bash Bish Falls,** a 275-foot (84-meter) natural waterfall where, , legend has it, an Indian maiden jumped to her death after being spurned by her lover. When the moon is full, her ghost may be seen walking through the mountain laurel to wade in the pool beneath the falls.

A Literary Heritage

Austen Riggs Center at Stockbridge.

North of Great Barrington is **Monument Mountain,** a craggy, hump-backed peak whose summit is a pleasant half-hour hike from the carpark at its base. The mountain is a Berkshire literary landmark of considerable repute. Poet William Cullen Bryant sang its praises while practicing as a Great Barrington attorney in the 1830s.

Monument Mountain is best known as the site of an extraordinary literary encounter between Herman Melville and Nathaniel Hawthorne. On Aug. 5, 1850, the two writers were invited to join a hiking party organized by Dr. Oliver Wendell Holmes, Boston essayist and father of the Supreme Court justice. The party, numbering 10 in all, scaled the peak just as a thunderstorm unleashed a torrent of heavy rain. The group ran for shelter under a granite outcropping and waited out the storm while sipping champagne from a silver goblet.

Hawthorne and Melville met frequently after their day on the mountain, the scribe of the South Seas often traveling to Hawthorne's little red cottage in Lenox for refreshment and conversation. But the moody Hawthorne soon grew tired of the changeable Berkshire climate, and after only a brief stay, returned east to Boston. Melville,

whose fondness for the region endured, remained another 10 years and wrote his masterpiece, *Moby Dick,* while residing in the Berkshire Hills.

The Berkshires have, in fact, hosted a plethora of poets and writers over the years. Longfellow once hiked these trails, as did Emerson and Thoreau. Henry James visited frequently, and more recently, the county has been home to Thornton Wilder and Norman Mailer.

U.S. 7 is the most direct road to Stockbridge, but those with a little more time on their hands should consider the drive through the **Tyringham Valley.** From Great Barrington, take State 23 east to Monterey, then turn north onto Tyringham Road.

In the early years of this century, the beauty of the landscape transformed the valley into an artists' colony. Today Tyringham Art galleries are at home in the fairy-tale Gingerbread House. The tiny village of **Tyringham,** where a community of Shakers settled in the 19th Century, is charming and unspoiled, as is **Lee,** which appears frozen in time. Until recently, the one-room schoolhouse still functioned; the local church is a marvel of New England architecture. State 192 heads west from Lee to Stockbridge.

Stately Stockbridge

Stockbridge was incorporated an Indian mission in 1739. Its first missionary was John Sargeant, a young tutor from Yale who lived among the Indians for 16 years. He slept in their wigwams, shared their venison and spoke their language, all the while introducing them to the White man's ways. Eventually, Sargeant helped the Indians establish a town, build homes and cultivate the land. Some among the Mohican tribe held public office, serving alongside Whites in the town government.

The Stockbridge Mission was so successful, it became a model of Indian acculturation. Sadly, the experiment was not to last. As more White men moved into the area, the Indians were slowly deprived of their land. By 1783, the mission was history, and surviving Indians were forced to settle on the Oneida reservation in New York State. All that is left of that age of enlightenment is the **Old Mission House,** now a museum on Stockbridge's Main Street.

One century later, Stockbridge — as well as its sister city of **Lenox,** 7½ miles (12 km) north — gained a different kind of notoriety. The rich and super-rich discovered the Berkshire Hills, earning these communities a reputation for wealth and elegance. At first, the newcomers bought simple cottages and played contentedly at being country squires. But as "impressions" became important, neighbors constructed magnificent estates in which to pass the summer and fall months. Soon continental architecture crowded out the simplicity of the old colonial homes, and both towns became facsimiles of Newport, Rhode Island — inland resorts where blue mountains took the place of sand and rolling surf.

To name the wealthy people who spent time here is like reading from the pages of a turn-of-the-century *Social Register.* There were Harrimans, Stuyvesants, Westinghouses, Biddles, Vanderbilts, Carnegies and Sloans. Many of the old estates are gone now, made obsolete by income tax and the First World War. Some have been converted to private schools; others were destroyed by fire. A few — like **Wheat-**

A miniature Abraham Lincoln poses, left, at Chesterwood, home of Daniel Chester French, Lincoln Memorial sculptor, near Stockbridge. Right, city folk relax on the veranda of the Red Lion Inn.

leigh and **Eastover** in Lenox — now function as country inns.

Rockwell's Canvas

If the stately mansions and quaint shops located along State 102, the Main Street of Stockbridge, look familiar, it may be because their New England essence was captured on the canvases of that remarkable illustrator of American life, Norman Rockwell. Rockwell, who created more than 300 covers for *The Saturday Evening Post,* kept a studio in Stockbridge and made his home there until his death in 1978.

No visitor should make the mistake of considering himself too sophisticated for a visit to the **Old Corner House** on Main Street, which contains a fine collection of Rockwell originals. Reflecting a time when American ideals were simpler, Rockwell's portraits capture an age of innocence with humor, joy and a sense of wonder.

The **Red Lion Inn,** located in the center of Stockbridge at the intersection of U.S. 7 and State 102, is surely the *grande dame* of New England country inns. Its flower-laden front porch, complete with rocking chairs, is a mecca for Berkshire travelers.

Naumkeag, two miles north of Stockbridge, is a Norman-style mansion designed by Stanford White for Joseph Choate, U.S. ambassador to Great Britain in 1899. **Chesterwood,** the summer home of sculptor Daniel Chester French, is located two miles west of Stockbridge. It was here that French created his masterpiece, "The Seated Lincoln," now the focal point of the Lincoln Memorial in Washington, D.C. Casts of this work are displayed in the home, now a museum. French was fond of saying: "Six months of the year I live in paradise; the rest of the time I live in New York City."

The Sounds of Music

Is there anyone who vacations in the Berkshires without stopping at **Tanglewood,** summer home of the Boston Symphony Orchestra? This 200-acre (81-hectare) estate, located on State 183, 1½ miles west of Lenox, has been a haven for performers, students and music lovers since the orchestra first began its outdoor concert series in 1931.

Left, potter Richard Bennett shapes his wares at a Housatonic workshop. Right, the stone barn at Hancock Shaker Village near Pittsfield.

The 6,000-seat Music Shed, designed by architect Eero Saarinen, has excellent acoustics; but many visitors prefer to pack their dinners, come early and picnic on the lawn. They need blankets and plenty of warm clothes to counter the cool night air. The BSO season begins in late June and runs through August, with concerts on Fridays, Saturdays and Sundays.

Concert-goers with a literary bent might be interested in touring the replica of the little red cottage where Hawthorne lived and wrote *The House of the Seven Gables* and *Tanglewood Tales*. During the summer season, the cottage — which stands near the lawn at Tanglewood — is open to visitors.

Tanglewood is only the best known of several summer music, dance and drama festivals in the Berkshires. Travelers who wish to avoid crowds may find their musical tastes better served elsewhere. The **South Mountain Concert Series,** which features weekend chamber-music concerts, is located on U.S. 7 one mile south of Pittsfield. Such fine groups as the Beaux Arts Trio and the Juilliard Quartet are featured performers. Those who revel in Renais-

sance and Baroque music head for the **Aston Magna Festival** in Great Barrington. The festival was founded by harpsichordist Albert Fuller; performances on original instruments are given at St. James Church on several weekends in July.

When Ruth St. Denis and Ted Shawn established the **Jacob's Pillow Dance Festival** more than 50 years ago, modern dance was in its infancy, and many viewed the likes of Martha Graham and Merce Cunningham as a passing fad. Today, Jacob's Pillow — located on State 8 in hilltown **Becket,** southeast of Pittsfield — is an institution at which every major American and international company has performed.

Similarly impressive is the **Williamstown Theater Festival,** which consistently stages some of the finest summer theaters in the country in Massachusetts' (and the Berkshires') northwestern corner. Running the gamut from Greek tragedy to Restoration comedy, from Chekhov to Coward, Pinter to Pirandello, the festival also boasts a superb company of actors. Blythe Danner and Edward Herrmann are regulars, as are Frank Langella, Christopher

Ivy-covered academia at Williams College in Williamstown.

Reeve and Richard Dreyfuss.

At the **Berkshire Theatre Festival** in Stockbridge, the emphasis is on American classics. The main theater was designed by architect Stanford White, but sometimes the best productions can be seen in the company's big red barn, where new playwrights are invited to stage works-in-progress.

For fans of the Bard, there's **Shakespeare & Company** at **The Mount** in Lenox. A youth company of English and American actors performs Shakespeare outdoors during July and August, nightly except Monday. The Mount, open for tours during the summer season, was the 1890s home of Edith Wharton. Here she wrote her best-known novel, *Ethan Frome,* set in the Berkshire town of West Stockbridge.

Even avant-garde theater has found a foothold in the Berkshires. The **Lenox Arts Center** in **Interlaken,** just a short drive from Stockbridge, stages adaptations of Franz Kafka, operas by Gertrude Stein and original works, many of which find their ways to off-Broadway theaters in the fall.

The Simple Shakers

"'Tis a gift to be simple," says the old Shaker hymn. A visit to **Hancock Shaker Village,** on U.S. 20 three miles west of Pittsfield, is testimony to the simple virtues of Shaker living.

Originally called Shaking Quakers because of the dances they performed during religious ceremonies, the Shakers settled in Hancock during the late 1780s. By 1850s, there were 19 Shaker communities in the United States, and Hancock — with a membership of more than 300 — was one of the largest.

Life in the Shaker community was based on the principles of community property, equality of the sexes, public confession of sins, and separation from the outside world. Because members practiced celibacy, converts or New Believers were important. Orphans were frequently adopted by the Shakers, and many elected to adopt the faith.

The community prospered through farming, printing, selling garden seeds and herbs, and manufacturing their distinctly designed furnishings. The elegance and functionalism of Shaker architecture is exemplified by Hancock's famous round stone barn. Constructed in 1826, the barn was designed to enable one farmhand to feed an entire herd of cattle by standing at the center of the structure.

Shakers continued to live in Hancock until the 1950s. But by then the community had dwindled to a few staunch survivors, celibacy and changing times having led to their decline. The village is open for tours from May 30 through August.

Returning to U.S. 7, the northbound traveler passes through **Pittsfield,** the Berkshire County seat and largest city (population 52,000) and the town that General Electric built. Even today, when much of American industry has moved south, GE remains the city's largest employer.

To the north is the high country. Fourteen miles (22½ km) from Pittsfield rises **Mount Greylock,** at 3,491 feet (1,064 meters) the tallest peak in the Berkshires. Hardy travelers can ascend on foot, while those less energetic can drive to the summit via a steep and winding access road. From the top of Mount Greylock, Hawthorne looked down upon **Williamstown** — "a white village and a steeple set like a daydream among the high mountain waves."

Even today, Williamstown may be the loveliest of New England villages. A community of sleepy streets and tweedy professors, it is home to **Williams College,** founded in 1793. Its finest attraction is the exceptional **Sterling and Francine Clark Art Institute,** located on South Street just west of the town center. In the years between World War I and 1956, the Clarks amassed a superb private collection of European and American paintings, including works by Botticelli, Goya, Gainsborough and Fragonard. But the museum is best known for its impressionist collection, which includes Monets, Degas, Casatts and more than 30 Renoirs.

From Williamstown, the **Mohawk Trail** (State Highway 2) winds west to east across the top of Berkshire County. An old Indian path-turned-roadway, it offers some of the most rugged and romantic scenery in the Berkshires. The road leads through **North Adams,** a 19th Century mill town; past the white marble **Natural Bridge;** and along an especially rugged stretch leading to **Shelburne Falls**

A classic New England doorway: the Gateways Inn at Lenox

154

CONNECTICUT

"Connecticut always looks as if the maid has just been in to clean," a long-time resident once remarked as he drove admiringly through the neat-as-a-pin village of Guilford. There, as in so many of Connecticut's picturesque colonial villages, the carefully kept, white, clapboard homes and manicured lawns evoke an image of quiet wealth, propriety and old school ties.

Indeed, this most southern of New England states has always had something of a conservative mien. The Puritans who settled here were staunch Congregationalists, little given to the radical ideas of Roger Williams or the autocratic piety of John Winthrop. They may have been farmers and sea-farers, but they were primarily men of commerce and merchants who understood the value of a dollar and the importance of its proper investment.

Though generations have come and gone, this aspect of the Connecticut character has not changed. It has, however, been tempered with a pride for the place and a heartfelt sense of its history.

Many visitors make the mistake of traveling *through* Connecticut (pronounced *ke-NED-eket*) en route to vacations elsewhere in New England. Perhaps because its riches are so accessible, people tend to take them too much for granted. For those who exit from the highways and take to the back roads and small towns of Connecticut, there is a wealth of colonial heritage waiting to be explored.

With Long Island Sound as its southern border, Connecticut roughly forms a rectangle measuring 90 miles (145 km) from east to west and 55 miles (89 km) north to south. The Connecticut River, New England's longest, bisects the state; along with the Connecticut, the Thames and Housatonic rivers were vital in the settlement and later industrialization of the state.

'The Constitution State'

Adrian Block, a Dutch navigator, was probably the first to understand the possibilities of the region when he sailed along the coast and up the Connecticut River in 1614. Nineteen years later, the Dutch established a trading post near the future site of Hartford, naming their new colony Fort Good Hope.

Beaver and timber had attracted the Dutch first, but it was the British who, lured by fertile land and religious freedom, finally settled the region in 1635. By that time, the original colony of Massachusetts Bay was overcrowded and many newcomers arriving from England had to extend their search for arable land to the upper reaches of the Connecticut River. Added to economic causes were the personalities of strong-willed leaders such as the Reverend Thomas Hooker who, unwilling to submit to the autocratic theocracy of the Massachusetts colony, chose to lead his congregation to an area beyond the reach of any colonial authority.

By 1636, settlements had been established in Hartford, Windsor and Weathersfield. Calling themselves the Hartford Colony, the three towns adopted the Fundamental Orders of Connecticut on Jan. 14, 1639. This document, sometimes called "the grandfather of the Constitution" is regarded by many historians as the

Preceding pages: hot air and blue skies in northwest Connecticut. Left, clowning in Hartford. Right, patriot John Wadsworth hides the royal charter in the oak tree.

world's first written constitution. From that historical first comes the legend on her license plates, "The Constitution State."

In the years that followed, new settlements were organized along the shores of the Long Island Sound. Old Saybrook was first, followed later by New Haven, Guilford and Stamford. Later towns, hewing to the staunch Congregationalism of their settlers, took such Biblical names as Goshen, Sharon, Canaan and Bethlehem.

When the time came to fight in the American War for Independence, Connecticut soldiers were eager participants. No major battles were fought on Connecticut soil, but the state had its patriots. Among them were General Israel Putnam and Ethan Allen. Most famous was Nathan Hale, the Coventry, Connecticut, schoolteacher who, when hanged by the British as a spy, uttered the immortal words: "I regret that I have only one life to give for my country."

With the end of the Revolution, Americans returned home to set about building their new nation. But Connecticut citizens quickly realized that they could not make their fortunes in farming. The stony, glacial soil that covered most of the region was poorly suited to cultivation. With the exception of the upper Connecticut valley, where tobacco is still grown under wide, cheesecloth tents, the land could support only small dairy farms and family fruit orchards.

Undeterred, Connecticut citizens turned to commerce, and from the years 1780 to 1840, the Yankee peddler reigned supreme. His sturdy wagon, loaded with tinware, soap, matches, yard goods and tools, was a familiar sight up and down the Atlantic seaboard, over the Appalachians into Detroit and St. Louis, and even down to New Orleans. Success brought with it the demand for more and more products, and it was here that the Connecticut Yankee made major contributions to the American economy.

Ever since the U.S. Patent Office opened in 1790, Connecticut inventors have filed more patents per capita than any other state in the nation. Hats, combs, cigars, seeds, clocks, kettles, furniture and firearms — all came out of the factory stamped with the label "Made in Connecticut."

New products called for new systems

Colonial piper at a birthday party in West Hartford.

Hartford, the
city of
insurance,
sleeps
soundly.

of manufacture: Eli Whitney, inventor of the cotton gin, first introduced the use of standardized parts at his firearms factory in New Haven. With the introduction of interchangeable parts came the creation of the assembly line — and the rise of the Industrial Revolution. No longer would manufacturing rely on the talents of a few, skilled craftsmen. Mass production had entered the marketplace, and the American economy prospered accordingly.

Not surprisingly, industry made Connecticut's fortune. In Hartford, entrepreneur Samuel Colt gave his name to the Colt. 45 revolver, the "gun that won the West." Winchester rifles were manufactured in New Haven, hats in Danbury, clocks in Bristol and brass in Waterbury.

New industry meant new workers, and the late 19th and early 20th centuries saw waves of immigrants settle in such manufacturing centers as Bridgeport, New Haven and Torrington. While Connecticut may present a colonial face to the casual traveler, those who remain long enough appreciate the contributions of Italians, Germans, Portuguese and Eastern Europeans to the Connecticut character.

Connecticut's past is also its present, and today the state continues to rely on industry for its economic good fortune and the highest per capita income in the nation. Airplane engines are manufactured in East Hartford, helicopters in Stratford; nuclear submarines are designed and built in Groton.

Despite its industry, Connecticut has remained a largely rural enclave. With manufacturing concentrated along the south shore and in Hartford, 75 percent of the state is given over to small towns and deeply forested woodlands. Narrow, winding roads lead the visitor from one charming village to another, to communities proud of their colonial heritage and seemingly untouched by modern times.

Capital of Connecticut

In any game of free association, the name of **Hartford** immediately elicits the response, "insurance." And, indeed, the skyline of Connecticut's capital city is dominated by the steel-and-glass skyscrapers of the nation's largest insurance companies. Today

more than 40 are located in the Greater Hartford area, together employing more than 10 percent of the total workforce.

The first insurance policy, covering a shipowner's losses in the event his ship didn't make it safely back to port, was written in the 18th Century. The early industry served the maritime trade, but as shipping declined during the 19th Century, Hartford's insurance companies expanded their coverage to fire and casualty.

Hartford's reputation is well-founded; from their earliest days, the insurance firms honored their commitments. In 1835, New York City suffered a disastrous fire that destroyed more than 600 buildings. Unable to pay the claims, many New York insurance companies folded. Not so the Hartford Insurance Company, however. Its president traveled to New York to personally guarantee payment of every claim. Similar incidents in Boston and Chicago as well as the 1906 San Francisco earthquake consolidated the reputation of Hartford's insurance companies.

But Hartford is more than insurance companies. It is also Connecticut's oldest city, settled in 1635 by a group of Puritans from the Massachusetts Bay Colony. Its location on the navigable waterways of the Connecticut River has made Hartford a major force in the political, economic and social development of the region.

In 1662, a royal charter was drawn up uniting the colonies of Hartford and New Haven and guaranteeing their independence. Sir Edmund Andros, appointed governor of Connecticut in 1687, had the charter revoked. In defiance of this move, Hartford patriot John Wadsworth stole the charter and hid it in the trunk of an oak tree standing at the center of the town. Two years later, upon the accession of William III, Andros was recalled to England and the charter was reinstated.

A plaque at Charter Oak Place, in the south end of the city, marks the spot where the magnificent oak stood until 1856, when a windstorm felled it. Hartford's museums are filled with items supposedly made from the wood.

Any tour of the downtown area should begin with a visit to the **Old State House**, located at the intersection of Main Street and Asylum Avenue. The roadside stand, a backroad tradition.

The oldest state house in the nation, it was the first public commission for architect Charles Bulfinch, who would later design the state capitols of Maine and Massachusetts. Neither compares to his Hartford creation, which stands as a supreme example of Federalist architecture.

Directly south of the State House, also on Main Street, is the **Wadsworth Atheneum,** the first public art museum in America. Built in the Gothic Revival style, the Atheneum was erected to house the library and art gallery of Daniel Wadsworth. Numerous additions have been made since, and the museum's collection — which includes paintings by Goya, Rubens, Rembrandt and van Dyck, in addition to works by American masters such as Thomas Cole and John Singer Sargent — remains a proud part of the city's cultural heritage.

The **Connecticut State Capitol,** a Gothic wedding cake of turrets, gables, porches and towers, was designed by Richard Upjohn in 1879. Though some might question its good taste, there is no doubt that its ornate interiors of hand-painted columns, marble floors and elaborate stained-glass windows were designed to reflect the wealth and prosperity of the community it served. Located on Capitol Avenue overlooking Bushnell Park, the Capitol is flanked by the **State Library,** which maintains an excellent collection of Connecticut clocks and firearms; and the **Busnell Memorial Auditorium,** a center for concerts, ballet, opera and theater.

More modern in concept, but respectful of the grace and dignity of its downtown district, is the **Hartford Civic Center** and **Constitution Plaza.** Completed in 1975, the Civic Center offers visitors a full range of convention services and ·is home to the New England Whalers ice-hockey team.

Constitution Plaza, a 12-acre complex completed in the 1960s, provides Hartford with an open mall, a vast array of shops, office buildings and the starkly modern, elliptically shaped **Phoenix Mutual Life Insurance Building,** so familiar to the Hartford skyline.

Traveler's Tower, the tallest building in the city, has an Observation Deck which offers an excellent view of the Hartford area. The Traveler's Insurance Company was founded in 1683,

Sitting pretty.

when Colonel James Bolter insured his life for $5,000 to cover his lunchtime trip from home to the post office; his premium was two cents.

Mark Twain's Home

Mark Twain, the riverboat pilot-turned-author, spent the happiest years of his life in Hartford. Although Twain, whose real name was Samuel Clemens, originally moved to Hartford in 1874 merely to be close to his publisher, he frequently sang the praises of his adopted city: "Of all the beautiful towns it has been my fortune to see, this is the chief. ... You do not know what beauty is if you have not been here."

Twain settled in Hartford soon after his marriage to Olivia Langdon, and it was in their home at 351 Farmington Avenue that the couple raised their three daughters, Clara, Jean and Susy. It was also in Hartford that Mark Twain penned his most successful novels, including *The Adventures of Tom Sawyer, The Adventures of Huckleberry Finn* and *A Connecticut Yankee in King Arthur's Court.*

The family home was situated in **Nook Farm,** the intellectual center of Hartford settled in the last half of the 19th Century. Twain's home is easily the largest, a great Victorian mansion designed by Edward Tuckerman Potter in 1874. Exquisitely decorated by Louis Comfort Tiffany and his associates, the house very much reflects the character of its owner. Outdoor porches and balconies give the impression of a Mississippi riverboat, while the interiors are grand and whimsical. Of particular interest is the upstairs billiard room, where Twain did much of his writing.

The author remained in Hartford until 1891, when poor investments forced him to move to Europe or face bankruptcy. The family always intended to return, but after the sudden death of his daughter Susy in 1896, Twain could not bear to return to the site of their happiest memories. He sold the Hartford home in 1903.

Nook Farm is located just north of exit 46 on the Connecticut Turnpike, less than two miles from downtown Hartford. Now a busy residential area, little of the community's pastoral charm remains but both the Twain house and

Leaves blaze a fiery yellow on a fall day in Essex.

Harriet Beecher Stowe's home have been expertly restored.

Timely Bristol

Hartford's environs include a number of historic towns and villages that provide worthwhile destinations for day trips.

Bristol, 18 miles (29 km) west, was the 19th Century clockmaking capital of the country, producing more than 200,000 clocks in a single year. The neighboring towns of **Terryville** and **Thomaston** were named for Eli Terry and Seth Thomas, craftsmen who at one time put a clock on every mantle in America. The **America Clock and Watch Museum** is located on Maple Street in Bristol, and houses a superb collection of the region's finest timepieces.

Farmington, a village situated on the Farmington River just 10 miles (16 km) west of Hartford, is considered by many to be one of the loveliest towns in New England. Certainly, its elegant 18th and 19th Century mansions display a clarity of architectural detail seldom equaled.

Hill-Stead Museum, located at 671 Farmington Avenue, is a particular gem. Designed by architect Stanford White, Hill-Stead was originally conceived as a retirement home for wealthy industrialist Alfred Atmore Pope. A self-made man, Pope was a personal friend of artist Mary Cassatt and a great admirer of the French Impressionist school of painters. Pope's home, which remains what it had been in the early 1900 s, reflects his taste in art. Scattered throughout the mansion are a number of familiar canvases. These include several paintings from Monet's "Haystack" series, Manet's "The Guitar Lady," and Degas' "The Tub." Whistler and Cassatt are also well-represented.

Wethersfield, located on the Connecticut River just south of Hartford, is one of the oldest villages in the state. More than 150 of the 17th and 18th Century homes in its downtown area have been preserved and restored. Take a look at the **1760 Congregational Meeting-house** on Main Street; then visit the **Webb-Deane-Stevens Museum,** three 18th Century homes that show the differces in lifestyles among a wealthy merchant, politician and craftsman.

The River Museum, Essex.

Hikers' Housatonic

The Housatonic River is a handsome river, crystal clear and freckled with trout — the kind of river that makes one want to roll up one's trousers and go wading. It rises in Vermont, flows through the Berkshire Hills of western Massachusetts and tumbles into Connecticut at the northwest corner of the state. As the river courses through the rustic communities of **Falls Village**, **West Cornwall** and **Cornwall Bridge**, the surging waters tear at the shoreline, creating small islands of pine trees and hardwoods.

To see the full beauty of this region, follow the river from **Kent** north on U.S. Highway 7 to **Canaan**. Then head west on U.S. 44 to **Salisbury**. Hikers may want to follow the **Appalachian Trail** from Kent to Canaan. The Housatonic is a canoeist's river, and those who wish to spend a day on its waters will find a convenient rental service in Falls Village.

The Connecticut highlands, thickly wooded and crisscrossed with old stone walls left over from the days when farmers tried to till the soil, were settled somewhat later than the southern reaches of the state. The mountains made access difficult, and many of those who came soon packed their wagons and headed for the more fertile regions of Ohio and Illinois.

With the discovery of iron ore in the Litchfield Hills during the 18th Century, the valley enjoyed a brief period of prosperity. Forges, like the old furnace at Kent, produced pig iron until the discovery of coal in Pennsylvania made Connecticut's ironworks obsolete.

Visitors to present-day Kent, now an artists' colony, may examine the ruins of the Old Kent Furnace at the **Sloane-Stanley Museum** located on U.S. 7. Also on view is an extensive collection of early American wood and iron tools gathered by writer and artist Eric Sloane.

North along the twisting and turning roadway of U.S. 7 from Kent are many well-preserved 18th and 19th Century homes. In the especially picturesque village of West Cornwall, look for the covered bridge, erected in 1836 across the Housatonic.

The return journey down U.S. 44

Ernie Tolx cooks planked shad in Old Saybrook.

166

through Salisbury and **Lakeville** offers an even grander display of traditional 19th Century mansions. Open during the summer months, the **Holley-Williams House** in downtown Lakeville is an excellent example of a Classical Revival house built by one of the area's more prosperous "Iron Barons."

Lovely Litchfield

Approximately 15 miles (24 km) east of Kent lies the historic New England community of **Litchfield**. The Litchfield green, graced by the tall-steepled Congregational Church, forms the meeting point of the village's four main streets. Lining North and South streets are handsome, white, clapboard houses, which can be toured only on Open House Day in mid July.

On South Street (State Highway 63) stands the **Tapping Reeve House**, behind which is a small building that housed the nation's first school of law. Visitors can see the desks where many a distinguished jurist learned his trade, among them Aaron Burr and John C.

Calhoun, two vice presidents of the United States. This simple schoolroom also graduated six cabinet members, 28 senators and more than 100 Congressmen.

Litchfield merchants prospered during the early days of the China trade when their money backed the sailing ships of Mystic and New Haven, but industry faltered when a new railroad bypassed the town center. Commerce was relocated to the more industrialized communities of Waterbury and Naugatuck. Litchfield was left as a sleepy town nestled in the past and today, it remains one of the loveliest examples of 18th Century New England.

Cruising the Connecticut

Beginning as a mountain stream tumbling from its source near the New Hampshire-Canada border, the Connecticut River travels 410 miles (660 km) through four states and ends its journey to the sea as a broad and majestic tidal estuary. The Indians named it "Quinnituckett," which means "the long, tidal river." Throughout

Connecticut River anglers. wait until dark when the fish bite best, left. Shad roe, right, is a prime regional delicacy.

history, the Connecticut has linked valley residents with the outside world. A fertile floodplain has made this area a center for agriculture, and water power has generated energy for a variety of small industries. Lovely and scenic, stately and calm, the river is well worth a day's exploration.

A tour of the Connecticut Valley can begin near the river's mouth with a visit to **Essex**, founded in 1645 and a long-time center of maritime activity. From the Connecticut Turnpike, take exit 67 (old Saybrook) to State Highway 9 north. Exit 3 leads into the village.

Essex developed as an important shipbuilding center during the 18th Century. The *Oliver Cromwell*, America's first warship, was launched in 1775 from its docks. Yachts and cabin cruisers still make their berths at various Essex marinas, where tall masts and yards of tackle lend the town a distinctly nautical air. Contained in its dockside museum is an exact replica of the *American Turtle*, the nation's first submarine. Invented by David Bushnell, a native of **Old Saybrook**, it was employed in 1776 by Yankee forces to sink an English battleship during the blockade of New York Harbor. Though unsuccessful in its mission, the *Turtle* incorporated a number of engineering ideas that Robert Fulton later adopted in the design of the *Nautilus*.

The **Old Griswold Inn** on Main Street has been in operation since 1776. The rare collection of maritime prints hanging in its tap room makes the inn worth a special visit.

Those who desire a first-hand glimpse of the Connecticut River may take an old-fashioned journey by steam locomotive and riverboat. Board the old steam train at Essex Depot, and ride along the river through the villages of **Chester** and **Deep River**. At Deep River, leave the steam train and board a riverboat similar to the hundreds of passenger ships that ferried travelers between Old Saybrook and Hartford more than 100 years ago. Along the way, look out for landmarks such as the East Haddam opera house and Gillette Castle. The total time required for the train ride and cruise is approximately two hours.

Those who continue their journey up the Connecticut Valley may cross the river by car ferry at Chester. The five-

Marsh grass, western Connecticut.

Connecticut Coast

minute crossing is a bargain at 75 cents. It is a charming excursion that brings you to **Hadlyme**, home of the spectacularly eccentric **Gillette Castle**.

William Gillette (1853-1937) was a much admired American actor whose portrayal of Sherlock Holmes brought him fame and fortune. It was Gillette who first took to wearing the deerstalker hat, a distinctive Sherlock Holmes' trademark; and it was he who first uttered those memorable words, "Elementary, my dear Watson."

Gillette was born and raised in Hartford and, when he decided to build the house of his dreams, the actor selected a hilltop aerie that commanded a breathtaking view of the Connecticut River and its surrounding countryside. Work began on the 122-acre (49-hectare) site in 1914, and it took five years and over $1 million before Gillette's architectural vision was completed.

The results were whimsical and bizarre. The stone-and-concrete castle is filled with hand-hewn oak furnishings and specialized gadgetry. Javanese mats line the walls and light fixtures are fashioned from numerous bits of colored glass. Outside, Gillette was free to develop his favorite hobby — trains and locomotives. He constructed his very own railroad on the estate grounds, and while the tracks have long since been dismantled, portions of the old roadbed make excellent hiking trails.

Now a state park with excellent picnicking facilities, Gillette Castle is open daily from May 31 to October 12.

Directly north of Gillette Castle, on Route 82, is the charming Victorian town of **East Haddam**. Still standing along the shoreline are the great rambling hotels (some of them now private homes) that served riverboat passengers during the 19th Century. Before the introduction of the railroad, East Haddam was a point of embarkation for the many passengers who traveled by steamboat across the Long Island Sound to New York City.

The **Goodspeed Opera House**, which sits so majestically on the banks of the Connecticut River, is a reminder of the heyday of steamboat travel. Many a citizen paused here for a bit of entertainment before continuing his journey downriver. Beautifully restored, the Opera House presents musical revivals,

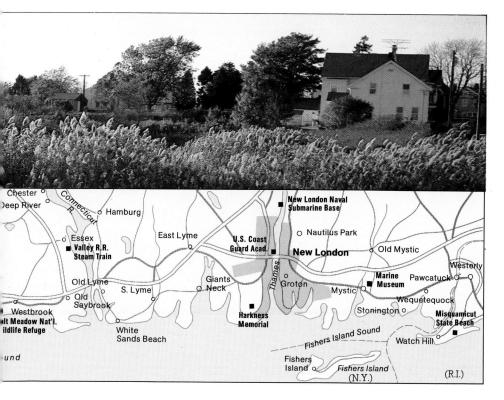

as well as original productions, from April through November.

Coastal Connecticut

From the harbors of New Haven, New London, Mystic and Stonington, China clippers and Yankee whalers sailed out to seek their fortunes. Such associations may be merely historical, but residents of the cities and towns along Connecticut's coast still retain a fondness for salt air and a genuine love of the sea. Most towns have at least one marina, and on a clear summer's day, the horizon of the Long Island Sound is filled with billowing sails.

For those planning to explore this region, there are several routes available. Most efficient is the Connecticut Turnpike (Interstate 95), the major highway linking New York and Boston. But what one makes up in time is definitely lost in charm. The more casual approach is the scenic Merritt Parkway from New York to New Haven, where a connection can be made with U.S. Highway 1. Now known as the Post Road, this rural roadway meanders through most of the towns mentioned here.

Greenwich, **Cos Cob**, **Stamford**, **Darien** and **Rowayton** — to the thousands of Connecticut residents who work in New York City, this is a railroad conductor's litany. Forty minutes to an hour away from Manhattan by train, the Connecticut suburbs are among the most luxurious bedroom communities in the nation. Many of New York's wealthiest business executives make their homes here, attracted by the pleasant, countrified locale and a government that collects no state income tax.

By the time one reaches **Bridgeport**, however, the New York influence recedes. For here is one of Connecticut's major industrial centers: Bridgeport is a town that manufactures everything from clothing to electrical appliances. In recent years, increased competition from the South and Sunbelt states has brought hard times to the area, but the city's workers continue to be some of the most skilled laborers in the country.

At **Stratford**, the **American Shakespeare Theatre**, which is modeled after the Globe Theatre in London, has mounted many a proud production of the Elizabethan classics. The theater is located on the shores of the Housatonic River, and many patrons begin their evening with a picnic along the riverbank.

Town and Gown

New Haven, settled by Puritans in 1638, was an independent colony until 1662 when it merged with the Hartford settlement. In the early 19th Century, the port brought prosperity to the town and, during that period, more than 100 ships regularly sailed along the coast to the West Indies and the Orient.

However, it was not until the Industrial Revolution that the town made the big leap to becoming a major manufacturing center. Eli Whitney first instituted a system of mass production in his firearms factory. Since that time, New Haven has pioneered such inventions as the steel fish hook, the meat grinder, the corkscrew and the steamboat.

New Haven is perhaps best known not as an industrial center, but as a center of learning. It is the home of

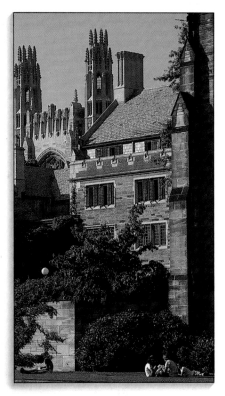

Yale University, which dominates much of the city's cultural life. Founded in 1701 by a group of Puritan clergymen, Yale was originally located in nearby **Saybrook**. In 1716, the school was moved to New Haven and, two years later, it took the name of wealthy merchant Elihu Yale, its benefactor.

Yale's undergraduate community is divided among 12 colleges, each of which has its own dormitories, library and dining halls. Including students enrolled in the 11 graduate programs, the school's total enrolment numbers approximately 10,000. Alma mater to famous personalities such as Eli Whitney, Nathan Hale and Noah Webster, Yale has pursued a policy of commissioning leading architects to design her buildings, among them Louis Kahn (the Art Gallery and the Center for British Art), Eero Saarinen (Morse and Ezra Stiles colleges, the Co-Op and the Ingalls Hockey Rink) and Philip Johnson (the Kline Biology Tower). The dominant architectural style on the campus is Gothic Revival, and there is more than enough greenery creeping up the walls to qualify the college as genuine Ivy League.

To make a thorough tour of Yale, inquire at the University's public information office. Otherwise, even an abbreviated stroll should include visits to the excellent museums and libraries. Start from the **Beinecke Rare Book and Manuscript Library** on Wall Street where an edition of the Gutenberg Bible is on display. Two blocks south is the Yale University Art Gallery which contains well over 100 paintings by patriot artist Jonathan Trumbull. The Gallery houses impressive collections of African and pre-Columbian art, as well as canvases by Manet, Van Gogh, Corot, Degas and Matisse.

Across the street stands the Yale Center for British Art, containing a vast collection of British paintings, (including works by Constable and Turner), drawings and sculpture donated in 1966 by industrialist Paul Mellon.

Adjacent to the university is the **New Haven Green**, a 16-acre (six-hectare) common surrounded by a trinity of churches. Although these houses of worship were constructed within three years of one another, they each have a distinctive architectural style — Gothic Revival, Georgian and Federal.

A ferry crosses the lazy Connecticut River.

New Haven has rich cultural offerings available. The **Yale Repertory Theater** on campus and the **Long Wharf Theater** on the downtown waterfront mount some of the finest productions in the country. The New Haven Symphony Orchestra, one of the finest small orchestras in America, frequently performs at **Woolsey Hall** on the Yale campus.

Guilford and Madison

Up the coast from New Haven are two of the loveliest communities along this shore, the villages of **Guilford** and Madison. Of the two, Guilford is the older, having been settled in 1639 by the Reverend Henry Whitfield. Whitfield's home still stands and is, in fact, the oldest stone dwelling in New England. Located on Old Whitfield Street, the house is open to visitors from January 15 to December 15.

Guilford's town green, one of the purest in New England, is bordered by many of its original 18th Century homes. Several of these homes are now museums, including **Hyland House** and

Dockside scene in quiet Stonington.

Griswold House, both located on Boston Street, east of the green.

Nearby **Madison** has always turned with one face toward the sea, and along its beachhead stand some of the most beautiful summer and year-round homes in the state. **Hammonasset Beach State Park**, located just two miles east of town, is the longest public beach in Connecticut.

Of all the towns on the Connecticut shore, **Old Lyme** has done the most to preserve its colonial heritage. There was a time when "a sea captain lived in every house," but in later years the community came to be known primarily as an artist's colony. Bridging the two pursuits, Florence Griswold was the daughter of a sea captain and a patron of the arts. Her house, located on Lyme Street next to the **Lyme Art Association**, served as a boarding house and an artist's retreat. Paintings done by her boarders, many of them American Impressionists, can be seen at the neighboring Art Association. The boarding house features exhibits of American fine and decorative arts.

Whales and Submarines

New London, with Nantucket and New Bedford, was one of the busiest whaling ports in the nation. In the early days of the 19th Century, more than 80 ships sailed from her docks and many a vast fortune was accumulated by her merchants. Evidence of this wealth can be seen in **Whale Oil Row** on Huntington Street, where four Greek Revival mansions were built in the 1830s.

When oil was discovered in Pennsylvania in 1859, the whaling industry went into a sharp decline, and manufacturing became New London's chief occupation. But the city maintained its ties to the sea and today is best known as the home of the **U.S. Coast Guard Academy**. Located on State 32, just a mile north of I-95, the Academy is open to visitors daily. An excellent walking tour of the Academy is available and those in luck may see a full-dress parade and tour the *Eagle*, the pride of America's tall ships.

Across the Thames River from New London stands the city of **Groton** known as the "Submarine Capital of the World." The U.S. Atlantic submarine fleet and the Electric Boat Division of

General **Dynamics** call Groton their home port, and the manufacture of nuclear submarines is the town's major industry. Those who wish to view the interior of a submarine may visit the **U.S.S. Croaker Memorial**. Launched from Groton in 1944, the *Croaker* is a veteran of six Pacific patrols during World War II. Tours of the craft are given by ex-submariners.

Mysterious Mystic

The village of **Mystic**, an old maritime community of trim white houses, sits at the tidal outlet of the **Mystic River**. For generations, Mystic was the home of daring mariners and fishermen and was feared by the British during the Revolution as "a cursed little hornet's nest" of patriots.

The village teemed with activity during the Gold Rush days of 1849, when shipbuilders vied to see who could construct the fastest clipper ships to travel round Cape Horn to the boom town of San Francisco. It was the *Andrew Jackson*, a Mystic-built clipper launched in 1860, that claimed the world's record — making the journey in 89 days and four hours, nine hours faster than the famous *Flying Cloud*.

Today, Mystic is best known as the home of **Mystic Seaport**, a living replica of a 19th Century waterfront community during the heyday of sailing ships. Restoration of Mystic Seaport began in 1929 and, since that time, the project has expanded to include a complex of more than 60 buildings covering 17 acres (seven hectares). A full day and plenty of stamina are required to tour the entire seaport properly.

The restoration imparts a vivid sense of how life was lived by Mystic's residents in the 1860s. Visitors are encouraged to wander along the wharves and streets of the village, and taste the old seafaring way of life. Visit the shops, the bank, the print shop, the tavern, the church and the schoolhouse. Stop at the ship's chandlery where seamen outfitted for their long outgoing journeys. Sometimes a craftsman may be seen giving a demonstration on scrimshaw, the fine art of etching on whalebone.

Save time for a visit to the *Charles W. Morgan*, the last surviving vessel of America's 19th Century whaling fleet. The *Morgan* served for more than 80 years and made 37 voyages, some of them lasting three or four years. Work is currently underway to make the *Morgan* seaworthy again.

Also board the *Joseph Conrad*, which was built in 1882 by the Danish as a training vessel. The *Conrad* is today serving its original purpose. Be sure to stop at the **Stillman Building**, a museum housing an impressive collection of ship's figureheads, scrimshaw, ship models, log books and other seafaring memorabilia. Drop by the **Mystic Marinelife Aquarium** with its outdoor exhibit of seals and sea lions; and hourly performances by dolphins, whales and sea lions.

One final caveat: don't make the same mistake that most other tourists make by ending your tour at Mystic. Travel just a few miles farther east and come to the charming old whaling port of **Stonington** huddling at the edge of the state near the Rhode Island border. Stonington was once the third largest city in Connecticut and an important seaport. Though considerably reduced in circumstances, the village remains one of the prettiest coastal enclaves in New England.

Left, around and around at the Durham Fair. Right, a stately church in Guilford.

RHODE ISLAND

Like the littlest kid on the block, Rhode Islanders have always had to contend with being the smallest state in the nation. People say that if one doesn't slow down when driving from New York to Boston, he'll miss Rhode Island altogether. But they also say good things come in small packages, and Rhode Island is no exception.

The turn-of-the-century millionaires who built their legendary summer "cottages" in Newport recognized Rhode Island's magnetic allure. The mansions they left behind still gleam, like jewels from the Gilded Age, on their cliff perches high above the ocean.

Centuries earlier, the Reverend William Blackstone had found the area equally attractive. Blackstone, who had been living as a hermit, fled to Rhode Island when a group of Puritans appropriated his land for their settlement of Boston.

Next came Roger Williams, the founder of Providence. On being driven out of Salem for preaching religious tolerance, Williams established a settlement here where all were free to practice their own faith. Anne Hutchinson and others from Massachusetts followed.

Soon people from even farther afield flocked to Rhode Island's shores. A large number of Quakers made Newport their home, and Jews from Portugal and Holland settled here as well. Through the years came Italians, Irish, Russians, Poles, French, Swedes, Greeks, Armenians, Chinese and Cape Verdians. By 1960 Rhode Island was the most densely populated state in America with 859,000 inhabitants crowded into 1,214 square miles (3,144 sq km). Today with its 947,154 residents, Rhode Island is a bustling little state. And a glance at the phone book will turn up names like Ricci, Balzano, Silva, O'Keefe, Gregoire, Nathanson and Najarian.

'The Ocean State'

Narragansett Bay dominates Rhode Island. Taking a dinosaur bite out of the New England coast, it gives the state a shoreline out of all proportion to its

Preceding pages: lavish Rosecliff manor at Newport. Below, Roger Williams, the founder of Providence.

land area. Rhode Island is only 48 miles (77 km) long and 37 miles (60 km) wide, yet end to end it claims 400 miles (644 km) of coastline.

With such an abundance of water at their disposal, Rhode Islanders have returned to the sea for their livelihood. Two of the nation's leading seaports in the early days of the republic were Providence and Newport. Using Rhode Island as a base, pirates raided merchant ships in the North Atlantic; the notorious Captain Kidd is rumored to have buried his cache of gold doubloons in Jamestown.

Divine wisdom may have influenced William's choice of a name for the state. Perhaps, like the little kid with an inferiority complex, its size demanded the longest name of any state in the Union. Its official moniker is "State of Rhode Island and Providence Plantations." Few people call it that, preferring instead "Little Rhody," "The State of the Independent Man," "The Ocean State" (a refrain appearing on car license plates) and "Biggest Little State in the Union."

Rhode Island is a land of contradictions. Founded as a haven of religious liberty, it was once a world-class slave trade center. Despite its heritage as a sanctuary for pirates, it gave birth to the United States Navy in Newport. (The Naval War College remains, although much of the Navy pulled out in 1974.) Although Rhode Island contributed heavily to the success of the American Revolution, it was the last holdout among states ratifying the U.S. Constitution. Notorious for its exploitation of child labor, Rhode Island became a bastion of New Deal social ideals.

Until 1854, it couldn't even decide which city would be its capital. Each year the General Assembly packed up its belongings and moved lock, stock and barrel to one of the five places contesting for the honor. Eventually, after a raucous battle in 1900, Providence won out over Newport. It remains the capital, although Newporters contend their city by the sea is truly the heart of the state.

The First and the Biggest

If little Rhode Island is a land of contradictions, it is also a land of superlatives — which itself may be a contradic-

Restored sea captains' homes on Benefit Street, Providence.

Restored sea captains' homes on Benefit Street, Providence.

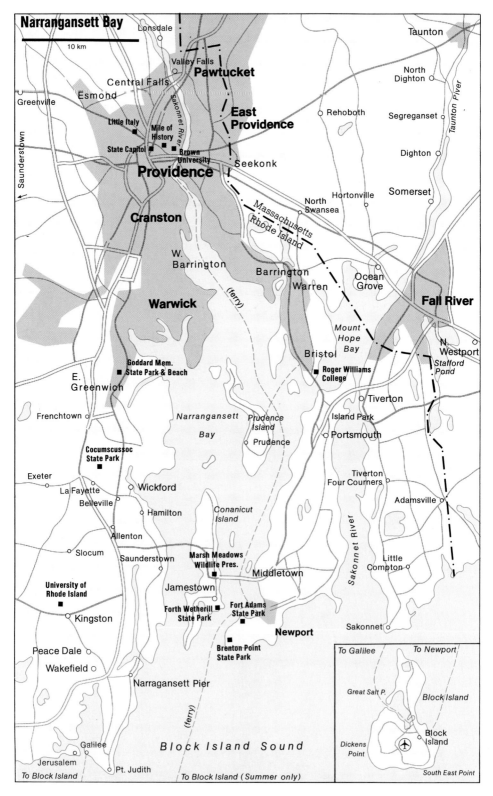

tion. The world's widest bridge is in Providence; and only operational water-powered snuff mill in the United States is in Saunderstown; the world's only known monument to a chicken (the Rhode Island Red) is in Adamsville. The state boasts the country's first synagogue, first department store and first enclosed shopping mall. And lest it be forgotten, the first two-week paid vacation on record was spent in Rhode Island. In 1524, the Italian navigator Giovanni da Verazzano was exploring the North American coast when he spotted Narrangansett Bay. Working for the King of France, Verazzano was "so enthralled ... he lingered for a fortnight."

Rhode Island, in the singular, is a misnomer. In fact, there are 35 islands within the state, the only one named after a Greek isle. Within and without Narrangansett Bay are the four principal islands of Aquidneck, Block, Conanicut and Prudence; there are also Hen, Hog, Rabbitt, Boat, Old Boy, Patience, Hope and Despair. In and about these islands, sportsmen enjoy boating, sailing, surfing and fishing.

Throughout the state — generously scattered through cities and towns like Providence, Wickford, Bristol, Little Compton and Newport — are lovely old homes, religious edifices and commercial buildings. Although Rhode Island is heavily populated, its size keeps everything on a human scale. Rhode Island is a state where people still know their elected officials personally.

It takes a little less than two hours to drive from one end of the state to the other. A visitor can walk its historic city streets in the morning, picnic in a far corner of its woods at noon, and savor the delights of its shores by moonlight.

Revitalized Providence

In its early days, **Providence** was the port of call for ships engaged in the lucrative Triangular Trade — New England rum for African slaves for West Indies molasses. In 1781, John Brown, one of the four brothers whose family was to dominate Providence for some years to come, sent the first of many ships to China. However, the maritime trade began to decline following a series of international wars which resulted in embargoes and protectionism. Public interest and investment shifted toward industry. Techniques of factory production were pioneered and groundwork for the development of the region's textile industry was laid in 1789, with the construction of **Slater Mill** by Moses Brown. (Now fully restored as a historic site, the mill offers visitors a rare look into bygone industry at **Pawtucket,** north of Providence).

A major industrial and financial center throughout the 19th Century, Providence was dubbed "the cradle of American industry." Its huge plants were known worldwide — Brown & Sharpe (machinery and tools), Nicholson (files), Grinnel (sprinkler systems), Gorham (silverware), Davol (rubber goods) and so on.

The 20th Century brought hard times. With the Great Depression and the textile industry's exodus to the south, Providence lost its preeminence as an industrial center. Although no longer the giant it once was, Providence has recently enjoyed a revitalization of business and is now a leading manufacturer of both costume and gold-filled jewelry.

Along with its rejuvenated industry, Providence began to turn its attention

The Arcade, a Greek Revival-style "temple of trade."

to revitalizing its downtown, the center of its business district. Here, residents have gotten used to stumbling on a Victorian office building, or an old industrial complex jazzily accented in pink, purple or chartreuse, right next to a seedy remnant from the 1930s. The skyline is dominated by the 28-story **Rhode Island Hospital Trust Building** and the **Fleet National Bank,** rumored to be the building over which Superman leaped in a single bound.

A Two-legged Tour

Visitors never take long to realize that the city, given its maddening network of highways and one-way streets, is best seen on foot. Begin at **Kennedy Plaza.** To the east stands the recently restored **railroad station,** worth a visit for a glimpse back to the times when train travel was a grand affair. Across the plaza is the **Biltmore Plaza,** a 1920s showpiece that deteriorated into a shabby eyesore until, in 1979, it was refurbished to become the first-class hotel it is today. With its three restaurants — the elegant L'Apogee on its 18th floor, the Cafe on the Terrace and Goddard's — the hotel is once again becoming the city's favorite haunt.

Around the corner from Kennedy Plaza, a fountain sits just outside the Rhode Island Hospital Trust Building. On warm days, workers from Providence's financial district congregate here to eat their lunch, people-watch and listen to musicians who perform here. Across the street are the **Turk's Head Building,** a 1913 landmark with an ornate stone head over its entrance; and the **Customs House** (1856), with a dome and lantern that once welcomed ships returning from China.

Theater and architecture buffs will want to head toward the refurbished **Ocean State Theater** on the Weybosset Street. This Hollywood extravaganza, built in the heyday of movie theaters, sports a great deal of gilt, a terra-cotta facade and a "Moorish sand castle" side entrance. Saved in the nick of time from total decay, it provides the city with a string of major performances and top stars throughout the year. Several blocks away is the **Lederer Theater,** home of Trinity Square Repertory Company, one of the country's finest. Like the Ocean State, the Lederer has an ornate terra-cotta facade, along with

a three-story arched entrance, floral swags and a false balcony. (Other buildings of architectural note or special historical value are listed in *Looking Up Downtown*, a Providence Preservation Society brochure.

For shopping or snacking and a bit of history, visit the **Arcade** situated between Weybosset and Westminster streets. This "temple of trade" and granddaddy of indoor shopping malls was built in 1828 in the Greek Revival style. Its three-story granite columns (said to be the second largest in America, after those at the Cathedral of St. John the Divine in New York) were cut from single pieces of stone, which required 15 yokes of oxen to move.

A City of Hills

Like Rome, Providence was built on seven hills. Most people remember three — College (officially, Prospect), Federal and Constitution. The other four — Tockwotten, Smith and two now-leveled hills — seem to disappear into the metropolitan sprawl. Constitution Hill is hard to miss because of the dominance of the **State Capitol** at its

Brown University on College Hill.

crest. And both College and Federal hills, on opposite sides of the downtown area, are favorite haunts of tourists and natives alike.

At the foot of College Hill, along the canal, stands **Market House,** a red-brick Colonial built in the 1770s. The wharves that fronted it are paved over now, and the building serves as a part of the **Rhode Island School of Design** (RISD, pronounced "rizz-dee") complex. But Market House was once the city's political nerve center. From its wharves in 1775, Rhode Islanders threw their own version of the Boston Tea Party. Instead of dumping the tea into the river, they burned 300 pounds of it.

Plaques on Market House and other downtown buildings record the high-water level of the 1815 storm that brought Providence to its knees with tides reaching nearly 12 feet (3.6 meters) above mean high-water level. The storms of 1938 and 1954 caused similar flooding in the city; today, the **Fox Point Hurricane Barrier,** south of Market House toward the mouth of the Providence River, stands as testimony to the devastation. A very unusual dam, its gates (usually open) face down-

stream and are closed only when a hurricane threatens.

On North Main Street, one block up the steep hillside from Market House, is the **First Baptist Church.** Designed by one of the Brown brothers, Joseph, this church is a lovely example of the Colonial style. The **Mile of History,** as the Preservation Society calls it, begins here. All along Benefit Street and adjacent blocks are more than 200 restored 18th and 19th-Century buildings. Originally built by sea captains and merchants, the old houses, churches and schools still bear bronze plaques identifying their first owner and date of construction. Affluent bankers, lawyers, businessmen and professors now live in these houses, which form a sort of "living museum." At twilight, gaslights and brick sidewalks, installed a decade ago, are a charming evocation of the past.

'For the Benefit of the People'

The **John Brown House,** built in 1786 at Power and Benefit streets, still lives up to John Quincy Adam's description as "the most magnificent and elegant

private mansion that I have ever seen on this continent." Converted into a museum, it now displays priceless old furniture, dolls, silver and items brought back from China in the 18th and 19th centuries. The slide show presented here gives a good sense of early Providence life.

Further north on Benefit Street is **Sullivan Dorr Mansion,** owned in the 1830s and 1840s by state legislator Thomas Dorr. The leader of Dorr's Rebellion (1841-42), he and his supporters instituted a new state government — unrecognized by the existing government — when their reform efforts failed. After a short time, Dorr was tried for treason and spent a year in jail.

Nearby is the **Sarah Whitman House.** Whitman, a poetess, captured the heart of Edgar Allen Poe; but she refused to marry him because he couldn't stay sober. It was at the **Providence Atheneum,** the Greek Revival structure at 251 Benefit St., that Poe courted Whitman. The Atheneum is worth a visit for its own sake, if only to perceive the time when libraries were the special province of the cultured few.

Benefit Street was once a twisting dirt path informally known as Back Street because it led around the back side of homes to the family graveyards. When at last a communal burial ground was marked out and ancestral bones duly transferred to it, Back Street was straightened out and "improved for the benefit of the people of Providence."

Other streets have similar tales about the origins of their names. The Preservation Society guides who lead walking tours through this area know all the stories.

Competing with the old houses on College Hill are the buildings of the RISD and the ever-sprawling **Brown University.** The heart of the College Hill shopping area is Thayer Street, a few blocks east of Benefit. Seen here and on the college green are Ivy Leaguers, bearded professors, the not-so-occasional celebrity parent checking up on his or her undergraduate offspring, aspiring artists in paint-spattered overalls, street musicians, conservative Yankee housewives and hippies from a bygone era. They come for the restaurants, bars, shops, bookstores and proliferation of specialty ice-cream parlors.

Private marina near Newport.

Old World Enclaves

Continue south down Thayer Street and encounter one of Providence's best kept secrets — **Fox Point.** Home to the city's Portuguese community, Fox Point speaks with an Old World accent. On holy days, devouts parade with statues of the Virgin Mary while solemn-looking children, dressed in their best suits and crinolines, follow along. Early morning brings to Fox Point the tantalizing scent of Portuguese sweetbread. Stop at one of the bakeries to pick up a loaf or two of this mouth-watering treat.

Perched on Federal Hill across the city is Providence's **Little Italy.** Welcoming visitors are the large stone archway at its entrance and the pinecone at the top. Wander along Atwells Avenue with its red, green and white stripes — colors of the Italian flag — down the middle of the street. The aroma of crusty Italian breads, cheeses, pastas, herbs and spices has long been fixtures in the area.

Some people come for traditional Italian deli delights like Gorgonzolas, Romanos, homemade pork sausages and prosciutto. Others come for restaurants, espresso shops and the general ambience. Without a doubt, Federal Hill is the friendliest part of all Providence. While the warmth and color of Italian life on the hill are perhaps inevitably blended and soured by the widespread notion that major figures in organized crime operate from somewhere in the neighborhood, visitors needn't be concerned. Its streets are among the safest and most orderly in the entire city.

Newport: Domain of Wealth

During World War II an anti-submarine net was strung across the entrance of the bay guarding Newport. It was effective. But, then, the elite of the city are expert at guarding their privacy. In the halcyon days of the Gilded Age, Newport was the domain of the very wealthy. Huge palaces built on expansive grounds were surrounded by mammoth fences and patrolled by guards and dogs. Now, however, with some 4 million visitors a year streaming over the Newport Bridge, the city has been transformed. And each year, locals wonder whether, next year, they'll be able to recognize it.

Summering in Newport first became fashionable before the Revolution among Southern plantation owners escaping the heat of Georgia and the Carolinas. After the Civil War, the nation's wealthiest families — Astors, Morgans, Fishers, Vanderbilts — discovered its charms. They hoped to legitimize their newfound wealth by duplicating the palaces and chateaux that had so awed them on their grand tours of Europe. Didn't Edward Bewind, the son of poor German immigrants, enter the ranks of aristocracy with **The Elms,** his home patterned after the Chateau d'Asnières outside Paris?

Extravagance became obligatory. Harry Lehr hosted a formal dinner at which a monkey, complete with tuxedo and princely title, numbered among the guests. James Gordon Bennett, the man who bought a Monte Carlo restaurant when it refused him a table, rode stark naked in his carriage through Newport's streets. The Coogans invited everyone who was anyone to a grand ball to celebrate the completion of their "summer cottage." When no one showed up, the Coogans simply walked out — leaving food, drink and furniture — and

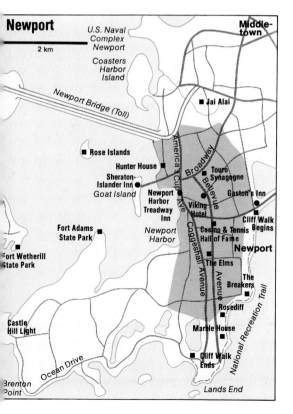

never returned.

Visitors to the city by the sea today may know nothing of Lehr, Bennett or the Coogans, but they recognize the setting for a perfect summer vacation. There's so much to see and do in Newport's 10 square miles (26 sq km) that the list of activities — sightseeing, shopping, swimming, sailing, dining, concert-hopping and more — is overwhelming. Always remember that, if Newport has one lesson, it's that there's always a tomorrow. Before doing anything else, just relax and breathe the salt air.

Golden Age Grandeur

Still, a trip to Newport has to include a tour of at least some of the mansions, the most impressive of which line Bellevue Avenue and Ocean Drive. Although literally hundreds of these establishments existed during Newport's Golden Age, only 70 remain now.

Most of them are no longer occupied by private individuals; many now house schools and charitable institutions. The Newport Preservation Society pays the grand sum of $1 a year to rent **The Breakers.** Considered the most magnificent of the Newport cottages, this Italian Renaissance palace took only two years to build. Cornelius Vanderbilt II commissioned American architect Richard Morris Hunt to build the mansion, whose 70 rooms are extravagantly adorned with marble, alabaster, gilt, mosaic, crystal and stained glass. The Grand Salon was constructed in France, and later dismantled and shipped to Newport, where it was reassembled.

Marble House, another of Hunt's design, was built for William K. Vanderbilt and styled after Grand et Petit Trianons of Versailles. And the list goes on: coal-rich Edward Julius Berwind commissioned The Elms; Mrs. Herman Oelrichs hired Stanford White to design **Rosecliff,** an imitation of Versailles' Grand Trianon; China trade merchant William S. Wetmore built **Chateau-sur-Mer,** another Hunt-designed mansion; while Mrs. Astor, the *grande dame* of American society, held court at **Beechwood Mansion.**

Strollers can examine the backyards of the Bellevue Avenue mansions from the **Cliff Walk,** a 3½-mile (5½-km) path that overlooks Rhode Island Harbor.

Sound as it crushes on the rocks below. Crusty Rhode Island fishermen saved this path for public use by going to court when wealthy mansion owners tried to close it. Visitors who do not wish to walk the length of this path can start at the end of Narrangansett Avenue and reach the water by way of the **Forty Steps**; or wander down to **Brenton Point**, a state park on the island's southernmost tip and an ideal place to watch gulls, picnic or just enjoy a sunset.

For a visual feast of Newport's great architectural wealth, tour **The Point** and the **Historic Hill**, the oldest colonial sections of the town. Among the favorites are the white clapboard **Trinity Church** (1726) on Queen Anne Square, based on designs of Christopher Wren; **Hunter House,** a 1748 Georgian building considered one of the 10 best examples of colonial American homes; **Touro Synagogue** (1759), America's first, also of Georgian style; **Colony House,** seat of the state's first government; and **Redwood Library,** inspired by Roman temple architecture.

The World's Yachting Capital

Newport is the scene of many yachting events. The prestigious America's Cup were held in Newport waters 24 times from 1851 through 1983, when the Cup was lost (for the first time) to the Australians. The 685-mile (1,102-km) Bermuda-Newport Race, held every other year, begins here; and the grueling Single-Handed Transatlantic Race, which starts in Plymouth, England, ends in Newport. To many, Newport is the yachting capital of the world.

Newporters love sailing. Yacht clubs abound, and a stroll through the town reveals a decidedly salty air blown in from the surrounding sea. Stop by a loft and watch sailmakers at work; see boats being prepared in shops along the wharves; visit the **Ebenezer Flagg Company,** where a hand-crafted emblem can be ordered, and listen to proprietor Leo Waring expound on the subject of flags: "Flags are symbols that move people. They make people think about our heritage, whether we're living up to our ideals."

When the sea has saturated one's interest, head for the **Newport Casino,** America's most exclusive country club when it was built in 1880. Today it contains the **Tennis Hall of Fame** and the

grass courts where the first Men's U.S. Lawn Tennis Association tournament was played in 1881.

Study the **Old Stone Tower,** a landmark variously said to have been left behind by the Vikings, Portuguese, Irish or even Phoenicians. Then tour the **Newport Automobile Museum** for a display of classical and antique cars. The museum houses the 1947 Mercury convertible that was Jacqueline Bouvier Kennedy Onassis' first car and the 1941 Alfa-Romeo Mussolini presented to Hitler on his 52nd birthday. Drive to nearby Portsmouth to visit the **Green Animals Topiary Gardens,** with its 80 tree sculptures representing everything from an ostrich to a camel.

Newport is also surrounded by fine beaches. The choice ranges from **First, Second** and **Third** beaches in Middleton (just north of Newport) to the more exclusive **Bailey's, Hazard's** and **Gooseberry.**

As night falls, brush off the sand and head for the waterfront. The parade of strollers on Bower's Wharf will remind some of a prep-school reunion, others will think back to the days when Newport hosted the Jazz Festival (moved to New York in 1971). Most action centers on the wharf and the bars, cafés and restaurants along Thames Street. The music is outrageously loud in places like **One Pelham East;** crowds spill out of the **Black Pearl** and the **Candy Store** to the cobblestones that lead to the water's edge.

Newport doesn't disappoint those who wish to dine on fine seafood while soaking in the sea breeze. Restaurants and bars may come and go, but many of the best and most popular remain. Pick up a copy of the *Newport Restaurant Guide* at the Chamber of Commerce Information Center at Brick Market Place and then ask a friendly local for some "inside advice" on the best. Some venerable eateries include the **White Horse Tavern,** the **Clarke Cooke House, Christie's,** the **Chart House,** and **The Inn at Castle Hill.** Others, like **The Ark, Southern Cross** and **Cafe Zelda,** are new but are attracting a lot of attention.

The Island Off Rhode Island

When Rhode Islanders want to get away from it all, they head for **Block Island,** the four-by-seven mile (six-by-

11 km) island some 12 miles (19 km) south of Narragansett Bay. Whereas Newport is packed to the gills with people, cars, boats, restaurants and notables, Block Island is a nearby hideaway yet overlooked by developers and fast-food chains. Block is the least accessible of the state's islands: although regular or chartered planes fly out of Westerly, R.I., and points in Connecticut (a 10-minute hop), most people take the ferry, a 1½-hour trip from Galilee, R.I.

Greeting arrivals are fine beaches, popular fishing grounds, tranquility and the romantic allure of aging Victorian hotels with huge verandas and a sense by bygone splendor. Dutch settler Adrian Block discovered the island in 1614; so little has changed since then that Block would probably still recognize it today.

The island's claim to fame in maritime annals is the large number of shipwrecks off its coast. More than 1,000 luckless captains saw their vessels come to misery along the coast of New England; almost half were wrecked on the submerged rocks and sandbars around "The Block." Scavenging goods from the holds of wrecked ships became such a lucrative trade that some islanders helped the wrecks to occur by placing lanterns and flares to confuse the ships. Many island place names commemorate the wrecking trade; at Cow Cove, for instance, a cargo of cows from a wrecked ship waded ashore, and on Calico Hill, bolts of cloth collected from another disaster were hung out to dry.

Life in the early days was hard. In the turbulent years of the late 17th Century, the island was constantly under siege from pirates. (Sarah Sands, the first doctor in the English colonies, lived on the island and most certainly had her hands full tending the sick and wounded.) During the Revolution, Rhode Island's mainland was inaccessible to the islanders, who nearly stripped Block Island of trees in order to build their houses and ships.

In 1842, tourism arrived. The first hotel was opened, and the first party of visitors — seven men from Newport — checked in for a stay. Ten years later, the **Spring House** opened its doors and is still accommodating visitors today. Spending time in this antique of a summer hotel, with its expanse of long cor-

A trio of yachts brave the waters en route to Block Island.

ridors and simply furnished rooms, is to be caught in a time warp. From its perch high on a hill, gaze out over the Atlantic Ocean and breathe the beneficent sea air just as wealthy tourists from New York and Baltimore once did.

Beaches and Bluffs

The island has several fine sand beaches. **Surfers Beach,** as its name suggests, is for specialists; **State Beach** and others on the east are the calmest and attract most visitors. The westerly strands are windswept and, more often than not, deserted. One trek not to be missed is the hike to **Mohegan Bluffs.** Here, the entire Mohegan tribe met its doom at the hands of the Manasees, who either enslaved them or drove them over the 200-foot (61-meter) cliffs.

Fishing for flounder and other species in **New Harbor** (formerly Great Salt Pond) can absorb an entire day. So can wandering along the roads and over the hills, looking for wildflowers and Indian relics. Shops in **Old Harbor,** the island's only town, sell the usual souvenirs as well as local specialties, such as candles, jellies and wool watchcaps. Check out the **Block Island Kite Company,** whose beautiful merchandise fly over the nearby beach.

Evenings are quiet, but that's part of the island's charm. It's time for a good ghost story. As the fog puts a shroud over the rock where the *Palatine* went down in 1739 with a load of German immigrants, look hard: some insist they have glimpsed this ghostly burning ship still moving through the waters.

Back on the mainland, take a short detour to **Jamestown** on Conanicut Island. The southern tip of the island offers New England scenery at its most picturesque. Don't miss **Mackeral Cove,** the **Beaver Tail Lighthouse** and the view from **Fort Wetherhill.**

From Jamestown, follow U.S. 1A along the coast. From **Narragansett Pier,** an elegant resort town during the 19th Century, proceed south to **Scarborough,** the beach most popular with Rhode Island's teenage crowd. The sheltered beach at **Galilee** is the perfect spot for passing a languid summer afternoon, while **East Matunuck State Beach** offers somewhat rougher surf. In late July the Blessing of the Fleet ceremony is held in this area.

Mohegan Bluffs, Block Island.

VERMONT

Vermont is a great green slice of high ground, a measured wedge of American Pie left over, wrapped up and set aside as a souvenir of the homemade, agrarian utopia America was once meant to be.

Fatally vertical, down-west and upstream, "the land in-between" was a rocky byroad up and away from the parade route of national destiny. Vermont had its brief, booming share of speculators, cash-croppers, side-wheelers, mother lodes and iron horses. But there was always something wildly tentative about the sweep and dash of its struggle to keep up with the American pageant, something mildly tragic in its slapdash network of railways, turnpikes and fine rural academies.

The farmer's son saw his way clear of the proud and frowzy hometown, and joined the march West. Before the hill towns could settle down properly, the exodus had begun. Vermont is a land of transience and experiment, a bottomland repeatedly reclaimed by nature, a country outstripped by the bigger wheels of progress, a land imperfectly subdued by man — and delightfully so.

Put the Vermonters ahead and keep the column well closed up.
— General John Sedgewick at the Battle of Gettysburg

The Civil War decimated Vermont. No other state gave as large a share of its sons to the cause of Union. The year 1865 marked the beginning of its decline in population; until 1960, it grew older and smaller, gradually but inevitably.

The only substantial benefit Vermont got from the Civil War was the fame President Lincoln and his family lent to Manchester-and-the-Mountains. Choosing the area as their vacation spot, the First Family helped make it a fashionable resort. Other visitors soon discovered the subtler pleasures of what 19th-Century British historian Lord Bryce called "the Switzerland of North America." "Setting and viewing," fishing and strolling among the green hillsides became *de rigeuer* during America's Gilded Age; Manchester, Burlington and Woodstock were simply the great places to summer and be seen summering.

At the height of the season, the population approached its pre-war numbers. By putting up city folk, boiling and peddling "sweet water" (maple syrup), and enclosing more of their land for pasturage, Vermont farmers got by without hired hands. Some of their neighbors, like marble baron Redfield Proctor and William Dean Howell's fictive paint king, *Silas Lapham,* simply turned the fallow land over and made a mint out of bedrock mined by cheap foreign labor. But by the time the railways gave way to the automobile, tourism had become the state's unofficial No. 1 industry.

America's Playground

"Vermont, Designed by the Creator for the Playground of the Continent," read a 1911 brochure published by Vermont's state publicity bureau, the first such in the nation. "Development" became the 20th-Century battle cry, and roadside attractions outflanked each other from Brattleboro to Morses Line. Natives and visitors alike started

Preceding pages: a forest road near Danby and a Green Mountains landscape. Left, honoring an old Vermont pastime — pipe smoking. Right, time passes slowly in Brattleboro.

grumbling in the Thirties, when rolling pastures and grassy meadows quietly gave way here and there to a lakeside resort, a new rambling "summer cottage," another country club or (finally) the slim Interstate highway. Stories began to circulate; the farmer and his 12-gauge shotgun versus a brigade of the Conservation Corps and their backhoe. But the lawmakers in Montpelier didn't notice until, nearly overnight in the early Fifties, the ski industry blew land taxes through the rooftop. Suddenly the land of milk and honey was overflowing with New Yorkers from solstice to solstice. The real boom had finally begun.

In 1965, Vermont lost its distinction as the state with more cows than people. Today, very few natives make a decent living off the land. But the new gentry — the seasonal country gentleman with his Morgan horse, his 30 head of sheep on 40 taxable acres and his A-frame in the valley — is determined to reconstitute and preserve his township's special flavor, its fallow charm, its pastoral innocence, from latecomers. He has formed a shaky coalition with his neighbors — the disgruntled patrician, once the Republican pillar of his community; the refugee from the Sixties, artisan and journeyman of the post-industrial era; the seventh-generation Vermonter, whose trailer home, pickup truck and snowmobile have become the attributes of the native son. This is the backwoods elite — the holy alliance keeping the lobbyists and the developers at bay.

The toughest anti-pollution law in the nation, a dizzying array of zoning ordinances, new wilderness designations, a "no off-premise billboards" mandate and even a touch of urban renewal, have made Vermont an unquestionably better place to live. Ironically, the innovative minority have promoted it as being among the best places to visit.

The Connecticut River Valley

The long, lazy Connecticut River forms the entire boundary between the states of Vermont and New Hampshire. Vermont's southernmost outpost on the river is **Vernon.** Home of the state's only nuclear power plant and, consequently, the center of much controversy, Vernon has been transformed

Jacob Estey's Brattleboro organ factory was in its heyday in the 19th Century.

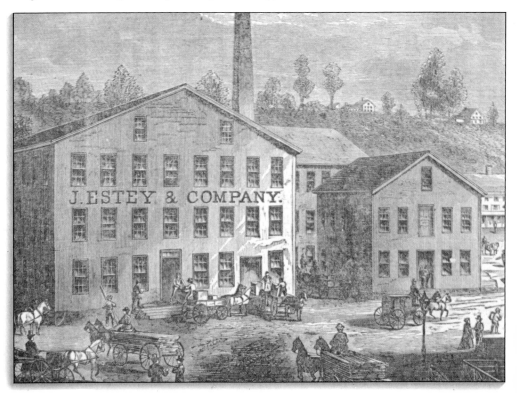

from a wide spot in the road into something of a sore spot for Vermonters. Just north of Vernon is the lake formed by the hydroelectric **Vernon Dam,** which was built in 1907 and which left the site of Fort Dummer — Vermont's first permanent settlement — nothing but a marker on the shore.

A byroad above Vernon leads west to U.S. 5, the Calvin Coolidge Memorial Highway, and to **Guilford,** a sleepy village that was once the most populous town in the territory. Just a throw north, the brisk town of **Brattleboro** rises from the Connecticut River Valley in a chain of ledges facing Wantastiquet Mountain on the opposite shore. A jumble of slate sheds are all that remain of the mammoth organ works of Jacob Estey, maker of the black-walnut parlor fixture every respectable 19th Century homemaker dreamed of owning.

"Winter has chased all these really interesting people south," lamented Rudyard Kipling from his Dummerston homestead on the Brattleboro town line, recalling a season when gypsies and itinerant artisans dared to cross just this far into peddler country. Lately, a new wave of rootless folk has washed

Purity and light: the Common in Newfane.

upstream. The back-to-basics crowd, in dirndls and headbands, variously tagged "wire-rimmers" and "sprout-heads," have set up shop for good in and around Brattleboro. They — and changing local tastes — support at least one genuine health emporium, two thrift shops, and a string of fine eateries on renovated Eliot Street. The **Common Ground,** in particular, seems less·a restaurant than a regional mecca, featuring a second-floor solar terrace

Naulahka, the ship-shaped manse where Kipling wrote the first two *Jungle Books* and *Captains Courageous* in the 1890s, is a private home at 19 Terrace St. Kipling, an Englishman born in India, married a Vermonter named Carrie Balestier, the sister of a young man he had come to know in London.

Puttering Putney

The new Brattleboro may have had some encouragement from **Putney** in the north, the most genuinely funky town in Vermont. Its riverside fields have been heavily farmed since the mid 18th Century, but this village in the center of apple country still lives off the

land. One of its two wildflower nurseries was begun by George Aiken, who as dean of the U.S. Senate in 1967 advised President Lyndon Johnson to "simply declare the Vietnam War won and pull out the troops." In 1975, after 34 years in Washington, this wise old owl returned home to Putney Mountain, next door to neighboring elder stateman Ellsworth Bunker, where he still trades yarns and tends to business.

More than 50 craftspeople ply their trades in Putney, manning a number of sculpture studios, an iron forge, and the ecologically pure Green Mountain Spinnery, where visitors can watch fleece from local sheep being scoured, carded and skeined for market. The community boasts the oldest bicycle club in the state, and the world's most unusual Santa's Land.

U.S. 9 to the west of Brattleboro is a crowded stretch leading to **Marlboro** and the ski resort towns of **Wilmington** and **West Dover.** Bohemian-born Rudolph Serkin directs chamber works for the renowned Marlboro Music Festival in July, and the music lingers until mid August over the **Marlboro College** campus — the first of three experimental colleges founded in Vermont by educator Walter P. Hendricks.

Hogback, Haystack and Mount Snow resorts loom west and north along Vermont's ski highway, State 100. Just far enough south to have escaped overdevelopment of the Fifties, the village of **Whitingham** boasts **Lake Sadawga** and **Harriman Reservoir**, both of which are well-stocked with fish. A small marker on Stimpson Hill reads:

Brigham Young Born
On This Spot 1801
A Man of Much Courage
And Splendid Equipment

State 30 out of Brattleboro follows the West River northwest for a short distance to the county seat of **Newfane.** Though next door to Putney via the old town road, the two towns couldn't be less alike. Its broad common lined with shady elms and its town green distinguished by stately public houses, Newfane fairly reeks of New World charm. Alistair Cooke considered Windham County Courthouse on the green "the exquisite symbol of what Americans could do in wood with Greek forms." Longtime summer visitors George McGovern and John Kenneth Galbraith will say that the town hall, church, huge country stores and formal inns are none too shabby, either. Stone No. 6 on old Newfane Hill attests to more than a century of civility: here in 1805 "the last woman" was whipped in public.

The Village Square in **Bellows Falls** reminds one of Brattleboro without all the fuss—quiet upscale shops and cafés on Westminster Street, and one of a dying breed of railroad hotels on the corner. Up-country ingenuity built America's first canal here in 1792 to bypass the falls, long the favorite fishing ground of the fierce Abnaki Indian tribe. A large boulder covered with ritual petroglyphs marks the spot where, swore one contemporary, "shad and salmon swarmed so thick a person could walk across the Connecticut on their backs." A set of steps leads down to the paper mills, where the **Old Gristmill Museum** documents town history, including the great turn-of-the-century log drives, which gave to the English language such terms as "logjam" and "haywire."

Scenic backroads thick with antique shops connect the Falls with **Grafton**

Memories in The Old Tavern, Grafton.

and **Chester** to the northwest. When "Aunt Pauline" Fiske left her fortune to the town of Grafton; her nephews put the town and the architects of Old Deerfield, Massachusetts, back to work reroofing and winterizing the Old Tavern, a cheese company, and the general store, generally resurrecting Grafton's long-dormant entrepreneurial spirit and its reputation as one of Vermont's loveliest small villages.

Under slate roofs and Bulfinchian towers, Chester village is a curious little strand of Victoriana on the Williams River. The ornate National Survey Charthouse, a cottage clothing industry and an outstanding village bakery are all on Main Street overlooking the slender village green. An 1850s vintage stone village features 30 homes on North Street faced in gneiss ledgestone.

Precision Valley

The covered bridge is almost a Vermont symbol.

A center of invention during the 19th Century and today home of a thriving machine tool industry, the towns of **Springfield** and **Windsor** form Precision Valley, a living testament to the severity of Vermont's winter — through which more than one cabin-feverish farmer has whittled, puttered and contrapted his way to world fame and wealth. Rising steeply from both banks of the Black River, Springfield gained most by Windsor's early tinkering with pumps and grinders and is finally, but for Barre, Vermont's only largely industrial area. Terrace upon terrace of homes overlook the large but tidy factories on the river, most of them innovative offshoots of J&L Machine, all open to the curious. The descendants of hundreds of pre-Revolutionary Russians maintain the most active Orthodox Church in the state. The town's Art and Historical Society exhibits an unusually fine collection of American Primitive portraits.

Even though Windsor boasts a healthy number of machine shops by the river, it rests its reputation on yesteryear. The Old Constitution House was founded on Elijah West's Publick House in 1772 — five years before delegates met there to establish the Free and Independent Republic of Vermont, draw up a constitution and create a Council of Safety to protect the new country as much from the 13 states as

from the Crown.

Windsor owes its industrial preeminence to native genius and patriotism, having long been a vital cradle of arms and other tools for the Union. The **American Precision Museum** on U.S. 5 is chock-full of all the gadgets, whatsits and thingamabobs that have made Windsor and Springfield famous. The Windsor-Cornish Covered Bridge, spanning the Connecticut River to lovely **Cornish,** New Hampshire, is the longest covered bridge in the United States.

"I live in New Hampshire so I can get a better view of Vermont," explained Maxfield Parrish from his home in Cornish. He did sneak a considerable piece of that view into most of his paintings, notably **Mount Ascutney,** which looms south of Windsor. The largest monadnock in New England, Ascutney plays year-round host to climbers, skiers and hang gliders.

There is no presidential library at **Plymouth Notch,** and the price to wander about the **Coolidge Homestead** is still only $1. But that doesn't mean this hilltop shrine to Silent Cal — the only President born on the Fourth of July, that self-styled "Puritan in Babylon" — isn't worth a look-see.

The Wiles of Woodstock

Woodstock's older money can, from time to time, be heard to lament late inroads made by what one observer has called the "suburban gold-coast mink-and-manure set." Upscale shopping sprees along the reappointed downtown blocks of Cabot and French streets have replaced placid strolls up Mount Tom's Bäden-Bäden-style cardiac walks as the fashionable summer pastime. But in general, the enlightened despotism of Laurance Rockefeller has preserved the tone of the town — complete with village idiot — much as it must have been in the Thirties, when Rockefeller met his future wife, Mary French, while summering on the green.

A passion for maintaining a graceful balance between man and nature has long been the keynote to Woodstock's renown. Mary's grandfather, Frederick Billings, returned from his lucrative law practice in San Francisco to become a pioneer in reforestation and a zealous model farmer in the 1890s. The slopes

Brookfield's extra-ordinary floating bridge.

200

of **Mount Tom** and **Mount Peg** and the newly remodeled **Billings Farm Museum** are testaments to his love for rural Vermont. Growing up on the elder Billings' farm in the 1830s, George Perkins Marsh — later to become a noted linguist and diplomat — remarked the effect of the clearing of the land on the rise and fall of the Ottauquechee River. More than 100 years after its publication, his landmark treatise *Man and Nature* remains the ecologist's New Testament.

The Rockefellers' **Woodstock Inn** on the elliptical green remains *the* place to do nothing — though the Robert Trent Jones golf course, Stanley Steamer foliage tour and Suicide Six ski area offer optional amusements year round. On the other side of the green, the last genuine covered bridge built in Vermont (1969) leads to Mountain Avenue, a well-preened redoubt of old summer cottages, and a park at the base of Mount Tom. Trails to the summit overlook, a guided floral walk through the Rockefeller estate grounds, and the **Vermont Institute of Natural History** keep Woodstock a comfortable spot to browse.

The hills surrounding Woodstock are horse country. Since 1926, the Green Mountain Horse Association in **South Woodstock** has been a mecca for well-heeled equestrians, and nearby stables offer the dude unusually expert training. At the fairgrounds in **Quechee** to the east, polo matches are played every Saturday afternoon during the height of the summer season. Quechee Gorge, "Vermont's Little Grand Canyon," also hosts a colorful ballooning festival in late June and a Scottish Festival at the end of August.

Since steamboat days, **White River Junction** has been a major crossroads. Today, Interstates 91 and 89, Amtrak lines and the high road to Dartmouth College (New Hampshire) all converge here, keeping a seafood restaurant, a rock 'n' roll club and the Hotel Coolidge, an old whistle-stop, in business.

"A man can easily hear strange voices," said Kipling of the lonely Vermont winter, "the Word of God rolling between the dead hills; may see visions and dream dreams...." On the top of **Dairy Mill Hill,** about a mile outside of South Royalton, Joseph Smith was born in 1805. The Mormons here maintain a 38½ foot (11.7-meter) obelisk and a museum devoted to the founder of the Church of Jesus Christ of Latter Day Saints. Vermont gave a whopping seven saints to the early Church, and the Mormons hold a Pioneer Days jamboree at this 360-acre preserve on the last Sunday in July.

The brand new **Vermont Law School** has put **South Royalton,** once a busy freight depot, back on the map. Over the river and up State 110 hide the towns of **Tunbridge** — cozy site of the world's smallest World's Fair since 1761, a real country treat in mid September — and **Chelsea,** a rural trading post where time has pretty much stood still since the turn of the century. The old bobbin shop is in some disrepair, but Vermont's oldest business, **Ackerman's Store** (1797), still dominates one of Chelsea's two greens, and Fred still sells a scoop of maple butternut ice cream for 25 cents at his general store, one of the twin 1818 brick buildings which form the center of town.

A conspicuous model statehouse next to Victoria's Restaurant in **Randolph** testifies that neighboring **Randolph Center,** three miles east, was carved out

of the hills with the idea that it should be the state's capital. With its wide tree-lined and mansion-littered Main Street, this oldest of "the Randolphs" still has the feel of optimism about it.

As State 12 creeps closer to the capital, don't overshoot the village of **Brookfield,** the geographical center of the state and perhaps the most unspoiled four corners in New England. In 1812, a floating bridge was built across **Sunset Lake,** the pond at the center of town, because it was too deep for a pillared span. The Highway Department refitted this one-car-at-a-time bridge — part of State 65 — with styrofoam pontoons a few years ago. One of the last ice harvests in the east is now an annual festival on the lake, held the last Saturday in January

The Smallest Capital

Home to about 9,000 souls, **Montpelier** is the smallest state capital in the nation. And — with the green ridge of Hibbard Park rising behind its gold-leaf dome — the **Vermont State House** has to be the most charming of the 50. The original nine-sided building was abandoned in 1836. Although its imposing stone successor was gutted by fire in 1857, the Doric portico and native granite walls withstood the flames to form a shell for the present structure. The Senate Chamber is rightfully considered the most beautiful room in the state.

The "Steamboat Gothic" Pavilion Hotel — "the Grand Old Lady of State Street," where so many lawmakers bedded down for the session — was demolished in 1966. But a skillful replica now occupies its place beside the State House lawn and houses a collection of Vermont icons which once decorated the capitol building. This, the **State Museum,** is a must-see mishmash of Green Mountain artifacts, including the last cougar shot in Vermont and Ethan Allen's blunderbuss.

The Barre-Montpelier Road — three miles of U.S. 302 — is a Vermont oddity unto itself. It is a strip of modern Americana complete with malls, fast-food joints and motels. To Vermonters, it is a bit of an embarrassment, an example of what recent legislation was drawn up to prevent.

In a state dominated by staunchly

Autumn light on Joe's Pond near Walden.

Vermont Athanaeum, St. Johnsbury.

202

Republican Yankees, lively **Barre** has been a city apart for more than a century. Since railroad access for the granite industry swelled its ranks tenfold between 1880 and 1910, this bottleneck on the Winooski River has been a vigorous melting pot of European stonecutters and artisans. Scotsmen erected the statue of poet Robert Burns at the heart of City Park. Italian craftsmen, who made up one-half of Barre's population by 1918, were largely responsible for the election and reelection of a Socialist mayor in that decade. And a steady influx of French-Canadians has made it one of the few predominantly Catholic communities in Vermont.

State 14 climbs steeply south out of town to **Graniteville,** "Granite Center of the World." The Rock of Ages firm owns nearly all of the quarries on and around Millstone Hill, which provide the nation with one-third of its memorial stones. The operation has long been a tourist-oriented showcase, with free access to the polishing and sculpting factory, and tram tours skirting the fully operational quarry a mile up the hill. Free granite specimens off the scrap heap make for weighty souvenirs.

Yesterday's architecture today... and yesterday. Left, a stony Robert Burns stands guard in Barre. Right, the Atheneum in St. Johnsbury as seen in an old postcard.

The Northeast Kingdom

Head northeast on U.S. 2 to St. Johnsbury, hub of the land of round barns and square meals. The Kingdom — that is, the Northeast Kingdom — is a land of crystal lakes and climax forests, of greater natural wealth and manmade poverty than anywhere else in the state. The nearly 2,000 square miles (over 5,000 sq km) of Caledonia, Essex and Orleans counties are sparsely populated and without industry, except for the scaleworks in St. Johnsbury, paper company holdings in the far east corner, and about 15 lake resort towns.

By the end of August, autumn reds and yellows have begun to creep across the Canadian border. By mid September, the face of Caledonia County goes flush with 50 hues, and the sleepy villages around "St. J" come alive in celebration. Each of the six hamlets — **Plainfield, Marshfield, Cabot, Walden, Peacham** and **Barnet** — has its own day in the weeklong Fall Foliage Festival at the end of September.

The same trees that bring the vibrant fall foliage yield Vermont's sweetest product — maple syrup. When the sap

begins to rise in early spring, buckets are hung out on the trunks of the sugar maples. Farmers insert a tube into the trunk to collect the sap, which boil down into syrup in the sugarhouse. Making maple syrup is no easy affair. 30 gallons of sap gives one gallon of syrup.

The village green in **Danville** has been the seat of up-country hospitality since the 1830s, when it boasted the only inn with four-poster beds in the Kingdom. For more than 100 years, the town has played host to the American Society of Dowsers — more than 2,000 firm believers in the powers of the divining rod. The society still meets here, in its red clapboard hall, and their gathering every September attracts curious observers.

East of St. J, the wilderness outpost towns of **Victory** and **Granby** conceived their mid September Holiday in the Hills in 1959 to convince Ma Bell and Public Service of their sincere desire for phone service and electricity. In conjunction with foliage fever, the recently resurrected St. Johnsbury & Lamoille County (a.k.a. "the Slow, Jerky & Latecoming") Railroad runs scenic excursions from St. J west to **Walden** **Station** and **Greensboro Bend** and back — 57 serpentine miles (192 km) — twice on festival weekends.

The city of **St. Johnsbury** gracefully weathered the multinational takeover of its Fairbanks Morse Scales factory in the Sixties, to remain a vibrant pocket of Victorian charm. From the bank buildings downtown to the Fairbanks mansion on the Plains overlooking the valley, the stamp of architect Lambert Packard and his wealthy patrons is visible everywhere. Thaddeus Fairbanks started making the world's first platform scale here in the 1830s, and he and his sons reinvested the fruits of their precision instrument into the quality of civic life. The Atheneum is a tastefully combined library, music chamber and art gallery dominated by the huge skylit *Domes of the Yosemite* by Hudson River School artist Albert Bierstadt. This is the oldest intact art exhibit in the country and so long as threats to sell the Bierstadt amount to nothing, it should remain one of the most inviting in the East. With a collection of more than 3,000 stuffed fauna and its own vintage planetarium, the Romanesque **Fairbanks Museum** is a little bastion of

The Black River valley near Craftsbury, Orleans County.

natural history erected by the Fairbanks family in 1890. Begun in 1904, the **Cary Maple Sugar Factory** quickly became the world's largest maple candy factory. The attached **Maple Grove Museum** is one of the more interesting of five or so throughout the state.

Diminutive **Lyndonville** boasts all five of the covered bridges in the lakes district. **Burke Mountain** rears its verdant head to the northeast. Burke is called "the Vermonter's Mountain" because, though top-notch, its trails are relatively free of New Yorkers. The ski academy here claims to have trained more Olympians for the U.S. Ski Team than any other American center, making **East Burke** a vibrant, up-beat village all year round.

'Where the Rivers Run North'

State 114 makes for a very scenic detour north to **Island Pond,** a lonely highland town commanding the eastern hinterland. Of a number of surprisingly good restaurants in town, the **Common Sense** is the most interesting because it is owned and run by the controversial Kingdom Church. A congregation of

300 or so primitive Christians, the church migrated to this desolate spot from Tennessee in the 1970s. Their strict interpretation of Biblical discipline has been the cause of some friction with Island Pond natives.

On the last weekend in August, the Bread & Puppet Theater troupe set up the Domestic Resurrection Circus in a meadow across from their farmhouse home and museum in the town of **Glover.** Thousands attend this free revel and revue of weird puppet gnomes, ogres and demons, all designed by Master Peter Schumann to illustrate the horrors of war and wonders of life.

In the last decade, Howard Frank Mosher of **Orleans,** has been infecting all of New England with the bold, pig-headed, bolt-upright Kingdom spirit. His restrained celebration of Vermont's upstream vernacular has set the tone for the northeast's latest literary renaissance. Regular pieces in *Yankee* magazine, and a fine collection called *Where the Rivers Run North,* wring a novel folklore out of backwater characters heretofore unsung.

The **Old Stone Museum** in **Brownington** was stacked together single-

Gliding near Burlington in Vermont's friendly skies.

handedly between 1827 and 1830 by "Uncle" Alexander Twilight, claimed by Middlebury College as the first Black American college graduate, Class of 1823. This Old Athenian rural academy is now the ambitious Orleans County Historical Society, with each of its 11 rooms devoted to one township.

Once a fashionable watering hole on the frontier, **Lake Memphremagog** lost most of its following in the 1920s with the retirement of the *Mountain Maid* and *Lady of the Lake* steam liners, but none of its international charm. **Newport,** "the Border City," is a busy and enterprising town noted for its easy mingle of Canadian day-trippers, contented locals and southerly summerers strung along Cape Elizabeth Bluffs at the lake's eastern shore. Smelt, smallmouth bass and walleyed pike are common catches over the Line — the Derby Line, that is, where the only Ammex Tax-Free Shop in Vermont beckons off Interstate 91, Exit 29.

To the west State 242 climbs from **Jay Village,** over the county line at the shoulder of **Jay Peak,** and down into **Montgomery Center.** By far Vermont's largest lift, the 60-passenger aerial tramway at Jay runs winter and summer to its 3,861-foot (1,177-meter) summit. With the Long Trail running through **Hazen's Notch** to the border, a 200-mile (322-km) network of ski-touring centers and one of New England's premier canoeing outfitters (located in Montgomery), Jay and environs are an outdoorsman's paradise.

The Snow in Stowe

Stowe had been trying hard to capitalize on the superlative height of **Mount Mansfield** in its backyard for 100 years before the Civilian Conservation Corps cut Nose Dive Trail through an old logging stand in 1933. Soon the enthusiastic Mount Mansfield Ski Club was attracting so many ski celebrities to Stowe that it was being called — especially by its promoters — "Ski Capital of the East." With three excellent slopes and a high concentration of well-known inns (among them, the **von Trapp Family Lodge,** still run by Maria of *Sound of Music* fame) and nightclubs, the Stowe area still deserves that distinction. But the town of Stowe has evolved into a very sophisticated all-weather resort; as

Early season powder at Killington.

206

the Federal Writers Project put it, "Stowe is a 'smart' place to be seen and many snowtime visitors are not skiers." The Stowe Winter Carnival makes mid January a good time not to ski. A classic-car rally — one of the best — crowns the summer season in early August.

Mount Mansfield resembles the silhouette of a human face. At "The Chin," this highest of the Green Mountains is 4,393 feet (1,339 meters) tall. A century-old toll road from the Inn at the Mountain climbs to the "Nose," where well-trodden trails trace a sturdy profile from "hairline" to "Adam's apple."

The northwest border with Canada, between **Alburg** and **Morses Line,** was a favorite route for smugglers in the steamboat era. But the notorious smuggling center of **Highgate** didn't get its mean reputation until Prohibition, when bootleggers began running their nag brigades and motorcades right into Franklin County. The springs at Highgate were long revered for their curative powers.

Over the years since 1609, when Samuel de Champlain discovered the lake that now bears his name, the islands at its foot (the waters flow north) have been compared to every place from the Isle of Man to the Louisiana bayou. Just fertile enough to support a few orchards and some grazing Jerseys, and just far enough out of the way to suffer no outright quaintness, the **Four Brothers Islands** — Alburg, Isle la Motte, The Two Heroes and Grand Isle — stretch 30 beautiful miles (48 km) south to the widest reach of **Lake Champlain.** "Vermont's Cape Cod" is strewn with arcadian preserves, lakeshore drives, and sleepy little towns. But **Isle la Motte,** with its exquisite marble deposits, "the oldest coral reef in the world" (littered with sunken steamboats and bobbing scuba buoys) and the St. Anne Shrine to America's first French settlement (1664), is the most satisfying of the islands. Bridges and ferries north and south draw New York, the Isles, Canada and Vermont snugly together about Champlain.

Franklin County was the center of Vermont's rise to eminence as a dairy state. The city of **St. Albans** puts up a parti-colored Main Street facade on

Ski racing in a blizzard at Stratton Mountain.

U.S. 7. Though it lacks the vivacity it had as a major railyard on the way to Montreal, St. Albans is a proud and forward-looking community, having engineered such zany publicity stunts as the world's tallest snowman and the world's largest ice-cream cone in 1982. Chester A. Arthur, the 21st and least-quoted President, grew up five miles east in **Fairfield.** A replica of his father's parsonage is open to the inordinately patriotic.

'Big City' Burlington

"The most miserable of one-horse towns," complained the young wife of an Army recruiting officer upon making their home here in the 1840s. "Startling incidents never occur in Burlington. None ever occurred there, and none probably ever will." Well, there is no accounting for temperament. By the Civil War, fiercely competitive steamboat lines and a busy lumber trade were beginning to make **Burlington** a plucky little inland port of entry. By the turn of the century, the wharves were teeming with businessmen, seekers of pleasure and ships' crews.

True, the decline of Champlain as a principal route for log drives, the death of steam culture, and a succession of waterfront fires in the 1930s nearly reduced the town back to one horse. But one couldn't say nothing ever happened here, nor, with the recent revitalization of the city's industrial base, could one say nothing ever will.

Today, trendy dockside restaurants, a natty open-air marketplace lined with cafés and oyster bars, "the best ice cream in the world" (**Ben & Jerry's** homemade, according to *Time*), and other symptoms of acute regentrification have changed the Burlington outlook. But the view remains the same. From Battery Park or The Cliffs, the sunset over the Adirondacks and Lake Champlain is still — as novelist William Dean Howells maintained — "superior to the evening view over the Bay of Naples." "Parties of pleasures" are again threatening to outnumber commuters on the 6 o'clock ferry to Port Kent, New York. But the Yankee spirit of getting things done prevails as it did when John Dewey grew up here during the Civil War. Dewey studied philosophy under a fellow Vermonter,

Spring colors near Rutland

Professor George Sylvester Morris, at Johns Hopkins University, and went on to become America's most influential pragmatic thinker.

A piecemeal past and the new metropolitan tone mingle to make the core of Vermont's "Queen City" (population 38,000) a commercial and cultural nexus not unlike Boston's Government Center. The Ethan Allen Firehouse and a polished marble-face bank/eatery round out the four traffic-free blocks of Church Street Mall. Gray's Carriage Factory, long a dockside landmark, is just one of the brick buildings souped up for business along Battery Street, a historical district in which restored old-time trolleys will soon be running. UVM (a pleasant acronym for *Universitas Viridis Montis*) and the State Symphony collaborate in twilight concerts, a Mozart Music Festival, and the Champlain Shakespeare Festival — lacing the cool summer air with civic solos and soliloquies. In addition to offering regular ferry services, the King Street Dock features an unusual freshwater aquarium and two vintage charter schooners sailing Lake Champlain from Vergennes to Rousses Point.

Fly fishing for trout on the Battenkill River.

There's a lot worth doing within Burlington's widening metropolis. When the famous woolen industry moved south, the sister city of **Winooski** over the Onion (now Indianized to "Winooski") River went completely bottom up. But in 1978, the huge mill was revamped and refitted with a bay of shops–the **Champlain Mill Mall.** Next door, **Essex Junction** is beginning to catch the tide of renewal. **Discovery Museum,** on Park Street, is an educational playland for the kids; the Vermont Wildflower Farm attracts thousands from mid May to Christmas; and the Champlain Valley Fair held here in late August has begun to entice a variety of upbeat exhibitors and class acts from around the country. In late March, the Maple Sugar Square; and Round Dance Festival is held in honor of the sweetest product of Vermont's hills.

Called "the collection of collections" or, locally, "Electra's Complex," the **Shelburne Museum** is *not* another living museum. It is very much a park — a welcome bit of green off the strip of U.S. 7, south of Burlington. Sugar baron H.O. Havemeyer and his wife,

collectors of European Art, were dismayed when their daughter, Electra, began to show the first signs of a preference for primitive Americana. But what can one do with a girl who simply must have this covered bridge or that Pullman sleeper? In fact, Electra and her husband, J. Watson Webb, saved more New England landmarks from certain demise than anyone else. One can spend a whole day wandering across these landscaped lawns and through the 35 buildings transplanted from all over the East. Champlain side-wheeler *Ticonderoga* is the gem of the collection, resting in her final berth alongside the Colchester Reef Light Light House.

Shelburne town's own landmark is the Webbs' 100-room "cottage" on the lake. Carved from 22 lakeside farms by Frederick Law Olmsted, this rambling estate is now **Shelburne Farms,** a center for rural conservation research. The mansion and its lawns are open to the public on special occasions.

The Monster of Lake Champlain

The ferry landing from **Charlotte** to Essex, New York, is a good place to appreciate the slim waist of southern Lake Champlain, and an excellent vantage from which to catch a glimpse of "Champ," Vermont's version of the Loch Ness monster, oft-sighted between Essex and Burlington since de Champlain described her undulating humps in his logbook. Champ has lately been the object of serious underwater exploration.

Lake Champlain becomes little more than a wide brook below Crown Point, New York. From **Larrabees Point,** Ethan Allen led a handful of skiffs across the lake to capture Fort Ticonderoga from the British on May 10, 1775, less than a month after the official start of Revolutionary hostilities. In this, the very first offensive action of the war, Allen captured the arms later used against the British in Boston. The fort itself, rebuilt brick by brick by a descendant of one of Allen's raiders, is worth a short trip across the lake.

Couched in the hills that rise east to the Green Mountain National Forest, **Bristol** and **Middlebury** are clean and pleasant crossroads towns serving farmers and mountain folk north of Rut-

land. Bristol sits at the gateway to the ski-crazy Mad River Valley. **Middlebury College** runs a popular foreign-language program in the summer, so sidewalks, pubs, the famed Vermont Book Shop, and the hilltop green are always bright and lively. **Frog Hollow** at the Otter Creek Falls is a steep drive topped with boutiques and the most inviting of Vermont crafts centers.

"The Morgan," boasted one celebrant, "can outrun, outpull, and outlast any other breed, just as you would expect a Vermont horse to do." There's no better place to trace the descent of this barrel-chested steed than the **UVM Morgan Horse Farm** just north of Middlebury in **Weybridge.** Training demonstrations and guided tours of the Victorian barn stables and paddocks are given May through October.

Poet Robert Frost moved to Middlebury in the Thirties, and into a log cabin in **Ripton,** not far from **Bread Loaf,** where he founded the prestigious Bread Loaf Writers' Conference. The Frost Wayside and Nature Trail — laid in 1976 — is a lonely mile of footpath

A break between classes at Bennington College.

through field and wood near the old cabin.

Rutland in a Rut

Aside from the Vermont State Fair in early September and New England's biggest Halloween Parade a bit later, there isn't much doing in **Rutland**, Vermont's second biggest city (population about 18,000). But its immaculate marble-plated downtown was recently crowned with a shiny Opera House Mall, keeping Rutland the shopping center for Sherburne Pass (Killington and Pico peaks) and points west.

Vermont's obstinate Republicanism is often attributed to its rural, small-town intransigence. But the leaders were industrialists — the railroad governors, as early as the 1840s, and then the marble governors, from the time Redfield Proctor built the town of **Proctor** in 1871. A Swiss multinational bought out the last of the Proctors in 1976, but the Vermont Marble Company carries on the tradition of quality that made Washington's Lincoln Memorial and the U.S. Supreme Court. Marble mining now involves underground shafts

An old postcard view of the Bennington Battle Monument.

350 feet (107 meters) deep, so watching the operations is out of the question. The exhaustive **Marble Exhibit,** however, is a fascinating experience and rates high among New England's biggest tourist attractions. The Tiffany window at the back of **Union Church** is easily the most stunning portrait of Mount Mansfield in existence.

Fair Haven, Poultney and **West Pawlet** are slate country. Some abandoned quarries are starting up again to meet a slowly growing market of re-roofers. Horace Greeley grew up in **West Haven,** still the most desolate corner of the state south of the Kingdom. After fleeing his father's farm to apprentice in a Poultney printing shop (from which he further escaped to found the *New York Tribune),* Greeley had these words for Vermont: "The moral I would deduce from my experience is simply this. Our farmers' sons escape their fathers' calling whenever they can, because it is mad, a mindless, monotonous drudgery, instead of an ennobling, liberalizing, intellectual pursuit."

When the railroad was built through Manchester on its way to Rutland in 1852, Levi Orvis' son got an idea: why

Mount Anthony and Battle Monument, Bennington, Vt. 404822

not put up a breezeway between the house and Dad's store, slap on a piazza and call it a resort hotel? With some whitewash and a few reservations, Equinox House was elegant and **Manchester-and-the-Mountains** was born of the hotel and its lush embrace of hills. As little brother Charles watched the piazza creep around the corner, he had another idea: why not put all these idle hands to work on the river? Less than 10 years after he sold his first bamboo flyrod, Manchester was to gentle sportsmen and their gentler wives *the* place to get away from it all.

To the Equinox's most famous guest, Abraham Lincoln, who spent his last summer vacation at the resort, getting away from it all was getting away from the Civil War. Mary and son Robert Todd cherished understandably fond memories of the mountains. Todd returned to build an estate, **Hildene,** under the shadow of Mount Equinox.

Today, paved with slab marble walks and decked with beautiful homes, Manchester Village is as tranquil and as foreign to Vermont as ever. The Equinox has been shut tight for a decade now, caught in the throes of another idea: why not go condo? But the Charles F. Orvis company has made the Battenkill River famous. It offers three-day fly-fishing lessons on its banks, the best equipment north of Abercrombie & Fitch and a history-of-the-art museum next door.

The **Williams Department Store,** just south of **Dorset Village,** is perhaps Vermont's most authentic country store, stocking everything from timber to rose water and talc. Home to playwright John Nassivera *(Sweeny Todd)* and the respected Playhouse equity troupe, Dorset had pretty much stolen Manchester's cultural banner with more artists in residence than many cities.

Arlington doesn't look like much from U.S. 7. But some poking around in this Revolutionary capital and one-time home to five *Saturday Evening Post* artists will reveal some of the rural cheer that made Norman Rockwell famous. The **Rockwell Gallery,** in the town's activity center, displays a large number of *Post* covers and lesser known prints, in which local uncles and grandmas figure largely. Dorothy Canfield Fisher needs no introduction to Vermonters: in an opus of down-home novels and her glorious *Vermont Tradi-*

tion, the Biography of an Outlook on Life, Fisher celebrated the spirit of fairness and community that has given Vermont its dignified complexion. The **Martha Canfield Library,** named after Dorothy's grandmother, holds a rich store of the author's memorabilia.

The Bennington Experience

Bennington, the state's southwesternmost most city, sprawls east from near the New York state border. Though no longer the most progressive school in America, **Bennington College** is certainly one of the most expensive. Bennington's splendid elevation, small size and open curriculum once attracted the likes of Bernard de Voto and W.H. Auden; bright ultramodern studios and the "Bennington Experience" still draw serious students and innovative instructors to a wide spectrum of the arts.

Old Bennington sprawls west from the city. Free of any commerce but the ancient Walloomsac Inn, it is an immaculate open-air museum running along Monument Avenue. The outstanding **Bennington Museum** fills an entire wing and schoolhouse annex with Grandma Moses primitives and memorabilia; née Anna Mary Robertson, Grandma passed all of her 100 years in nearby Altamont, New York. A rotating exhibit regularly features classic Vermonter crafts, contemporary landscapes, woodcuts and prints.

At its north end, Monument Avenue climbs Mount Anthony, on top of which is the 306-foot (93-meter) **Bennington Battle Monument.** This blue limestone obelisk, today a lookout, marks the site of a colonial supply dump that was the goal of General Burgoyne in 1777. His troops were turned back by General John Stark and 1,800 ragtag Hampshiremen across the Walloomsac River in Hoosick Falls, New York. The Battle of Bennington was the beginning of the end for Burgoyne, whose subsequent indecision made possible the decisive American victory at Saratoga. Bennington Battle Day is a Vermont state holiday. Every August 20, latter-day Continentals from all over New England reenact the skirmishes and charges from their encampment just west of Old Bennington. The performance is a spirited display of arms and frustrated talent.

Copper and iron: an old-fashioned American hearth at the Blue Hill Farm, Blueberry Hill.

212

215

NEW HAMPSHIRE

Once every four years, New Hampshire trundles out of general obscurity to perform one of the classic song-and-dance acts of American politics. The New Hampshire Presidential Primary is the first in the nation, the supposed diviner of political fortunes and for many, a make-or-break event. Back in 1968, George Romney received a less-than-enthusiastic welcome from the New Hampshire public and pulled out of the race before the voting even started. In the same year, Eugene McCarthy became a credible candidate, for a while at any rate, by hitting it off with New Hampshire's Democrats (and with a good number of Republicans, who declined to root for their own team and wrote him in instead).

Though typically disdainful of such ephemeral trivia as fame and public attention, the people of New Hampshire jealously guard their self-appointed right to keep the nation's elections reasonably honest. Vermont (New Hampshire's perennial competitor for glories about which no one else much cares) once hinted that it might steal the primary limelight by sneaking its elections in before New Hampshire's. Retaliation was swift and decisive: New Hampshire passed a law stipulating that its primaries will be held on "the Tuesday preceding the date on which any other New England state shall hold a similar election." So there.

Crafty Massachusetts made its move in 1975, waiting until only a few months before the 1976 primaries began to announce that it would vote on the same day as New Hampshire—the second Tuesday of March. New Hampshire promptly pushed its date up to the last Tuesday in February, even though this resulted in the inconvenience of voting in the primaries one week and then getting back together for Town Meeting Day the next (the two events had formerly been something of a political double-header). Though it's highly unlikely that many New Hampshirites lie awake nights worrying over the fact that the rest of the nation is reminded of their existence only once every four years, the Presidential primary is their moment

centerstage and they intend to keep it.

Politics in New Hampshire is definitely a participatory (and contact) sport. New Hampshire's state legislature, the General Court, is the third-largest governing body in the English-speaking world. The United Kingdom's House of Commons has 630 members; legislators in both houses of the U.S. Congress total 485; New Hampshire manages to get by with 24 senators and 400 representatives (one for every 2,062 men, women and children).

The Acid Test

Much of the state's business, however, is conducted by that venerable, fundamentally American institution, the Town Meeting. Each Town Meeting Day, every eligible voter with an opinion on any part of that year's agenda has the opportunity to speak his or her piece and cast a vote. This is politics in the revolutionary vein which first shaped the nation. Without the camouflage of cloakroom deals, press-conference equivocation or media hype, the Town Meeting is pure, sim-

ple democracy, out in the open and accessible to immediate response, whether praise or scorn. The signatures of only 10 voters are required to place an issue on the agenda. It's not an especially efficient system, but it is difficult to corrupt.

It's no surprise, then, that New Hampshire is something of an acid test for Presidential hopefuls. Most of the voters are amateur politicians themselves, and they are not easily fooled. They're also pretty accurate in anticipating the nation's mood. Since its first primary in 1952, New Hampshire has picked the candidates nominated by both parties seven out of eight times. In 34 of the 47 contested elections in the nation's history (George Washington ran unopposed), New Hampshire has voted for the winner.

All this hands-on governmental process both reflects and, no doubt, fosters the feistiness that is deeply ingrained in the state's collective temperament. New Hampshire has yet to institute a general sales tax or state income tax. Instead, it rather deviously allows outsiders to make sizable donations by deriving over half of its general-fund revenue from tax-free liquor sales, state-run gambling and other "sin taxes." And New Hampshire's constitution retains (in its Bill of Rights) the right of revolution when "all other means of redress are ineffectual."

This is not to suggest that New Hampshire is a haven for rampant radicals. In fact, the state is decidedly right-of-center on most issues, yet fervently independent. Though predominantly Republican, New Hampshire has voted for Democratic candidates in four of the past 12 Presidential elections. The Republican predominance is kept in check by a nearly equal (if not entirely opposite) force of registered Independents. Public opinion falls mostly between the two poles represented by the state's two most significant newspapers—the *Manchester Union-Leader,* with its inflamed and imflammatory rhetoric, and the more subdued and liberal *New Hampshire Times.*

Yankee Ingenuity

The rugged individualism which typifies the people of New Hampshire is intricately bound up in both their land and their history. The first settlers came not to escape religious or political pressures, as with many of the other original colonies, but simply to have a little space in which to productively apply their Yankee ingenuity. They encountered and eventually subdued a land that was obstinate and rugged—with thin, "cold" soil; fresh crops of rock pushing through the surface each year; a forested wilderness that had to be cleared before settlements and farming were possible; long, hard winters; and Indians who soon learned that the arrival of these foreigners was no blessing.

The main assets of the region at the beginning of the colonial period were the deepwater port and surrounding shores of what is now Portsmouth; and the tall, straight pines, which became highly prized in the construction of ships. Fisheries, established along the coast, prospered from the sale of salt cod and other catches, hauled from the Atlantic as far north as the Grand Banks off Newfoundland.

The impetus behind these first forays was provided by Sir Ferdinando Gorges, head of the council established by King James to govern all of New England, and Captain John Mason, an early governor of Newfoundland. They obtained grants to an ill-defined territory lining the coast from the Naumkeg to the Sagadahock rivers and extending roughly 60 miles (97 km) inland. With capital obtained from English shareholders in their Laconia Company, Gorges and Mason proposed to foster a variety of commercial enterprises that would return healthy dividends to investors.

It never really paid off. Lack of supplies limited the scheme's progress, the company eventually collapsed, and the settlers simply divided the land up among themselves and proceeded to amass their own fortune, without giving much thought to the niceties of property laws.

At first, relations with the Indians, primarily Abenakis and Pennacooks, were harmonious and mutually rewarding. In exchange for coats, shirts, kettles and other goods, and in anticipation of assistance in repelling assaults by other tribes and of a market for their furs, the Indians granted the settlers access to the land between the Piscataqua and Merrimack rivers, in-

A rocky brook gurgles through southern New Hampshire hills.

cluding the rich fishing bases of the Isles of Shoals. In principle, the Indians were to retain the right to hunt, fish and farm in the area.

The original deal was reasonably fair to both parties. Soon, however, the settlers became more ambitious. They built dams which obstructed the migration of salmon along the rivers, conducted lumbering operations which frightened off game, introduced livestock which wandered into and consumed Indian crops, and clogged the waterways with sawdust from mills. Realizing that they had been taken, the Indians banded together in 1675 and unleashed "King Philip's War," named for Philip, chief of the Wampanoags. For one year, they raided settlements and garrisons, disrupting the facade of harmony and touching off nearly a century of tragic feuding.

Throughtout this period, New Hampshire's commercial reputation and prosperity rested primarily on its supplies of mast pines. Soaring 150 to 200 feet (46 to 61 meters), as much as six feet in diameter and up to 10 centuries old, these massive shafts of wood required as many as 100 oxen to haul them from the forest. But they were invaluable to the expanding fleets of England's merchant marine. The best of them were reserved solely for the use of the King, providing in due course one of the motives that led to the Revolution.

Settlement and Revolution

Strong-willed settlers, gradually pushing their way inland from Portsmouth and up the Connecticut River from the south, laid claim first to the lush valleys, then to the harsher hillsides, and finally to the forbidding mountains in the north. The first man to lend the colony some cohesion was John Wentworth, a prosperous merchant appointed by the King in 1717 to govern the province of New Hampshire. Though hardly an altruist (his land grants always reserved a portion for himself, a token 500 or more acres), he did begin the process—later carried on by his son and nephew—of stabilizing the province, encouraging settlement and promoting commerce. Largely through their enthusiasm for gracious living, the Wentworths helped

Pumpkin patch approaches the autumn harvest season.

transform Portsmouth into a genteel oasis, traces of which are still in evidence.

For most of the settlers, however, life was anything but genteel. When not warring with the Indians, they cleared land, produced crops without much help from either climate or terrain and, by sheer obstinance, endured. Matters were not improved by the unresponsiveness of their government, and when the Revolution came, New Hampshire joined early in the fight, less from any political fervor than from a general acknowledgement that change could hardly be for the worse. With their training in years of conflict with Indians, New Hampshire's militia were particularly skilled at the guerrilla warfare tactics which the orderly British were ill-equipped to combat.

Despite its active involvement in all the major campaigns of the war, New Hampshire, alone of the 13 original colonies, was spared the task of fighting the British within its own boundaries.

Among its Revolutionary credits, New Hampshire was the first colony to assert its independence from England (establishing its own government on January 5, 1776) and the first to suggest the idea to the Continental Congress in Philadelphia (in 1775). Late in 1774, alarmed by an edict from the King forbidding the shipment of gunpowder to the colonies, and informed that a British ship was on the way to fortify Fort William and Mary near Portsmouth, 400 New Hampshire rebels invaded the garrison, locked up the British guard and stole 100 barrels of gunpowder, later put to good use at Bunker Hill.

Following the Revolution, the people of New Hampshire went back to the task of coming to terms with their land. The push inland was by now extending up into the White Mountains, already rich with Indian myth and soon to generate new legends of the crusty men and women settling the region. Revolutionary fervor gave way to the more tiresome task of transferring high ideals to workable practice. Due to the combination of a terrain ill-suited to plantation farming and an innate resistance to the idea of constraint, New Hampshire resolved the issue of slavery for itself by effectively abolishing it early in the 19th Century. An unfortunate pragmatism,

Rural farms such as this are a common sight in southern New Hampshire.

however, kept the only New Hampshire-born U.S. president, Franklin Pierce, from advocating abolition throughout the country. He argued that slavery was morally wrong, but that the issue should be decided by the states practicing it.

By the middle of that century, it was becoming evident that New Hampshire's weak soil and short summers could not support competitive agriculture. Farmland was abandoned as people moved West in hopes of greater success. Textile mills were established and logging operations continued, but the most notable shift in New Hampshire's economy resulted from the discovery that it possessed one asset that promised a good return for relatively little investment or labor—scenery.·

The Summer People

By the 1850s, "summer people" were a well-established industry. Executives on hoilday, retired librarians with a little nest-egg set aside, and an assortment of temporary bohemians came to sit on farmhouse porches in rocking chairs, dine in the lavish resort hotels newly built in splendid surroundings, or hike the expanding network of trails leading through the hills and mountains. Others, professedly more serious in intent, came to paint or sculpt or write. Among them were sculptor Augustus Saint-Gaudens, playwright Thornton Wilder, novelist Willa Cather, painter Benjamin Champney, essayist Ralph Waldo Emerson, writer Nathaniel Hawthorne and others.

The ranks of summer people have steadily swelled and spilled over into other seasons as well. Autumn draws connoisseurs of vibrant foliage which reaches its peak in early October to the north, then proceeds south. And New Hampshire's heavy snowfalls provide for superb skiing. The state boasts over 100 ski areas; the largest are Waterville Valley, Mount Sunapee, Cannon Mountain and Mount Cranmore, each with a lift capacity of 5,000 or more skiers per hour. Of the 35 major resorts, virtually all have chairlifts, and few need bother with snowmakers as there is generally more than enough snow to go around.

New Hampshire's rivers, streams and lakes are kept well-stocked with game

An old-fashioned toboggan ride.

222

fish—brook trout, smallmouth and largemouth bass, salmon, pickerel, perch, whitefish and shad, among others, Hunters track deer (close to 7,000 are taken each year), bear (about 150 annually), ruffed grouse, hares and rabbits, pheasant, gray squirrel, raccoon, wildcat, lynx and migratory birds. There is even a bounty on porcupines of 50 cents each.

In addition to the White Mountain National Forest (of which nearly 700,000 acres 283,000 hectares are situated in New Hampshire, roughly 40,000 acres in Maine), there are 32 state parks in New Hampshire, with some 1,000 campgrounds in the 11 largest. Depending on location, these parks offer swimming, noating, fishing, cross-country and downhill skiing, snowmobiling, hiking, camping and picnic facilities.

Local enterprise has also resulted in an impressive crop of roadside attractions—compact amusement parks, miniature golf courses, "trading posts" and just about anything else that might by some stretch of the imagination be termed "entertainment." Although not always in the best taste, and rarely

sophisticated, they do at least ensure that no one can complain for lack of anything to do, and besides, most of them are fun.

Beauty and Elegance

Finally, the tour sites themselves. Though New Hampshire's primary appeal is its quiet country life and scenic beauty, there are, of course, some places that stand out. There are particularly elegant flourishes of nature, such as the Old Man of the Mountain, the Flume, the notches and Mount Washington; there are examples of human ingenuity and history, like the Cog Railway, Shaker Village and Mystery Hill. And there are such local specialties as covered bridges. More than half of the covered bridges in New England are in New Hampshire, including the nation's longest—the 460-foot span crossing the Connecticut River from Cornish—and very likely the shortest—a 12-foot expanse on a private estate in Alstead.

From the outset, New Hampshire has appealed to visitors not so much as a place in which to do or see anything

Youngsters line up for a ski lesson at Waterville Valley.

in particular, but as a place simply to *be.* It is the ambiance of the state that attracts, more than any tour roster.

Due in part to its relative isolation and lack of leading industries, New Hampshire has always been slow to receive and absorb developments originating elsewhere. This cultural sluggishness has now come into its own: while so much of the country has progressed into a wasteland of "miracle miles" and economic frenzy, New Hampshire has retained a calmer, more dignified pace and quality. Here, there are still long, slow days to sit idle on a shaded porch or inside by the fire; evenings with the stars clear overhead and the startling silence of the countryside; neighbors with the time and inclination to chat about how the snow (or rain or heat) this year is nothing like it was back in '64 (or '42 or last year); old farms with pastureland arching down to a barn with a pond beside it; small towns where everybody is on a first-name basis with everybody else; and forests where the only signs of the 20th Century are what the visitor brings in.

New Hampshire's town fairs still feature ox-pulls and taffy-pulls, exhibits of handmade quilts, the rapid-fire patter of auctioneers hawking antiques, beans baked in a pit in the ground, homespun games involving baseballs and milk bottles, and a prize for the best pig.

From Mystery Hill
To the State Capitol

Driving north from Boston, the first tour site off Interstate 93 (after it crosses the border into New Hampshire) is, appropriately enough, also the oldest. According to recent radiocarbon dating, **Mystery Hill,** otherwise known as America's Stonehenge, is at least 4,000 years old—though who built it and why are still unanswered questions.

Although lacking the grandeur of its British namesake, the site is thought to have served much the same purpose as Stonehenge—a giant calendar tracing the movements of the sun, stars and moon. There is quite enough here to justify a few leisurely hours of exploration and speculation.

To reach Mystery Hill, turn off onto State Highway 111 toward Kingston, then follow the signs. Directly above the parking lot is a small lodge with a cafeteria and an exhibit of some of the more intriguing finds of the area—stones carved with hieroglyphs, ancient tools and other artifacts. Guided tours (included in the price of admission) are offered daily in summer and on weekends in spring and autumn.

A series of stone buildings and passageways, altars, walls, chambers and carvings are surrounded by an expansive ring of three-foot standing stones that pinpoint solstices, equinoxes and other astronomical occurrences. The identity of the site's builders and the specific purpose it served are matters of more or less pure speculation. Indeed, much of its charm derives from there being more questions here than answers: your guess is as good as anyone's. The site's creators have been variously designated as Native Americans, ancient Greeks, Phoenicians and Celts—take your pick.

Further north on I-93 is **Manchester,** one of several New Hampshire cities (including Nashua to the south) that, as centers of textile manufacturing, attracted large numbers of French-Canadian immigrants to work in the mills. Manchester still retains much of its French-Canadian legacy, including a large bilingual population and the nation's most comprehensive archives of material on French-speaking Canadians, **l'Association Canado-Americaine,** founded by a Manchester grocer in 1918. The **Currier Gallery of Art** features fine collections of European and American paintings and crafts.

Some 15 miles (24 km) north of Manchester is **Concord,** a pleasant, rather sleepy city, notable chiefly as the state capital. The gold-domed **State House,** the centerpiece of the downtown area, is fronted by statues of New Hampshire's political luminaries (Daniel Webster, Franklin Pierce, General John Stark and others) striking imperial poses in bronze. For the historically minded, the Coach and Eagle Trail provides a self-guided tour through the capital's major architectural landmarks, including the **New Hampshire Historical Society Museum** and the gallery of the **League of New Hampshire's Craftsmen.**

Shakers and Strawbery Banke

Though reminders of New Hampshire's colonial past are largely confined to the occasional restored farm-

Miss International Zucchini, queen of an annual festival in Harrisville.

224

225

house and barn, the state does offer two opportunities (both within easy distances of Concord) to experience that past in greater depth—the Shaker Village at Canterbury and Strawbery Banke in Portsmouth.

Located about 17 miles (27 km) north of Concord (off I-93), **Shaker Village** is an eloquent testament to the ingenuity and gentle faith of the Shakers, one of the religious sects that took root in the new world of America. Devoted to orderliness, community, productive labor and such progressive notions as sexual equality and industrial innovation, the Shakers established communal "Families," here and elsewhere, blending religious discipline with craftsmanship and business acumen to produce both spiritual and fiscal prosperity. They believed all should be made welcome, a commitment that continues today as the Family's two surviving members greet each visitor.

The 1½-hour tours of the Village provide a rare glimpse into skill and faith of this remarkable community. Crafts on display (some reproductions of which are available for purchase) include basketry, tinsmithing, wood-working and "the sewing arts." In addition, there is the simple grandeur of Shaker architecture, a host of intriguing inventions and a cafeteria offering specialties of Shaker cooking.

A little more than 40 miles (65 km) east of Concord, **Portsmouth**—New Hampshire's only seaport — has preserved 10 acres at the site of its original settlement. **Strawbery Banke** (so named for the profusion of wild strawberries that greeted the English settlers) is an ongoing restoration project that recaptures the look and feel, and some of the activities, of this old seaport neighborhood. The primary attraction is the houses: five (illustrating changes in architectural style between 1750 and 1811) are fully restored and furnished; some contain displays of construction and restoration techniques; others are still in the process of being restored.

Several serve as workshops and sales outlets for independent artisans. Robert Chace is at work on his elegant watercolors of the New Hampshire coast in one; the Batchelder family fashion baskets in another; and one of the oldest boat shops in America continues to produce dories, skiffs and

Dartmouth College, Hanover.

other vessels employing archaic copper clench nails.

Strawbery Banke is literally an open-air museum. Tours are self-guided, permitting one to browse and linger at will.

West of Concord

Fifty miles (80 km) southwest of the capital, via U.S. 202 and State 9, is the manufacturing center of **Keene.** Its noted 19th Century glass and pottery are now exhibited in the **Colony House Museum.** A short distance east of Keene are **Mount Monadnock** (3,165 feet or 968 meters) — which attracts about 100,000 people a year to climb to its summit for the view — and the lovely **Cathedral of the Pines,** a war memorial chapel near Jaffrey.

Northwest of Concord, I-89 weaves past **Sunapee Lake** (site of two major ski areas and the recreational facilities of the lake itself) and arrives in **Hanover,** home of **Dartmouth College.** One of the bastions of Ivy League tradition, Dartmouth was founded in 1769, primarily for "the education and instruction of youth of the Indian tribes

Daniel Webster's House at Strawberry Banke, Portsmouth.

of this land." The college retains much of its colonial appearance while, at the same time, accommodating such modern touches as Hopkins Center with its art galleries and impressive theater repertoire. Hanover is very much a college town, and none the worse for that. Among its finer points are the Dartmouth Bookstore, the stately, gracious Hanover Inn and Peter Christian's, an unusually captivating restaurant and pub (it has published its own cookbook, although the mustard recipe is still a closely guarded secret).

South of Hanover is the **Saint-Gaudens National Historic Site**—the summer residence, garden and studios of Augustus Saint-Gaudens, one of America's most celebrated classical sculptors. Farther south is **The Fort at Number 4,** a reconstruction of a fortified village dating back to 1746. Inside are demonstrations of such colonial crafts as candle-dipping, weaving and the molding of musket balls; exhibits of Indian canoes, colonial tools and other artifacts; and, on specified dates, Muster Days and encampments which recreate the life and times of the colonial militia.

Winnepesaukee And The Lake Country

State 11 branches east off I-93 north of Concord to reach the heart of New Hampshire's "Lake Country." **Lake Winnepesaukee** sprawls in convoluted splendor with 183 miles (294 km) of shoreline and 274 habitable islands, the centerpiece of a cluster of lakes and ponds scattered among rolling hills. According to legend, Winnepesaukee means "Smile of God," the name given it by Chief Wonotan on the occasion of his daughter's marriage to a young chief from a hostile tribe. Wonotan had grudgingly consented to their union, and he regarded the overcast sky on their wedding day as a bad omen. Just as the two lovers were departing, however, the sun broke through the clouds, the waters of the lake sparkled, and Wonotan concluded that the marriage was a fine idea after all—and gave the lake its name.

Weirs Beach (named for the weirs, or fishnets, which Indians once stretched across a narrow channel there) brings a touch of Atlantic City to Winnepesaukee's western shore, with its boardwalk, shops, marina, exotic miniature-golf links and mock casino. Other attractions include "New England's largest water slide" (there's a competition for this?) and the Mount Washington ferry, which offers a 3½-hour cruise around the lake, including dinner-dance specials on some evenings.

In 1982, the **Gunstock Recreational Area** (a 2,000-acre campground south of Weirs Beach) was the site of a neo-Woodstock music festival. In this case, the event was the "Great Northeast Arts and Energy Festival." The "energy" was provided by a photovoltaic solar generator that supplied all the electricity required for the three-day festival. Music ranged from politicized sing-along folk ballads to straight-ahead rock. Among the sideline diversions were arts, crafts and (for lack of a better term) consciousness-raising booths, gourmet fast-food and mime performances. The mood throughout was cordial, bordering on euphoria, as crowds spilled up ski-slope meadows and basked in the sun and music. Although it was not clear whether the festival will return to the Gunstock grounds in future years, such events have become

The Homestead Country Inn, Sugarhill.

228

something of a New England (and occasionally New Hampshire) tradition.

Of course, Winnepesaukee is a big lake, and there are many less public locations where one may pitch a tent or park a Winnebago and fish or swim in peace. Looking down over the lake from the north, **Castle in the Clouds** stands as an imposing monument to one man's idyllic vision of bucolic tranquility. Built in 1910 by eccentric millionaire Thomas Gustave Plant, this mansion is set in a 6,000-acre (2,430-hectare) estate with waterfalls, ponds, streams, miles of forest trails and magnificent views out over the surrounding countryside. Seasonal activities include camping, nordic skiing and horseback riding.

On Winnepesaukee's southeastern shore, the **Wolfeboro Railroad** offers a 24-mile (39 km) round-trip ride on restored antique steam and diesel trains, through countryside that is particularly stunning in the fall foliage season. The entire trip takes two hours. Lunch is available, and, on Fridays and Saturdays during the summer, "Sunset Dinner Specials" are served, complete with music and liquor.

On the lower edge of the White Mountains, and just west of I-93, is an impressive reminder of the glaciers that once ground their way across the state. The **Polar Caves,** a popular tour site since 1922, are what was left when the glacial ice covering Mount Haycock began to thaw and recede north. Massive slabs of granite, which the glacier split and quarried from the mountain's lee side, were unceremoniously dumped at the base of a cliff. There they formed caves, narrow passages and an artful pile of rubble dubbed the "Rock Garden of the Giants." The Pemigewasset Indians, who had a large settlement just across the Baker River, are said to have used these caves as a haven from attack or other threats.

A Walk on the Wild Side

Continuing north, travelers now begin their ascent into the **White Mountains**—first the Franconia Range, clustered along an east-to-west axis, then the Presidentials, running to the northeast up toward Maine, culminating in Mount Washington.

Long a forbidding wilderness, the White Mountains have evolved into a

virtually autonomous region of the state, with an ambiance as distinct as the landscape. This is the domain of the Appalachian Mountain Club (AMC), which provides trails and shelter for purists who come to hike and enjoy the serenity of vast stretches of untrammeled (though no longer forbidding) nature. It is also the domain of a thriving tourist industry, which provides just about anything else one might reasonably desire. Fortunately, there is room for both.

The tourism faction is, by law and convenience, contained in pockets along the major highways. All the rest is reserved (and preserved) for the purists. Those inclined to side with the tourism faction will certainly find plenty to do. But all visitors would be well-advised to at least dabble in the "wild side."

These mountains are not, for all their beauty and massiveness, too demanding. Many summits can be reached with an hour or so of fairly leisurely walking. The trails are well-kept, and the overnight accommodations of the AMC lodges (generally referred to as huts) are pleasant, if not luxurious. Contact an AMC Information Center for as-

sistance in selecting a trail suited to your endurance and schedule.

A typical trail leads from the highway directly into the forest, within range of a parking lot. It then proceeds over gradually inclining terrain, up tree-covered slopes—past a stream, perhaps, or along a ridge that looks down into the the rapids of a gorge. Trails are marked with color-coded blazes cut into tree trunks at regular intervals, so there's little risk of taking a wrong turn. Twisted dwarf pines and boulders mark the treeline. Above is the summit, from which adventurers gaze down over the world spread at their feet, savoring that peculiar sense of accomplishment that comes with putting one self on top of a mountain.

There are too many trails (1,128 miles of them) for even a partial listing to be attempted here; a full and detailed roster is available in the AMC Guide, an indispensable publication for those planning more than a single-day trip. One of the most rewarding excursions (in terms of view obtained relative to energy expended) is the short (45-minute) romp up **Mount Willard,** from the top of which one looks out

Left, youngster and friend at the Fantasy Farm; and right, the thrilling Flume.

over the magnificent panorama of Crawford Notch—a particulary splendid view at sunrise. Reservations at the AMC huts, by the way, must be made in advance. (A day or two is usually adequate.)

Mountain Motoring

The first major intersection of roads in the White Mountains occurs, not surprisingly, at a cluster of natural and contrived tour sites. The first of these, sequentially, is **Clark's Trading Post,** a venerable tradition dating to 1928 and a conspicuous landmark, its trained bears lolling on platforms perched high above U.S. 3. The price of admission to the ground entitles one to watch the bears go through their cumbersome paces and to spend half an hour riding behind a wood-burning steam engine along the Pemigewasset River. Other features include a photo parlor where you can don period costume for a sepia-toned portrait; a museum devoted to historical firefighting equipment; the American Building with, among other mechanical curiosities, a nickelodeon that plays eight instru-

ments, more or less simultaneously; and the song-and-dance cajolery of "Dr. Dare's Traveling Medicine Show." And, of course, there is the trading post itself, reputedly the region's largest.

Though more elaborate than most, Clark's Trading Post typifies the theme parks scattered through the mountains. Others include **Fantasy Farm,** just ahead on U.S. 3, with an assortment of livestock and rides; **Six Gun City,** along U.S. 2 near Jefferson, with high-noon duels and other borrowings from the Old West; **Santa's Village,** also near Jefferson, with a year-round Christmas theme; and **Heritage,** on State 16 south of Jackson, where talking mannequins provide on overview of colonial life.

Just south of Clark's, State 112, under the name of **Kancamagus Highway,** winds its scenic way east along the Swift River to Conway. The road is narrow enough to put one on intimate terms with the surrounding wilderness. The views, especially during the fall or at sunset, are spectacular.

West of Lincoln, State 112 leads to **Lost River,** formed (like the Polar Caves) by the passage of glaciers. Here the ice first gouged a deep gorge; as the

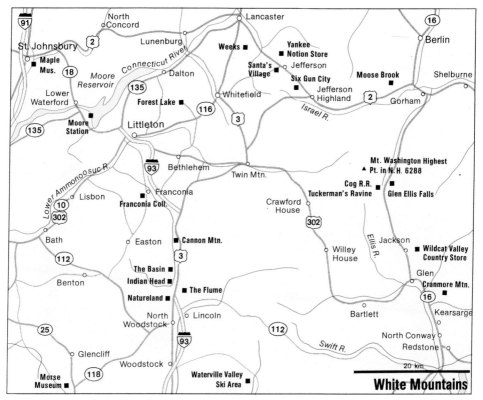

White Mountains

glacier receded, it deposited boulders in the ravine. The Lost River can be glimpsed amongst the boulders, which create an intriguing and beautiful maze of caves, passageways and sculpted granite.

North on U.S. 3 (with which I-93 merges), **The Flume** is considered by many to be the most beautiful cascade in the world. Popular credit for its discovery, in 1803, goes to 93-year-old Aunt Jess Guernsey, who happened on it while she was out fishing. The name refers to the 700-foot (214 meter) long, 70-foot (21-meter) high canyon through which the cascade falls. There was originally a mammoth boulder suspended between the canyon's walls above the waterfall, but an 1883 flood dislodged it and deposited it farther downstream.

Faces of Franconia Notch

Moving on up through **Franconia Notch,** look west to see **Indian Head** brooding from the side of the mountain with his prominent nose, scowling brows and "mohawk" of pines. Long obscured by pine growth on the surrounding hillsides, this natural visage

went undiscovered until a forest fire unveiled it. The head measures 98 feet (30 meters) from chin to forehead. It is traditionally associated with Pemigewasset, an Abenaki chief who is said to have used the top of the (then invisible) profile as a lookout post.

Soon **Cannon Mountain** (named for a cannon-shaped rock perched on its ridge) rises on the left. As the road curves around its base, travelers can look over their left shoulders to catch a glimpse of the **Old Man of the Mountains.** Also known as the Profile and the Great Stone Face, this impressive piece of nature's craftsmanship is noteworthy not so much for its size— it measures 40 feet (12 meters) from top to bottom—as for the fine detailing of its features. That first glance may be disappointing, but look more carefully, ideally from the shores of **Profile Lake,** just off the highway. The Old Man has generated a sense of reverence over the years. The jutting brow, regal nose, lips slightly pursed as if in meditation, and sharp line of the bearded chin—all conspire to produce more than just a striking resemblance to a human face. They convey character as well. It was

The White Mountain foothills in fall.

this that led Nathaniel Hawthorne to wax poetic in his short story *The Great Stone Face:* "...all the features were noble, and the expression was at once grand and sweet, as if it were the glow of a vast, warm heart, that embraced all mankind in its affection, and had room for more."

Though credit for its discovery is rather presumptuously ascribed to a road-survey team in 1805, no doubt the region's Indians were acquainted with the Old Man long before then. According to some sources, they saw in it the features of Manitou, the Great Spirit, and reserved for their chiefs the right to view it—and, even for them, only in times of crisis. Legend has it that the face was not always as stern as it now appears, but became so through sorrow over the conflicts and cruelty of the human race.

A few miles north of the Old Man of the Mountains, I-93 veers off to the west, bypassing **Bethlehem** (a small town noted for the Maplewood golf resort and the Hasidic community that gathers here in considerable numbers each summer) and continuing on to **Littleton,** one of the major towns in the

region and a center for shopping and other indulgences in civilization.

Mount Washington

U.S. 3 bears off to the east, connecting with U.S. 302, which curves down through Crawford Notch to the Conway area, and provides one of two access roads to the base of **Mount Washington.** Depending on the weather (low-level clouds commonly shroud the higher peaks), Mount Washington will appear first as wedge poking above the horizon, then as a looming presence in the distance. Hawthorne (who played an important role in promoting and preserving the region) accurately pointed out that the White Mountains, and particularly the Presidential Range, are "majestic, and even awful, when contemplated in a proper mood, yet by their breadth of base and the long ridges which support them, give the idea of immense bulk rather than of towering height." Mount Washington is high enough in its own right—6,288 feet (1,917 meters), the highest summit north of the Carolinas and east of the Rockies—but it is the mountain's mas-

Left, the Mount Washington hotel; and right, the brooding 'Old Man of the Mountains.'

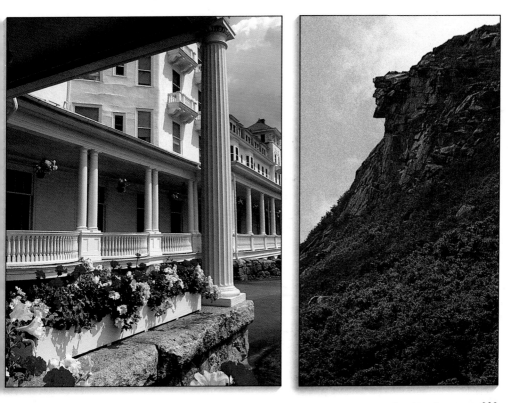

siveness that most impresses, at least from the bottom. To appreciate its height, get on top of it.

There are three ways to get to the top —by car, by train ... or by foot. This last option is, of course, the preference of purists, but it is not easy and (unless one knows what one is doing) can be extremely dangerous, even deadly. The summit is climatically in the Arctic. Its topographic isolation results in alarmingly abrupt changes in weather, including blizzards in summer. The highest velocity winds ever recorded (231 miles, or 372 km, per hour) were recorded here, and some summit buildings are chained down to prevent them from being blown off.

So long as one has the humility to turn back at the first sign of hazard, the climb need not pose any threat, nor is it exceptionally difficult. But a number of people have died up there, due primarily to their failure to acknowledge the dangers.

Driving is certainly easier—and safer —but can be hard on one's car. The local shibboleth that a car sporting a "This Car Climbed Mount Washington" bumper-sticker is an abused vehicle (soon to be scrap metal and spare parts) is less true now than it once was, due to improvements in the road. Still, eight miles (13 km) of braking is no picnic. (There is a shuttle service for those who choose to leave their cars at the base.)

Uphill by Cog Railway

Finally, there is the train. Completed in 1869, the **Cog Railway** bears testimony to American ingenuity in the pursuit of diversion. The train serves no more noble purpose than that of carting tourists up and down the mountain, but it does so with an admirable inventiveness.

The average grade is 25 percent (one foot in four), reaching 37.4 percent on "Jacob's Ladder," one expanse of trestle that supports the track for most of its 3¾ miles (six km). The train is propelled by a rack-and-pinion system, in which a cogwheel (the pinion) locks into slots in a rack bolted to the crossties. Two independent pairs of cylinders in each engine ensure against breakdowns. The passenger cars precede the locomotive uphill and follow it

The Mount Washington Cog Railway

down for safety; each car is equipped with powerful friction brakes and two cogwheels of its own, just in case. The only accident (with the exception of some fatal daredevil stunts involving other vehicles on the track) was caused by "Old Peppersass," the original engine, which failed on a ceremonial ascent years after it had been retired from active service, injuring the engineer and killing a photographer intent on recording the accident.

The railroad was devised by Sylvester March, a local inventor who hoped to capitalize on the tourist trade attracted to the mountain. He obtained a charter to build the railroad from decidedly skeptical Concord legislators and completed it in three years. It was the first railroad of its kind and has since been emulated, though outdone only once by an even steeper version in the Swiss Alps.

Just beyond the entrance to the Cog Railway stands one of the few remaining symbols of the age of luxurious resorts which flourished in New Hampshire—the **Mount Washington Hotel.** With its genteel grandeur still intact, this impressive structure continues to harbor wellheeled visitors in a manner to which all might wish to become accustomed.

With the shimmering expanse of its white stucco facade, octagonal turrets capped with red tile, the crystal chandeliers and Doric columns of its lobby, and the 900-foot (274-meter) veranda set with white-wicker lounge chairs for absorbing the view in style, the Mount Washington takes its place with disarming grace in that elite fraternity of resort hotels that are worthy destinations in their own right. Without leaving the hotel grounds, guests may apply themselves to golf (on an 18-hole PGA course), swimming (in indoor and outdoor pools), bicycling, croquet, tennis (11 clay courts), badminton, horseback riding, fishing, jogging and even horseshoes. Those who select the hotel's main dining room for their evening meal will be serenaded by the Brettonians, a musical ensemble whose members double as waiters and waitresses. All the food is, of course, fresh, including fish brought in from Cape Cod.

If luxurious appointments, fine cuisine and impeccable service aren't sufficiently impressive, the Mount

Cattle in the barnyard of a Jackson farm.

Washington also has a place in history. The hotel was the site, in 1944, of the "Bretton Woods Conference" at which representatives of 44 nations established the gold standard, instituted the International Monetary Fund and World Bank, and stabilized currency and exchange rates in the aftermath of World War II. (Visitors with no intention of staying the night are, by the way, most welcome.)

Pioneers of Tourism

From the Cog Railway base station, U.S. 302 cuts south through **Crawford Notch,** a narrow pass named for the region's most notable early entrepreneurs. The notch was "discovered" 1771 (more or less accidentally) by Timothy Nash, who was tracking a moose at the time. When Nash informed Governor Wentworth of his discovery, the skeptical governor offered to grant him a tract of land including the notch if Nash could bring a horse through it and present the animal, intact, at Portsmouth. When Nash complained for lack of a horse, Wentworth provided him with one.

Enlisting the aid of fellow hunter Benjamin Sawyer, and employing a block-and-tackle to transport the horse over obstacles in the trail, Nash eventually arrived in Portsmouth, delivered the emaciated horse, and received his grant. At the same time, he opened up the White Hills (as the mountains were then called) to a steady influx of settlers —and tourists.

Among the first to anticipate and capitalize on the area's potential for tourism were Abel Crawford and his son, Ethan Allen Crawford. They blazed the first path to the summit of Mount Washington (in 1819), advertised both it and their services as tour guides, and established inns to accommodate their clients and other travelers —thereby masterminding the White Mountains' debut as a visitor attraction. Both men were as rugged as the mountains. In his 80s, Abel is said to have hiked five mountainous miles each morning to his son's house for breakfast. He was 75 when he made the first ascent of Mount Washington on horseback. Ethan was known as the "Giant of the Hills" (he was nearly seven feet, or 2.13 meters, tall), was fond of wrestling bear and lynx, could carry a live buck home on his shoulders, and once lectured a marauding pack of wolves on their bad manners and thus dissuaded them from dismembering him.

At the southern end of Crawford Notch, U.S. 302 merges with State 16, continuing south to **Conway** and on to Portsmouth. Another group of tour sites (Heritage, Story Land and the Conway Scenic Railway) and ski resorts (Attitash, Mount Cranmore, Black Mountain and Wildcat) are clustered around this intersection. Also located near here is the headquarters of the Appalachian Mountain Club, lc **Pinkham Notch.**

The North Country

State 16 also swerves north, continuing up through the White Mountains, passing the entrance to the Mount Washington Auto Road, and winding along the banks of the serene Androscoggin River through **Berlin** (a small industrial city) into the sparsely populated North Country.

The isolated region is one of New Hampshire's better-kept secrets. The landscape is as stunning as any in the state, if less than inviting during the long months of winter. Even in a car, one feels absorbed in the vast stretches of forest that cover most of the region and provide its primary industry—logging. A lacework of lakes, rivers, ponds and streams offers a delicate counterpoint to the craggy presence of hills and mountains. It is up here that the Connecticut River has its source, in a string of lakes just a few miles from the northern tip of the state, in a corner so out of the way that its allegiance was not decided, nor its boundary with Canada fixed (and then, by force), until 1840.

There is one major resort up here— **The Balsams,** at **Dixville Notch,** with recreational facilities (golf, tennis, skiing) spread out over an area the size of Manhattan Island. Dating back to the 1870s, the Balsams has earned its cultured patina, and the right to charge accordingly.

From there to Canada, it's a world of forest, water and occasional towns scattered along quiet highways, a world well-suited to (and perhaps requiring) an exploring spirit. Those prepared to explore an environment like this don't need a guide to tell them how to do it.

Clowning around in the Laconia Christmas Parade.

MAINE

The typical Maine Yankee is characterized as a weather-beaten, taciturn individual with a twinkle in his eye and a hankering for toying with "outta state folks":

"Excuse me, how do I get to Portland?"

"You can't get there from here."

"Where does this road go?"

"Don't go nowhere, stays right where she is."

"Is Portland far?"

"Waal, the way you're facing, I'd say about 30,000 miles."

Don't misunderstand; if your car breaks down or you're in any real trouble, Mainers are almost without exception helpful and resourceful. And there's a good chance they'll invite you in for supper when it's all over.

But Maine does think of itself as a state apart, and its residents take a stubborn — and well-justified — pride in their state and themselves. For Downeast life can be rugged: it is said that the only seasons here are July and winter. Survival calls for endurance and self-reliance, and Mainers should not be faulted by their bemusement at the uninitiated "summer people."

Larger in area than the other five New England states combined, but less populous than any one of them, Maine bears little resemblance to her southern neighbors. The "Pine Tree State" — 87 percent forestland — was recognized by Henry David Thoreau 150 years ago as the last remaining wilderness area east of the Mississippi River. Why go West, asked that great author and naturalist, when Maine has everything — coastline, wild rivers, rugged mountains, freshwater lakes. There is boating and swimming in summer, skiing and snowmobiling just a few months later. No other East Coast state has managed to keep its natural beauty so unspoiled.

Drowned Valleys And Red Paint

Traditionally, the Maine coastline has been the focus of the state's commercial and cultural activity. It extends 228 miles (367 km) straight as the gull flies, yet traces almost 3,500 miles (5,633 km) following every indentation and cove. Geologists call it a drowned coastline: the original coastline sank thousands of years ago, its valleys becoming Maine's harbors, its mountains the hundreds of islands that trace the coast from the New Hampshire border to New Brunswick, Canada. While the coastline was sinking, receding glaciers dumped countless tons of granite, which gives Maine's mountains their peculiar pink coloring and provides a valuable building material.

The first known residents, 11,000 years ago, were the Paleo Indians, who hunted and fished along the coast. Other tribes followed, including a race known as the Red Paint People because lumps of red clay — thought to have been a religious sacrament — have been found in the grave sites of this tribe. The first Indians to greet European explorers in the 15th and 16th centuries were the Abenaki.

European explorers to the New World, not immediately recognizing the value of Maine's abundant forest and seafood resources, passed them up for more obvious treasures like Inca gold. John Cabot is known to have come to

Preceding pages: a sunrise canoe expedition near Calais, and the magnificent Portland Head Light. Left, Jeanne and Steve Rollins return home after a day of lobster fishing off Monhegan Island. Right, the Old Gaol at York.

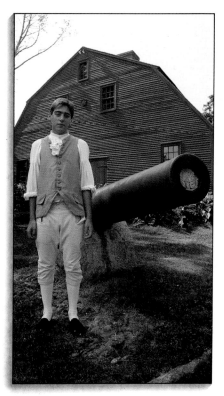

Maine in 1497 (his voyage established all future British claims to the land), but it wasn't until Captain John Smith (of Pocahontas fame) sounded "about 25 excellent harbors" that the "Father of Maine," Englishman Sir Ferdinando Gorges, was granted a charter to establish British colonies there.

Rival French explorers claimed parts of Maine and Canada, and these territorial disputes eventually led to the French and Indian Wars of the 18th Century. In the meantime, Maine became a part of the Commonwealth of Massachusetts and remained so until 1820, when it became, as patriotic residents still call it, the State of Maine.

The Western Coast

The best way to see Maine is to start at the southern tip, Kittery, and work your way north along the old coastal highway, U.S. 1. Interstate 95 is bigger and faster, but, as any Mainer will tell you, you don't get to see anything. While the coast is only a tiny fraction of the state, 45 percent of Maine residents call it home, and the overwhelming majority of visitors to "Vacationland," as the license plates have it, go someplace on the shore. The coast divides into three primary areas — weste n, middle and eastern — each with its own unique character and flavor.

The first natural division extends from Kittery to a rocky jut of land called Cape Elizabeth, just south of Portland. The earliest settled part of the state, Maine's western coast combines the historical ambiance of colonial Virginia with the mass-market accessibility of Coney Island. Many onetime fishing towns have been seduced by the more lucrative prospects of the tourist industry. The western coast's un-Mainelike sandy beaches and relatively warm water, as well as its proximity to the rest of New England, make it the best-known and most heavily traveled area of the state.

Just across the New Hampshire border from Portsmouth, **Kittery** is only a shadow of the shipbuilding center it once was. Kittery's Portsmouth Navy Yard, still in use, built the first ship ever to fly the Stars and Stripes. Christened the *Ranger*, it was the maiden command in the great naval career of John Paul Jones and received the first foreign salute to an American flag.

Neaby Fort McClary on Kittery Point was originally built by Maine's powerful Pepperell family for defense against the frequent Indian attacks common along the entire coastline. The fort's large blockhouse and granite seawall still stand. The fort was last defended against attack in the Revolutionary War and now serves primarily as a vantage point for yacht races in Portsmouth Harbor.

Off the coast of Kittery are the **Isles of Shoals,** named for the fish that schooled ("shoaled") off their shores. Four belong to Maine and three to New Hampshire. The first of hundreds of islands along the coast, the Shoals were settled earlier than the neighboring coast but were considered an unsavory, unreputable place by mainlanders, who looked down on their island brethren as uncivilized. The islanders were accused of harboring pirates in their midst and setting false navigation lights on rocks to lure unwary ships to their doom, after which they would loot the cargoes. The Isles' reputation improved only after the construction of a manned lighthouse, the Isles of Shoals Light. When the keeper's son-in-law became a pub-

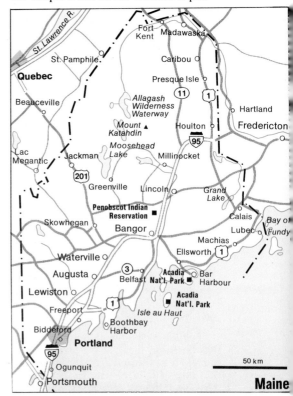

Maine

lished poet in the *Atlantic Monthly,* the Isles became a literary enclave frequented by such luminaries as Nathaniel Hawthorne, James Greenleaf Whittier and Harriet Beecher Stowe. Any lowlifes left on the islands quickly moved away, perhaps to prote their reputations.

Dingy Cells, 'Kumfy Kabins'

The territory that is now the Yorks was granted to Gorges in 1639. The charter stated that the area "shall forever be called the province and County of Maine and not by any other name whatsoever." This was the first recorded official use of the name Maine.

York became a center of rebel spirit and indignation during the Revolutionary War. The York chapter of the Sons of Liberty decided to hold their own tea party when a British ship carrying tea anchored in York Harbor. A number of residents disguised themselves as Indians and sneaked aboard the ship at night. Like most Mainers, they were more practical than their Bostonian counterparts — none of the hijacked tea

was wastefully poured into the harbor.

The Yorks epitomize that odd blend of historical preservation and beach-oriented tourism typical of the lower Maine coast. **York Village,** on State Highway 1A north of Kittery, features several restored buildings and a cemetery from the colonial period. The best known of the buildings, the Old Gaol, overlooks the village from a grassy knoll in the center of town. Built in 1653 and believed to be the oldest English stone public building still in use, the Gaol is now a museum housing a collection of Indian and early American artifacts. The Gaol is replete with cramped, dingy cells and small windows bordered with sawteeth to dishearten would-be escapees. Visitors can also see the pit, a wet hole in the ground darker and more horrible than the cells, where disciplinary cases were sent.

The other side of York, physically and philosophically, is **York Beach.** Residents of the Village look down their historically preserved noses at the Beach's "hot dog and Kumfy Kabin" approach to tourism. A popular family vacation area, York Beach is a narrow mile-long strip of fine clayish sand and

Baxter State Park reminds visitors to preserve the wilderness.

occasional rocks. A small area is reserved for surfing. Lining the beachfront drive is every imaginable type of fast-seafood shack and family-entertainment facility. It's not typical Maine, but it doesn't pretend to be.

Spiderman's Nemesis

North of York on State 1A is a rocky jut of land called **Bald Head Cliff.** You can walk over the cliff — something of a rarity this far down the coast — via a short, steep path. Don't try climbing straight up the face, however. In summer 1983, police arrested Kittery resident Dan "Spiderman" Goodwin, conqueror of New York and Chicago skyscrapers, for trespassing when he attempted to scale the dangerous ledges overhanging the water.

Following State 1A farther north brings travelers to **Perkins Cove,** once one of many small fishing villages in this area. It was "discovered" by artist Charles Woodbury of Boston, who liked to paint the colorful fishing boats that tied up in the harbor. When Woodbury let word slip about this "artists' paradise," other artists moved in as

well. The many small galleries and crafts shops that still crowd this area sprang up soon afterward.

A similar tale may be told of **Ogunquit,** which can be reached by following Marginal Way, a scenic one-mile walk along the cliff. The name Ogunquit is a corruption of an Indian name meaning "beautiful place by the sea," and a quick look will reveal what has attracted Indians, artists and tourists alike. When the first artists arrived, they used to sneak off into the woods to paint nature scenes. Residents suspected the artists were in seclusion to paint nude models and treated the artists with due scorn. When the painters displayed their landscapes, the humbled and perhaps disappointed natives treated them with ever greater disdain. Nowadays, so many artists live here that no one takes much notice.

Ogunquit's long strip of sandy beach backed by grassy, gently sloping dunes is reminiscent of Cape Cod beaches and rather unlike anything else in Maine. Those who like to swim should take advantage of the beaches on this part of the coast. Farther on, the coast becomes much rockier and the water never warmer than 55 degrees Fahrenheit (13°C).

For fishermen, the Ogunquit Tuna Club sponsors deep-sea voyages in quest of bluefin tuna and horse mackerel, the largest quarry sought by Maine sport fishermen. Giant tuna can weigh anywhere from 300 to 1,000 pounds (136 to 454 kilograms) and often require hours of struggle between man and fish before a victor is determined. Less effort is required to snare cod, halibut, mackerel, pollock, haddock and flounder on chartered expeditions.

Ogunquit's Summer Playhouse, among the oldest in Maine, features an adjunct acting school, The Workshop, that attracts theater students from around the country and stages several shows each summer.

Wedding Cake and a Boardwalk

Once the shipbuilding center of York County, the town of **Kennebunk** lies north of Ogunquit on U.S. 1 Shipbuilding has long since given way to fishing and tourism, but the legacy of past days remains in the town's stately elms and handsome white houses. To get a closer look at these buildings, take

Left, a moose in a bog outside Greenville. Right, the night shift at the Bath Iron Works, among the world's fine shipbuilding centers.

the architectural walking tour conducted by the Brick Store Museum, an old general store now devoted to exhibits about local history. The Seashore Trolley Museum offers another glimpse into the past with its collection of more than 150 vintage trolleys and a mile of track over which visitors may ride.

Also in Kennebunk, the Wedding Cake House, so named because of the elaborate carved wooden scrollwork adorning its face, may well be the most photographed house in the state. Legend holds that the house was the gift of a sea captain to his young bride, who had missed out on her real wedding cake when the groom was hastily summoned away to sea.

Further north on U.S. 1 are the twin cities of **Saco** (pronounced "sock-o") and **Biddeford,** the largest population centers south of Portland. Chiefly industrial centers, the cities lie just to the west of **Old Orchard Beach,** one of the most popular resorts on the coast. Formerly known for its promenade and dance hall with big-name swing bands, the original pier has been replaced by a large boardwalk and amusement park with rides and funhouses. The Old Orchard Historical Society also arranges public exhibits on the background and history of the town.

Portland: Phoenix of Maine

On the shores of Casco Bay lies the most populous city in the state, **Portland.** To city-dwellers who feel lost in the vast open spaces of Maine, Portland is a friendly reminder of home. To rural Mainers with a distaste for crowds and traffic, Portland is the only urban center fit to enter. Although its population is barely one-tenth that of Boston, peninsular Portland is the cultural and commercial center of the entire state of Maine.

Founded as Casco in the middle of the 17th Century, the city immediately became a center of international commerce. It is a natural port for trade, located more than 100 miles (160 km) closer to Europe than any other major U.S. port. Its sheltered, deep-water harbor is a natural stopping point for large ocean-going vessels and boats traveling along the coast.

Yet Portland's sea of success has

American enterprise starts young: a roadside blueberry stand near Rockport.

often been choppy and beset by sudden storms. Three times the city was burned completely to the ground — by the Indians in 1675, by the British in 1775 and by accident in 1866. Three times the city, like its symbol, the Phoenix, rose quickly from its ashes, improved and rejuvenated. After the last fire, the city was replanned. Streets were widened, and Portland's elaborate network of municipal parks was developed to alleviate the claustrophobic feeling of a large metropolis. The city stands today as one of the best planned in the world.

Modern Portland faces the same problems as the rest of the state. Continued economic distress caused by the decline of the pulpwood and shipbuilding industries and overfishing of lobster has meant difficult times for Maine residents. In addition, the tourist industry, which falters with the nation's economy, can be an unreliable source of income. As the business center of the state, Portland suffers for the rest.

Portland's attempts to progress with the times are perhaps best-exemplified by the recently completed waterfront development program. Many of Portland's wharves and piers, built during

'The Lobster From the Dark Lagoon' — a whimsical Maine advertisement.

the heyday of cargo ships, lay decaying and useless in the era of air and land freight. While some are still used for commerce, others have been refurbished and now house small shops and inexpensive restaurants specializing in seafood.

Portland sports a wide range of cultural activities. The city has become a theater town of some repute ever since it saw the repeal of an old Puritan statute which stated that plays "have a pernicious influence on the minds of young people and greatly endanger their morals by giving them a taste for intrigue, amusement and pleasure." Portland also houses some fine art museums. The Portland Museum of Art was renovated recently and a new wing, donated by Charles Shipman Payson, was added. The wing contains a number of Winslow Homers, as does the L.D.M. Sweat Museum, which also exhibits works of contemporary Maine artists.

South of Portland on **Cape Elizabeth** is the oldest lighthouse on the eastern seaboard, the Portland Head Light. It was commissioned by President George Washington in 1791 in the hope of mak-

ing safer the treacherous, rocky waters leading into Portland harbor. More than 200 islands can be seen from the original tower, which stands 100 feet (31 meters) above Casco Bay. Even people who have never been anywhere near the sea are no doubt familiar with Portland Head Light. Its likeness has been photographed and painted countless times and has appeared on all manner of trinkets and souvenirs, ranging from playing cards to cocktail napkins.

Casco Bay's Calendar Islands

Eighteen miles (29 km) wide at the mouth, Casco Bay holds within its waters the **Calendar Islands** (there are 365 of them). You can catch a cruise to the islands from the Custom House Wharf in Portland: the Bailey Island Cruise (four hours round-trip) includes a stopover on Bailey Island, while the U.S. Mail Boat Cruise (three hours round-trip) calls at several islands without allowing passengers to disembark. The islands — some no more than a few square yards of exposed rock and others, like **Peaks Island,** heavily populated suburbs of Portland — fall into three parallel bands, and the scenery grows generally more wild and beautiful as you reach the more remote regions.

The islands of Casco Bay, like many on the Maine coast, are rumored to have pirate treasure buried on them. Much time and money has been spent looking for Captain Kidd's buried treasure on **Jewell Island**, the outermost large island in the bay, although historians have determined that Kidd came nowhere near the place. Hard-core treasure seekers have consulted mediums, used divining rods, and poured the blood of sacrificial lambs on areas suspected of containing buried treasure

So far, the only treasure has turned up on **Bailey Island.** It was a real-life *Beverly Hillbillies* tale: while hunting wild duck to feed his family, a poor farmer shot what turned out to be an iron pot full of Spanish gold coins. While the treasure enabled him to support his wife and children for a while, the man apparently never really learned what to do with his newfound wealth and ended up poor and unhappy.

Bailey Island is connected to neighboring **Orr's Island** by a clever structure known as a cobwork bridge.

The only one of its kind in the world, the bridge is supported by a honeycomb structure of granite blocks allowing tides to flow freely.

Bean's Boots

On the shores of the bay, atop a hill overlooking the little town of **Freeport,** stands a living legend. **L.L. Bean Inc.** employs hundreds of people and furnishes tens of thousands more each year with $165 million worth of anything from camping supplies to woolen doggie beds. Open 24 hours a day, 365 days a year, it is furthermore a mecca of fashion to which members of the Preppie faith hope to make a pilgrimage at least once in their lifetime. And it all began 70 years ago as one man's idea for a better hunting boot.

Leon L. Bean had barely reached adulthood in 1912 when he sent an advertisement for an improved outdoors boot to a number of Maine hunting-license holders. Along with the boot came a guarantee of money back if not completely satisfied. As the legend goes, on 90 of the first 100 pairs, the soles separated from the leather uppers. True to his word, Bean replaced the defective boots with pairs of improved design and — after absorbing the healthy financial loss — began building the legendary L.L. Bean empire that he controlled until his death in 1967.

Bean lived long enough to see the store (which wasn't built until 1951) grow from a hunting and outdoors outfit to a distributor of fashionable shoes and sweaters as well. In addition, the store has become a social and even cultural center, sponsoring free courses in outdoor skills and health care. Its effect on tiny Freeport has been marked and drastic: many other Maine companies have moved here to sop up the Bean overflow. L.L. Bean has made Freeport one of the most recognized spots on the Maine map.

Brunswick, a few miles north an I-95, works very hard to be more than a college town. Every year, it hosts a number of fairs and outdoor shows, of which the annual Bluegrass Festival has gained national attention for the quality of performers attracted. The city has generated interest in her history by setting up the Pejepscot Historical Society Museum, a showcase of seafaring relics including a restored sea captain's home.

Brunswick is also home of the Bowdoin Pines, a small forest of tall, straight pines of the sort once used for masts on schooners during the shipbuilding days. Last, and probably least, Brunswick boasts Maine Street, the state's widest street at 198 feet (60 meters). It was built big in the hope of discouraging Indians from lurking about on dark corners and in alleyways.

Yet Brunswick has always been best known as the home of **Bowdoin College**. Founded in 1794, Bowdoin was originally slated to be built in Portland, but the college's benefactors found that that city offered too many "temptations to dissipation, extravagance, vanity and various vices of seaport towns" for impressionable young minds. The college became home to literary figures such as Hawthorne, Longfellow and poet Robert Peter Tristram Coffin. Harriet Beecher Stowe wrote the 19th Century masterpiece *Uncle Tom's Cabin* in Brunswick after seeing a vision of a Negro slave while listening to her husband preach at the town church. Guided tours of the Bowdoin campus begin at Longfellow Hall.

East of Brunswick on U.S. 1 sits the town of **Bath,** once the shipbuilding capital of the state. For a time during the last century, Maine's shipyards were responsible for one-third to one-half of all ships on the high seas. Timber cut north of Augusta was floated down the Kennebec River to Bath, where the riverbank slopes perfectly for laying keels into the water.

The era of the wooden ships ended on the day the iron hull was invented. Not ready to give up a lucrative business, Bath constructed the Bath Iron Works, today one of the country's busiest producers of Navy ships. The shipyard is off limits to civilian personnel for security reasons, but a good view of the towering cranes and other equipment can be obtained from the bridge over the Kennebec.

The history of shipbuilding in Bath and other coastal towns is preserved in the Maine Maritime Museum, the largest of its kind in the state. Exhibits of nautical tools and gadgets capture the flavor of seafaring days, while a working boatyard demonstrates techniques of different stages of shipbuilding. The price of admission includes a boat ride up the Kennebec to the Iron Works.

Surf washes on the rocks at Two Lights State Park near Portland.

Land of the Lobster

For some Maine residents, Downeast Maine doesn't start until the middle coast, which extends from Cape Small in the west to the easternmost end of Penobscot Bay. Of course, exactly where Downeast Maine lies is an entirely subjective, judgment, so finding it is mostly a matter of personal taste. The word "downeast" comes from seafaring days: sailing downwind, ships traveled east to Maine. Today, it is used mostly to assure tourists that they're experiencing the real thing.

The rocky coastline and ice-cold waters for which the state is known begin along the middle coast. Lobstermen hereabouts contend that the lobsters living in these waters are the best in the world. The waters farther north, Mainers say, are so cold and so deep that they produce a sluggish lobster with inferior meat. Canadian lobstermen, no doubt, say otherwise.

Homarus Americanus, as the Romans would have called it, is native to the waters from New Brunswick, Canada, down to Maryland. The Romans, in fact, probably never heard of lobster, and that's too bad, because it is the quintessential food for orgiastic dining. The taste of sweet lobster meat, carefully extracted from the protective shell and smothered in drawn butter, is unequaled in succulence.

The Maine lobster was not always the expensive pound-and-a-quarter of ecstasy it is today. Lobsters used to be much larger — four to six pounds average — and they sold for two or three cents each. No one used to get too excited over them because there were so many, they would just wash up on shore. In the days of colonial exploration, indentured servants would have it written into their contracts that they would not be fed lobster more than four or five times a week.

Purists say the only way to prepare lobster is by steaming it for a crucial amount of time, though no one can agree how long that time should be. There must be a lot of non-purists around, judging from the list of recipes that call for stuffing lobsters with crabmeat and broiling them, drowning lobster in Newburg sauce, or adding mayonnaise and making lobster salad. However they're prepared, Maine

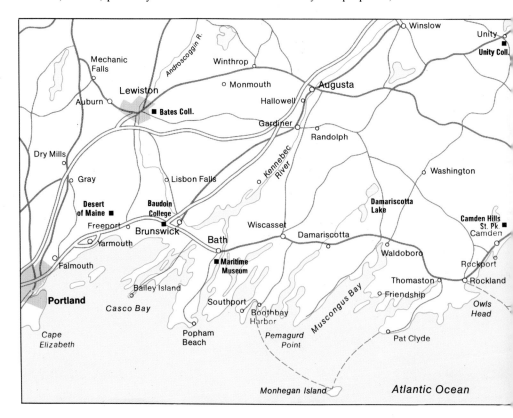

lobsters will always be first in the hearts and mouths of seafood lovers.

Boothbay Harbor

Although the tourist industry in this part of the state is more dignified than on the western coast, there are some exceptions — among them **Boothbay Harbor,** possibly the best known and most popular resort in Maine. In summer, over 50,000 visitors throng the streets of this former fishing village: they inspect shops, sample seafood delicacies, and charter boats to explore offshore islands with names such as The Cuckolds and The Hypocrites. There are yacht and golf clubs, flower shows, auctions and clambakes to pass the time. Antique buffs should look into the Boothbay Railway Museum, located on State 27. In addition to a rideable miniature railroad, the large outdoor museum features a restored turn-of-the-century small-town barbershop, bank, and country store as well as an antique auto museum. An authentic Grand Banks schooner, the *Sherman Zwicker,* is maintained by the museum at the harbor; a guided tour reveals the close

quarters endured by sailors in earlier days.

Wiscasset and **Damariscotta,** north of Boothbay on U.S. 1, are as quaint as any villages in New England. Wiscasset bills itself as "the prettiest little village in Maine," and boasts many fine homes built during the days when seafaring men spent extended shore leaves here. Bothe Wiscasset and Damariscotta sponsor an open-house day each year when all the homes in the town are open to public inspection at a small fee. Many of the houses still contain relics from the exotic and distant lands to which Maine sailors once voyaged.

South of Damariscotta on State 130 is **Pemaquid Point,** a rocky peninsula at the tip of which stands the Pemaquid Light, built in 1827. With powerful surf constantly breaking on the rocks, the point is a favorite spot for painters and photographers. The Fishermen's Museum, located next to the lighthouse in the old keeper's residence, displays a large variety of fishing and lobstering equipment donated by fishermen over the years.

In the same way car buffs get choked up over Model T's and Packards, so do

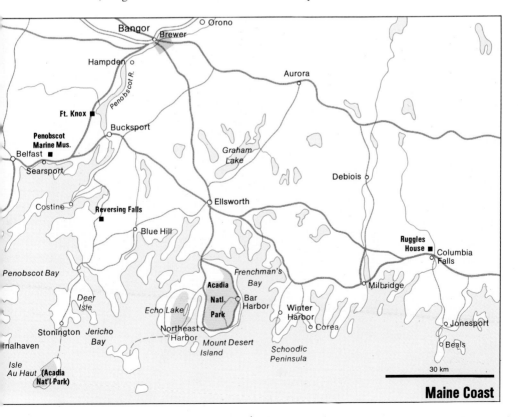

Maine Coast

many coastal Mainers have a soft spot for old boats. Whereas most of today's yachts have painted fiberglass hulls, older boats were made of sanded and stained wood. They didn't move as quickly as today's boats, nor were they built as inexpensively, but there is much to be said for the careful handcrafting and woodwork that went into their design.

'A Great Island, Backed Like a Whale'

The king of the old wooden sailboats is the Friendship Sloop, built in the tiny town of **Friendship,** southeast of Damariscotta on State 220. This small, all-purpose boat — strong, sturdy and dependable — was the Ford pickup of its day, the turn of the 20th Century. It may not have been the best-engineered boat ever, but it remains one of the most popular and recognizable. In this age of powerboats, the Friendship Sloop is relegated mostly to pleasure duty. Friendship Sloop races are held in Hatchet Cove off the coast of Friendship during the last week in July.

An early European explorer named David Ingram, known to historians as one of the greatest liars of all time, astounded Europe with tales of the marvelous peoples and cities he encountered on a walk from the Gulf of Mexico to Canada. A group of Germans were, in fact, lured by such reports to come settle the town of **Waldoboro,** north of Damariscotta. In the center of town is a plaque that reads: "This town was settled in 1748 by Germans who immigrated to this place with the promise and expectation of finding a prosperous city, instead of which they found nothing but wilderness." So when Ingram reported the existence of "a great island that was backed like a whale" 10 miles out to sea, nobody took him very seriously.

But for once, he had been telling the truth. The cliffs of **Monhegan,** 10 miles (16 km) south of **Port Clyde,** do indeed lend the island the appearance of a whale, and, although the island is only a mile long, its history and natural beauty are considerable. Almost everyone agrees that, if you're going to visit only one island off the Maine coast, Monhegan should be your choice.

Twice a day the most famous mail boat on this coast, the *Laura B.*, ferries

An ornamented window in Boothbay Harbor.

254

passengers between Port Clyde and Monhegan. Step on the shore of the island and you will touch the same ground on which, some say, the Vikings walked 1,000 years ago. European settlers — here as early as 1605 — noticed immediately that Monhegan's waters were even better stocked with fish than other Maine waters. They caught and dried tons of them to send home. Explorers and fishermen from many nations made Monhegan their home; perhaps because of the island's remote natural beauty, they managed to live together harmoniously.

The families that live on Monhegan today are also a close-knit group: Monhegan is the only fishing community in Maine that puts a season on lobster-trapping. No lobsters are caught from sunset on June 25 until Trap Day, January 1. If any of the town's lobstermen is unable to begin at the appointed time, the beginning of the season is postponed. No outside fishermen are allowed within two miles of the island. Since the lobsters have more growing time, they are bigger then average and thus command higher prices.

Monhegan is still best known for its

The Ruggles House, Columbia Falls.

scenery. In the Cathedral Woods, pines tower overhead while wildflowers carpet the meadows. Departing island guests are traditionally given bouquets of these flowers as going-away presents.

Penobscot Bay

On the west end of Penobscot Bay is **Rockland,** the largest city on this part of the coast. Originally called Thomaston, the name was changed in honor of the limestone deposits that supported the town's economy and its foundation. Rockland was once a great limestone producer, but has now built its economy around the lobster: the town is the world's largest distributor of lobster. During the first week of August, it hosts the annual Maine Seafoods Festival.

North of Rockland on U.S. 1 is the town of **Rockport.** A small fishing town, Rockport makes headlines once a year upon the arrival of André the Seal. Spending most of the year at the Boston Aquarium, André swims up the coast to his native waters in Rockport Harbor every summer. There he entertains fishermen, tourists and members of the press, who sometimes wait days for his

unpredictable arrival.

Camden, the publishing capital of Maine, is the home of a number of Maine periodicals, including the popular *Downeast Magazine*, and the headquarters of the Maine Publicity Bureau. Whenever something happens in Maine, Camden residents are sure to know about it.

When they're not busy writing or running presses, Camden residents might be found on board one of the authentic Windjammer Fleet of sailing vessels that cruise along the coast and make Camden their home port. With sails billowing from their two- or three-masted frames, the windjammers are a throwback to a past era and are unlike anything else on the water today. Boats like the *Stephen Taber*, believed to be the oldest sailing vessel in continuous use, are manned by crews of tourists seeking the thrill of sailing and navigating old-time sailboats.

The Outward Bound School, located on **Hurricane Island** in Penobscot Bay, offers summer people another way to get out on the water and learn new skills. The program promises its students "the hardest, most miserable, most wonderful days of your life." This dubious-sounding advertisement describes a rugged program including backpacking, cycling and voyaging in old-style pulling boats, which can be rowed as well as sailed. Navigating from island to island for periods of two weeks or more, the students, aged 16 to 60, learn new and forgotten outdoor and survival skills.

Breathtaking Mount Desert

If the state of Maine stands apart from the rest of New England, then **Mount Desert Island,** in the waters east of Penobscot Bay, stands apart from the rest of Maine. Explorer Samuel de Champlain spotted the mountains of Mount Desert — the highest coastal mountains on the Atlantic seaboard — and called the place "L'isle des monts deserts," the island of wilderness mountains. The French pronunciation has remained, so be sure to pronounce it "dessert" if you want to sound properly Downeast.

Mount Desert's largest town, **Bar Harbor,** existed for decades as a small local resort and farming area. Then in

A logging truck in Millinocket near Baxter State Park. Timber is a mainstay of the Maine economy.

the 1870s, Thomas Coles, founder of the Hudson River School of naturalist painting, put the island on the map. He came to capture on canvas Mount Desert's breathtaking landscapes — the mountains blend into forest and the forest into open sea. Coles' paintings revealed something in addition to scenic beauty — miles and miles of undeveloped waterfront property. By the turn of the century, Bar Harbor had gained a reputation as a "playground for the rich." In 1916, some of the more conservation-minded residents got together and purchased some 33,000 acres (13,350 hectares) of land on Mount Desert and nearby **Isle au Haut** and **Schoodic Point** and donated it to the government as **Acadia National Park,** the only national park in the New England states.

In 1947 — in what European socialist newspapers called a peasant rebellion against the landed aristocracy — much of Bar Harbor burned to the ground in a fire that actually began at a garbage dump. It was one of the worst fires in Maine's history. The fire burned above and below ground for almost a month before it was brought completely under control. Scorch marks were visible on the ground and trees for years afterward. Over a third of the island was wiped out and many of the great estates destroyed. The fire accounts for the island's high concentration of coniferous trees, the first to grow into a barren area. Bar Harbor was quickly rebuilt but lost much of its reputation as an "upper class only" resort. Smaller and cheaper hotels were built, and the town is now accessible to more people.

A visit to Mount Desert Island is not complete without a tour of Acadia National Park. From flat walks along carriage roads donated by John D. Rockefeller to steep climbs up rock mountain faces, Acadia offers something for everyone's outdoor tastes. Try hiking up the Precipice Trail, along which ladders and handrails have been placed to ease the ascent, and you will reach the summit of **Champlain Mountain,** where there are excellent views of Bar Harbor and Schoodic Point. The Jordan Cliffs walk leads from the fashionable Jordan Pond House inn to the top of **Penobscot Mountain**; a half-mile from the summit, refreshing Sargent Pond attracts swimmers. Or you can

Left, mythical lumberjack Paul Bunyan stands tall over Bangor. Right, guide Martin Brown poles down the rapids of the St. Croix River.

walk over Acadia and St. Saveur mountains, around the less traveled west side of Mount Desert, to cool off in **Somes Sound,** a natural fjord.

The highest point on Mount Desert is **Cadillac Mountain,** visible for more than 60 miles (97 km) out to sea. Located on the east side of the island, Cadillac *can* be climbed by foot ... but it's something of a letdown to reach the summit and find a crowd of tourists who drove up in their cars. The Cadillac road is one of the best conceived and engineered mountain roads in the world: it never attains a gradient of more than seven degrees.

The Far East

From atop Cadillac, the entire island comes into view. The mountain is only 1,530 feet (466 meters) high, but on a clear day you can see far out to sea and 100 miles inland to Mount Katahdin, Maine's highest peak. Sunsets are spectacular. Often hundreds of people gather on the mountainside to watch the fiery orange-red sun melt into the sea. Especially beautiful sunsets are hailed with applause, which in turn is followed by embarrassed laughter.

Contrary to popular tourist travel patterns, the coast of Maine does not end at Bar Harbor. Eastern coast residents aren't happy about being neglected by tourists, but their relative remoteness gives them little opportunity to draw visitors. Certainly, beyond Mount Desert, tourism takes a back seat to lobstering and the cultivation of blueberries and Christmas trees, the only profitable crops in this fog-enshrouded tundra.

For hard-core Mainers, the eastern coast is true Maine. Here, there's no question about it: you *are* Downeast. While accommodations are available, visitors never get the feeling that anything has been altered or preserved especially for tourist consumption. It has been said of Maine that things never change; on the eastern coast, they move more slowly than that.

Small, unspoiled fishing towns dot the eastern coast. **Winter Harbor** is among the most accessible, just across Frenchman's Bay from Bar Harbor on State 186. Boasting a small and extremely well protected harbor, this town also sponsors annual blueberry

A Coast Guard cutter breaks the ice at the mouth of the Kennebec River.

and lobster festivals. The Fishermen's Co-op, tucked away on the town wharf, serves lobster, live or boiled, literally fresh out of the ocean. The old salts who hang around here — and some not so old, though one never hears anyone described as a young salt — delight in talking about the sea and life in a coastal fishing town.

Machias, east of Winter Harbor on U.S. 1, was once a haven for pirates and smugglers. Early in the Revolution, outraged citizens assembled at Burnham Tavern (still standing) before capturing the British warship *Margaretta,* lying just offshore. Piracy was a natural outgrowth of Revolutionary privateering, which was really government-sanctioned piracy. The pirate Samuel Bellamy worked out of Machias but was captured during what he had planned to be his final voyage before hanging up his sword and eyepatch.

Lubec is a long way to go for a vacation. It bills itself as the easternmost town in the United States. (The easternmost American soil is **Quoddy Head State Park,** just south of Lubec.) As an international port of entry, Lubec mixes American and Canadian people

and customs freely. Just across a small bridge is **Campobello Island,** New Brunswick, onetime home of the Franklin Roosevelt clan and now open to the public. All the original Roosevelt furniture and artifacts are still in place.

Lubec's sister town, **Eastport,** is three miles (five km) from Lubec by water or 40 miles (64 km) by land. Outside Eastport is the **Passamaquoddy Indian Reservation,** which on occasion stages authentic Indian dances and rituals in full dress and makeup.

The North Country

Bangor is the northernmost bastion of New England culture and civilization in Maine. To the north and west are nothing but the woods and potato farms of Aroostook County, half the size of Connecticut; and to the east are small towns that have more in common with their cousins across the Canadian border than with anyone in Maine.

Once the center of Maine's world-leading timber and paper industries, Bangor has declined along with the pine trees. It has neither the cultural attractions of Portland nor the charm of the

Majestic Mount Katahdin, seen from Baxter State Park.

smaller towns nearby. Most visitors to Bangor seem to be on their way elsewhere, usually to the great wilderness areas of the north and west.

Just north of Bangor in the Penobscot River is **Indian Island,** home of the Penobscot Indians. They are probably the wealthiest Indians in the country, thanks to a federal court's ruling that the U.S. government owed them millions of dollars for lands illegally seized as the country was being consolidated and developed.

While Maine's wilderness is slowly shrinking, the state has tucked away hundreds of thousands of acres in which moose and black bear roam. Many lakes, rivers and other areas in the north are just as they have been for centuries. Many still bear the names given them by Indians long ago.

In the center of this wilderness lies **Moosehead Lake,** the largest lake in New England. At **Greenville,** on the lake's southern shore, guides can be hired for canoeing trips along the **Allagash Wilderness Waterway.** The waterway stretches 92 miles (148 km) from Telos Lake to Twin Brook and offers some of the most scenic, exciting

and dangerous whitewater canoeing in the United States.

Gift of a Governor

Baxter State Park, 75 miles (121 km) directly north of Bangor, was donated to the state by former Maine Governor Percival Baxter with the stipulation that it forever remain a natural, undeveloped area. The park contains dozens of ponds and lakes, and 45 peaks over 3,000 feet high. All manner of wildlife call the park home, including moose, which can usually be found feeding in Sandy Stream Pond at the southern end of the park.

Baxter's main draw is **Mount Katahdin,** the highest peak in Maine and the second tallest in New England. This pile of glacially discarded granite boulders has three peaks, the highest of which is Baxter Peak (5,267 feet; 1,605 meters). Connecting Baxter to Pamola Peak is a narrow, mile-long strip of rock known as the Knife Edge. Only a few feet wide in spots, the Knife Edge is an acrophobe's nightmare — 3,000 feet straight down on one side, 4,000 feet on the other. Would a person fall straight down to the bottom? No, a park ranger reassures. You'd bounce a couple of times. Don't cross it in high winds.

Pamola Peak is named for the Indian god Pamola, who was supposedly banished to that peak after stepping out of line with the other gods who hung out at Baxter Peak. In his *Maine Woods,* Thoreau warned of another Indian legend — that Pamola, who has the wings and talons of an eagle but the arms and torso of a man, becomes angry with mortals who reach the top of Katahdin and thus enter the territory of the gods. Anyone who has ever tried to climb Katahdin, with its high winds and unpredictable weather, might be persuaded that Pamola still keeps an eye out for potential troublemakers.

The most difficult trails up and down Katahdin are the Cathedral and Dudley trails. They present the most rugged and difficult rock-climbing possible without using ropes and pitons. Allow eight to 10 hours for a full circuit climb. Good boots, food and water as well as warm clothes for the top are necessities. Katahdin marks the northern end of the Appalachian Trail, 2,000 miles (over 3,200 km) north of Springer Mountain, Georgia.

Left, Father German Cuiba, Russian Orthdox priest, at the altar during a service in Richmond. Right, dusk at Pemaquid Point.

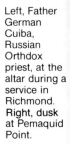

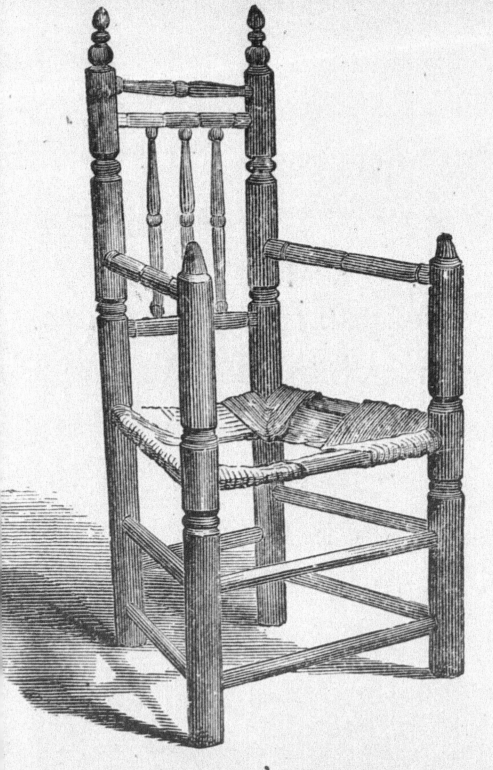

CARVER'S CHAIR.

BREWSTER'S CHAIR.

Shingles and clapboards, gables and steeples — an array of traditional architectural images forms in the mind's eye at the mention of New England. Buildings capture the essence of New England's character; they sum up what was at once noble and humble about the ambitions of the region's forefathers. And the charm of the old houses and churches is not lost on today's New Englanders, whose tireless efforts have succeeded in preserving much of the architectural traditions of the past.

A visitor to New England might stand in wonder at the palatial splendor of The Breakers at Newport, but nowhere in that building can the true character of the region be found. That mansion symbolizes a departure from the honesty and utility that inspired the first 200 years of New England building. The work of those years, from the mid-17th to mid-19th centuries, holds the secret to New England's appeal and charm. Styles changed over that period but these changes refined rather than departed from tradition.

To learn New England, read her buildings, for they tell tales rich in wisdom about the lives of their builders and inhabitants. Always aware of its heroic past, New England has wisely held on to enough of its architectural heritage to sketch a vivid picture of a distinguished history. Studying its buildings will not only stimulate the mind and seize the imagination; it will delight the eye as well.

Purity and Practicality

Beauty is not the strong point of New England homes of the 17th Century, although in their simplicity can be found a certain comeliness. The heavy, somewhat medieval feel of early Yankee houses caused one writer to note as early as 1848 that "happily ... they will not much longer remain to annoy travelers" in New England. Fortunately, her prediction did not come to pass, for enough 17th Century structures have been preserved throughout to tell much — in however basic a vocabulary — about their beginnings.

The stark simplicity of the earliest houses, those built by the first several generations of settlers, is a testament to the unaffected motivations of the people. Stylistic vestiges of English country homes governed housing design and construction, but none of these was applied for decorative effect. On the contrary, there is virtually no indulgence in ornament in Massachusetts houses such as the 1637 Hoxie House in Sandwich or the Whipple House of 1640 in Ipswich. After all, when one was living for the glory of God and laboring for the good of community, there was little room for excess.

The Hoxie and Whipple houses and the handful like them were in fact nothing more than offspring of the homes the Pilgrims left behind in southeastern England. Simple oblong boxes, they were framed painstakingly and filled with the wattle-and-daub left visible on the half-timbered country homes of England. Clapboards, which provided an extra blanket of protection against the New England winters, created a stern, dark appearance that was relieved only by small, randomly placed windows. The steep roof and the massive central chimney, shared by the two lower and two upper rooms, crowned the house with an air of authority.

In the very early homes, the second floor extended slightly beyond the first, creating an overhang that served no purpose but to make construction more difficult. The 1683 Capen House in Topsfield, Massachusetts, offers a marvelous example of this device. The overhang, perhaps recalling English townhouses where the first floor stepped back in deference to the street, was among those features that were dropped as housing designs began to accommodate expansion and reflect the colonists' growing sense of security. Those peering, diamond-paned windows were replaced by a double-hung variety that substantially brightened the facade as well as the interior. Roofs were extended to add more room on the first floor, and the style resulting was dubbed "salt box."

Coming of Age

With a growing sense of confidence, the colonists began adding some flourishes to their humble homes. At the turn of the century, commerce was growing beyond the borders of the town and with expanding horizons came a more excited, adventurous spirit among the people and a weakening of the strict principles of religion that had dampened individual expression.

Economic change was gradual and the

architectural symbols of this change vary in their message, depending on the place and time. Along the coast, where maritime trading and fishing were making their mark on the landscape, money and the exposure to new styles from abroad combined to produce splendid mansions. Inland, where farmers and· craftsmen produced almost anything that the increasingly far-flung marketplace would absorb, the changes in building style were more subtle and slower to peak.

The inspiration for the new Georgian

generations of English architects. In this country, Palladian ideas spread through the publication of Palladio's *Four Books of Architecture* as well as scores of other imported design handbooks. With these guides in hand, the first tentative but unmistakable steps were taken towards the establishment of a conscious aesthetic in this country. Not insignificantly, a style was born that is as often termed Colonial as it is Georgian, and the modern American landscape certainly attests to its staying power.

Symmetry, a sense of strength and a qual-

style of architecture, as the pre-Revolutionary period of 18th Century design has been named, stemmed from misfortune back in England. London burned in 1666, and out of the ashes rose buildings in a completely new style, tributes to the ideas of the 16th Century Italian architect Andrea Palladio. Palladio's work recalled the classical architecture of antiquity and restated it in a refreshing, heroic way. Inigo Jones and, later, Christopher Wren championed this Renaissance spirit in London, and their works inspired

Preceding pages, handcrafted chairs are among the most notable of Shaker folk arts. Above the gristmill at Longfellow's Wayside Inn is a classic study in the use of materials in simple form.

ity of ease characterize the Georgian style. The Georgian house was a simple two-story rectangle, but classical elements gave it definition: scrolled, often broken pediments capped doorways and windows; fluted attached columns marked the entrances of houses; and, in the grander examples, bulging cornerstones bracketed the corners of the structures from the eaves to the foundations. Many of these same Georgian touches were built out of granite or sandstone in Europe, and the simulation in wood was carried off precisely by the skilled carpenters of New England.

The plan of the Georgian home expanded to allow greater room and privacy. One of the most notable changes was the use of two separate chimneys servicing the two, now larger halves of the house. Four full rooms both upstairs and down were the norm. The massive central chimney was replaced by two leaner towers, adding to the elegance and richness outside and leaving room for a hallway where the chimney had formerly stood.

Georgian Charm

Examples of Georgian buildings abound in New England. In Deerfield, Massachusetts, stand several charming examples of early renderings of Georgian ideas. At the north end of a marvelous mile of 18th Century historical structures stand the 1733 Ashley House and the 1743 Hawks House.

reached during the bitter days of winter.

By mid-century, activity at the coastal ports was in full swing, and the houses of the captains and merchants suggest that business was decidedly profitable. Many of the houses built in this era were late remodeled to keep up with architectural styles, making it sometimes difficult to find the purely Georgian. Portsmouth, New Hampshire, is blessed with unsullied originals in its 1763 Moffat-Ladd House — as handsome as any to be found — and the delightfully understated Wentworth-Gardner House of 1760, where it is hard to resist touching the facade to verify that it is, indeed, wood and not stone.

Aspects of Georgian architecture, particularly Palladian motifs, remained in the

There is something about the precision of the barest Georgian proportion and detail exhibited in these buildings that exudes calm and assurance. At the same time, their dark, unpainted clapboards suggest a ruggedness absent in later painted facades. Indians were regularly raiding Deerfield, and several bloody massacres had occurred, but when your eyes rest upon these buildings, you feel no sense of trepidation, and the marvelous doorways welcome visitors warmly. Equally gracious is the Dwight-Barnard House of 1754. This rambling residence is a lovely example not only of Georgian architecture but also of the common New England practice of interconnecting the house, the barn and any other outbuilding that had to be

language of New England design beyond the 18th Century, but for the most part the style had run its course by the time of the Revolutionary War. One lovely exception is the handsome town of Litchfield, Connecticut, where pristine homes lining the roads north and south of the village green compose the perfect picture of the idyllic New England town. Some of the finest homes were built or remodeled after 1780, when the Litchfield China Trading Company brought wealth and increased notoriety to the town.

A trademark of the Federal style of architecutre, left, was the semicircular portico over the door, supported by columns. The house in Litchfield, right, is refined Georgian architecture.

266

The residence of one of the company's founders, a Mr. Deming, and the remodeled Sheldon's Tavern are impeccably Georgian, down to the three-part Palladian window not commonly used before 1780. All other buildings in the borough of Litchfield are meticulously preserved, although not necessarily in their original state. The predominantly white exteriors date from a later 19th Century taste that has stuck not only in Litchfield but throughout New England and conveys a considerably different feel than would the yellow, blue or red hues that comprised the Georgian palette.

No style since the Georgian has lingered for so long a time in New England. Deriving as it did from familiar forms, with simply more space and embellishments added, it

was adapted with ease by New England builders. If it was a long time before the Georgian style matured into its successor, the Federal, it was surely a result of the many preoccupations of a nation in adolescence, rather than an absence of native architectural acumen. The century that followed was to prove that.

The Federal Style

Despite the debilitating physical and economic affects of the war, the remarkable victories of the Revolution gave birth to a vigorous self-confidence across the new nation. Litchfield's homes of the 1790s were a last provincial gasp of Georgian charm, for

as the 19th Century approached, a new sophistication was exhibited in buildings that, for the first time, were the work of native American architects.

Elsewhere in the colonies at the turn of the 19th Century, visiting architects from abroad, as well as native sons like Thomas Jefferson, drew from their academic knowledge of European architecture to design daring buildings of Roman inspiration. In New England, where few foreign architects traveled, a less radical transformation took place, fueled by the accumulation of wealth and the booming economy along the coast.

Optimism must indeed have been palpable in the harbors of Salem and Boston. Even inland, whaling, shipbuilding and the expansion of trade brought the sea into the lives of many New Englanders as the coastal merchants commanded the goods and natural resources of the whole region. But no country carpenter could rival the skills of Salem's Samuel McIntire or Boston's Charles Bulfinch, whose combined work represents the finest of the period.

The Salem of Samuel McIntire's time was a far cry from the city that had been home to hysterical witch-hunters 100 years earlier. Success in the pepper trade and other undertakings made wealthy men of captains and cabin boys alike. It is fortuitous that McIntire and Salem grew together, for the local carpenter may otherwise have had no outlet for his self-taught architectural proficiency.

In McIntire's work are the clearest notations of the Federal style. While New England's roofs had lost some of their cant in the Georgian period, their Federal counterparts virtually disappeared behind delicately carved balustrades. The effect was urbane, as evidenced by the 1804 Gardner-Pingree house, a rather neat summation of Federal motifs. Although boxy and still, its facade is relieved by the semi-circular portico, its refined columns and the arching fanlight over the door — a signature of the Federal era.

McIntire performed his own carpentry with a skill that left him in constant demand up until his death in 1811. His inspiration was Robert Adam, the English architect who raised the art of interior decoration to exquisite heights with his dainty stucco reliefs. McIntire introduced these same embellishments to Salem, as can be seen inside the Gardner-Pingree house.

The full impact of McIntire's work on the rest of Salem is best grasped on Chestnut Street, which in its entirety has been designated a National Historic Landmark. Up and down both sides of this majestic street are stunning Federal-style mansions, built in the early 1800s when the sea captains decided to move a short distance away from the noise and clutter of the port. Elsewhere in Salem, a 1970s' facelift has not only turned around a declining city but, in doing so, reversed plans to topple many Federal-era buildings, which have been renovated and put to new use. A similar turnabout, has occurred in nearby Newburyport where, in an almost miraculous rescue mission, life and charm have been reintroduced into its previously dilapidated, deserted commercial buildings.

The Brilliance of Bulfinch

The Federal era peaked with the work of Charles Bulfinch. Bulfinch pursued architecture first as an activity of leisure and then as profession. Building — or his speculations in it — bankrupted him twice. One can only surmise, however, that misfortune fired rather than smothered his talents. Unfortunately, many of his more daring buildings have been destroyed, but the jewel among those standing, his State House, rests atop Beacon Hill. Here is as grand a composition as any Bulfinch realized, and to picture it surrounded by open land is to begin to appreciate what a dazzling paean to the promise of government it must have appeared to the Bostonian of 1800.

The classical State House, again very Palladian in inspiration, has been extended twice in two contradictory styles. The 1890 addition to the back of the building is a lumpish but highly mannered Baroque echo of its opposing side. The second addition of 1914 totally neutralized the first by blotting it out, at least from the front, behind two thoroughly impassive marble wings — dull perhaps, but a mute backdrop to the golden-domed Bulfinch original.

The State House is vintage Bulfinch. His easiest work to take in — not because it is any less accomplished than his other buildings — stands sprinkled among the many elegant homes of Beacon Hill. Bulfinch was in on the beginning of Beacon Hill speculation, and the three homes he built for the investor Harrison Gray Otis summarize not only his growth but the maturation of the Federal residential style. The first house, now the headquarters for the Preservation of New England antiquities, is the least developed, a harmonious but basic expression of Federal-style concepts. In the second building, Bulfinch took a few cautious steps to animate the street facade — the first floor windows are recessed inside well-defined brick arches. By the third house, Bulfinch's

confidence had been established. This Beacon Street residence, of noble proportions and refined detail, projects a sophistication that was repeated in his other work on Beacon Hill and, indeed, set the tone for the rest of the neighborhood.

The uniqueness of Beacon Hill and Bulfinch's contributions to it was recognized long ago by its citizens, who established the Beacon Hill Historic District in 1955. This organization has overseen not only the preservation of a beautiful cluster of buildings but has also protected a rare haven of tranquility in the heart of busy, modern Boston.

Tranquility is what so much of New England is about, and among the emblems of this serenity are the scores of white steeples, visible on every horizon as landmarks for

travelers. The source for this ubiquitous New England image is traced back to one of the most influential forces in turn-of-the-century New England architecture — Asher Benjamin, an architect and writer. It was in the first of Benjamin's seven widely read architectural handbooks that he rendered a steepled church that became the basis for decades of church design. The simple classicism of the facade changed little over time, but the detailing, particularly of the steeple, incorporated changing architectural fashions

Early American carpenters styled furnishings like the staircase, left, from detailed descriptions taken from English books. Victorian homes, like the one at right, were a departure from austerity.

over the decades and can be a handy clue to the era in which a given church was built.

At Home with Homer

It was Benjamin who, in his final 1830 volume, judged New England ready for the Greek Revival style that elsewhere in America was already vying with the Gothic. The same sense of self-importance that had characterized the Federal era, along with the influence of learning and intellectualism, gave the imposing Greek style a certain snob appeal. New England allowed the style in but without totally letting go of the integrity of its architectural traditions. Particularly in non-residential examples, the Greek Revival style produced buildings that were a logical

or Paris," an apt compliment to its crisply colonnaded and handsomely detailed facade. Inside, the two-story, sky-lit interior has been beautifully restored, its cast-iron balconies once again offering passage for shoppers in an intimate, elegant setting.

Charismatic Faneuil Hall

Certainly the most celebrated New England project of its kind, the restored Faneuil Hall Markets (also known as Quincy Market) is now a consumer's cornucopia, with food and every kind of specialty store galore. The renovation has been done with care and charisma; although the sober Greek references of Alexander Parris' 1825 domed building are generally overwhelmed

extension of the refinements made during the Federal era. Greek Revival houses proved less successful.

The economy of Greek architecture gives it its superior air, and scale is key to its grandeur. Civic buildings, institutions and halls of commerce lent themselves to the heroic Greek scale; houses were dwarfed by it. Although New England is not particularly rich in examples of the style, two of its more exemplary Greek Revival buildings, both of them marketplaces, happen to be among the most clever and renowned examples of recently restored and reused 19th Century buildings.

The Providence Arcade of 1828 has been described as "something worthy of London

by their surroundings, it seems somehow fitting that this hive of activity be housed in such sublime splendor.

The addition of heavy columns and crushing pediments did little for otherwise well-proportioned Federal and Georgian homes. Neither remodeled nor new Greek Revival houses carry themselves with particular ease, but one of their fundamental features was assimilated into the vocabulary of vernacular New England design quite effortlessly — the passion for white paint, stemming from the association of white with Greek temples. Some fine examples of everyday Greek Revival can be found in Grafton, Vermont, a quiet town remarkable less for its architecture than for the story of its rescue over the past 20 years by the Windham Foundation, which has invested substantial sums into the restoration of this once-bustling town.

Not far from Grafton, a very different vision from the 19th Century survives. Harrisville, New Hampshire, is an untouched, unchanged emblem of how pervasive the textile industry was in New England after 1830. The handsome granite and brick mills, boardinghouses and storehouses — now being used to house light industry — are essentially all that comprise a town that is an abridged version of the story of the rapid rise and fall of New England's mill towns, a story that began with windmills and small-town enterprise and climaxed with building of entire towns designed solely to support the textile industry. The effects on the social

fabric of New England were profound and lasting.

Historic Lowell

It is appropriate that in Lowell, Massachusetts, named after one of the fathers of the power loom, aggressive efforts are underway to preserve an extensive architectural legacy of the industrial past. Ten short years of intense activity have resulted in the creation of the Lowell National Historic Park and the Lowell Historic Preservation District, each chartered with the task of preserving and interpreting the town's rich heritage. Dozens of factory buildings, designed in the boxy, brick, frugal industrial

version of the Federal style, line the city's intricate canal system, with the rows of boardinghouses for the legendary "mill girls" standing nearby. These and many once-abandoned commercial buildings are being renovated and reused at a remarkable pace.

As a result of foresight and dedication on the part of many people, Lowell is once again a healthy and active city, a rich visual lesson in the architecture of a tumultuous chapter of our history. Fortunately, the Lowell Mills are among many in New England that are being saved from the wrecking ball and reused for housing, commercial and retail purposes. Towns like Fall River, Manchester and Pawtucket are the richer for it.

The Loss of Innocence

The opening of the industrial age marked the closing of an era of architectural innocence in New England. For its first 200 comparatively stable years, New England architecture had been governed by conservative principles that emphasized function first; form existed to serve the central purpose of shelter. While European ideas had clearly dictated design, they had been tempered by restraint. But by 1850, something had changed. Perhaps for no other reason than boredom with symmetry, scale and four-square plans, architecture took off in all directions, most in opposition to the language of the past.

Gothic and Italianate, Renaissance and Romanesque — even Egyptian — are among the labels attached to the late 19th Century architectural revivals. In the hands of architects like Henry Hobson Richardson and McKim, Mead and White, or many lesser known but dextrous carpenters, these styles could be expressed with unparalleled success. But the spiritual link to New England grew remote; these buildings have only distant kinship with the native builders.

The Shingle style of the late century is an ironic illustration of how far architecture was to journey: begun in New England, its source is none other than the region's Colonial coastal homes of the early 18th Century. New England architects had circumnavigated a stylistic globe, only to find inspiration in their own backyards.

A brick house on Boston's Chestnut Street, left, displays an urbane Federal style with a recessed door. The Martha's Vineyard church (1843), right is of Greek revival style with Gothic columns.

THE PURITANS' INTELLECTUAL LEGACY

The Puritans did more than settle New England; they created her. Out of the calvinistic beliefs in man's inherent evil and the predestination of the soul grew a society that was stern and uncompomising. The Puritans' was a hard creed at its best, an ultimate faith that required everyone — from the most prominent minister to the humblest child — to strain toward an ineffable God. In his fallen state, argued the Puritan, man could never know God and could thus never truly know the state of his own soul. Salvation came not through human action, but through God's mysterious grace. Abject though man may be, he must always examine his conscience, always repent his inevitable sin, always attempt a just life.

The Puritans' difficult faith stood them well: seeing discipline and hard work as spiritual values, these early settlers labored long for the greater glory of God — and incidentally accumulated wealth and built prosperous communities. At their worst, the Puritans came to identify worldly success with godliness, nonconformity with devil-worship. Their faith found little room for gentleness or pleasure.

The many world-class schools and colleges found in New England stand as tangible reminders of that legacy. Education was essential to the Puritans' vision of what their new society in America was to be. Most of the settlers were well-educated; four officers of the Massachusetts Bay Colony — John Winthrop, Sir Richard Saltonstall, Isaac Johnson and John Humphrey — had been educated at England's Cambridge University. For them, the journey to the New World was more than an adventure to a new frontier; it was a chance to transport their old society in purified form to a new land. Discontented in a country where they were persecuted for their religious practices, they came to America to build an ideal society, their "city on a hill." These men knew that unless they provided for the education and training of clergymen, they would quickly lose the new (and perfect) England.

In America, as in England, class distinctions were important. But the Puritans, eschewing such worldly signs of status as expensive clothes and fancy carriages, had to

Harvard students are dwarfed by the pillars of the Widener Library. The largest university library on earth, it is indicative of the long-term importance placed on education in New England.

devise other more subtle ways of indicating social class. The title "Master" was reserved exclusively for educated men.

A society in which education established one's credentials before God and the world was destined to develop an impressive school system. As early as 1635, Boston voted a declaration that "our brother, Mr. Philemon Pormont shal be intreated to become scholemaster for teaching and noutering of children with us." He established Boston Latin School, the first secondary school in the country and today one of Boston's finest high schools. Several years later, in 1642, the General Court of the Bay Colony voted to institute a new law requiring every town to see to the education of its youth. By 1671, all colonies but Rhode Island, ever the renegade, had instituted compulsory education.

Higher Education

Still the settlers had yet to provide their colony with an institution of higher learning. In 1636, the Bay Colony's General Court voted to £40 toward a public "school or college." What then was New Town, Massachusetts, was chosen as the site for the institution, which opened as Newtown College in 1637. In 1638, John Harvard, a graduate of Emmanuel College at Cambridge and a recent immigrant to America, died and left his library and half of his fortune to Newtown College. The school was subsequently renamed Harvard College, and New Town was renamed Cambridge to signify the town's new role as the colony's university community.

Throughout the rest of the 17th Century, the college served primarily as a training ground for the Puritan clergy. But in the early years of the 18th Century, Harvard — feeling the effects of Enlightenment — liberalized and added Locke and Newton to its curriculum.

In 1701, decrying the change in their alma mater's educational philosophy, James Pierpont and several other Harvard graduates — all congregational ministers — founded the Collegiate School in Saybrook, Connecticut. The school moved to New Haven in 1716 and two years later was renamed Yale College in honor of Elihu Yale, its benefactor.

More colleges were to follow Harvard and Yale. In 1764, Nicholas Brown, one of the prominent Brown family of Rhode Island whose fortune was made in the molasses, rum and slave trade, founded Rhode Island College as a Baptist school. Relocated from Warren to Providence several years later, the school was renamed Brown University after its founder in 1804.

Dartmouth College, founded in 1769 by the Reverend Eleazar Wheelock, was originally chartered "for the education of Youth of the Indian Tribes" as well as for "English Youth and Others."

In 1778, Samuel Philips and his uncle, Dr. John Phillips, complaining of "a growing neglect of youth in our time," founded the Phillips Academy at Andover, Massachusetts. Several years later, Dr. Phillips established a similar school, the Phillips

Exeter Academy in Exeter, New Hampshire. Exeter's charter is a revealing commentary on the Puritan mind: the school's purpose was "to promote piety and virtue" in its students and "to learn them the great and real business of living." Virtue and business, the twin obsessions of the Puritans, were perhaps their most enduring legacy to New England.

A far less benign and more compelling expression of the Puritan character were the Salem witch trials of 1692, which continue to fascinate people nearly 300 years later. Salem (whose name ironically comes from the Hebrew word for peace, *shalom*) had never been, since its founding in 1626, a bastion of tolerance and goodwill: it was from Salem that the founder of Rhode Island, Roger Williams, had been exiled for preaching religious freedom. And it was in Salem that the "witches" were hanged.

The 'Witches' of Salem

The story begins in the home of Salem's minister, the Samuel Parris, a graduate of Harvard and a former merchant. With him in the parsonage lived his wife; his daughter, Elizabeth; and her cousin, Abigail Williams; as well as two slaves Parris had purchased in Barbados, John Indian and his wife, Tituba. Tituba's account of voodoo so fascinated Elizabeth and Abigail that the two invited some of their friends, all young girls of the village, to listen.

The 12-year-old daughter of the parish clerk, three servant girls and four other young girls joined in these sessions. Meetings of such a nature, being strictly forbidden in the Puritan Salem, held an illicit and daring appeal that the girls must have found difficult to resist.

No doubt, they also found their guilty pleasure difficult to live with. Elizabeth Parris and Abigail Williams, later joined by the others, began to have seizures. Making rough, choking sounds, the girls took to crawling on the floor. They complained of feeling as though needles were piercing their flesh. The town doctor was called in to examine the girls and, after the medicine he administered failed to cure them, diagnosed them as victims of witchcraft. Ministers from the surrounding area were summoned to participate in a fast and prayer meeting to drive Satan from the town. But the girls did not respond, and so began the long chain of accusations and trials.

The girls were examined once more, and, when the Rev. Mr. Parris suggested that Tituba might be their tormentor, Elizabeth responded, "Tituba." Parris took this as an accusation, and the slave was charged with witchcraft. Accused with her were two women unpopular in the village, Sarah Osborne and Sarah Good, who were charged with everything from bewitching cattle to using voodoo dolls.

At her trial, Tituba confessed to being a witch. She claimed to have seen the girls being tormented by Osborne and Good, and, on another occasion, being molested by a tall gentleman from Boston who was

Left, John Winthrop, Cambridge-educated Puritan leader. Right, a plaque marks the site of Nathaniel Hawthorne's "Tanglewood" home near Lenox, where he wrote many of his stories.

accompanied by witches. Tituba went on to give a vivid account of being ordered by Satan to kill the girls and, on her refusal, being beaten by the other witches. The pain, she said, had driven her to torment the girls.

The witch scare started in earnest. More than 200 people were accused of witchcraft. Those judged by the magistrates to be witches — about 150 people — were jailed. The accused waited for trial in cold, damp cells; several of the accused women died in jail, and others suffered nervous breakdowns. Those found guilty, 19 in all, were hanged.

Nor did the hysteria limit itself to Salem: officials in Andover, Massachusetts, asked to borrow the girls to hunt down witches there. Throughout the state, 400 people were accused of witchcraft before the hysteria died. In the end, the scare was retarded by the number of judges who refused to take the charges seriously. By Christmas 1692, the governor of the Massachusetts Bay Colony ordered the release of all accused witches.

Always ready to discover depravity in someone else, the Puritans sat in eager judgment of the accused, many of whom were simply the town misfits. Unrelenting in their desire to purge their world of evil and in their arrogant belief in their own righteousness, they sent innocents to their death. The Salemites, too late, repented of their actions: in 1693, the Salem jurors wrote that they humbly begged the forgiveness of everyone who had been harmed by their actions.

Hawthorne and Transcendentalism

The arrival of the 19th Century brought the intellectual flowering of New England. Flushed with the success of the Revolutionary War and the founding of the nation, growing prosperous from the lucrative China trade, the Puritan temperament seemed transformed. The sweet optimism of transcendentalism, a mystical philosophy that argued the existence of an Oversoul unifying all creation, and which preached the primacy of insight over reason and inherent goodness over man, was a far cry from the dour outlook of the Puritans.

The movement spawned several experiments in living: the best known is, no doubt, Henry David Thoreau's solitary life on Walden Pond. Brooke Farm and Fruitlands, where adherents of transcendentalism lived communally, promised escape to a simpler life; neither community, however, survived for very long.

Led by Ralph Waldo Emerson, the transcendentalist movement attracted some of the brightest minds of the day — including, for a short while at least, Nathaniel Hawthorne. Hawthorne sort of dabbled with Emerson's philosophy and was, in fact, one of the founding members of Brooke Farm. His disillusionment with this experiment reinforced his essentially somber cast of mind. Far from being sweetly optimistic, his writing broods on human sin and quiet.

The descendant of Salem Puritans, Hawthorne grew up with a family legend of a Judge Hawthorne who, as a magistrate at the witchcraft trials, was cursed by a woman he convicted. The later Hawthorne was to use this story in his *House of Seven Gables.*

In fact, much of Hawthorne's work, even fantastic, was based on the stories of real people. In *The Minister's Black Veil,* an 1836 tale of a minister who always wore a black veil covering his face, the character explains: "If I hide my face for sorrow, there is cause enough, and if I cover it for secret sin, what mortal might not do the same." Hawthorne was, no doubt, familiar with the story of the Reverend Joseph Moody of York, Maine. After accidentally shooting and killing a friend while on a hunting trip, Moody became morbidly frightened of having his friend's family and fiancée look upon him. So he refused to show his face, covering it with a black handkerchief.

Young Goodman Brown, perhaps one of Hawthorne's greatest tales, draws on the story of the Salem witches. In what may be a dream, Goodman Brown, wandering in the dark forest, comes upon the devil, who boasts: "I have a very general acquaintance here in England. The deacons of many a church have drunk the communion wine with me; the selectmen of divers towns make me their chairman; and a majority of the Great and General Court are firm supporters of my interest. The governor and I, too — but these too are state secrets." To prove his power, Satan leads Goodman Brown to a clearing in the woods where the village people are worshipping the devil; among the congregation is Faith, Goodman's wife. In this masterful tale, Hawthorne depicts a world sunk in evil: if Goodman Brown's vision is true, the devil rules; if not and if Goodman has imagined innocent people in Satan's service, he reveals, like the Salem Puritans, the depth of his own corruption.

Banned in Boston

As the 19th Century continued, New England grew more and more prosperous. Shipping fortunes became manufacturing fortunes, and the region — with Boston at its hub — continued as America's industrial and intellectual center. Prosperity brought with it change; the liberalization of culture, represented by the transcendentalists in the early years of the century, continued.

New England's early settlers, like everyone else in the 17th Century, would have been shocked by the idea of educating women. But the Industrial Revolution created a class of wealthy and leisured young women, the daughters of America's new entrepreneurs, freed from the usual social responsibilities borne by the rest of their American sisters. America now had a class of women who, not needing a husband to ensure their financial security, did not need to concentrate their minds on homemaking.

The first women's school to open was Vassar Female College in 1861 in Poughkeepsie, New York. Vassar was followed, in 1875, by Wellesley College and Smith College in the Massachusetts towns of Wellesley and Southampton. Two other important Massachusetts women's colleges later joined them — Mount Holyoke in Holyoke and Radcliffe in Cambridge.

Despite this liberalization, the Puritan strain, much changed by the growth of industry, the waves of immigration and simply by time itself, nonetheless persists. Not quite able to forget its origins, New England has remained a deeply moral, and occasionally moralistic, society.

At their worst, New Englanders banned books they deemed offensive to public taste. Plays — and especially actors — were looked upon with suspicion and were considered to exert a pernicious influence on impressionable minds. Blue laws, the old Puritan statutes forbidding anyone to do much of anything on Sunday, lasted well into the 20th Century. Only recently, in fact, have Boston stores been permitted to open on Sundays.

At their best, New England's politicians and thinkers have been at the vanguard of reform. In the years before the Civil War, they worked strenuously for the abolition of slavery. (It must be admitted, however, that the health of the region's economy, unlike that of the South, did not depend on "the peculiar institution.") William Lloyd Garrison published his anti-slavery newspaper, *The Liberator,* here, and Harriet Beecher Stowe delivered one of the Abolitionist movement's most effective tracts with her best-selling novel, *Uncle Tom's Cabin.* Such zeal lives on, and today, New England is the home of many a would-be reformer. This is an ironic turn of events — the heritage of the conservative and moralistic Puritans yielding one of the country's most progressive regions.

Summer students park their bicycles outside the foreign-language studies classrooms at Middlebury College, Vermont.

MARITIME NEW ENGLAND

The little ship had been at sea for two months. It was November of the year 1620 in the North Atlantic, not a kind season to a vessel barely bigger than a pleasure yacht. The passengers and crew, more than 100 people, had been squeezed into this one little ship after its sister ship had proven unseaworthy. They were headed for the English colonies in America.

At last, the call arose, "Land ho!" The weary passengers who crowded the railings could barely make out the tops of several small islands on the horizon. As the ship drew closer, they discovered that the "islands" were actually hills arising above a long bar of sand. Weary from the months at sea and eager to set foot in the New World, the Pilgrims disembarked at the tip of Cape Cod to rest and reconnoiter. After five weeks on land, they set sail again for Virginia, but the sea had other plans for them. Battered by storms that seemed endless, the tiny but sturdy barque *Mayflower* was driven across Cape Cod Bay and into the mainland at a place the Pilgrims named Plymouth.

The sea had allowed these early New Englanders to escape the spiritual confines of the old country. It had brought them to the New World. But it had not given them any choice about their landing place. Down through the centuries, the sea — more than any other force — has written the history of New England and determined the destiny of its people.

The sea could take a man speedily between continents — or condemn him to frigid, watery grave. It has toppled granite buildings, even torn away the land itself; and it has made men fabulously wealthy overnight. A rich merchant, pillar of his community, might come into his warehouse on Boston's Long Wharf one morning only to find that his entire fleet and all its cargo had been swept away and lost forever, and that he was no better than a beggar. Or a lonesome beachcomber slowly tracing the sinuous miles of Cape Cod's sandy shores might come upon 100 gold doubloons washed up only minutes before by a whim of the sea.

Baptism by Sea

Even today, no matter how far man progresses in science and industry, subduing mighty rivers and moving great mountains, he cannot control this most vast and elemental of all earthly forces. All he can do is learn to live with it, by it and from it, to understand its strict rules and to abide by them. New Englanders have had no choice. The sea brought them here, the sea nourished them, and, if it did not destroy them, the sea made them rich. Only one of the six New England states (Vermont) has no maritime coastline. To all the rest, the outlet to the sea is a condition of life, the source of their prosperity.

From the beginning, New Englanders relied on the sea. The first generation of

Europeans in America all had the same "baptism by sea": a two-month voyage across the stormy North Atlantic. Most of the settlers who came were landlubbers, many of whom had never seen the ocean before.

Shipbuilding was one of the first activities for the early colonists. Ships maintained the connection to the homeland and provided an income from trade. The vast virgin forests of the New World supplied ready-at-hand

Preceding pages: reenactment of a naval battle off Fairhaven, Massachusetts (near New Bedford). Left, the *Beaver,* famed as the Boston Tea Party ship. Right, an old book recalls the trials of a 19th Century lobsterman.

materials for their construction. One hundred years after the Pilgrims stepped on Plymouth Rock, New England's coastal shipyards were launching a ship a day. With labor and lumber costs so cheap compared to those in England, American-made ships flooded and dominated the market.

For the early colonists, the sea brought news from home, fresh legions of colonists to do battle with the wilderness, and ships in the Triangular Trade among ports in Africa, New England and the Caribbean. The vast virgin forests of colonial Maine seemed an

land's livelihood, the "Sacred Cod" — a stuffed fish mounted on a board — was enshrined in the Massachusetts Colony House. It is still there today, hanging in the House Chamber of the State House on Beacon Hill.

The Whaling Industry

The lamps of colonial New England were fired by vegetable and animal oils. Candles were made from animal tallow. The light was dim and the lamps were smoky until someone made a fortuitous discovery: the

inexhaustible storehouse of straight, lofty white pines for the masts of the Royal Navy. The fishing grounds along the coasts teemed with marine wealth.

One of the first important acts of the Great and General Court of Massachusetts over 250 years ago was to set standards for the regulation and encouragement of the fishing industry. Early on, fishing was seen as a prime source of the region's prosperity. In fact, many settlers came not so much to enjoy religious freedom as to catch fish. Codfish, high in protein, iodine and Vitamin A, nourished and strengthened not just the New England colonists, but those in Mid-Atlantic and Southern towns and even in many ports of Europe. As the basis of New Eng-

blubber from a beached whale could be rendered, and the oil thus extracted would provide a clearer, brighter light.

Whales beached themselves frequently on the New England shores during the early colonial days, and whaling got its start as a shore activity. Teams of townsfolk gathered whenever they saw a whale, tethering the creature to a stake to prevent the tide from taking it out to sea. The blubber was cut away, rendered in the kettles of a "tryworks" set up on the beach; and transformed into a high-quality oil which could be burned in the town's lamps or traded for other goods.

The demand for this excellent oil became so great that fishermen, hoping to get rich from the sale of oil, began to pursue whales and gave birth to New England's famous whaling industry.

Whaling ships out of New Bedford, Nantucket and other ports were complete processing plants. They roamed the seas throughout the world in quest of their gigantic prey. When sighted, men in small dories pursued and harpooned the whale and then braced themselves for the "Nantucket sleighride" which followed. The hapless whale dragged the men in the dory many miles before exhausting itself. Tied up alongside the whaling ship, the whale carcass was stripped of blubber. Rendered in a tryworks right on deck, the oil was then stored in casks in the hold. Whalebone, or "baleen," was also collected, prized for use

The sea formed the path from England to America, and served as the road system from one point in America to the next. In colonial times, roads were expensive to build and maintain, and the colonies did not have the resources to establish a good system of roads. Nor did they have the need. Coastal freighters and passenger boats carried colonists and their wares from Boston to New York and Philadelphia. Every young American knows the story of Master Benjamin Franklin, a loaf of bread under each arm, arriving from Boston on the docks in Philadelphia, where he would make his fortune.

Dozens of boats out of Salem harbor headed for home with decks full of salt cod. But the enterprising captains headed south, where they unloaded their cod at Philadel-

in making stays for corsets and collars.

Until the end of the 19th Century, the sea was the world's great proven oil reserve. Whalers out of Nantucket and New Bedford pursued their mammoth quarry for months, even years, until the holds were completely filled with barrels of the oil that would fire the nation's lamps. Distinctions were even made among grades of oil. That of the sperm whale was purest and lightest, and Nantucket whalers came to specialize in the pursuit of sperm whales. For a close look at this fascinating chapter in maritime history, visit the last remaining whaler, the *Charles W. Morgan*, tied up at Mystic Seaport in Connecticut, or take a turn through the whaling museums in New Bedford or Nantucket.

phia or Annapolis and took on corn and flour, beans and barrels of pork, which could be sold at a greater profit in the home port than could codfish. New England never produced such goods in sufficient quantities. Cod she had in abundance.

Coastal Connections

Though a boon to New England's maritime economy, the coastal trade, like fishing and whaling, was not an easy way to make a living. Every trip between Boston

New Englanders continue their love affair with the water at the "Whatever Race," an annual affair on the Kennebec River at Gardiner, Maine.

and ports to the south involved a voyage around Cape Cod, and the weather which had so discouraged the Pilgrims was a constant threat. Ships and men were regularly lost to the ravages of the sea.

Though fishing and the coastal trade helped New England employ its people and pay its bills, the region was not a rich one. Because New England always imported more goods than it exported, ways had to be found to balance the trade deficit. New endeavors were always welcomed, and Yankee ingenuity was always coming up with new ideas.

Merchants and sea captains from New England towns saw themselves as the world's transport agents: if they couldn't produce the goods from their rocky soil and primitive industries, at least they could carry the goods produced by others. Like the whalers that roamed the world for years in search of their fortune, New England merchant vessels undertook long and arduous voyages to Europe, Africa and the Orient. And not just the cargoes were put up for sale: the ships themselves were frequently on the auctioning block, bringing added revenue to their builders back home in New England.

Trade was good to New England. While the pioneer towns of inland America were primitive and rough, New England seaports took on the polish of wealth and culture. Fortunes made at sea were translated into fine mansions and patronage of the arts. From the profits of their voyages, captains brought home art treasures, luxury goods and curiosities from China, Zanzibar, Indonesia and the Turkish empire. The Peabody Museum of Salem is filled with the incredible wealth that came to New England on returning merchant ships.

Clocks, Shoes and Ice

As time went by, the new republic developed industries that produced goods for trade. Connecticut's household utensils, machines, clocks, pistols and rifles, plus shoes and cloth from Rhode Island and Massachusetts, ultimately made their way around the world.

Perhaps the most ingenious export of all was ice. Cut from freshwater ponds, rivers and lakes, ice was packed in sawdust, loaded into fast clipper ships and sent off to Cuba, South America and beyond. The rulers of the British Raj in India sipped drinks cooled by ice from New England ponds! In exchange for a commodity that was free for the cutting, New Englanders brought back

spices, fine porcelain, silks and other items.

The volume of New England's trade soon fell behind that of the Southern ports on the coasts of the Atlantic and the Gulf of Mexico. But trade continued to be important in maintaining the region's economy and its cosmopolitan outlook.

The Taming of the Sea

The end of the 19th Century saw profound changes in the way New Englanders put to sea. The speedy sloops, or clipper ships, with small holds, were economical only for high-profit items (such as ice). For a while, the profits shifted to larger, heavier craft such as the great schooners with four, five and even six masts. But the magnificent six-masted schooners that could carry huge payloads of coal went nowhere when the wind died, and the newfangled steamships went anywhere, anytime, on schedule. Steamships could sail placidly around Cape Cod, ignoring the winds that had caused so much trouble since the time of the Pilgrims.

With the coming of steam came the railroads, and maritime trade went through another great change when the Atlantic and Pacific coasts were finally connected by steel rails. Where once the ships had sailed all the way around South America to reach California, rail transport steamed West in a straight line, undaunted by storms.

Yet transport by sea, for both goods and passengers, hung on in New England well into the 20th Century. What finally laid it to rest was not the railroad but the highway — the truck and the automobile.

Safer Waves

Today, the sea is still a major source of income for New Englanders — and at a much lower price in lives lost to storms. Though yachts, motorboats and fishing fleets fill the harbors, a disaster at sea is a rarity. A century ago whole families, even most of a town, might be lost to a single ferocious storm. There are still tragedies at sea — oil tankers breached, pleasure craft wrecked, swimmers drowned — but the sea has been tamed as much as it can be. Trackless fog can be pierced by radio beacons and radar, and stricter safety precautions help prevent many an accident.

The taming of the sea has allowed New Englanders to put it to other uses. Dependable passenger service by steamship opened up the coasts to vacation travelers in the early part of this century. Newport, Block Island and Bar Harbor, difficult to reach by road or railroad, became flourishing resorts when they became accessible swiftly, comfortably and safely by sea.

But it was not just these new settlements which benefited from the taming of the sea. The whalers and clipper ships are gone, but the beautiful port towns built by the wealth of maritime commerce survive. Tourists come in droves to stroll among the handsome sea captains' houses of Nantucket, Salem, Provincetown and Newport. Having seen the houses, they explore in museums the world of the seafaring men who built them.

A Salty Playground

In other times, a New Englander either went to sea or remained a landlubber. Now

lost ships. Today, the beaches serve another purpose. Hundreds of miles of Cape Cod's sandy beaches have been set aside as the Cape Cod National Seashore, one of the great tourist attractions of New England. The beaches of Connecticut, Rhode Island, New Hampshire and Maine are booming.

The whalers that sailed out of New Bedford and Nantucket are long gone. Or are they? Boats from a dozen New England ports still head out each day in search of whales, but now it's the camera lens and not the harpoon which "captures" the whale for good. Whale-watching cruises are among the most popular summer activities at sea. It's ironic, and heartening, that the leviathans that once made New England "oil-rich" should still be helping her economy.

every New Englander is part mariner, taking a motorboat or yacht out for a Sunday cruise or climbing aboard a launch for a tour of Boston harbor. There is direct service by sea between Boston and Provincetown each summer, and Nantucket, Martha's Vineyard, Block Island and other islands are all served by ship.

In fact, New England's seacoast has become a major playground, and the variety of maritime sports seems limitless. As in so many other realms, the world of work has become the world of play, and occupations once perilous or tedious are now pursued just for fun. One hundred years ago, "wreckers" used to trudge the beaches of New England with a keen eye for the remains of

Seafood Feasts

Fishing, both commercial and amateur, is booming. Conservation and regulation maintain New England's fishing grounds and guarantee supplies for the table. The gathering of clams, mussels, oysters, scallops and lobsters is closely monitored by each town and state so that future generations may enjoy the bounty of New England's waters. Many a full-time lawyer, tailor, teacher or

Left, night lights at Maine's Bath Iron Works, one of the world's finest shipbuilding centers. Right, another mightly Bath product rolls into its maiden voyage. Following pages, sunset on Pemaquid Beach, Maine.

administrator is a part-time lobsterman or clamdigger. A heap of clamshells outside a restaurant is an echo, over the space of 400 years, of similar heaps stacked outside Indian dwellings.

Perhaps the clearest indication of the taming of the sea is this: the perilous voyage undertaken by the Pilgrims in 1620 is now done for sport. TransAtlantic yacht racing began over a century ago when the *Henrietta* raced the *Vesta* to England in 1866. In 1851, the schooner *America* won the Royal Yacht Squadron Cup, and the America's Cup became the great event of yachting with the first race held in Newport in 1870. The beauty and science of yacht design and racing is pursued passionately in Newport and in dozens of other ports along the coast.

New England's waters are particularly suited to the sport: Long Island, off the coast of Connecticut, protects spacious Long Island Sound from the dangers of the Atlantic seas; Nantucket does the same for Nantucket Sound; and Cape Cod Bay has provided calm sailing ever since the days of the Pilgrims. With the cutting of the Cape Cod Canal and the establishment of the Intracoastal Waterway, coastal cruising has been made safer and more enjoyable than ever. No more is it necessary to brave the storms off Cape Cod to travel between New York and Boston.

The highpoint of coastal cruising in New England is undoubtedly the rocky shore of Maine. The jagged coast, cut with bays, inlets, coves, peninsulas and islands, is 2,500 miles (4,000 km) long, and blessed with exceptional beauty. One of the most thrilling ways to see it is aboard a windjammer out of Camden. Since 1935, these sturdy sailing ships have taken "dude" crews out into the cold waters to share the real life of New England's maritime heritage.

New England's relationship with the sea is changing. The codfish has yielded to the computer as the most important element in New England's economic life; the schooner and whaler have yielded to the yacht and the motorboat. Over the years ahead, New Englanders will no doubt discover new ways to enjoy and profit from the sea. (Witness the recent popularity of Windsurfing.)

Facing the Future

Scientists say we have barely begun to tap the wealth of the sea, and that the potential is enormous. To explore that potential, New England has its own research facilities at Woods Hole, Massachusetts. Just south of the old town of Falmouth, Woods Hole is visited by thousands of tourists each summer. Most of them are just passing through to board the ferryboats to Martha's Vineyard and Nantucket. However, a knowledgeable few (including, in recent years, Emperor Hirohito of Japan) come specifically to visit or to work at the Woods Hole Oceanographic Institute. Established by a Rockefeller grant in 1930, the Institute carries out studies of marine life and explorations of the ocean's currents and topography of the seabed. Nearby are the Marine Biological Laboratory and the National Marine Fisheries Service. As in the past, New Englanders use the sea as their connection with the rest of the world. The work being done at these institutions deals with all the oceans, not just those off the New England coast. The Japanese Emperor, himself a noted marine scientist, paid tribute to that global work with his visit.

Whatever shape the future may take, New England will observe it across the surface of the water. News now comes by satellite, not by barque. In these days of containerized freight and supertankers, the Triangular Trade is only a memory. Ships no longer need white-pine masts, and whale-oil lamps are rarer than the whales themselves. But New England depends upon the sea as much as ever. For native New Englanders, what began as a stormy love affair is now a marriage; as in all good marriages, this one is based on closeness, dependence, affection and respect.

GUIDE IN BRIEF

Traveling to New England

By Air

Most major U.S. carriers service the New England states. However, depending upon the state and point of origin, schedules and even size of aircraft can vary considerably. While **Logan International Airport** in Boston has the greatest number of arriving and departing flights serving many domestic and international regions, other smaller regional airports may be more convenient for local areas. Principal airports include the **Bradley International Airport** near Hartford, Connecticut, and **Bangor International Airport** in Maine.

Many international airline companies serve New England. If traveling with one of those airlines that do not serve Boston, travelers can route a trip through New York where there are many connecting flights to the New England area. Visitors are advised to consult a travel agent before choosing a flight. A variety of discount fares and special deals are offered. The Eastern Shuttle from New York to Boston runs daily every hour from 7 a.m. to 9 p.m.; tickets may be purchased on board. Air New England (Tel. 800-225-3640) also links New York City with points in New Hampshire, Massachusetts, Connecticut and Vermont. Such special flights can significantly reduce a standard fare to and from the New England area.

By Land

Amtrak offers slow but efficient rail service to New England both from southern points such as Washington, D.C., and New York, routing through Connecticut; Rhode Island and terminating in Boston; and from northern points, also terminating in Boston's South Station. From here, a variety of commuter trains service smaller local towns and cities throughout New England. For information on all rail service to New England, call Amtrak's toll-free number: (800) 368-8725.

Greyhound and **Trailways** bus companies provide service to New England. Other smaller companies include **Bonanza** and **Peter Pan**. Many bus terminals, however, tend to be in "problem areas," thus necessitating caution when traveling to and from stations and when venturing from the terminals on solitary walks.

Travel Advisories

Visa Regulations

A passport, a passport-size photograph, a visitor's visa, evidence of intent to leave the United States after your visit and, depending upon your country of origin, an international vaccination certificate, are required for entry into

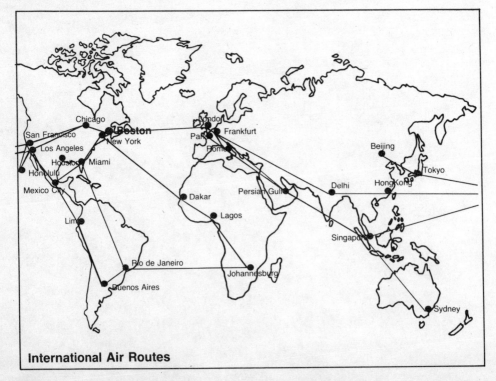

International Air Routes

the United States by foreign nationals. Vaccination certificate requirements vary, but proof of immunization against smallpox or cholera may be necessary.

Canadian and Mexican citizens, as well as British residents of Canada and Bermuda, are normally exempt from these requirements but it is always wise to check for specific regulations on international travel in your home country at time of visit.

The use of American dollars traveler's checks is advised; they can be used for payment and are easily cashed in most hotels, restaurants and stores throughout New England. More importantly however, they can be replaced if lost or stolen. Despite the small fee which is generally 1 percent of the cash value of the checks, traveler's checks are a good way to avoid unnecessary problems and complications.

Visitors to New England may encounter problems exchanging foreign currency. A large number of banks throughout New England, including **Baybanks** and **Merchant's** banks, offer foreign-exchange service, but the practice is not universal. Banks generally close by 5 p.m. on weekdays, by 1 p.m. on Saturdays and are close on Sunday.

Getting Acquainted

Climate

One of the most appealing aspects of New England is the dramatic change in seasons, not only in terms of temperature and weather conditions, but also in terms of appearance, atmosphere and recreational attractions. Autumn is perhaps the most beautiful season marked by brilliantly colored leaves of the many different types of trees which abound throughout the New England states.

Temperatures do drop severely during the winter months, sometimes as low as −25°F (−32°C), especially in the mountains in Vermont, New Hampshire and Maine. Generally, in the less extreme areas, the winters are only a little below the freezing point and are by no means unpleasant. The brisk, cold air in a small New England town, combined with a light snowfall, has a special charm and an overall exhilarating effect.

Come March, the temperature begins to rise, often reaching the upper 40s (8°C) and, the 50s and 60s (12°C and 16°C) by April. Yet, temperatures in New England are always erratic and can never be conclusively characterized; for instance in 1977, after a warm spring, it snowed in the beginning of May.

But many beautiful summer days may be expected. Whether relaxing in the mountains of Vermont on a 70-degree (21°C) day or sunning by some beautiful beach in Rhode Island in 90-degree (32°C) weather, summers are rarely oppressively hot. During the day in a few cities, it is possible to get a beautiful suntan.

Clothing

Clothing styles in New England vary from state to state, and then from region to region. Styles in New Hampshire, Maine, Vermont and the Berkshires in Massachusetts tend to be casual and geared towards outdoor life. The standard attire in most other New England cities in Massachusetts, Connecticut and Rhode Island is more traditionally oriented. Trends in clothing have affected New England as every other region in the States. It is not uncommon to see a group of young people clad in anything from the latest fashions from Italy to pseudo "punk" attire.

To be safe, one should try to bring a variety of clothing from sportswear to formal attire. For men, a jacket and tie, although not a suit, is standard dress for most nicer restaurants, while a cocktail dress or pants ensemble is acceptable in most instances for women. Some warm clothing, like sweaters and jackets, should be packed even during the summer in case of cool evening temperatures, especially in the mountain areas, where temperatures dip unexpectedly during the fall and spring. Winters necessitate heavy outerwear, including scarves, gloves and hats.

Time Zones

New England is within the Eastern Time Zone, which is one hour ahead of Chicago and three hours ahead of California. On the last Sunday in April the clock is moved ahead one hour for Daylight Savings Time, and on the last Sunday in October the clock is moved back one hour to return to Standard Time.

Without Daylight Savings Time adjustment, when it is noon in New England, it is ...

7 a.m. in Hawaii
9 a.m. in San Francisco
11 a.m. in Chicago
12 noon in New York and Montreal
5 p.m. in London
6 p.m. in Bonn, Madrid, Paris and Rome
7 p.m. in Athens and Cairo
8 p.m. in Moscow
10.30 p.m. in Bombay
12 midnight in Bangkok
1 a.m. (the next day) in Singapore and Hong Kong
2 a.m. (the next day) in Tokyo
3 a.m. (the next day) in Sydney

Weights and Measures

Given below are the U.S. equivalents of metric units:
1 inch (in) = 2.54 centimeters (cm)
1 foot (ft) = 0.305 meters (m)
1 mile = 1.609 kilometers (km)

1 square mile = 2.69 square kilometers
1 U.S. gallon = 3.785 liters
1 ounce (oz) = 28.35 grams (g)
1 pound (lb) = 0,454 kilograms (kg)

Electricity

Most wall outlets have 110-volt, 60-cycle, alternating current. If you plan to use European-made electrical appliances, be sure to step down the voltage with a transformer.

Liquor Laws

The legal age for both the purchase and the consumption of alcoholic beverages differs within the six-state region of New England; in Vermont, it is 18; in Connecticut, it's 19; and in Massachusetts, Rhode Island, Maine and New Hampshire, it's 20.

Alcoholic beverages are sold by package in state liquor stores and by drink at licensed establishments in all the six states. On Sundays, however, no package sales are allowed except by drink only at specified hours.

Again, interstate import limits differ from state to state: one gallon for Connecticut and Maine; two gallons for Vermont; three quarts into New Hampshire; while in Massachusetts, import of liquor is totally prohibited.

Public Holidays

During the holidays listed below, some or all state, local and federal agencies may be closed. Local banks and businesses may also be closed.
New Year's Day — January 1
Martin Luther King, Jr.'s Birthday — January 15
Abraham Lincoln's Birthday — February 12
Susan B. Anthony's Birthday — February 15
Easter Sunday — April 8, 1984 (first Sunday after the first full moon following the spring equinox)
Patriot's Day — April 15
Memorial Day for Veterans of All Wars — last Monday in May
Independence Day — July 4
Labor Day — first Monday in September
Columbus Day — second Monday in October
General Election Day — November 6, 1984 (first Tuesday after the first Monday in November of even-numbered years.)
Veterans Day — fourth Thursday in November
Christmas Day — December 25

In addition to these, there are certain holidays which are observed by a particular state only. For example, Rhode Islanders celebrate their **Independence Day** on May 4 and **Victory Day** on the second Monday in August; Vermont holds its **Town Meeting Day** on the first Tuesday of March and its **Bennington Battle Day** on August 16; New Hampshire's **Fast Day** falls on the fourth Monday of April; and Massachusetts' **Lafayette Day** is on May 20.

Tourist Information

Tourist information and useful literature may be obtained from the tourist board of each specific state. The following are the addresses of these boards:

Connecticut
Connecticut of Economic Development, 210 Washington Street, Hartford, CT 06106

Maine
Maine Publicity Bureau, 97 Winthrop St. Hallowell, ME 04347

Massachusetts
Massachusetts Department of Commerce and Development, Division of Tourism, 100 Cambridge Street, Boston, MA 02202

New Hampshire
New Hampshire Office of Vacation Travel, Box 856, Concord, NH 03301

Rhode Island
Rhode Island Department of Economic Development, Tourist Promotion Division, 7 Jackson Walkway, Providence, RI 02903

Vermont
Vermont Travel Division, Agency of Development and Community Affairs, 61 Elm St., Montpelier, VT 05602

State Information Centers

Besides the tourist boards, each state maintains its own information center which gives assistance to travelers trying to find their way about that respective state. Most literature and maps are available free.

Check the telephone directory for addresses and phone numbers.

Transportation

Domestic Air Travel

Several airline companies operate flights within New England. These flights, while providing a convenient mode of traveling within the area, can be expensive too. The following is only a sample of the many airlines which service the area:

Bar Harbor Airlines, Tel. (800) 343-3210, and **Delta** each has daily flights to Portland and Bangor, Maine.

U.S. Air, Tel. (800) 428-4322, flies daily to Burlington, Vermont.

Bar Harbor and **Precision Airlines** each makes it daily to Manchester, New Hampshire.

Ransom, Tel. (800) 345-4321, craft call at Providence, Rhode Island.

Pilgrim Airlines, Tel. (800) 243-0490, covers New Haven, Connecticut, and Provincetown, Massachusetts.

Boston Airlines has several commuter flights to Provincetown.

Schedules change often, so check before planning a trip.

Buses

Bus companies, like Greyhound and Trailways, operate an efficient fleet of buses which plies the network of well-paved roads in the New England area daily.

Several companies offer a variety of sightseeing tours, the specifics of which a travel agent can provide. Again, travelers should exercise caution when venturing to and from bus terminals.

In Boston, contact:

Greyhound, 10 St. James Avenue, Tel. (617) 423-5810;

Trailways, Inc., 555 Atlantic Avenue, Tel. (617) 482-6620; or

Bonanza, 10 St. James Avenue, Tel.(617) 423-5810.

Railway

For rail travel, make enquiries at **Amtrak's** toll-free number: (800) 368-8725.

Waterway

Coastal cruise ships, *Independence* and *America*, offer seven- and 10-day trips between July and October. There are trips to Newport, Nantucket, Martha's Vineyard and Block Island, along the New England coast, as well as trips from Connecticut to Maine, and up the Hudson River.

Or take the regional cruises available, such as an elegant seven-day round trip cruise around the Maine coast, departing from Rockland to visit the historic ports of Castire, Belfast, Boothbay Harbor and Wiscasset.

For more information on these cruises and a variety of others, contact **America Cruise Lines**, Haddam, CT 06438; Tel. (800) 243-6755. In Connecticut, call 345-8551 collect. Other cruise operators in most major coastal cities offer short trips and other types of cruises on New England waterways and seas. Check local literature or with a travel agent for time schedules and rates.

Taxis

Taxis are available throughout New England, although they are seen more frequently in major tourist attractions and less in smaller towns. Rates are subject to change but rides tend to be expensive for long distances.

Car Rentals

The automobile is a popular and convenient means of getting around New England. Although the bus, train and taxi service within the area is fairly reliable, an automobile proves to be the best way to negotiate a trip, especially when venturing to a remote country inn or to a winter ski lodge in the mountains.

Visitors wishing to rent or lease an automobile after arriving in New England will find offices of all U.S. firms, including Hertz (800-654-3131), Avis (800-331-1212) and Budget (800-228-9650), in most tourism centers, at most airports and in hotels.

Shop around for the best rates and features. Often, smaller local rental firms outside the airports offer less expensive and more desirable conditions than the large national companies. But be sure to check insurance coverage provisions before signing anything.

Most automobile rental agencies require drivers to be at least 21 years old (sometimes 25), and to hold a valid driver's license and a major credit card, before permitting them to drive off in any of their cars. Some will take a cash deposit, sometimes as high as $500, in lieu of a credit card. Foreign travelers may need to produce an international driver's license or a license from their own country. Liability is not included in the terms of your lease, so advertised rates usually do not include additional fees for insurance. Also check with an airline, bus or rail agent or travel agent for special package deals that provide rental cars at reduced rates.

Motoring Advisories

In general, state laws apply to the New England driver. However, each state has specific laws and special regulations regarding parking, speed limits and the like. Check with its tourism board or with the state motor-vehicle department.

New England states maintain their inter-state highway system in fine condition. Speed enforcement, at 55 miles (89 km) per hour, is quite strict throughout the state of Maine and in certain parts of Connecticut, especially between Hartford and New Haven. The other states seem more lenient, although it is always wise to be wary when driving fast. Speed limits on some highways and other roads are usually posted, ranging from 20 miles (32 km) to 55 miles (89 km) per hour.

Unless otherwise noted, a right-hand turn at a red light is permitted throughout New England. The driver, on sighting a school bus that has stopped to load or unload children, must stop his vehicle completely before reaching the bus and may not proceed until the warning signals on the school bus have been switched off or until he is directed to do so by a police officer or other authorized person on duty.

Hitchhiking is discouraged; so is picking up hitchhikers. If planning to drive, learn what areas of cities to avoid before starting out. Ask questions of your rental clerk at the airport when you arrive or check with tourist offices before taking a drive.

Accommodations

New England provides an especially diverse set of accommodation alternatives. The options vary in terms of location, price, amenities, atmosphere and orientation.

Perhaps the most uniquely New England type

of lodging is the famed **country inn**. If tired of the monotony of motels and hotels, and willing to forego certain conveniences for more simple pleasures, country inns are a wonderful option. Country inns can be stereotyped only to the degree that they provide year-round good lodging and country fare throughout the New England states. They range from weathered farmhouses with huge fireplaces and relaxing music like Connecticut's **Griswold Inn**, to the grand elegance of the **Whitleigh** in Lenox, Massachusetts, to the golf courses, shops and pools of the **Spalding Inn Club** located in Whitfield, New Hampshire. Other country inns offer many or all of these attractions, some offer even more; the common trait shared by all of them is one of high-quality service and hospitality.

Of course New England also offers the more traditional types of lodging — from **Holiday Inns** to full-service grand hotels like Boston's **Ritz-Carlton**, from numerous **roadside motels** in all of the states to low-budget **bed and breakfast inns** and **youth hostels.** See the Appendix for a listing of accommodations.

Telegrams & Telex

Western Union and International Telephone & Telegraph (ITT) will take telegram and telex messages by phone. Check the local phone directory or call local information for the toll-free numbers of their offices.

Telephones

Public telephones are generally located in hotel lobbies, restaurants, drugstores, street corners, garages, convenience stores and other general locations throughout New England. The cost of making a local call ranges from 10 to 25 cents depending on the state. Long distance call rates decrease after 5 p.m., decrease further after 11 p.m. and are lowest on weekends. Several countries can be dialed directly from many areas in New England, without operator assistance. For all specific information concerning telephone rates and conveniences, simply call the local operator "0" and inquire.

Communications

Postal Services

Post-office hours vary in central big-city branches and in smaller cities and towns. Hotel or motel personnel will answer questions about the business hours of the nearest post office. If you do not know where you will be staying in a particular town, you can receive mail simply by having it addressed to you, care of General Delivery at the main office in that town. But you must pick up such mail personally. Check with postal officials about charges and the variety of mail delivery services available.

As of mid 1984, postage rates are as follows:

letters inside the United States, or to Mexico and Canada, are 20 cents for the first ounce and 17 cents for each additional ounce;

postcards inside the United States, or to Mexico and Canada, are 13 cents;

surface letters to other foreign countries are 30 cents for the first ounce and 17 cents for each additional ounce;

airmail letters to other foreign countries are 40 cents for each half-ounce;

postcards to foreign destinations are 19 cents for surface mail and 28 cents for airmail; and

aerograms require 30 cents postage.

Stamps may also be purchased from vending machines installed in hotel lobbies, in shops and airports, and at bus and train stations.

To facilitate quick delivery within the States, always be sure to include the five-digit zip code when addressing communications. Zip code information may be obtained from post offices.

Health and Emergencies

Hospitals and Medical Services

It's not cheap to fall sick in America. Make sure you're covered by medical insurance while traveling in New England. An ambulance costs about $200; an emergency room treatment costs a minimum of $50; and an average hospital bed costs at least $300 per night. If cost is a concern, turn first to the county hospital which gives good service and will not charge patients who are indigent.

Most hospitals have 24-hour emergency rooms. You usually have a long wait before you get to see the doctor but the care and treatment is thorough and professional.

Security and Crime

Many parts of New England are best enjoyed on foot and it is generally safe to walk the streets. But as with newcomers to any place, it pays to exercise extra caution when moving about sightseeing, shopping, and so forth.

Whenever possible, travel with another person, especially in the night. Women, particularly, should avoid deserted or poor areas alone. Clutch your bag close to you; never allow it to hang loosely over your shoulder.

If not driving, lock your car and never leave luggage, cameras or other valuables in view. Lock them in the glove compartment or in the trunk. At night, park in lighted areas. And when returning to your parked car, have your car keys ready and do not start fumbling for them only when you reach the car.

Never leave your luggage unattended. While waiting for a room reservation, a cab or a rental car, always keep your property in plain view. Better still, check if you can deposit your luggage with the front desk of a hotel, restaurant or department store. Turn in your room key at the desk when going out and never leave money or valuables in your room, even it is only for a short time.

Do not carry more cash than you need. Whenever possible, use credit cards and traveler's checks and be discreet when pulling out money to pay for your purchases.

Emergencies

Telephone numbers for police, fire and ambulance in New England are as numerous as the number of cities. The best policy in case of emergency is to dial the operator "0," state the nature of the emergency, and clearly give your name and address. Another option, time permitting, is to turn to the inside front cover of a local telephone directory which lists emergency numbers. Other vital telephone numbers are generally contained on a detachable yellow page near the front.

Dining Out

"The way to a man's heart is his stomach," and New England restauranteurs seem to work by this rule of thumb with much success. Among New England's many attractions are its inns and restaurants which serve authentic home-cooked meals.

Not surprisingly, a favorite among New Englanders is seafood, available in great abundance off the coast. First, try the **fish**, fresh from the sea and prepared in varied ways. Recipes handed down from the earliest settlers are still in use and the resulting dishes continue to whet both local and foreign appetites. There are broiled, baked and fried fish; haddock, pollack, scrod, flounder, sole, trout, cod and bass. **Fish cakes**, crispy on the outside and smooth on the inside, and **fish chowders** are found almost everywhere.

Shellfish literally scooped from New England waters include **mussels, clams** and **scallops**. A regional favorite is the famous **clambake**, a dish originating with the Indians: fresh clams with corn and potatoes are covered with a layer of seaweed, which is soaked with salty sea water. This wrapped-up mixture is cooked over a charcoal fire built with rocks on a sandy beach.

Most waterfront restaurants and fast-food places serve **lobster** prepared in many ways — from **boiled lobster** served with butter, to **lobster chowder**, to **lobster salad**, to **lobster rolls**.

Those with a sweet tooth must not miss **Boston cream pie**, a cake made with custard and chocolate icing; **Indian pudding**, made with molasses, cornmeal, milk and spices; and the many kinds of fruit pies, made with pumpkin, blueberries, cran-

berries, apples or pecans. The perfect dressing for New England pancakes is golden-brown **maple syrup**. It is also perfect for ice cream and puddings and is commonly used in baking cookies, pies and cakes. Other New England delicacies include cornmeal **Johnny cake** and tasty **apple cider**.

Shopping

New England provides a greater range of offerings for shoppers than any other area in the country — large department stores which resemble those found in any urban center throughout the United States, local country auctions, antique shows, craft stores and bargain factory outlets.

Antique stores abound throughout New England and antiquing in these shops can be both fun and inexpensive. Nonetheless, it is always a good idea to keep certain guidelines in mind. If considering value, it is important to make sure that the entire piece is in its original condition and to get a *written* bill of sale which guarantees the authenticity of the item.

American handicrafts are experiencing a renaissance throughout the country and especially in New England. There are probably more handicraft items being produced now than at any time since the Industrial Revolution. Throughout New England, thousands of craftspeople thrive, having "escaped from the rat race" to make smaller, but perhaps more fulfilling incomes with their own hands. Crafts, whether pottery, weaving, scrimshaw or woodworking are usually less expensive when bought directly from the craftsman's studio, and are of a better quality when purchased from a juried crafts show where only a limited number of craftspeople are selected to exhibit their wares.

Factory outlet stores are a phenomenon which has also increased in popularity over the past few years. Many companies have come to recognize the sales potential of offering their products at discounted prices right at the mill, thereby reducing handling costs. Some outlets, such as the famous **L. L. Bean** in Freeport, Maine, which specializes in outdoor wear and gear, operate only a mail-order business in addition to their one outlet. Most outlets, however, are merely the source of brands and labels seen in retail stores. Finally, many outlets carry irregular or slightly damaged items at discounted prices. In such cases, look for the irregularity before buying to make sure the savings is worth it.

Tours and Attractions

Connecticut

Avon

Talcott Mountain Science Center, Montevideo Road.

For students interested in astronomy, meteorology, geology and chronobiology. Open all year, Monday to Saturday, 8 a.m. to 10 p.m., by appointment only; Tel: (203) 677-8571.

Bridgeport

Bridgeport-Port Jefferson Ferry, Union Square Dock, off Interstate 95 exit 27.
A cruise to Port Jefferson, Long Island; also overnight excursions. For reservations and for schedules and times of departure call (203) 367-8571.
Museum of Art, Science and Industry, Park Avenue off Route 15 exit 47.
Indian Gallery with furniture, paintings, exhibits, duPont Planetarium and a special gallery with Braille labels. For rates and opening hours, call (203) 372-3521.

Bristol

American Clock and Watch Museum, 100 Maple Street.
Large display of foreign and American clocks and watches dating from the 17th Century. Call (203) 583-6070.

Canton

Roaring Brook Nature Center, 70 Gracey Road, 1½ miles north of junction of routes 44 and 177.
Center with seasonal displays and dioramas over six miles of marked trails, field, forest and live animals. Call (203) 693-0263 for rates and opening hours.

Coventry

Nathan Hale Homestead, South Street.
Built in 1776; original furnishings and family heirlooms can still be seen. Call (203) 742-6917 or (203) 247-8996.

East Granby

Old New-Gate Prison and Copper Mine, 115 Newgate Road.
Formerly a copper mine until 1773 and then, later, the first state prison in the United States. Call (203) 653-3563.

East Haddam

East Haddam Historical Society, Route 149.
Changing exhibits on local history, costumes, accessories, photographs and country store can be seen. 50 cents donation requested. Guided tour available. Open Memorial Day weekend through Labor Day, Wednesday through Sunday 12.30 to 4.30 p.m.; after Labor Day through mid October, weekends 12.30 to 4.30 p.m.
Gillette Castle State Park, River Road off Route 82.
Estate of actor William Gillete, famed for his portrayal of Sherlock Holmes. For enthusiastic hikers and picnickers. Call (203) 526-2336.

Goodspeed Opera House, Goodspeed Landing, off Route 82.
A restored 1876 building, performances, guided tours and facilities for handicapped available. Call (203) 873-8664.

East Haven

Branford Trolley Museum, 17 River Street., off Interstate 95.
A trolley ride, a car-barn tour of an area perfect for picnicking. Call (203) 467-6927.

East Windsor

Connecticut Electric Railway Association Warehouse Point Trolley Museum, 58 North Road (Route 140).
A collection of cars from 1905 to 1947 can be viewed. Gift shop and free parking. Call (203) 668-7190.

Essex

Valley Railroad Company, Route 9 exit 3.
Trips on a vintage steam train offered from Essex to Chester; evening excursions available during season. Call (203) 767-0103 for information on departure times.

Fairfield

Connecticut Audubon Headquarters, 2325 Burr Street., off Interstate 95 exit 21.
Features a 4,000-volume naturalist library, a wildlife rehabilitation facility and a renewable energy resource room; solar energy and organic gardening demonstrations can also be seen. Call (203) 259-5606.

Falls Village

Music Moutain, Music Mountain Road, near junction of routes 63 and 126.
Concert Hall in a rural setting, with performances by the Manhattan String Quartet and guest artists. Call (203) 482-8505 for information on concert schedule.

Farmington

Hill-Stead Museum, Mountain Road off Route 10.
Works by great artists like Monet, Manet, Degas, Whistler and Cassatt; antique furniture, Chinese ceramics and Japanese prints can be viewed. Call (203) 677-4787 or (203) 677-9064.
Stanley-Whitman House, 37 High Street.
A National Historic Landmark featuring furniture, decorative objects, herb gardens and special exhibitions. Call (203) 677-9222.

Groton

Enviro-Lab, Thames Street at Croaker Submarine Memorial.
Hands-on oceanographic tour offered. Call (203) 448-1616.

Hel-Cat Fishing Parties, 181 Thames Street, off Interstate 95.

One-day deep sea fishing trips available. Call(203) 535-2066 or (203) 535-3200 for information on departure times.

Henry Whitfield Museum, Whitfield Street off Route 77 and Broad Street.

17th Century antiques, weaving equipment and a tower clock on display; also, herb garden. Call (203) 453-2457.

Haddam

American Cruise Lines, One Marine Park.

Cruise ships *America* and *Independence* have seven-day cruises to Newport, Nantucket, Martha's Vineyard and Block Island. Call (203) 345-8551 or (800) 243-6755 for information.

New England Steamboat Lines, One Marine Park.

Daily cruises to Greenport and Sag Harbor, Long Island. Also, Connecticut River excursions. Call (203) 345-4507.

Hartford

Bushnell Park Carousel, downtown Hartford.

Beautiful hand-carved carousels with brightly painted horses. Call (203) 525-1618.

Butler-McCook Homestead, 396 Main Street.

1782 home featuring 18th and 19th Century American art, toys, Japanese armor, bronzes and Egyptian crafts. Call (203) 522-1806.

Connecticut State Library and Supreme Court Building, Capitol Avenue opposite State Capitol.

State history museum housing collections of Colt firearms and library research materials. Call (203) 566-3056.

Mark Twain and Harriet Beecher Stowe Houses, 77 Forest Street, Interstate 84 exit 46.

Tour of "Nook Farm," authors' homes with original furnishings still intact. Call (203) 525-9317.

Old State House, 800 Main Street.

Another National Historic Landmark where the Constitution in the United States was written. State history exhibits, monthly exhibits by artists and craftsmen can be viewed. Outdoor concerts and farm markets are also available in season. Call (203) 522-6766.

Wadsworth Atheneum, 600 Main Street.

Paintings, sculpture, porcelain, silver, glass and furniture are displayed. Call (203) 278-2670.

Kent

Sloane-Stanley Museum, Route 7, about two miles north of Kent.

Early American tools, log cabin, ruins of Kent Iron Furnace can all be seen. Call (203) 927-3849.

Litchfield

White Memorial Foundation, off Route 202.

Camping, fishing, picnicking, canoeing; boat rental available. Also, hiking, birding and horseback riding. Exhibits, live animals, dioramas and a nature library can be found in the Conservation Center. Foundation office: (203) 567-0857. Conservation Center: (203) 567-0015.

Manchester

Lutz Children's Museum, 247 South Main Street.

Exhibits about history, science, ethnology, art, and nature, live animal exhibits. Call (203) 643-0949.

Middlefield

Lyman Orchards, routes 147 and 157.

Extensive fields of fruits and vegetables, golf course, restaurant and farm store. Call (203) 349-3673.

Moodus

Amasa Day House, on the green.

Restored 1816 home with original decorations and collections of 18th and 19th Century American furniture, pewter, ceramics, mirrors and clocks. Call (203) 873-8144.

Mystic

Denison Homestead, Pequotsepos Road off Route 27.

An 18th Century building; a colonial kitchen, Revolutionary War bedroom, Federal parlor, Civil War bedroom, early 20th Century living room. Family heirlooms also displayed. Call (203) 536-9248.

Memory Lane Doll and Toy Museum, old Mistick Village.

Vast collection of antique dolls from 1700 to the present are featured; also, a completely furnished 19th Century farmhouse. Call (203) 536-3450.

Mystic Marinelife Aquarium, Interstate 95 exit 90.

2000 specimens of undersea life, training sessions of dolphins, sea lions and the only whales in captivity in New England. Call (203) 563-3323.

Mystic Seaport Museum, exit 90 off Interstate 95.

A maritime museum featuring a 19th Century whaling village with carefully preserved buildings and ships. Also, steamboat rides, craft demonstrations, whaling talks and planetarium shows can be enjoyed. Call (203) 572-0711.

Old Mistick Village, Interstate 95 exit 90.

A shopping village. Call (203) 536-4941.

New Britain

New Britain Museum of American Art, 56 Lexington Street, off Interstate 84 exit 35.

Collections of American art, sculpture, graphics and illustrations as well as changing exhibits. Call (203) 229-0257.

New Haven

Beinecke Rare Book Library, Yale Campus.
Collections of rare books and manuscripts housed here. Call (203) 436-8438.

Creative Arts Workshop, 80 Audubon Street.
An art school with an exhibit gallery. Call (203) 562-4927.

Long Wharf Theatre, 222 Sargent Drive, exit 46 off Interstate 95.
A major American regional theater. Call (203) 787-4282 for information on admission charges and schedule of shows.

Yale Center for British Art, 1080 Chapel Street.
Museum featuring British art, culture and literature. Exhibits of paintings, drawings, prints, rare books and sculpture are also displayed. Call (203) 432-4594.

Yale Repertory Theater, 222 York Street.
A professional theater presenting nine shows annually. Call (203) 436-1600 for information on schedule of the performances and admission prices.

Yale's Peabody Museum of Natural History, 170 Whitney Avenue, off Interstate 91 exit 3.
Collection of fossils including dinosaurs, the 110-foot *Age of Reptiles* mural, invertebrates, birds of Connecticut and North American habitat groups. Call (203) 436-0850.

Yale University Art Gallery, 1111 Chapel Street, off Interstate 95 exit 47.
An old art museum with collections of paintings of the Revolutionary War period, African art, Near and Far Eastern art and decorative arts. Also featured are paintings, prints, drawings and photographs. Call (203)436-0574.

Yale University Collection of Musical Instruments, 15 Hillhouse Avenue.
Vast collection of musical instruments representing Western and non-Western traditions: strings, harpsichords, guitars, lutes and woodwinds. Call (203)436-4935.

New London

Connecticut Arboretum, William Street, Connecticut College.
Features collections of native woody plants of North America; grounds available for hiking. Call (203) 447-7700.

Lyman Allyn Museum, 625 Williams Street.
Paintings, sculpture, drawings, prints, decorative arts and costumes are housed here. Call (203) 443-3433.

Monte Cristo Cottage, 325 Pequote Avenue.
Childhood home of the American dramatist Eugene O'Neill; Special exhibitions are also held. Call (203) 443-0051.

New London-Orient Point Ferry, off Interstate 95, exit 83 or 84.
A crossing to Orient Point, Long Island. Call (203) 443-5281 or (203) 443-5035 for inquiries on ticket prices and reservations.

Tale of the Whale Museum, 3 Whale Oil Row.
Whales, arts, crafts and an authentic whaleboat are displayed. Call (203) 442-8191.

Norwalk

Lockwood-Mathews Mansion Museum, 295 West Avenue, off Interstate 95.
National Historic Landmark; a Victorian mansion with octagonal rotunda housing beautiful crafts and a gift shop. Call (203) 838-1434.

Norwich

Slate Memorial Museum, Norwich Free Academy campus, 108 Crescent Street.
Displays of Greek, Roman and Renaissance casts, American art, furniture and Indian artifacts, Oriental and African art and a gun collection. Also, Converse Art Gallery. Call (203) 887-2505 ext. 218.

Ridgefield

Aldich Museum of Contemporary Art, 258 Main Street.
Exhibitions of contemporary paintings, sculpture and graphics. Call (203) 438-4519.

Riverton

Hitchcock Museum, Route 20.
Collections of antique furniture and a chair-making factory with craftsmen displaying their skills in woodwork. Call (203) 379-1003.

Rocky Hill

Dinosaur State Park, West Street off Interstate 91 exit 23.
Over 500 dinosaur tracks; nature trails with a 300-foot broadwalk. Call (203) 529-8423.

Simsbury

Massacoh Plantation-Simsbury Historical Society, 800 Hopmeadow Street.
Features six buildings representing three centuries of living in a New England town. Call (203) 658-2500.

Stamford

Stamford Museum and Nature Center, 39 Scofieldtown Road. At junction of High Ridge Road, off Merritt Parkway.
Includes nature trails, historic farm with live animals, "Farmer's Year" tool exhibition, country store and picnic facilities. Museum has an art gallery fossil and Indian exhibits, and a planetarium. Call (203) 322-1646.

Warehouse Point

Connecticut Electric Railway, 58 North Road (Route 140).
Features antique trolley and railway equipment and 1½ miles of track. Call (203) 623-7417.

Washington

American Indian Archaeological Institute Visitor Center, Route 199, off Interstate 84 exit 15

Center for the study of prehistoric man; features 12,000-year-old mastodon, Paleo-Indian artifacts, an Indian longhouse and nature trail. Call (203) 868-0518.

West Hartford

Children's Museum of Hartford, 950 Trout Brook Drive.
A natural-history museum, aquarium and a live animal center with small mammals, birds, reptiles and a planetarium. Summer Science Academy classes and live animal demonstrations available. Call (203) 236-2961.
Noah Webster Museum, 227 South Main Street, off Interstate 84 exit 41.
Home of the famous lexicographer, the museum displays changing exhibits with special educational programs. Call (203) 521-5362.

Wethersfield

Webb-Deane-Stevens Museum, 203-215 Main Street.
A three-house complex of restored 18th Century homes of Webb, Deane and Stevens; furnishings and memorabilia of the inhabitants can also be seen. Call (203) 529-0612.

Windham Center

Fruit Hill Farm, Ballamhack Road.
An apple orchard. Call (203) 423-2847.

Windsor

Brown's Harvest, 60 Rainbow Road, three miles north of Interstate 91 exit 38.
Farm offers strawberries, peas, red raspberries and pumpkins at various times of the year; wagon rides also offered. Call (203) 683-0266.
Fyler House and Wilson Museum, 96 Palisado Avenue.
17th Century house featuring period furniture, early American and Indian artifacts with historical and genealogical exhibits. Call (203) 688-3813.

Windsor Locks

Bradley Air Museum, off Route 75, west side of Bradley International Airport.
Exhibits of more than 40 different types of aircraft; also, large transports and bombers. Souvenir shop and free parking. Call (203) 623-3305.

Woodstock

Bowen House, on the Common Route 169.
19th Century structure with period furnishings, original outbuildings. Call (203) 928-4074.

Maine

Augusta

Maine State Museum, Route 201, in State House complex.

Exhibits on Maine's environment and history. Call (207) 289-2301.

Bath

Maine Maritime Museum, 963 Washington Street, off Route 1.
An 1844 church, shipbuilders' family home, shipyard and a schooner under restoration can be viewed. Call (207) 443-6311.

Boothbay

Boothbay Railway Village, Route 27.
Has narrow-gauge railroad rides; museum house displays which relate to steam railroading era: general store, firehouse and hotel. Also, an antique auto display. Call (207) 633-4727.

Boothbay Harbor

"Argo" Cruises, Pier 6, Fisherman's Wharf.
Two- and three-hour cruises, nature cruises and supper sails. Call (207) 633-5090.

Brunswick

Pejepscot Museum, 159 Maine Street.
Regional history museum. Call (207) 729-4622.

Bucksport

Allagash River Canoeing.
An eight-day camping excursion in the wilderness. Call (207) 469-7151 or (207) 326-4096.

Camden

Maine Windjammer Cruises, waterfront off Route 1.
Seven-day cruises along Maine coast on schooners; meals and linens provided. Call (207) 236-2938.
Schooner "Stephen Taber," Head of the Harbor, off Elm Street.
Seven-day cruise aboard the oldest documented ship in the United States; meals and linen provided. Call (207) 236-3520.
Windjammer "Mary Day," Camden harbor, off Atlantic Avenue.
Seven-day cruises among islands of Penobscot Bay; meals/linens provided. Call (207) 236-2750.

Cranberry Isles

Beal and Bunker, Inc., Cranberry Isles.
Ferry service for whale watching trips, narrated excursions and special charters. Call (207) 244-3575.

Freeport

Wolf Neck State Park, Wolf Neck Road, off Bow Street.
Scenic nature spot for appreciation and hiking. Call (207) 289-3821.

Kennebunkport

St. Anthony Monastery and Shrines, Beach Street.
Franciscan monastery with shrines and a gift shop. Call (207) 967-2011.
Seashore Trolley Museum, Log Cabin Road, off Route 1.
Process of how electric mass-transit vehicles are preserved and restored can be seen. 20-minute trolley ride, slide show and a picnic area are available. Call (207) 967-2712.

Mount Desert Island

Acadia National Park.
Glacier-formed landscape consisting of mountains, lakes, forest and ocean; perfect for bicycling, horseback riding, bird watching, hiking, swimming and camping. Call (207) 288-3338.

Newfield

Willowbrook at Newfield, off Route 11.
19th Century village with buildings housing period furniture, crafts, tools and carriages. Call .(207) 793-2784.

Ogunquit

Finestkind Scenic Cruises, Perkins Cove.
Narrated cruises discussing history, geology, fishing and points of interest along coast. Charters are available. Call (207) 646-9476.

Owls Head

Owls Head Transportation Museum, Knox County Airport, Route 73.
Museum housing collections of restored air and ground vehicles; also, restoration workshop. Call (207) 594-9219.

Portland

Casco Bay Lines, Custom House Wharf.
One-hour and all-day excursions available. Call (207) 774-7871.
M/S "Scotia Prince," International Ferry Terminal.
A 10-hour deluxe cruise to Yarmouth, Nova Scotia. Call (207) 775-5616.
Portland Museum of Art, Congress Square.
19th and 20th Century paintings, works on paper, art, sculpture and furniture are displayed. Call (207) 775-6148.

Rockland

American Cruise Lines, State Ferry Service Terminal.
Seven-day cruise to Castine, Belfast, Boothbay Harbor, Bath and Wiscasset; superb cuisine provided. Call (203) 345-8551 or (800) 243-6755.
Rockland-North Haven Ferry, Route 1.
A trip past picturesque Pulpit Harbor. Call (207) 594-5543.
Rockland-Vinalhaven Ferry, Route 1.

A trip to Vinalhaven; tour of the island. Call (207) 594-5543.
Schooners Isaac H. Evans and **Lewis R. French**, off Route 1.
Seven-day cruise with meals and linen provided. Call (207) 594-8007.

Rockport

Maine Windjammer Association.
Display of authentic 19th Century ships and seven-day excursions along Maine coast. Call (207) 236-4867.

Searsport

Penobscot Marine Museum, Church Street off Route 1.
Houses exhibits of marine paintings, shipbuilding tools, navigational instruments and charts, and whaling artifacts. Call (207) 548-6634.

Springfield

Maine Wilderness Canoe Basin, on Pleasant Lake.
Guided canoe trips, cabins, tent sites, swimming, fishing, hiking and berry-picking available. Call (207) 348-2339 or (207) 989-3636, ext. 631.

Wells

Wells Auto Museum, Route 1.
Display of 70 cars, antique bicycles, motorcycles and license plates. Also rides in 1911 Model T Depot Hack. Call (207) 646-9064.

West Forks

Kennebec Dories, Route 201.
Day trips on Maine's beautiful rivers. Call (802) 649-2998.

Massachusetts

Boston

Arnold Arboretum, Arborway, Jamaica Plain 02130.
Exhibits of north-temperate woody plants. Call (617) 524-1718.
Black Heritage Sites.
History of Beacon Hill's Black Community is traced here.
Boston Common.
A 48-acre park, it was formerly a pasture land and militia training ground.
Boston Tea Party Ship and Museum, Congress Street Bridge, Museum Wharf.
Boston's historic protest is recreated here. Costumed guides available and complimentary tea served. Call (617) 338-1773.
Bunker Hill Pavilion, "Whites of their Eyes," 55 Constitution Road, Charlestown.
In this theater, the Battle of Bunker Hill is recreated. Call (617) 241-7575.
Charlestown Navy Yard.
Opened in 1800, it built, repaired and supplied

the ships of the U.S. Navy. It also restores some of their ships.

Children's Museum, Museum Wharf, 300 Congress Street.
"Handson" exhibits can be seen. Call (617) 426-8855.

Copp's Hill Burying Ground.
A former cemetery, it was later used by the British as an emplacement for cannon that fired on the Americans.

Faneuil Hall.
Its lower floor used as a market, its second floor as a meeting place and the third floor houses the Ancient and Honorable Artillery Company and their museum.

The Freedom Trail.
A three-mile round trip where you can walk or take a sightseeing bus. Information concerning this trail can be obtained from the Visitor Center and the Charlestown Navy Yard.

Harvard University Museum, 24 Oxford Street, Cambridge.
Four museums are housed here: The Peabody Museum of Archaeology and Ethnology, The Museum of Comparative Zoology, The Botanical Museum and The Mineralogical, all in one building. Exhibits include pre-Colombian art to dinosaurs and rare gems. Call (617) 495-2341.

John Fitzgerald Kennedy Library, Columbia Point, Dorchester.
This new museum features information on the life and times of the late President. Call (617) 929-4523 or (617) 929-4567.

John Hancock Observatory, Copley Square.
It is New England's tallest building, providing a spectacular view. Call (617) 247-1976.

King's Chapel.
Founded in 1688, it received vestments and silver gifts from Queen Anne and King George III.

Museum of Fine Arts, 465 Huntington Avenue.
Features Chinese, Japanese, Indian, Egyptian, Greek, European and American collections, silver, period room and musical instruments. Also gallery talks, library, lectures and films. Call (617) 267-9300.

Museum of Science, Science Park.
Science Center which covers a wide range of subjects including the human body, live animals and Maya culture. Call (617) 723-2500.

Museum of Transportation, Museum Wharf, 300 Congress Street.
The history of the development of transportation from the 1600s to the present is traced here. Call (617) 426-7999.

New England Aquarium, Central Wharf.
Displays of 200 species of aquatic life like dolphins, sea lions, giant turtles, sharks and many other fish. Call (617) 742-8830.

Old Corner Bookstore.
The center of literary Boston in the 1800s.

Old North Church.
Built in 1723, it was the City's oldest standing church.

Old South Meeting House.
The largest meeting house in Boston.

Old State House.
Formerly the seat of the colonial government of Massachusetts.

Paul Revere House.
Built in 1676, it is the oldest surviving house in Boston.

Quincy Market.
Situated across Faneuil Hall, it is a newly restored shopping and dining center, and is a leading tourist attraction.

The Skywalk, 50th floor Observation Deck, Prudential Center.
It offers a panoramic view of Boston and beyond. Call (617) 3318.

Society for the Preservation of New England Antiquities, Harrison Gray Otis House, 141 Cambridge Street.
This society manages 23 historic house museums throughout New England. Call 227-3956 for further information.

State House and Archives.
Many original documents, like the Charter of the Massachusetts Bay Company and the Massachusetts Constitution of 1780 are housed here.

"Where's Boston?" Show & Exhibit, 60 State Street.
The city and people of Boston are portrayed in a historical and contemporary setting in this 200-seat theater with the aid of slides and a superb sound system.

USS Constitution Museum, Charlestown Navy Yard.
Exhibits, art and preservation galleries recreate the life aboard this great fighting ship in the 1800s.

Brewster

Cape Cod Museum of Natural History, Route 6A.
Collections of birds, mammals, aquatic life together with a natural history library and marked nature trails are all found here. Call (617) 896-3867.

Drummer Boy Museum, Route 6A.
Provides a detailed review of the American Revolution through life-sized scenes. Call (617) 896-3823.

Chatham

Monomoy National Wildlife Refuge, Morris Island Road.
Wilderness area suitable for hiking, birdwatching and fishing. Monomoy Island is accessible by boat and contains 252 bird species. Call (617) 465-5753.

Cummington

Cummington Farm, South Road, off Route 9.
Musical events and the annual Berkshire Balloonfest are held. Call (413) 634-2111.

Dalton

Crane Museum, 30 South Street.
The history of American paper making, as well as the making of paper for stocks, currency and bonds are traced here. Call (413) 684-2600.

Deerfield

Historic Deerfield, routes 5 and 10 off Interstate 91.

12 museums are housed. Call (413) 774-5581.

East Falmouth

Ashumet Holly Reservation, Ashumet Road, four miles east of Route 28 on Route 151.

Acres of American holly and other plants can be viewed. Call (617) 563-6390.

Framingham

Macomber Farm, 450 Salem End Road.

Features farm animals, computer games, picnicking; snack bar and gift shop available. Call (617) 879-5345.

Gloucester

Beauport, 70 Eastern Point Boulevard.

25 museum rooms containing American, European and oriental antiques can be viewed. Call (617) 283-0800.

Gloucester Sightseeing Cruises, Rose's Wharf, 415 Main Street.

Whale watching and evening cruises available. Call (617) 283-5110.

Holyoke

Holyoke Museum, 335 Maple Street, 2nd floor of public library.

Western paintings, Western and oriental decorative arts are all housed here. Call (413) 534-3350.

Jamaica Plain

Arnold Arboretum of Harvard University, junction routes 1 and 203.

Internationally significant collection of plant-life. Also, 1872 paintings. Call (617) 524-1718.

Lenox

Berkshire Sanctuaries, 472 West Mountain Road.

Two wildlife sanctuaries — Pleasant Valley has trails, uplands and beaver ponds; Canoe Meadows has woods, wetlands and fields. Also canoe launching sites. Call (413) 637-0320.

Lexington

Museum of Our National Heritage, 33 Marrett Road, junction Route 2A and Massachusetts Avenue.

Changing exhibits which feature American life and historic events; films, lectures and concerts are also available. Call (617) 861-6560.

Lincoln

DeCordova and Dana Museum and Park, Sandy Pond Road.

Center for visual and performing arts with changing exhibits that focus on contemporary art. Call (617) 259-8355.

Littleton

Nagog Hill farm, Nagog Hill Road.

Pick your own apples during season. Call (617) 486-3264.

Lowell

Lowell National Historic Park.

Historic Park set up to commemorate Lowell's role in the Industrial Revolution. Exhibits and presentations can be found at the visitor center. Call (617) 459-1000.

Milton

China Trade Museum, 215 Adams Street.

Features collections of Asian crafts and arts and artifacts which document America's early trade with China. Call (617) 696-1815.

Nantucket

Whaling Museum, Broad Street.

Displays from the whaling era — scrimshaw, rigged whaleboat, outfitting shops and paintings. Call (617) 228-1984.

New Bedford

New Bedford-Cuttyhunk Ferry, Pier 3.

A 1½-hour trip to a scenic island. Call (617) 992-1432.

New Bedford-Martha's Vineyard Ferry, Leonald's Wharf.

Weekend moonlight cruises available. Call (617) 997-1688 for information on departure times and rates.

New Bedford Whaling Museum, 18 Johnny Cake Hill.

Take Interstate 195 to Route 18 to downtown exit. Museum of whaling history, art and local history. Call (617) 997-0046.

Newburyport

Parker River Wildlife Refuge, Northern Boulevard, Plum Island.

A wildlife habitat with nature trails, it is an ideal spot for migratory birds. Call (617) 465-5753.

Northampton

Arcadia Nature Center and Wildlife Santuary, at Northampton-Easthampton town line off Route 10.

Vast acres of sanctuary lands for nature appreciation; nature center has a library, auditorium and a classroom. Call (413) 584-3009.

Look Memorial Park, 300 North Main Street.

Beautiful landscape; boating, swimming, tennis, miniature zoo, restaurant, picnic facilities and a children's theater are all featured here. Call (413) 584-5457.

North Andover

Merrimack Valley Textile Museum, 800 Massachusetts Avenue.
Exhibits relevant to the growth of the American textile industry are displayed. Call (617) 686-0191.

Pitttsfield

Arrowhead, 780 Holmes Road., off Route 7.
Home of author Herman Melville; houses period furnishings. Call (413) 442-1793.
Berkshire Museum, 39 South Street. (Route 7).
Early to contemporary art, sculpture, silver; rooms on animals, biology, history with live exhibits, a gift shop and a cinema. Call (413) 443-7171.
Hancock Shaker Village, Route 20, five miles west of Pittsfield.
A village museum with exhibits and restored buildings relating to Shaker communal life. Call (413) 443-0188.

Plymouth

Cape Cod Bay Cruises, Mayflower II State Pier, adjacent to Plymouth Rock.
Call (800) 242-1304; in Massachusetts (617) 747-2400 or (617) 747-2401 for information on rates and schedules.
Cranberry World Visitors Center, Water Street off Route 44.
History of cranberry and its uses, the kind of tools used, ancient and modern, are featured here. Call (617) 747-2350.
Mayflower Experience, Water Street.
History museum. For further inquiries, call (617) 746-6562.
"Mayflower II," State Pier.
A replica of the ship that brought the Pilgrims to the New World; costumed guides will answer queries. Call (617) 746-1622.
Pilgrim Hall, 75 Court Street.
Pilgrims' possessions like paintings, furniture, arms and armor are housed here. Call (617) 746-1620.
Plimoth Plantation, off Route 3 exit 4.
A re-creation of 17th Century Plymouth, with costumed residents busy harvesting and building houses. Call (617) 746-1622.
Plymouth National Wax Museum, 16 Carver Street.
Pilgrim life is depicted here. Call (617) 746-6468.

Provincetown

Dolphin Fleet, MacMillan Wharf at town center.
Features whale watching. Call (617) 487-1900 for reservations.
Schooner *Hindu*, MacMillan Wharf, off Route 6.
Sailing trips available on a replica of a 19th-Century schooner. Call (617) 487-9123.

Rockport

Rockport Art Association, 12 Main Street.
Features changing exhibits, demonstrations and lectures. Call (617) 546-6604.
Essex Institute, 132 Essex Street.
Featuring a museum with records on the history of the people of Essex, and a reference library; it also maintains some 17th-Century houses. Call (617) 744-3390.
House of the Seven Gables, 54 Turner Street.
A collection of 17th-Century houses. Call (617) 744-0991.
Peabody Museum of Salem, East India Square.
Collections on maritime history, ethnology of non-European people and the natural history of Essex are featured here. Call (617) 745-1876 or 745-9500.
Pickering Wharf, corner of Derby and Congress streets.
A seacoast village consisting of shops, museums and restaurants; cruises and deepsea fishing available. Call (617) 745-9540.
Salem Maritime National Historic Site, The Custom House, Derby Street.
Features such buildings like the Custom House, Bonded Warehouse, West India Goods Store, Derby House, Derby Wharf and Central Wharf. Call (617) 744-4323.
Salem Witch Museum, 19½ Washington Square N.
The plight of the accused girls, the trials, the jails and the hangings are all brought to life. Call (617) 744-1692.

Sandwich

Dexter Grist Mill and Old Hoxie House, Water Street, adjacent to town hall.
17th Century mill where fresh cornmeal is ground and sold daily. 17th Century Hoxie House, Cape Cod's oldest house and an example of early Colonial construction. Call (617) 888-0352.
Heritage Plantation, Grove and Pine streets.
Plantation with beautiful gardens and trails; museum with collections of antique cars, firearms, early tools, folk art, Currier and Ives collections, a working 19th Century windmill and a carousel. Call (617) 888-3300.
Sandwich Glass Museum, 129 Main Street.
Display of Sandwich glass, period manuscripts, photographs and paintings. All types of glassware are also featured. Call (617) 888-0251.

Saugus

Saugus Iron Works, 244 Central Street off Main Street.
An iron-works House, museum with artifacts and a working blacksmith shop can be viewed. Call (617) 233-0050.

South Carver

Edaville Railroad and Museum, Route 58.
A ride through cranberry bogs on steam and diesel trains; museum with works and

memorabilia relating to railroads. Call (617) 886-4526.

Sturbridge

Norman Rockwell Museum at the Old Corner House, Main Street.
An 18th Century house with a collection of Rockwell paintings; changing exhibits relating to Rockwell and American art. Call (413) 298-3822.
Old Sturbridge Village, Route 20, off Interstate 90 exit 9.
The life of a rural New England village dating from 1790 to 1840 is depicted here with 40 historical houses, craft shops, churches and so forth. Call (617) 347-3362.

Wellesley

Wellesley College Museum, Jewett Arts Center, off Route 135.
Housed here are collections of classical, medieval, Renaissance and contemporary sculpture, 15th- to 20th-Century paintings, drawings and photographs. Call (617) 235-0320, ext. 2051.

West Brewster

Sealand of Cape Cod, Route 6A.
Marine aquarium and park featuring aquatic animals like dolphins, seals and sea lions; snack bar and picnic areas also available. Call (617) 385-9252.

Williamstown

Sterling and Francine Clarke Art Institute, South Street.
Collections of paintings by great artists as well as sculpture, prints, drawings and furniture can be viewed. Call (413) 458-8109.

Woods Hole

Woods Hole-Martha's Vineyard Ferry.
A ride to the island towns of Vineyard Haven and Oak Bluffs. Call (617) 540-2022 for information on schedules and auto reservations.
Woods Hole-Nantucket Ferry.
A three-hour trip to a resort island. Call (617) 540-2022.

Worcester

American Antiquarian Society, 185 Salisbury Street, junction routes 9 and 12.
Research library. Call (617) 755-5221.
Higgins Armory Museum, 100 Barber Avenue.
Features medieval suits and Renaissance armor; weapons, tapestries and artifacts from the Stone and Bronze ages. Call (617) 853-6015.
Worcester Art Museum, 55 Salisbury Street.
Collections of art works from early to contemporary times like 17th Century Dutch paintings and American paintings. Also restaurant. Call (617) 799-4406.
Worcester Science Center, 222 Harrington Way.

A vast complex with a museum, planetarium, nature trails, outdoor live animals exhibits. Call (617) 791-9211.

New Hampshire

Alton

Piro Brothers Vineyard, Halls Hill Road, off Route 140.
Pick-your-own grapes during season; grape juice for sale also. Call (603) 875-7256.

Bartlett

Attitash Alpine Slide, Route 302.
Chairlift ride up to Attitash Mountain; then a ride down in a sled. Call (603) 374-2369.
Attitash Aquaboggan Water Slide, Route 302.
A fun ride down the mountain and then through a cascade of water. Call (603) 374-2368.

Canterbury

Shaker Village, off Route 106 or Interstate 93 exit 18.
A Shaker community consisting of six historic buildings; craft demonstrations and gift shop available. Call (603) 783-9977 or (603) 783-9077.

Center Conway

Saco Bound-Northern Waters, Route 302.
Canoe and kayak trips, with lessons and rentals available. Call (603) 447-2177.

Charlestown

Old Fort No. 4, Route 11, off Interstate 91 exit 7.
Replica of original village with 10 buildings, stockade, great hall and watch tower. Early American crafts demonstrations are available. Call (603) 826-5094.

Chesterfield

Road's End Farm, Jackson Hill Road.
Working horse farm with areas for hiking and jogging. Collection of carriages and sleighs can be seen. Call (603) 363-4703.

Concord

State House, 107 North Main Street, off Interstate 93 exit 14.
Built in 1819, it is the largest state legislature in the United States. Murals, portraits and battle flags are housed here. Call (603) 271-2154.

Conway

Passaconaway, Kancamagus Highway at junction of Downes Brooke and Swift River.
A visitor's center, with sufficient areas for camping, fishing and hiking. Call (603) 477-5448.

Cornish

Saint-Gaudens National Historic Site, Route 12A.
Home and studios of American sculptor Saint-Gaudens; historically furnished rooms, sculpture and pieces of contemporary art. Call (603) 675-2175.

Derry

Robert Frost Farm, just south of intersection 28 and by-pass 28, near Derry-Salem town line.
Visit to poet's home and barn; Frost's life is illustrated through exhibits. Call (603) 271-3556.

Dublin

Friendly Farm, Route 101.
Featuring farm animals in their natural habitat. Call (603) 563-8444.

East Andover

Halcyon Hills Vineyard, Hale Road.
A walk through the vineyards with grapes available. Call (603) 735-5221.

East Hebron

Paradise Point Nature Center, North Shore Road, off Newfound Lake. .
Forestland with trails and exhibit center. Family programs and events available. Call (603) 744-3516.

East Sullivan

Apple Hill Chamber Players, Apple Hill Road., three miles off Route 9.
A music school with a concert barn. Call (603)847-3371.

Enfield

Lockehaven Schoolhouse Museum, Lockehaven Village off Route 3.
A 19th Century schoolhouse with equipment and photographs of that age. Admission free. Open mid June through September, Sunday 2 to 5 p.m.

Franconia

Cannon Mountain Aerial Tramway, Franconia Notch, Route 3.
A short summit ride, hiking trails and a fire tower are available. Call (603) 823-5563.

Jackson (Pinkham Notch)

Wildcat Mountain Gondola Tramway, Route 16.
A round-trip ride to the mountain summit on a gondola. Call (603) 466-3326.

Jaffrey

Silver Ranch, Route 124, one mile east of village.
Features horseback riding, bayrides and sleighrides. Call (603) 532-7363.

Keene

Cheshire Airways Scenic Air Ride, Dillant-Hopkins Airport terminal.
A flight over White Mountains, Surrey and Otter dams. Call (603)352-3951.
Colony House Museum, 104 West Street, off routes 9, 10 or 101.
19th Century home of H. Colony, Keene's first mayor. Exhibits of glassware, pottery and pewter are found here. Call (603) 357-0889.
Wyman tavern, 339 Main Street.
A historic tavern which marks the point where patriots marched from in the 18th Century. Call (603) 352-1147.

Laconia

White Mountain National Forest Headquarters, 719 Main Street.
Information on the forest in New Hampshire and western Maine can be found here. Call (603) 524-6450.

Manchester

The Currier Gallery of Art, 192 Orange Street.
13th to 20 Century paintings, sculpture, pewter, glass, tapesteries and furniture can be viewed. Also featured are concerts, films, lectures and exhibits. Call (603) 669-6144.

Mason

Parker's Maple Barn, Brookline Road.
A 100-year-old barn with restaurant, gift shop and a maple syrup house. If weather permits, horse and carriage rides during weekend mornings. Call (603) 878-2308.

Merrimack

Anheuser-Busch Brewery, 1000 Daniel Webster Highway, three miles north of Nashua.
Beer-making process can be seen and product sampling is permitted. Call (603) 889-6631.

Milford

American Stage Festival, Route 13 North.
A theater featuring plays and children's shows, arts and crafts festivals too. Call (603) 673-7515.

Milton

New Hampshire Farm Museum, Route 16, Plummer's Ridge.
Demonstrations of 18th Century farming methods, tools and artifacts are featured. Call (603) 652-7840.

Mount Washington

Mount Washington Cog Railway, off Route 302.
A ride on the world's first steam-powered cog railway, with an excellent view of the surroundings. Call (603) 846-5404.

Nashua

New Hampshire Children's Museum, 14 Court Street.
Museum where a village grocery store, a house and a fire station can be viewed. Call (603) 883-1506.

North Conway

Conway Scenic Railroad, Village Park.
An antique train ride through Saco River Valley. Call (603) 356-5251.
White Mountain Airways, routes 16 and 302.
Airplane, helicopter and old open-cockpit biplane rides. Tours available. Call (603) 356-2930.

North Hampton

Fuller Gardens, 10 Willow Avenue, off Route 1A.
A formal garden with an extensive collection of plants like rose-bushes, spring-flowering bulbs, tropical and desert plants. Call (603) 964-5414.

North Woodstock

Lost River Reservation, Route 112, Kinsman Notch.
Broadwalks through natural glacial gorge; caverns, waterfall and a granite pothole can all be viewed. Nature garden and a natural history museum. Call (603) 745-8031.

Portsmouth

Guild of Strawberry Banke, 93 State Street.
The historic preservation organization headquarters; a gift shop. Call (603) 436-8032.
Moffatt-Ladd House, 154 Market Street.
Period furnishings and gardens can be seen. Call (603) 436-8221.
Strawberry Banke, Marcy Street, off Interstate 95 exit 7.
Waterfront neighborhood with buildings, exhibit rooms and craft shops. Call (603) 436-8010.
Theatre by the Sea, 125 Bow Street, off Interstate 95 exit 7.
A theater located in a restored brewery. Call (603) 431-6660 or (603) 431-5846.

Rindge

Cathedral of the Pines, Cathedral Road off Route 119.
Built in 1945 to commemorate the American war dead. Call (603) 899-3300.

Sharon

Sharon Arts Center, Route 123.
Features demonstrations, exhibits on arts and crafts, workshops. Call (603) 924-7256.

Weirs Beach

M/V "Doris E." and " M/V "Sophie C.," Weirs Beach dock, Route 3.
Excursions on Lake Winnipesaukee with commentaries given enroute. Call (603) 366-5331.
M/V "Mount Washington," Route 3, Weirs Beach dock.
A scenic cruise around Lake Winnipesaukee; moonlight dinner cruise available with band, meals and refreshments provided. Call (603) 366-5531.

Rhode Island

Newport

Preservation Society of Newport County, 118 Mill Street.
Tours of Newport mansions available. Call (401) 847-1000.
Viking Boat Tours, Goat Island Marina, off Washington Street
A scenic cruise of Newport harbor and Narrangansett Bay with narration. Call (401) 847-6921.

Pawtucket

Slater Mill Historic Site, Roosevelt Avenue, off Interstate 95.
Museum of history and technology featuring working textile machinery and handcrafts demonstration. Call (401) 725-8638.

Providence

Museum of Art, 224 Benefit Street at Rhode Island School of Design, off Interstate 95.
Art, French and American paintings, American Indian and pre-Columbian artifacts are featured. Call (401) 331-3511.
Roger Williams Park Zoo, Roger Williams Park.
Nature center, farmyard, tropical American exhibits and polar bear exhibits. Call 467-9013.

Warren

American Canadian Line, 461 Water Street, Blount Marine Gate 4.
Three-day cruises through Long Island Sound, up the Hudson River to Erie Canal. Call (800) 556-7450.

Vermont

Bellows Falls

Allen Brothers, Interstate 91 exit 5.
Sweet corn, strawberries, apple cider, cheese, maple syrup and breads and pies from the farm bakery are available. Call (802) 722-3395.

Steamtown Foundation, Route 5.
Railroad museum; rides on a steam-powered train offered. Call (802) 463-3937.

Bennington

Bennington Battle Monument, 15 Monument Circle, off Route 9.
A stone monolith built in 1891 commemorates the Revolutionary War Battle of Bennington.

Brattleboro

Brattleboro Museum and Art Center, Main Street at Vernon Road, off Interstate 91 exit 1.
Features exhibits on regional history and arts. Call (802) 257-0124.

Burlington

Burlington-Port Kent Ferry, off Interstate 89 exit 14W.
A crossing to Port Kent, New York. Call (802) 864-9804.
Champlain Shakespeare Festival, Royall Tyler Theatre, University of Vermont campus.
Shakespeare's plays are performed here. Call (802) 656-2094 for information on rates and schedules.
Robert Hull Fleming Museum, University of Vermont campus.
Collection of art, sculpture, paintings, prints, artifacts and costumes. Call (802) 656-2090.

Center Rutland

Wilson Castle, West Proctor Road, off Route 4.
A 19th Century building with beautiful furnishings. Call (802) 773-3284.

Charlotte

Charlotte-Essex Ferry, Route F-5 off Route 7.
A crossing to Essex, New York. Call (802) 864-9804.

East Arlington

Equinox Sky Line Drive, Route 7, about four miles south of Manchester.
A sightseeing drive to the summit of Mount Equinox. Call (802) 362-1115.

East Hubbardton

Hubbardton Battlefield, East Hubbardton Road.
The only Revolutionary War battle in Vermont was fought here. Call (802) 828-3226.

East Rutland

Norman Rockwell Museum, Route 4, just past mall.
A large collection of the artist's works with a gift shop. Call (802) 773-6095.

Essex Junction

Discovery Museum, 51 Park Street (Route 2A), three miles north of Interstate 89 exit 12.
Children's museum with exhibits on natural and physical science, history and art. Live animals with a park, nature area and picnic facilities. Call (802) 878-8687.

Glover

Bread and Puppet Museum, Route 122 off Interstate 91 exit 24.
Vast collections of masks and puppets. Call (802) 525-3031.

Grafton

Bike Vermont, with various starting points in Vermont.
Guided five-day and weekend as well as overnight bicycle touring trips. Call (802) 843-2259.

Grand Isle

Grand Isle-Plattsburgh Ferry, off Interstate 89 exit 17.
A crossing to Plattsburgh, New York. Call (802) 864-9804.

Graniteville

Rock of Ages Quarries, off Route 14.
A tour of the working granite quarries and finishing plant. Call (802) 476-3115.

Healdville

Crowley Cheese Factory, Route 103.
Oldest cheese factory in Vermont featuring old time cheese-making. Call (802) 259-2340.

Jay

Aerial Tramway Rides, Jay Peak Ski Area, Route 242.
Scenic tram rides with views of Vermont, New York, New Hampshire and Canada. Call (802) 988-2611.

Killington

Killington Gondola, junction routes 4 and 100.
A round-trip ride to the summit. Call (802) 422-3333.
Killington Nature Trail, top of Killington Road, five miles from junction of routes 4 and 100 north.
A walking trail around summit of Killington Mountain. Call (802) 422-3333.

Ludlow

Black River Academy Museum, High Street.
Exhibits on crafts, agriculture and geology, regional history; also featured are American furniture, a 1900 schoolroom and a library room. Call (802) 228-5050.

Manchester

Hildene, Route 7.
Estate of Robert Todd Lincoln; original furnishings with family memorabilia. Call (802) 362-1788.

Middlebury

University of Vermont Morgan Horse Farm, just off Route 23.
Breeding, training and showing center for horses; park and picnic area. Call (802) 388-2011.
Vermont State Craft Center, Frog Hollow Area, near Mill Street.
Crafts like pottery, glass, fiber can be seen. Also, classes, workshops and demonstrations are available. Call (802) 388-3177.

North Bennington

Park-McCullough House, Park and West streets, off Route 67A.
A 19th Century mansion with Victorian exterior and garden. Call (802) 422-2747.

Pittsford

New England Maple Museum, Route 7.
Collection of sugaring artifacts with slide show demonstrating how sap is made into sugar. Call (802) 483-9414.

Plymouth

Plymouth Cheese Corporation, off Route 100A.
Cheese factory with sales room. Call (802) 672-3650.

Saint Johnsbury

St. Johnsbury Athenaeum, 30 Main Street at junction of routes 2 and 5.
Library and an art gallery with a collection of 100 works of art. Call (802) 748-8291.

Shelburne

Shelburne Museum, Route 7.
35 historic buildings where collections of toys, textiles, folk art, ceramics and furniture can be viewed. Also, a side-wheel steamer and a railroad train; Webb Gallery with paintings by great artists. Call (802) 985-3346.

Shoreham

Shoreham-Ticonderoga Ferry, Shorewell Ferries dock.
A crossing of Lake Champlain. Call (802) 897-7999.

Stowe

Bloody Brook School House, School Street.
Fully equipped one-room schoolhouse. Call (802) 253-7227.
Mount Mansfield Gondola, off Route 108 on Mount Mansfield.
An enclosed ride to the summit of Mount Mansfield. Call (802) 253-7311, ext. 288.
Stowe Alpine Slide, off Route 108 at Spruce Peak.
A double chair ride to the top of the slide, and then a sled ride down. Call (802) 253-7311, ext. 288.

Waterbury Center

Vermont County Cyclers.
Guided five-day, weekend and overnight bicycle touring trips in various parts of Vermont. Call (802) 244-5215.

Wilmington

Maple Grove Honey Museum, Route 100 north.
A conducted tour of maple syrup and honey packing plant; a short film on bee-keeping and honey making is shown. Call (802) 464-2913.

Woodstock

DAR House and Museum, on the green.
Museum houses a collection of local and regional artifacts.

Nightlife

New England offers a wide range of entertainment; there's something for everyone. The rural areas tend to be more slow-paced and relaxed during the evening, while Boston, among the New England cities, is the mecca of fast-paced, exciting nightlife.

Boston outgrew its staid image long ago. At night, the city sparkles with lively and sophisticated activity. Boston has its famed symphony orchestras as well as the equally impressive Boston Pops Orchestra which offers a more informal atmosphere. There are many other musical events throughout the year including performances by the Opera Company of Boston, other opera groups and hundreds of concerts from jazz to rock 'n' roll.

Boston and the surrounding areas also host many pre-Broadway shows and performances by other drama groups; experimental theater; traditional drama; summer and dinner theaters; as well as ballets. Many singles bars discotheques and dance clubs are found throughout the area. At **Quincy Market's** many bars, young single professionals congregate; the **Metro** is a popular discotheque; and the **1270, Spit** and **Buddy's** cater to younger, often "punk," gay or unconventional people looking for a good place to go to dance and to "party." The entertainment section of a local Boston newspaper will provide more specific information about current options for after-dark entertainment.

Sports

New England offers an abundance of both spectator and recreational sports. There are a variety of professional teams in all the major sports including baseball, basketball, football, hockey and tennis. Generally, the New England states are represented by Boston's teams — the Boston Celtics in basketball (Boston Garden, September to May), the Boston Red Sox in baseball (Fenway Park, April to September) and the Boston Bruins in hockey (Boston Garden, October to March). The major exception to this rule is football (August to December); the major team is the New England Patriots who originate from Foxboro, Massachusetts (Schaeffer Stadium). For up-to-date information on schedules and locations of games, one need only refer to the sports section of any local daily newspaper.

Depending on the season, one can indulge in almost any recreational sport. From skiing in Vermont to sailing on the Charles River in Boston, New England is a haven for the outdoor sports enthusiast, regardless of ability or experience. Throughout New England, one can swim, play tennis, horseback ride, mountain or rock climb, hunt, fish, sail or play golf, just to name a few of the many possibilities. For exact information, check with the Vacation Council in any state.

Boston Athletic Club; the former Boston Tennis Club, it now has facilities for tennis, racquetball, saunas, nautilus gymnastics and spas. The club is open Monday to Friday 6:30 a.m. to 11 p.m.; Saturday and Sunday from 8 a.m. to 10 p.m. Price ranges between $6 and $16 per court hour. Reduced rates are available on weekends and between 9 a.m. to 4 p.m. from Monday to Friday. Venue: 635 Summer St. Boston 02210, Tel. (617) 269-4300.

Suffolk Downs; thoroughbred racing in East Boston daily except Tuesday. Price ranges between $2.50 to $3.50; special rates for groups of 25 and more.

Yankee Greyhound Racing, at Wonderland Dog Track, Revere; dog racing six days and nights every week until September 5. Fall racing is on Thursday, Friday and Saturday evenings from 6 p.m.

Appendix

Accommodations

In the following listing, "inexpensive" lodging is generally considered to be that costing less than $30 per night; "reasonable" $30 to $55; "moderate" $55 to $80 and "expensive" over $80 a night. This is by no means to be regarded as an exhaustive list; it merely represents some of the better accommodations available.

CONNECTICUT

Avon
Avon Old Farms Hotel, junction Routes 44 & 10, 06001, tel. (203) 667-1651. 81 units. Moderate.

Berlin
Hawthorne Motor Inn, 2387 Wilbur Cross Hwy., 06037, tel. (203) 828-4181. 70 units. Moderate.

Bethel
Stony Hill Inn (Best Western), Route 6, 06801 (I-48, Exit 8), tel. (203) 743-5533. 36 units. Moderate.

Branford
MacDonald's Motel, 565 E. Main St., 06405 (I-95, Exit 56), tel. (203) 488-4381. 14 units. Inexpensive.
Sunset Motel, 309 E. Main St., 06405 (I-95, Exit 55), tel. (203) 488-4035. 19 units. Inexpensive.

Bridgeport
Sheraton-Bridgeport Hotel, 815 Lafayette Blvd., 06603 (I-95, Exit 27), tel. (203) 366-5421. 238 units. Expensive.

Brookfield
Candlewood Inn, 506 Candlewood Lake Road, 06804 (I-84, Exit 7), tel. (203) 775-1281. 16 units. Reasonable.

Chester
The Inn at Chester, 318 W. Main St., tel. (203) 526-9541. 22 units. Moderate.

Clinton
Lamplighter Motel, 231 E. Main St., 06413 (I-95, Exit 63), tel. (203) 669-8486. 14 units. Reasonable.
The Mornings, Blaisdell Point, Box 45, 06413 (I-95, Exit 63), tel. (203) 669-8541.

Cornwall Bridge
Hitching Post Country Motel, Route 7, 06754, tel. (203) 672-6219. 11 units. Reasonable.

Danbury
Danbury Hilton Inn & Conference Center, 18 Old Ridgebury Road, 06810 (I-84, Exit 2); tel. (203) 794-0600. 240 units. Expensive.

Ethan Allen Inn, 21 Lake Ave. Extension, 06810 (I-84, Exit 4), tel. (203) 744-1776. 199 units. Moderate.

Darien
Howard Johnson's, Ledge road, 06820 (I-95, Exit 11), tel. (203) 655-3933. 72 units. Expensive.

East Hartford
Holiday Inn, 363 Roberts St., 06108 (I-84, Exit 58), tel. (203) 528-9611. 130 units. Moderate.

Howard Johnson's, 490 Main St., 06108 (I-84, Exit 56), tel. (203) 569-1100. 85 units. Reasonable.

Imperial "400" Motel, 927 Main St., 06108 (I-84, Exit 56), tel. (203) 289-7781. 48 units. Inexpensive.

Madison Motor Inn, 393 Main St., 06118 (I-84, Exit 55), tel. (203) 568-3560. 60 units. Reasonable.

Ramada Inn, 100 E. River Dr., 06108 (I-84, Exit 53), tel. (203) 528-9703. 215 units. Expensive.

East Haven
Hostways Motel, 30 Frontage Road, 06512 (I-95, Exit 51), tel. (203) 469-5321. 59 units. Expensive.

Enfield
Harley Hotel, 1 Bright Meadow Blvd., 06082 (I-91, Exit 49), tel. (203) 741-2211 189 units. Expensive.

Essex
Griswold Inn (country inn), tel. (203) 767-0991. 19 units. Reasonable.

Fairfield
Fairfield Motor Inn, 417 Post Road, 06430 (I-95, Exit 22), tel. (203) 255-0491. 80 units. Expensive.

Merritt Parkway Motor Inn, 4180 Black Rock Turnpike, 06430 (Route 15, Exit 44E/45W), tel. (203) 259-5264. 42 units. Moderate.

Greenwich
Sheraton Motor Inn, 1114 Post Road, 06878 (I-95, Exit 5), tel. (203) 637-3691. 105 units. Expensive.

Showboat Inn, 500 Steamboat Road, 06830 (I-95, Exit 3), tel. (203) 661-9800. 105 units. Expensive.

Groton
Quality Inn, 404 Bridge St., 06340 (I-95, Exit 85N/87S), tel. (203) 445-8141. 98 units. Moderate.

Windsor Motel, 345 Gold Star Hwy. (I-95, Exit 86), tel. (203) 445-7474. 43 units. Reasonable.

Hartford
Governor's House Hotel, 440 Asylum St., 06103 (I-95, Exit 48W/47E), tel. (203) 246-6591. 96 units. Reasonable.

Holiday Inn, 50 Morgan St., 06120 (I-84, Exit 52; I-91, Exit 32), tel. (203) 549-2400. 359 units. Expensive.

Howard Johnson's, 7 Weston St., 06120 (I-91, Exit 33), tel. (203) 525-4441. 80 units. Moderate.

Koala Inn, 207 Brainard Road, 06114 (I-91, Exit 27), tel. (203) 249-5811. 70 units. Reasonable.

Parkview Hilton Hotel, 10 Ford St., 06103 (I-84, High Street Exit), tel. (203) 249-5611. 410 units. Expensive.

Sheraton-Hartford, 315 Trumbull St., 06103 (I-84, Main Street Exit W/Trumbull Street Exit E), tel. (203) 728-5151. 402 units. Expensive.

Summit Hotel, 5 Constitution Plaza, 06103 (I-91, Exit 31), tel. (203) 278-2000. 300 units. Expensive.

Milford
Best Western, 1015 Boston Post Road, 06460 (I-95, Exit 39A), tel. (203) 878-3575. 50 units. Reasonable.

Connecticut Turnpike Motel, 1083 Post Road, 06460, tel. (203) 874-3216. 14 units. Reasonable.

Holiday Inn, 1212 Boston Post Road, 06460 (I-95, Exit 39B), tel. (203) 878-6561. 107 units. Moderate.

Howard Johnson's, 1052 Post Road, 06460 (I-95, Exit 39A), tel. (203) 878-4611. 118 units. Moderate.

Inn on the Parkway, Wheelers Farms Road, 06460 (Route 15, Exit 55), tel. (203) 878-3521. 65 units. Moderate.

Mayflower Motel, 219 Woodmont Road, 06460 (I-95, Exit 40), tel. (203) 878-6854. 64 units. Moderate.

Mystic
Days Inn, Route 27, 06355 (I-95, Exit 90), tel. (800) 241-7200. 122 units. Moderate.

Harbour Guest House, Edgemont Street, 06355 (I-95, Exit 90), tel. (203) 572-9253. 5 units. Reasonable.

The Inn at Mystic, junction routes 1 and 27, tel. (203) 536-9604. 68 units. Moderate.

Whaler's Inne, 20 E. Main St., tel. (203) 536-1506, (800) 243-2588. 39 units. Moderate.

New Britain
Holiday Inn, 65 Columbus Blvd., 06051 (I-84, Exit 35), tel. (203) 244-9161. 120 units. Moderate.

New Canaan
The Roger Sherman Inn (country inn), tel. (203) 966-4541. 12 units. Reasonable. Closed Sundays.

New Haven
Colony Inn, 1157 Chapel St., 06511 (I-91 or I-95, Downtown Exit), tel. (203) 766-1234. 87 units. Expensive.

Holiday Inn at Yale, 30 Whalley Ave., 06511 (I-95, Exit 47; I-91, Exit 1), tel. (203) 777-6221. Expensive.

Howard Johnson's Long Wharf, 400 Sargent Dr., 06525 (Route 15, Exit 59), tel. (203) 387-6651. 123 units. Reasonable.

Park Plaza Hotel, 155 Temple St., 06510 (I-91, Exit 1; I-95, Exit 47), tel. (203) 772-1700. 300 units. Expensive.

New London

Colman Lodge, 14 Colman St., 06320 (I-95, Colman Street Exit), tel. (203) 443-1723. 25 units. Moderate.

Holiday Inn (I-95, Colman Street Exit N/ Frontage Road Exit S), 06320, tel. (203) 442-0631. 100 units. Moderate.

New Preston

The Hopkins Inn on Lake Waramaug (country inn), tel (203) 868-7295. 9 units. Reasonable. Inn open May to November,· restaurant open March through December.

Norwalk

Golden Crest Motor Inn, 596 Westport Ave., 06851 (I-95, Exit 16N/17S), tel. (203) 847-3833. 56 units. Reasonable.

Holiday Inn, 789 Connecticut Ave., 06854 (I-95, Exit 13), tel. (203) 853-3477. 267 units. Expensive.

Norwich

Sheraton Inn-Norwich, 179 Salem Turnpike, 06360 (Route 52, Exit 80), tel. (203) 889-5201 oɾ (800) 325-3535. 129 units. Expensive.

Old Lyme

Bee and Thistle Inn (country inn), tel. (203) 434-1667. 10 units. Moderate.

Old Saybrook

Admiral House Motor Inn, Spencer Plains road,, 06475 (I-95, Exit 66), tel. (203) 399-6273. 37 units. Expensive.

Heritage Motor Inn, 1500 Boston Post Road, 06475 (I-95, Exit 66), tel. (203) 388-3743. 15 units. Moderate.

Plainville

Holiday Inn, 400 New Britain Ave., 06062 (I-84, Exit 34), tel. (203) 747-6876. 109 units. Moderate.

Ridgefield

Stonehenge (country inn), tel. (203) 438-6511. 8 units. Moderate. Closed Tuesdays.

Salisbury

Under Mountain Inn (country inn), tel. (203) 435-0242. 7 units. Moderate. Closed in March.

Stamford

Howard Johnson's, 135 Harvard Ave., 06902 (I-95, Exit 6), tel. (203) 357-7100. 160 units. Expensive.

Le Pavillon Hotel, 60 Strawberry Hill Road, 06902 (I-95, Exit 8), tel. (203) 357-8100. 176 units. Expensive.

Merriott Hotel, 2 Stamford Forum, 06901 (I-95, Exit 8), tel. (800) 228-9290. 305 rooms. Expensive.

Stratford

Howard Johnson's, 36 Honeyspot road, tel. (203) 375-5666. 93 units. Reasonable.

Waterbury

Holiday Inn, 88 Union St., tel. (203) 575-1500. Moderate.

MAINE

Augusta

Best Western Senator Inn, 284 Western Ave., tel. (207) 622-5804. 85 units. Reasonable.

Holiday Inn (I-95, Exit U.S. 202), tel. (207) 622-6371. 128 units. Reasonable.

Susse Chalet Motor Lodge (I-95, Exit 15), tel. (207) 622-3776. 58 units. Inexpensive.

Bangor

Best Western White House, Cold Brook Road (I-95), tel. (207) 862-3737. 60 units. Reasonable.

Holiday Inn, 500 Main St., tel. (207) 947-8651. 125 units. Reasonable.

Ramada Inn, 357 Odlin Road, tel. (207) 947-6961. 118 units. Reasonable.

Susse Chalet Motor Lodge, 1100 Hammond St., tel. (207) 947-6921. 60 units. Reasonable.

Bar Harbor

Atlantic Oakes, Eden Street, 04609, tel. (207) 266-5218. 84 units. Moderate.

Bar Harbor Motor Inn, Newport Drive, 04609, tel. (207) 288-3351. 74 units. Expensive.

Golden Anchor Inn, Granite Point, 04609, tel. (207) 288-5033. 75 units. Moderate.

Villager Motel, Box 43, 207 Main St., 04609, tel. (207) 288-3211. 63 units.

Wonder View Motor Lodge, Eden Street, 04609, tel. (207) 288-3358. 87 units. Moderate.

Boothbay Harbor

Brown Brothers, Atlantic Avenue, 04583, tel. (207) 633-5440. 46 units. Moderate.

Fisherman's Wharf Inn and Motel, 42 Commercial St., 04538, tel. (207) 633-5090. 54 units. Moderate.

Pines Motel, Sunset Road, 04538, tel. (207) 633-4555. 29 units. Reasonable.

Rocktide Motor Inn, 45 Atlantic Ave., 04538, tel. (207) 633-4455. 52 units. Reasonable.

Blue Hill

Blue Hill Inn (country inn), tel. (207) 374-2844. 9 units. Reasonable.

Brunswick

Holiday Inn, Cooks Corner, 04011, tel. (207) 729-5555. 141 units. Moderate.

Siesta Motel, 130 Pleasant St., 04011, tel. (207) 729-3364. 37 units. Reasonable.

Center Lovell

Center Lovell Inn (country inn), tel. (207) 927-1575. 5 units. Expensive. Closed March 15 to May 15 and Oct. 15 to Dec. 15.

Cornish

The Carriage Inn (country inn), tel. (207) 625-4042. 4 units. Reasonable.

Dennysville
Lincoln House Country Inn, tel. (207) 726-3953. 6 units. Reasonable. Restaurant closed Mondays.

Kennebunk
The Kennebunk Inn (country Inn), tel. (207) 985-3351. 35 units. Inexpensive.

Village Cove Inn (country inn), tel. (207) 967-3993. 34 units. Moderate.

Kennebunkport
Austin's Sun Town Hotel, Dock Square, 04046, tel. (207) 967-4241. 10 units. Reasonable.

Captain Lord Mansion, Box 527, Pleasant and Green streets, 04046, tel. (207) 967-3141. 16 units. Reasonable.

The Colony, Box 511, Ocean Avenue, 04046, tel. (207) 967-3331. 139 units. Expensive.

White Barn Inn (country inn), Beach Street, tel. (207) 967-2321. 26 units. Reasonable. Open March through December.

The Yachtsman Motel, Ocean Avenue, 04046, tel. (207) 967-2511. 30 units. Reasonable.

Kingfield
Winter's Inn (country inn), tel. (207) 265-5421. 12 units. Moderate. Dining room only closed May and June, plus first three weeks of November.

Newcastle
The Newcastle Inn (country inn), tel. (207) 563-5685. 20 units. Reasonable.

New Harbor
Gosnold Arms (country inn), Northside Road, tel. (207) 677-3727. 25 units. Reasonable. Open mid-June to mid-September.

Ogunquit
The Cliff House Resort, Bald Head Cliff, off Route 1, tel. (207) 646-5124. 105 units. Reasonable.

Colonial Village Resort, Box 836, 03907, tel. (207) 646-2794. 51 units. Reasonable.

The Lemon Tree, 50 Shore Road, 03907, tel. (207) 646-7070. 21 units. Moderate.

The Old Village Inn (country inn), tel. (207) 646-7088. 6 units. Reasonable. Closed January and February. Dining room closed Mondays in winter.

Norseman Motor Inn, Black Street, 03907, tel. (207) 646-7024. 95 units. Moderate.

Sparhawk Resort Motel, Shore Road, 03907, tel. (207) 646-5562. 52 units. Moderate.

Old Orchard Beach
Carolina Motel, Roussin Street, 04064, tel. (207) 934-4476. 34 units. Moderate.

Royal Anchor Motor Lodge, Box 6E, Grand Avenue, 04064, tel. (207) 934-4521. 40 units. Moderate.

Gull Motel, 89 W. Grand Ave., 04064, tel. (207) 934-4321. 21 units. Reasonable.

Portland
Best Western Executive Inn, 645 Congress St., tel. (207) 773-8181. 120 units. Moderate.

Holiday Inn West, 81 Riverside St., 04103, tel. (207) 774-2601. 206 units. Moderate.

South Portland
Best Western Merry Manor Inn, 700 Main St., 04106, tel. (207) 774-6151. 100 units. Moderate.

Sheraton Inn, 363 Maine Mall Road, 04106, tel. (207) 775-6161. 124 units. Moderate.

MASSACHUSETTS

Andover
Andover Inn (country inn), tel. (617) 475-5903. 33 units. Reasonable. Closed last two weeks of August.

Sheraton Rolling Green Inn and Conference Center, 311 Lowell St., 01810, tel. (617) 475-5400, (800) 325-3525. 182 units. Moderate.

Auburn
Sheraton Yankee Drummer, 624 Southbridge St., 01501, tel. (617) 832-3221, (800) 325-3535. 102 units. Reasonable.

Bass River
Blue Water Resort, South Shore Drive, 02664, tel. (617) 398-2288.

Cap'n Gladcliff Motel, Route 28, Box 116, 02664, tel. (617) 394-9828. 30 units.

Cavalier Motor Lodge and Cottages, Route 28, 02664, tel. (617) 394-6575. Moderate.

The Dunes Motel, 170 Sea View Ave., 02664, tel. (617) 398-3062. Reasonable.

Ocean Mist Motor Lodge, South Shore Drive, 02664, tel. (617) 398-2633. 42 units.

Red Jacket Beach Motor Inn, South Shore Drive, 02664, tel. (617) 398-6941. 150 units.

Shore Side Apartments, South Shore Drive, P.O. Box 62, 02664, tel. (617) 398-6971.

The Surfcomber, South Shore Drive, tel. (617) 398-9228. 33 units. Moderate.

Village Green Motel, South Shore Drive, Box 39, tel. (617) 398-2167. 46 units. Reasonable.

The Windjammer, 192 S. Shore Dr., 02664, tel. (617) 398-2370. 50 units.

Becket
Bonny Rigg Motel, Route 20, 01011, tel. (413) 623-5314. 12 units.

Long House (bed and breakfast), High Street, tel. (413) 623-8360. 4 units.

The Maples Inn, Route 20, tel. (413) 623-5353. 7 units.

Bedford
Stouffer's Bedford Glen, 44 Middlesex Turnpike, 01730, tel. (617) 275-5500. 286 units. Expensive.

Boston
Back Bay Hilton Hotel, Dalton and Belvedere streets, 02115, tel. (617) 236-1100. 367 units. Expensive.

Beacon Inns, 248 Newbury St., 02116, tel. (617) 266-7142. 250 units. Inexpensive.

Berkeley Residence Club, 40 Berkeley St., 02116, tel. (617) 482-8850. Women only. 212 units. Inexpensive.

The Bostonian Hotel, 4 Faneuil Hall Market-place, 02109, tel. (617) 523-3600, (800) 343-0922. 153 units. Expensive.

Boston Marriott Hotel: Long Wharf, 296 State St., 02109, tel. (617) 227-0800. 400 units. Expensive.

Boston Park Plaza Hotel, 64 Arlington St., 02117, tel. (617) 426-2000, (800) 225-2008. 1,000 units. Moderate.

Bradford Hotel, 275 Tremont St., 02116, tel. (617) 426-1400. 350 units. Reasonable.

The Colonnade Hotel, 120 Huntington Ave., 02116, tel. (617) 424-7000, (800) 223-6800. 300 units. Expensive.

Copley Plaza Hotel, 138 James Ave., 02116, tel. (617) 267-5300, (800) 225-7654. 450 units. Expensive.

Copley Square Hotel, 47 Huntington Ave., 02116, tel. (617) 536-9000, (800) 225-7062. 158 units. Reasonable.

Eliot Hotel, 370 Commonwealth Ave., 02116, tel. (617) 267-1607. 100 units. Reasonable.

57 Park Plaza Hotel: Howard Johnson, 200 Stuart St., 02116, tel. (617) 482-1800, (800) 654-2000. 350 units. Moderate.

Holiday Inn: Boston Government Center, 2 Blossom St., 02114, tel. (617) 742-7630, (800) 238-8000. 304 units. Moderate.

Howard Johnson's Kenmore Square, 575 Commonwealth Ave., 02215, tel. (617) 267-3100, (800) 654-2000. 180 units. Moderate.

Howard Johnson's Motor Lodge, Andrew Square (Southeast Expressway, Exit 16), 02125, tel. (617) 288-3030, (800) 654-2000. 100 units. Reasonable.

The Lenox Hotel, 710 Boylston St., 02116, tel. (617) 536-5300, (800) 225-7676. 225 units. Moderate.

Logan Airport Hilton, Logan International Airport, 02128, tel. (617) 569-9300. 559 units. Moderate.

Meridien Hotel, Pearl and Franklin streets, 02102, tel. (617) 451-1900, (800) 223-7385. 328 units. Expensive.

The Midtown Hotel, 220 Huntington Ave., 02115, tel. (617) 262-1000. 160 units. Moderate.

Milner Hotel, 78 Charles St. S., 02116, tel. (617) 426-6220. 70 units. Inexpensive.

The Parker House, 60 School St., 02107, tel. (800) 228-2121. 546 units. Expensive.

Ramada Inn: Boston Airport, 228 McClellan Hwy., 02128, tel. (617) 569-5250, (800) 228-2828. 209 units. Moderate.

The Ritz-Carlton Hotel, 15 Arlington St., 02117, tel. (617) 536-5700, (800) 225-2620. 263 units. Expensive.

Sheraton-Boston Hotel, Prudential Center, 39 Dalton St., 02199, tel. (617) 236-2000, (800) 325-3535. 1,400 units. Expensive.

Braintree
Sheraton Tara Hotel, 37 Forbes Road, 02184 (Route 128, Exit 68), tel. (617) 848-0600. 386 units. Moderate.

Brewster
Inn of the Golden Ox (country inn), tel. (617) 897-3111. 6 units. Inexpensive.

Brighton
Ramada Inn, 1234 Soldiers Field Road, 02135, tel. (617) 254-1234. 113 units. Moderate.

Terrace Motel, 1650 Commonwealth Ave., 02135, tel. (617) 566-6260. 73 units. Reasonable.

Brookline
Beacon Plaza, 1459 Beacon St., 02146, tel. (617) 232-6550. 41 units. Inexpensive.

Travelodge Boston at Brookline, 1200 Beacon St., 02146, tel. (617) 277-1200, (800) 255-3050. 190 units. Moderate.

Buzzards Bay
Bay Motor Inn, 223 Main St. (routes 6 and 28), 02532, tel. (617) 759-3989. Inexpensive.

Cambridge
Holiday Inn: Cambridge, 1651 Massachusetts Ave., 02138, tel. (617) 491-1000, (800) 238-8000. 135 units. Reasonable.

Howard Johnson's Motor Lodge, 777 Memorial Dr., 02139, tel. (617) 492-777, (800) 654-2000. 205 units. Moderate.

Hyatt Regency Cambridge Hotel, 575 Memorial Dr., 02139, tel. (617) 492-1234, (800) 228-9000. 478 units. Expensive.

Sheraton Commander Hotel, 16 Garden St., 02138, tel. (617) 547-4800, (800) 325-3525. 175 units. Moderate.

Hotel Sonesta, 5 Cambridge Parkway, 02142, tel. (617) 491-3600, (800) 343-7170. 196 units. Moderate.

Chatham
Bow Roof House, 59 Queen Anne Road, 02633, tel. (617) 945-1346.

Captain's House Inn, 371 Old Harbor Road, 02633, tel. (617) 945-0127.

Chatham Bars Inn and Non-Housekeeping Cottages, 02633, tel. (617) 945-0096. Expensive.

Cranberry Inn at Chatham, 359 Main St., 02633, tel. (617) 945-9232.

Queen Anne Inn, 70 Queen Anne road, 02633, tel. (617) 945-0394.

Surfside Motor Inn, Holway Street, 02633, tel. (617) 945-9757.

Town House Inn and Lodge, 11 Library Lane, 02633, tel. (617) 945-2180. 20 units.

Cheshire
Hoosac Lakefront Homes, Hoosac Lake (Cheshire) and Pontoosuc Lake (Lanesboro), tel. (413) 620-7075.

Lewis II, Willow Lane, 01225, tel. (413) 743-0464. 2 units.

Concord
Colonial Inn, 48 Monument Square, 01742, tel. (617) 369-9200. 60 units. Moderate.

Cohasset
Kimballs Motor Inn, 124 Elm St., 02025, tel. (617) 383-6650. 60 units. Moderate.

Dalton
The Dalton House, 955 Main St., tel. (413) 684-3854.

313

Mid-Town Motel, Main Street, routes 8 and 9, tel. (413) 684-0860.

Danvers

Best Western Inn on the Pike, 50 Dayton St., 01923, tel. (617) 777-1700, (800) 528-1234. 125 units. Reasonable.

King's Grant Inn, Route 128, 01923, tel. (617) 774-6800, (800) 228-5151. 125 units. Reasonable.

Radisson Ferncroft Hotel and Country Club, Ferncroft Village, 01923, tel. (617) 777-2500, (800) 228-9822. 300 units. Moderate.

Dennisport

"By the Sea" Guests, Chase Avenue and Inman Road, 02639, tel. (617) 398-8685. Reasonable.

Innisfree of Dennisport, 32 Inman Road, 02639, tel. (617) 394-6041 or (617) 394-5356. Moderate.

Edgartown

The Charlotte Inn (country inn), tel. (617) 627-4751. 18 units. Inexpensive.

Falmouth

Best Western Admiralty, Route 28, Box 606, 02540, tel. (617) 548-4240, (800 352-7153.

Cape Colony Motor Lodge, Surf Drive, Box 609, 02540, tel. (617) 548-3975.

The Capewind, Maravista Avenue Exit (Route 28), Teaticket, tel. (617) 548-3400. Moderate.

Carleton Circle Motel, Sandwich Road, Box 54, 02541, tel. (617) 548-0025. Reasonable.

Falmouth Heights Motor Lodge, 146 Falmouth Heights Road, tel. (617) 548-3623. Moderate.

Falmouth Marina Motel, Robbins Road, 02540, tel. (617) 548-4300. 39 units. Moderate.

Great Bay Motel, Route 28, Teaticket (half-mile east of Falmouth Mall), tel. (617) 548-5410. 23 units. Reasonable.

Mostly Hall Bed-and-breakfast Inn, 27 Main St., 02540, tel. (617) 548-3786. Reasonable.

Sea Crest Hotel and Motor Inn, Old Silver Beach, North Falmouth, tel. (617) 548-3850. Expensive.

Sheraton Falmouth, 291 Jones Road, 02540, tel. (617) 540-2000, (800) 325-3535. 98 units. Expensive.

Town and Beach Motel, 382 Main St., 02540, tel. (617) 548-1380. Reasonable.

The Trade Winds, 12 Robbins Road, 02541, tel. (617) 548-4575. Reasonable.

Gloucester

Bass Rocks Motor Inn, 89 Atlantic Road, 01930, tel. (617) 283-7600.

Great Barrington

AAA-Lantern House Motel and Antique Shop, Route 7, tel. (413) 528-2350. 14 units.

Barrington Court Motel, 400 Stockbridge Road, Route 7, tel. (413) 528-2340. 12 units.

Berkshire Motor Inn, 372 Main St., tel. (413) 528-3150. 64 units.

Berkshire Chalet, 949 S. Main St., Route 7, tel. (413) 528-1690. 42 units. Reasonable.

Briarcliff Motor Lodge, Route 7, tel. (413) 528-3000. 16 units. Reasonable.

Elling's Bed-and-breakfast, RD#3, Box 6, Route 23 (half-mile west of Route 7), tel. (413) 528-4103.

Friendship Inn Monument Mountain Motel, Route 7, tel. (413) 528-3272. 18 units.

Searles Castle, 359 Main St., tel. (413) 528-3151.

Windflower Inn (country inn), tel. (413) 528-2720. 12 units. Moderate.

Harwichport

Country Inn, tel. (617) 432-2769. 7 units. Reasonable.

Hyannis

American Holiday Motel, Route 28, 02601, tel. (617) 775-5511. Reasonable.

American Host Motel, Route 28, 02601, tel. (617) 775-2332. 80 units. Reasonable.

The Angel Motel, Route 132, 02601, tel. (617) 775-2440. 30 units. Reasonable.

Anric Oceanside Motel, 549 Ocean St., Box 183, 02601, tel. (617) 771-5577. Reasonable.

Dunfey Hyannis Hotel (A Resort and Conference Center), West End Circle, 02601, tel. (617) 775-7775. Expensive.

Hyannis Inn Motel, 473 Main St., 02601, tel. (617) 775-0255. 72 units. Moderate.

Hyannis Motel, Route 132, 02601, tel. (617) 775-8910. Reasonable.

Hyannis Regency Inn, Route 132, 02601, tel. (617) 775-1153. 196 units. Expensive.

Hyannis Star Motor Inn, Route 132, 02601, tel. (617) 775-2835. 34 units.

Hyannis Travel Inn, 16 North St., 02601, tel. (617) 775-8200. Moderate.

Iyanough Hills Motor Lodge and Golf Club, Route 132, 02601, tel. (617) 771-4804. 104 units. Reasonable.

Rainbow Resort Motel, Route 132, 02601, tel. (617) 362-3617. 42 units. Reasonable.

Samurai Motor Inn, Route 132, 02601, tel. (617) 775-3324. Inexpensive.

Snug Harbor Motor Lodge, Route 28, 02601, tel. (617) 775-4085. 50 units. Moderate.

The Sands Motor Lodge, Route 132, 02601, tel. (617) 775-9000.

Terry's Inn and Cottages, Park Avenue and Glenwood streets, Hyannis Park, 02601, tel. (617) 775-9754. Inexpensive.

The Warburtons by the Beach, 388 Sea St., 02601, tel. (617) 775-4612.

Windrift Cottages and Motel, Route 28, 02601, tel. (617) 775-4697. Reasonable.

Lee

Chanterwood (near Tanglewood),tel. (413) 243-0585.

Gaslight Motor Lodge, Route 20, East Lee, tel. (413) 243-9701. Inexpensive.

The Inn on Laurel Lake, Tanglewood 4 miles, tel. (413) 243-9749. 20 units.

Lakeview Motor Court, on Laurel Lake, tel. (413) 243-1350.

Laurel Hill Motel, Route 20W (one-quarter mile from Massachusetts Turnpike Exit 2), tel. (413) 243-0813. 20 units.

The Morgan House (country inn), Main Street, tel. (413) 243-0181. 12 units. Reasonable.

Morpheus Arms Motel, Route 102 (two miles from Massachusetts Turnpike Exit 2), tel. (413) 243-0501. 12 units.

The Pilgrim Motel, 127 Housatonic St. (one-quarter-mile north of Massachusetts Turnpike Exit 2), tel. (413) 243-1328. 25 units.

1777 Greylock House, 58 Greylock St., tel. (413) 243-1717. 5 units.

Lenox

Brooke Farm Inn, 15 Hawthorne St., tel. (413) 637-3013. 11 units. Reasonable.

Candlelight Inn (country inn), 53 Walker St., tel. (413) 637-1555. 7 units. Moderate.

Cornell House, 197 Pittsfield Road, tel. (413) 637-0562. 16 units.

Eastover, 430 East St., tel. (413) 637-0625. 165 units.

Foxhollow Resort, Route 7, tel. (413) 637-2000.

Gables Inn, 103 Walker St., routes 183 and 7A, tel. (413) 637-3416.

Gateways Inn, 71 Walker St., tel. (413) 637-2532.

Lenox Motel, routes 7 and 20, P.O. Box 713, tel. (413) 499-0324. 17 units.

Quincy Lodge, 19 Stockbridge Road, tel. (413) 637-9750.

Susse Chalet Motor Lodge, routes 7 and 20, tel. (413) 637-3560. 60 units.

Underledge, 79 Cliffwood St., tel. (413) 637-0236. 6 units. Reasonable.

Wheatleight (country inn), tel. (413) 637-0610. 16 units. Expensive.

Lexington

Sheraton Lexington Inn, 727 Marrett Road, 02173, tel. (617) 862-8700, (800) 325-3535. 114 units. Expensive.

Nantucket

The Four Chimneys Inn (country inn), tel. (617) 228-1912. Closed in winter. 12 units. Expensive.

Jared Coffin House (country inn), tel. (617) 228-2400. 58 units. Reasonable.

Natick

Hilton Inn at Natick, Route 9 and Speen Street, 01701, tel. (617) 653-5000. 189 units. Reasonable.

Newton

Boston/Newton Marriott Hotel, 2345 Commonwealth Ave., 02166 (Route 30 at junction I-90, Exit 14, and Route 128, Exit 51), tel. (617) 969-1000. 433 units. Expensive.

Howard Johnson's, 320 Washington St., 02158, tel. (617) 969-3010, (800) 654-2000. 260 units. Moderate.

Northampton

Hotel Northampton, 36 King St., tel. (413) 584-3100. 83 units. Reasonable.

Northampton Hilton Inn, junction I-91 and Route 5, tel. (413) 586-1211. 125 units. Reasonable.

Pittsfield

Berkshire Hilton Inn (city center), tel. (413) 499-2000. 175 units. Reasonable.

Blythwood Farm, 360 Churchill St., tel. (413) 442-8750. 4 units. Reasonable.

Bonnie Brae Cabins and Campsites, 108 Broadway, tel. (413) 442-3754. Reasonable.

Ferris Tourist Home, 838 William St., tel. (413) 443-3947. 2 units. Inexpensive.

Heart of the Berkshires Motel, 970 W. Housatonic St., Route 20, tel. (413) 443-1255. 16 units. Reasonable.

Liberty Court Motel, Albany Road, Route 20 (five miles west of Pittsfield), tel. (413) 443-9431. 11 units.

Munro's (bed and breakfast), 306 South St. on routes 7 and 20, tel. (413) 442-0503.

Pittsfield City Motel, Route 20 (half-mile from city center), tel. (413) 443-3000 or (413) 445-4527. 39 units. Reasonable.

Town and Country Motel, 1350 W. Housatonic St., Route 20 (2½ miles west of Pittsfield), tel. (413) 442-8714.

Townhouse (bed and breakfast), 37 Pollock Ave., tel. (413) 443-6637. 4 units.

Traveldge Motel, junction routes 8 and 9, tel. (413) 443-5661. 48 units.

Plymouth

The Governor Bradford Motor Inn, Water Street, 02360, tel. (413) 746-6200. 94 units. Reasonable.

The Governor Carver Motor Inn, 25 Summer St., 02360, tel. (617) 746-7100. 82 units. Reasonable.

Provincetown

Anchor Inn Beach House, 175 Commercial St., tel. (617) 487-0432.

Antique Inn, 377 Commercial St. (on the waterfront), tel. (617) 487-1780.

Bradford House and Motel, 41 Bradford St., tel. (617) 487-0173.

The Cape Codder, 570 Commercial St., 02657, tel. (617) 487-0131. Inexpensive.

Courtland Guest House, 14 Court St., 02657, tel. (617) 487-2292. Inexpensive.

Holiday Inn, Route 6A, 02657, tel. (617) 487-1711. 139 units.

Oceans Inn (country inn), 386 Commercial St., 02657, tel. (617) 487-0385. 16 units. Reasonable. Closed December through March.

Provincetown Inn and Seaside Conference Center, 1 Commercial St., 02657, tel. (800) 352-3137, (800) 343-4444. 100 units.

Sandcastle Motor Inn and Condominiums, Route 6A, 02657, tel. (617) 487-9300.

Somerset House, 378 Commercial St. at Pearl Street, 02657, tel. (617) 487-0383. Inexpensive.

Wave's Landing, 158 Bradford St., 02657, tel. (617) 487-9198, (617) 487-9665. Reasonable.

Quincy

Quincy Bay Inn, 29 Hancock St., 02171, tel. (617) 328-1500, (800) 631-1601. 100 units. Reasonable.

Revere

Howard Johnson's Motor Lodge, 407 Squire Road, 02151, tel. (617) 284-7200, (800) 654-2000, 107 units. Reasonable.

Paul Revere I, 309 American Legion Hwy., 02151, tel. (617) 289-5911. 32 units. Reasonable.

Rockport
Seaward Inn, Marmion Way, 01966, tel. (617) 546 6792. 39 units. Reasonable.

Salem
Hawthorne Inn, 18 Washington Square W., 01970, tel. (617) 744-4080. 88 units. Reasonable.

South Yarmouth
Brentwood Motor Inn, Route 28, 02664, tel. (617) 398-8812. Reasonable.

Riverview Motor Lodge, 37 Neptune Lane, 02664, tel. (617) 394-9801. 110 units. Reasonable.

Riviera Beach Motor Inn, South Shore Drive, Box N, 02664, tel. (617) 398-2273. Moderate.

Soundview Cottages, South Shore Drive, 02664, tel. (617) 475-4064. Reasonable.

Terrel Cottages, Squanto Road, 02664, tel. (617) 398-6459.

Yarmouth Motel, 759 Route 28, 02664, tel. (617) 398-3122.

Springfield
Best Western Black Horse Motel, 500 Riverdale St., West Springfield, 01089 (I-90, Exit 4), tel. (413) 733-2161. 50 units. Reasonable.

Quality Inn and Conference Center, 296 Burnett Road, Chicopee 01020 (junction I-291 and I-90, Exit 6), tel. (413) 592-7751. 181 units. Reasonable.

Sheraton Inn-Springfield West, 1080 Riverdale St., West Springfield 01089 (U.S. 5 at I-91, Exit 13B), tel. (413) 781-8750. 204 units. Moderate.

Springfield-Marriott Hotel, Box 15729, Palmer Central Station 01115 (I-91, Exit 6N/7S), tel. (413) 781-7111. 265 units. Moderate.

Stockbridge
1896 House, Route 7, tel. (413) 458-8125. 16 units. Reasonable.

The Inn at Stockbridge (country inn), Route 7 toward Lenox, tel. (413) 298-3337. 7 units. Moderate.

The Red Lion Inn (country inn) tel. (413) 298-5545. 110 units. Moderate.

Stirling Moffat Guest House, Route 7, tel. (413) 298-5539. Reasonable.

Williams Inn, on the Green, tel. (413) 458-9371. 100 units. Moderate.

Sturbridge
Carriage House Motor Lodge, junction routes 20 and 131, 01566, tel. (617) 347-9000. 100 units. Reasonable.

The Old Sturbridge Village Motor Lodge, P.O. Box 481, 01566, tel. (617) 347-3327. 47 units. Reasonable.

Publick House (country inn), tel. (617) 347-3313. 21 units. Moderate.

Sudbury
Longfellow's Wayside Inn (country inn), tel. (617) 443-8846. 10 units. Reasonable.

Wakefield
Hilton at Colonial Conference Center and Resort, Audubon Road (I-95 and Route 128, Exits 31 and 32), 01880, tel. (617) 245-9300. 300 units. Moderate.

Ware
The Wildwood Inn (country inn), tel. (413) 967-7798. 5 units. Reasonable.

West Harwich
Commodore Motel, 30 Earle Road, 02671, tel. (617) 432-1180.

Manning's Efficiency Motel, 292 Main St., Route 28, 02671, tel. (617) 432-3958.

Wishing Well Motel, Route 28, 02671, tel. (617) 432-2150. 20 units.

West Yarmouth
Aladdin Motor Inn, Mill Creek Bay, Route 28, 02673, tel. (617) 775-5669. 86 units.

Beachway Motel, 498 Route 28, 02673, tel. (617) 775-0399. Reasonable.

Cape Holiday Motel, Route 28, 02673, tel. (617) 775-0962. 40 units. Reasonable.

Cape Sojourn Motel, Route 28, 02673, tel. (617) 775-3825. 60 units. Reasonable.

Cape Traveler Motor Inn, Route 28, 02673, tel. (617) 775-1225. 20 units.

Colonial Acres Resort Motel, Standish Way, 02673, tel. (617) 775-0935.

Englewood Hotel Motor Inn and Condos, 60 Broadway, 02673, tel. (617) 775-3900. Reasonable.

Green Harbor on the Ocean, Box 746, Baxter Avenue, 02673, tel. (617) 771-1126. Moderate.

Holly Tree Motel, 412 Main St., Route 28, 02673, tel. (617) 775-0012. 20 units. Reasonable.

Hunters Green Motel, Route 28, 02673, tel. (617) 771-1169. 74 units.

Irish Village: Cape Cod, Route 28, 02673, tel. (617) 771-0100. 70 units.

Mayflower Motel, 504 Main St., Route 28, 02673, tel. (617) 775-2758.

Thunderbird Motor Lodge, Route 28, 02673, tel. (617) 775-6322.

Town's Country Motor Lodge, Route 28, 02673, tel. (617) 771-0212. 150 units. Reasonable.

Williamstown
Four Acres Motel, State Road, Route 2, tel. (413) 458-8158. 36 units.

Le Jardin (country inn), tel. (413) 458-8032. 9 units. Moderate. Closed Tuesdays November through May.

Northside Inn and Motel, 45 North St., junction routes 7 and 2, tel. (413) 458-8107. 21 units. Reasonable.

The Williams Inn, Main Street, tel. (413) 458-9371. 100 units.

Winthrop
Governor Winthrop Motel, 600 Shirley St., 02152, tel. (617) 846-9700. 53 units. Inexpensive.

Worcester
Days Lodge, 50 Oriol Dr. 01605 (I-290, Exit 20), tel. (617) 852-2800. 115. units. Reasonable.

Marriott Inn, 10 Lincoln Square 01608 (I-290,

Exit 17E/18W), tel. (617) 791-1600. 250 units. Moderate.

Sheraton-Lincoln Inn, 500 Lincoln St. 01605 (I-290, Exit 20), tel. (617) 852-4000. 143 units. Moderate.

Yarmouthport
Old Yarmouth Inn (country inn), 223 Main St., Route 6A, tel. (617) 362-3191. 27 units. Moderate. Open April to December.

NEW HAMPSHIRE

Alton
King Birch Motor Lodge, Route 11D, tel. (603) 875-2222. 10 units.

Ashland
Black Horse Motor Court, RFD#1, Box L, 03217, tel. (603) 968-7116. 16 units. Reasonable.
Little Holland Court, route 3 and 175, 03217, tel. (603) 968-4434. 15 units.

Bartlett
North Colony Motel, Route 302, tel. (603) 374-6679. Reasonable.
Sky Valley Motel and Chalets, Route 302, tel. (603) 374-2322.
Villager Motel, Route 302, tel. (603) 374-2742. 10 units. Reasonable.

Berlin
Traveler Motel, 25 Pleasant St., 03570, tel. (603) 752-2500. 28 units. Moderate.

Bretton Woods
The Lodge at Bretton Woods, Route 302, 03575, tel. (603) 278-1000. 50 units.
Mount Washington Hotel, Route 302, 03575, tel. (603) 278-1000. 235 units. Expensive. Open June to mid-October.

Bridgewater
Blackberry Inn (country inn), Route 3A, Box 431, 03222, tel. (603) 744-3518. 15 units. Reasonable.
The Pasquancy Inn (country inn), Route 3A, 03222, tel. (603) 744-2712. 28 units. Inexpensive. Closed Oct. 15 to Christmas.
Sandybeach of Newfound, Whittmore Point Road, Box 670L, 03222, tel. (603) 744-8473. 12 units. Reasonable.

Center Sandwich
Corner House Inn (country inn), tel. (603) 284-6219. 4 units. Inexpensive.

Charlestown
Indian Shutters Inn (country inn), Route 12, 03603, tel. (603) 826-4445. 4 units. Inexpensive.

Chocorua
Stafford's in the Fields (country inn), tel. (603) 323-7766. 12 units. Moderate.

Concord
Brick Tower Motor Inn, I-93, Exit 12S, 03301, tel. (603) 224-9565. 51 units.

Concord Coach Motor Inn, 406 S. Main St. (I-93, Exit 12S), 03301, tel. (603) 224-2511. 40 units.
Daniel Webster Motor Lodge, routes 3 and 4, Boscawen (I-93, Exit 17, nine miles north of Concord), 03301, tel. (603) 796-2136. 20 units. Inexpensive.
Elmwood Lodge and Motel, routes 3 and 4 (I-93, Exit 17, nine miles north of Concord), 03301, tel. (603) 796-2411. 20 units. Reasonable.
New Hampshire Highway Hotel and Convention Center, Route 9 at I-93, Exit 14, 03301, tel. (603) 225-6687. 140 units. Reasonable.

Conway
The Darby Field Inn, Bald Hill Road, off Route 16, 03818, tel. (603) 447-2181 or (603) 447-2198. Moderate.

Dixville Notch
The Balsams Grand Resort Hotel, 03576, tel. (603) 255-3400. 232 units. Expensive. Open, June to October.

Dover
Ramada Inn, Spaulding Turnpike, Exit 8E, 03820, tel. (603) 742-4100. 80 units.

Durham
New England Center for Continuing Education, Strafford Avenue, 03824, tel. (603) 862-2810. Reasonable.

Eaton Center
Palmer House Inn (country inn), Route 153, 03832, tel. (603) 447-2120. Reasonable.
Rockhouse Mountain Farm (country inn), 03832, tel. (603) 447-2880.

Enfield
Mascoma Lake Lodge, off Route 4A, 03748, tel. (603) 632-7450. 18 units. Inexpensive.
Shaker Bridge Motel, off Route 4A (I-89, Exit 17), 03748, tel. (603) 632-4279. Inexpensive.

Etna
Moose Mountain Lodge, 03570, tel. (603) 643-3529. 12 units.

Exeter
Exeter Inn, 90 Front St. at Phillips Exeter Academy, 03833, tel. (603) 772-5901. 50 units. Reasonable.

Fitzwilliam
Fitzwilliam Inn (country inn), tel. (603) 585-9000. 21 units. Inexpensive.

Francestown
The Inn at Tory Pines (country inn), tel. (603) 538-6352. 32 units. Moderate.

Franconia/Sugar Hill
Franconia Inn (country inn), Route 116, Easton Road, 03583, tel. (603) 823-5542. 29 units. Moderate. Closed Oct. 15 to Dec. 15 and April 1 to May 25.
Gale River Motel, Route 18 (I-93, Exit 38), tel. (603) 823-5655. 12 units. Reasonable.

Hillwinds Inn, Route 18, 03583, tel. (603) 823-5551. 30 units. Reasonable.

The Horse and Hound Inn (country inn), tel. (603) 823-5501. Moderate.

Ledgeland (country inn), Route 117, Sugar Hill, 03585, tel. (603) 823-5341. 21 units. Moderate.

Lovett's Inn, Route 18, 03583, tel. (603) 823-7761. 18 units. Moderate.

Pinestead Farm Lodge, Route 116, 03583, tel. (603) 823-8121. 8 units.

Sunset Hill House, off Route 117, Sugar Hill, 03585, tel. (603) 823-5522. 35 units. Moderate.

Westwind Cottage, Route 18, 03583, tel. (603) 823-5532. Reasonable.

Glen

The Bernerhof (country inn), Route 302, 03838, tel. (603) 383-4414. 9 units. Inexpensive. Closed mid-November to mid-December and mid-April to May 30.

Best Western Storybook Motor Inn, junction routes 302 and 16, 03838, tel. (603) 383-6800. 54 units. Moderate.

Linderhof Motor Inn, Route 16, 03838, tel. (603) 383-4334. 33 units. Moderate.

Hampton Beach

Ashworth by the Sea, 295 Ocean Blvd., Routes 1A and 51, 03842, tel. (603) 926-6762. 100 units. Reasonable.

Hotel Kentville, 315 Ocean Blvd., 03842, tel. (603) 926-3950. 36 units.

Jen's Ocean Manoir, 753 Ocean Blvd., 03842, tel. (603) 926-9119. Winter address: 236 S. Main St., Newmarket, N.H. 03857. Reasonable.

Mainsail Motel, 40 Ashworth Ave., 03842, tel. (603) 926-4958. 37 units. Moderate.

McGovern's Boar's Head Inn (country inn), Great Boar's Head, off Ocean Boulevard, 03842, tel. (603) 926-3911. 12 units.

Rainbow Village Motel, 4 "P" St., The Lemerise's, 03842, tel. (603) 926-3380. 11 units.

Sheraton Lamie's, 490 Lafayette Road, Route 1, tel. (603) 926-8911. 30 units. Reasonable.

Hanover

Chieftain Motor Inn, Route 10, 03755 (two miles north of Dartmouth College), tel. (603) 643-2550. 22 units. Reasonable.

Hanover Inn, Main and Wheelock streets, 03755, tel. (603) 643-4300. 101 units. Expensive.

Intervale

Holiday Inn (country inn), tel. (603) 356-9772. 10 units. Reasonable. Closed late March to late May and late October to Dec. 26.

The New England Inn (country inn), tel. (603) 356-5541. 26 units. Moderate. Closed in April.

Jackson

Christmas Farm Inn (country inn), tel. (603) 383-4313. 27 units. Moderate.

Dana Place Inn (country inn), Route 16, tel. (603) 383-6822. 14 units. Moderate. Closed in April and November.

Eagle Mountain House, Route 16, tel. (603) 383-4347. 90 units. Reasonable.

The Wildcat Inn (country inn), tel. (603) 383-4245. 18 units. Inexpensive. Closed May and November.

Keene

Best Western Valley Green Motel, 379 West St., 03431, tel. (603) 352-7350. 60 units.

The Coach and Four Motor Inn, FRD#4, Route 12, 03431 (five miles south of Kenne), tel. (603) 357-3705. 22 units. Reasonable.

Coach House Motel, route 12S, Everett Decatur, 03431, tel. (603) 352-4208. 20 units. Inexpensive.

Motor Inn Motel, Route 12S, Lower Main Street, 03431, tel. (603) 352-4138. 8 units.

Ramada Inn, 401 Winchester St., 03431, tel. (603) 357-3038. 96 units. Moderate.

Winding Brook Lodge, Park Avenue, Box 372, 03431, tel. (603) 352-3111. 90 units Reasonable.

Laconia

The Anchorage on Lake Winnisquam, RFD#1, Route 3, 03246 (2½ miles from I-93, Exit 20), tel. (603) 524-3248. 32 units.

Bluebird Motel and Cottages, 67 Lake St., Route 3, 03246, tel. (603) 524-5806. 27 units. Reasonable.

Christmas Island Resort, Route 3, 03246, tel. (603) 366-4378. 61 units. Moderate.

Margate Resort, Route 3, 03246, tel. (603) 524-5210. 155 units.

Lincoln

Beacon Motel, Route 3, 03251, tel. (603) 745-8118, (800) 258-8934. 100 units. Reasonable.

Indian Head Motel Resort, Route 3, 03251, tel. (603) 745-8181. 132 units. Reasonable.

The Inn at Loon Mountain, Kancamagus Highway (I-93, Exit 32), tel. (603) 745-8341. 21 units. Reasonable.

Parker's Motel, Route 3, 03251 (two miles north of end of I-93), tel. (603) 745-8341. 21 units. Reasonable.

Village of Loon Mountain, Route 112, Kancamagus Highway, 03251, tel. (603) 745-3401. 150 units.

White Mountain Motel and Cottages, Route 3, 03251 (one mile north of I-93, Exit 32), tel. (603) 745-8924. 17 units. Reasonable.

Littleton

Edencroft (country inn), tel. (603) 444-6776. 6 units. Reasonable. Closed first two weeks in March.

Manchester

The Elms Resort, Brown Avenue, 03103 (two miles south of I-293, Exit 2), tel. (603) 625-6426. 64 units. Reasonable.

Holiday Inn, Route 3 at Amoskeag Bridge, 03102, tel. (603) 669-2660. 120 units.

Howard Johnson's Motor Lodge, Queen City Avenue, 03102 (I-293, Exit 4), tel. (603) 668-2600, (800) 654-2000. 104 units.

Susse Chalet Inn, 03103 (I-293/Route 101, Exit 1), tel. (603) 625-2020, (800) 258-1980. 102 units. Reasonable.

Merrimack

Appleton Inn, 03054 (Everett Turnpike, Exit 8),

tel. (603) 424-7500, (800) 258-1335. 116 units. Moderate.

The Hilton at Merrimack, Route 3, 03054 (Everett Turnpike, Exit 8), tel. (603) 424-6181. 200 units. Moderate.

Moultonboro
Bon Air Lodges, Clarks Landing Road, 03254, tel. (603) 544-2144. Moderate.

Kona Mansion Inn, Lake Winnispesaukee, Moultonboro Neck Road, 03254, tel. (603) 253-4900. Reasonable.

Mount Sunapee
Back Side Inn, RFD#2, Box 213, Newport 03773, tel. (603) 863-5161. 8 units.

Edgemont Motel, Route 103, 03772, tel. (603) 763-4401. 9 units. Reasonable.

Mount Sunapee Motel, Route 103, 03772, tel. (603) 763-5592. 22 units. Reasonable.

Nashua
Best Western Hallmark Motor Inn, Route 3, (Exit 1), 03060, tel. (603) 888-1200. 81 units. Reasonable.

Green Ridge Motor Lodge, Exit 1, Daniel Webster Highway, 03060, tel. (603) 888-2500. 58 units.

Hannah Dustin Motel, 172 Daniel Webster Highway, Exit 1, Route 3, 03060, tel. (603) 888-2315, (800) 343-4104. 25 units. Reasonable.

Howard Johnson's Motor Lodge and Restaurant, Everett Turnpike, Exit 5E, 03060, tel. (603) 889-0173. Moderate.

Lillian's Motel, Route 3N, 03060, tel. (603) 882-3451. 18 units. Reasonable.

Sheraton Tara Hotel, Route 3, Exit 1, 03060, tel. (603) 888-9700, (800) 325-3535. 240 units. Moderate.

Newbury
Lakewood Manor, Route 103, Box ST, 03255, tel. (603) 763-2231. 13 units.

New London
Hide-Away Lodge (country inn), off Route 11, 03257 (two miles north of city center), tel. (603) 526-4861. 12 units.

Lakeside Landing, Route 103A, 03257, tel. (603) 763-5541. 18 units.

Lake Sunapee Country Club and Inn, Route 11, 03257, tel. (603) 526-6040. 32 units.

Lamplighter Motor Inn, Route 11, 03257 (one mile west of city center), tel. (603) 526-6484. 14 units. Inexpensive.

Pleasant Lake Inn, North Pleasant Street, Box 1030, 03257, tel. (603) 526-6271. 12 units. Reasonable.

Twin Lake Village, Little Sunapee Road, 03257, tel. (603) 526-6460.

North Conway
Briarcliff Motel, routes 16 and 302, 03860, tel. (603) 356-5584. 21 units.

Cranmore Mountain Lodge, tel. (603) 356-2044. 17 units. Reasonable.

Crestwood Motor Lodge, Route 16, Box 3172A, 03860, tel. (603) 356-5492. 32 units. Moderate.

Eastern Slope Inn/Resort and Motor Lodge, Route 16, 03860, tel. (603) 356-6321. 74 units. Reasonable.

Fox Ridge Resort, Route 16, 03860, tel. (603) 356-3151. 136 units. Moderate.

Red Jacket Mountain View Motor Inn, Route 16, 03860, tel. (603) 356-5411. 152 units. Moderate.

The Scottish Lion (country inn), tel. (603) 356-6381. 8 units. Inexpensive.

Stonehurst Manor (country inn), Route 16, 03860, tel. (603) 356-3113. 26 units. Moderate.

North Sutton
Follansbee Inn, Keysar Street, tel. (603) 927-4221. 23 units. Reasonable.

Portsmouth
Howard Johnson's Motor Lodge, Interstate Traffic Circle (I-95, Exit 5), tel. (603) 436-7600. 135 units.

Inn at Christian Shore, 335 Maplewood Ave., tel. (603) 431-6770. 6 units. Reasonable.

Martin Hill Inn, 404 Islington St., tel. (603) 436-2287. 6 units.

The Meadowbrook Inn, Interstate Traffic Circle (I-95, Exit 5), tel. (603) 436-2700. 120 units.

Pebble Beach Motel, Ordione State Park, Box 4340, tel. (603) 431-5896, (603) 436-8244. Moderate.

Port City Motel, Interstate Traffic Circle at Route 1, tel. (603) 436-4378. 56 units.

River Bend Motel, White Mountain Highway, routes 4 and 16, tel. (603) 436-9708. 17 units.

Seabrook
Best Western Seabrook Inn, routes 107 and 95, 03874, tel. (603) 474-3078. 106 units. Reasonable.

Shelburne
Philbrook Farm Inn (country inn), tel. (603) 466-3831. 19 units. Reasonable. Closed during April and from late October to Dec. 26.

Snowville
Snowvillage Inn (country inn), Route 153, 03849 (five miles south of Conway), tel. (603) 447-2818. 14 units. Moderate.

Tilton
Tilton Inn, 03276 (I-93, Exit 20), tel. (603) 286-3003. Inexpensive.

The Wayland Motel and Cottages, Route 3 South, 03276 (I-93, Exit 20), tel. (603) 286-4430. 11 units.

Waterville Valley
The Inns of Waterville Valley (Landmark Lodge, Silver Squirrel Inn, Snowy Owl Inn, The Birches), 03223, tel. (603) 236-8366, (800) 258-4040. 100 units.

The Valley Inn and Tavern, Tecumseh Road, 03223, tel. (603) 236-8336. 50 units. Expensive.

Waterville Valley Condominium Vacations, 03223, tel. (603) 236-8211. 70 units. Moderate.

The White Mountains Resort, 03223 (seven miles from I-93, Exit 28), tel. (603) 726-3724.

Windsor Hill Condominiums, Route 49, 03223, tel. (603) 236-8321, (800) 343-1286. Moderate.

Whitefield
The Playhouse Motor Inn, Route 3, tel. (603) 837-2527. Reasonable.
Spalding Inn Club (country inn), tel. (603) 837-2572. 56 units. Moderate.

Wilton
The Ram in the Thicket (country inn), Maple Street, off Route 3, tel. (603) 654-6440. 9 units. Inexpensive.

Wolfeboro
Country Village Motel, Route 109, 03894, tel. (603) 544-3800. 12 units.
The Lake Motel, South Main Street, Route 28, 03894, tel. (603) 569-1100. 35 units.
Lakeshore Terrace Cottages, routes 109 and 28, 03894, tel. (603) 569-1701. 11 units. Inexpensive.
Lakeview Inn and Motor Lodge, Route 109 North, 03894, tel. (603) 569-1335. 14 units. Reasonable.
Pick Point Lodge and Cottage, on Lake Winnepesaukee, 03894, tel. (603) 569-1338. Expensive.
Piping Rock Cottages and Motel, North Main Street, 03894, tel. (603) 569-1915. 23 units.

Woodstock
Cascade Lodge (guest house), Main Street, North Woodstock, 03262, tel. (603) 745-2722. 13 units. Inexpensive.
Jack O'Lantern Resort, Route 3, 03293 (I-93, Exit 30), tel. (603) 745-8121. Moderate.
Montaup Motor Lodge, Route 3 South, 03262 (I-93, Exit 32), tel. (603) 745-6691. 12 units. Reasonable.

RHODE ISLAND

Block Island
Manisses Hotel, tel. (401) 466-2836. 18 units. Moderate. Open April to November.
Narragansett Inn, tel. (401) 466-2626. 45 units. Moderate. Open June to September.
1661 Inn, tel. (401) 466-2421. 26 units. Reasonable. Open year-round.

Middletown
Howard Johnson's, 351 W. Main Road, tel. (401) 849-2000. 115 units. Reasonable.

Newport
Brinley Victorian Guest House, 23 Brinley St., tel. (401) 849-7645. 16 units. Moderate.
Captain Samuel Rhodes Guest House, 3 Willow St., tel. (401) 846-5486. 4 units. Moderate.
Easton's Inn on the Beach, 30 Wave Ave. 02840, tel. (401) 846-0310. 41 units. Moderate.
The Inn at Castle Hill (country inn), Ocean Drive, tel. (401) 849-3800. 18 units. Moderate to expensive.
Newport Harbor Treadway Inn, America's Cup Avenue, tel. (401) 849-2600. 134 units. Expensive.
Sheraton-Islander Inn and Conference Center, Goat Island (Long Wharf), 02840, tel. (401) 849-2600. 254 units. Moderate.

Viking Hotel and Motor Inn, 1 Bellevue Ave., 02840, tel. (401) 847-3300. 183 units. Reasonable.

Pawtucket
Howard Johnson's, 2 George St., 02860, tel. (401) 723-6700. 100 units. Reasonable.

Providence
Biltmore Plaza, Kennedy Plaza (I-95, Exit 21), 02903,tel. (401) 421-0700. 350 units. Moderate.
Holiday Inn Downtown, 21 Atwell Ave., tel. (401) 831-3900. 275 units. Reasonable.
Marriott Inn, Charles and Orms Streets, 02904, (I-95, Exit 23), tel. (401) 272-2400. 350 units. Expensive.

Wakefield
Larchwood Inn (country inn), tel. (401) 783-5454. 15 units. Reasonable.

Warwick
Howard Johnson's, 20 Jefferson Blvd., tel. (401) 467-9800. 124 units. Moderate.
Sheraton Airport Inn, Post Road, tel. (401) 238-4000. 125 units. Moderate.

Watch Hill
Harbor House, Bay Street, tel. (401) 348-8998. 5 units. Moderate. Open June to October.

Westerly
Pine Lodge Motel, Route 1, tel. (401) 322-0333. Reasonable.
Pony Barn Motel, Shore Road, tel. (401) 348-8216. Moderate.
Shelter Harbor Inn (country inn), tel. (401) 322-8883. 18 units. Reasonable.

VERMONT

Arlington
Arlington Inn, U.S. 7, 05250, tel. (802) 375-6532. 13 units. Reasonable.

Barre
The Hollow Motel, 278 S. Main St., Route 14, 05641 (I-89, Exit 6), tel. (802) 479-9313.

Bennington
Bennington Motel, 143 W. Main St., 05201, tel. (802) 442-5479. Reasonable.
Bennington Ramada Inn, Route 7 and Kocher Drive, 05201, tel. (802) 442-8145, (800) 228-2828.
Best Western New Englander, 220 Northside Dr. (U.S. 7), 05201, tel. (802) 442-6311, (800) 528-1234. 51 units.
Fife'n Drum Motel, Route 7S, 05201, tel. (802) 442-4074. Reasonable.
Kirkside Motor Lodge, 250 W. Main St., 05201.
Knotty Pine Motel, 130 Northside Dr., 05201, tel. (802) 442-5487.
South Gate Motel, Route 7S, 05201, tel. (802) 447-7525. Reasonable.

Bolton Valley
The Black Bear, 05477 (20 miles from Burlington), tel. (802) 434-2126. 20 units. Moderate.

Brattleboro
Holly Motel, Canal Street, 05301 (I-91, Exit 1), tel. (802) 254-2360. 42 units.

Quality Inn, Route 5N, Putney Road, 05301, tel. (802) 254-8701. 100 units.

Red Coach Motor Inn, Putney Road, 05301 (I-91, Exit 3), tel. (802) 254-4583.

Susse Chalet Motor Inn, Route 5N, 05301 (I-91, Exit 3), tel. (802) 254-6007, (800) 258-1980, in New Hampshire (800) 572-1880. Reasonable.

Burlington
Anchorage Motor Inn, 108 Dorset St., 05401 (I-89, Exit 14E), tel. (802) 658-3351. 91 units.

Bel-Aire Motel, 111 Shelburne St., 05401 (I-89, Exit 13 to U.S. 7), tel. (802) 863-3116.

Best Western Redwood, 1016 Shelburne Road, South Burlington (I-89, Exit 13 to U.S. 7), tel. (802) 862-6421, (800) 528-1234. Moderate.

Howard Johnson's Motor Lodge (I-89, Exit 14E, at U.S. 2), tel. (802) 863-5541, (800) 654-2000.

Motel Brown, 165 Shelburne Road, 05401 (I-89, Exit 13 to Route 6N), tel. (802) 862-5708. 33 units.

Radisson Burlington Hotel, 05401, tel. (802) 658-6500. 200 units.

Ramada Inn, 1117 Williston Road, 05401, tel. (802) 658-0250. 130 units.

Sheraton-Burlington Inn, 870 Williston Road, 05401, tel. (802) 862-6576. Moderate.

Chester
Chester Inn (country inn), tel. (802) 875-2444. 31 units. Reasonable. Closed last three weeks of April and first two weeks of November.

Cranberry Inn (country inn), tel. (802) 875-2525. 11 units. Inexpensive. Closed in April.

Chittenden
Mountain Top Inn at Chittenden, P.O. Box 50, 05737, tel. (802) 483-2311. 48 units. Expensive. Open May 27 to Oct. 24 and Dec. 15 to April 15.

Tulip Tree Inn (country inn), 05737, tel. (802) 483-6213.

Craftsbury
The Craftsbury Inn (country inn), tel. (802) 586-2848. 10 units. Moderate. Closed in April and November.

Cuttingsville
Shrewsbury Inn (country inn), tel. (802) 492-3355. 3 units. Reasonable. Closed mid-April to mid-May and in November.

Dorset
Dorset Inn (country inn), tel. (802) 867-5500. 45 units. Reasonable. Closed October to Dec. 25 and late March to mid-May.

East Burke
The Old Cutter Inn (country inn), Burke Mountain Access Road, 05832, tel. (802) 626-5152.

Essex Junction
Baker's Motor Inn, 65 Pearl St., 05452, tel. (802) 878-3343. 40 units. Reasonable.

Fairhaven
Victorian Marble Inn (country inn), 12 W. Park Pl., 05743, tel. (802) 265-4376.

Grafton
The Old Tavern (country inn), tel. (802) 843-2231. 35 units. Moderate. Closed in April.

Greenboro
Highland Lodge (country inn), tel. (802) 533-2647. 22 units. Expensive. Closed April 1 to May 25 and November (after foliage season) to mid-December.

Jamaica
Three Mountain Inn (country inn), Route 30, P.O. Box 185 VG, 05343, tel. (802) 874-4140.

Killington
Alpine Inn, Killington Road, 05751, tel. (802) 422-3485.

Cascade Lodge, Killington Road, 05751, tel. (802) 422-3731.

Cortina Inn, Route 4, Mendon Mountain, 05751, tel. (802) 773-3331.

Edelweiss Motel and Chalets, Route 4, 05751, tel. (802) 775-5577. Reasonable.

Friendship Inn/Tyrol Motel, Route 4, 05751, tel. (802) 773-7485. Reasonable.

Grey Bonnet Inn (country inn), Route 100N, 05751, tel. (802) 775-2537. 44 units. Reasonable.

The Inn at Longtrail (country inn), Route 4, Sherburne Pass, 05751, tel. (802) 775-7181. 16 units. Closed April 15 to July 1 and from the end of foliage season to Thanksgiving.

Killington Resort, 241B Killington Road, 05751, tel. (802) 422-3261.

Mountain Meadows Lodge, 05751, tel. (802) 775-1010. Moderate.

Pico Peak Lodge, Route 4, 05751, tel. (802) 773-6331. 40 units.

Summit Lodge, Killington Access Road, 05751, tel. (802) 422-3535. Moderate.

Trailside Lodge, Coffee House Road, 05751, tel. (802) 422-3532.

Val Roc Motel, Route 4, 05751, tel. (802) 422-3881. 24 units.

The Vermont Inn (country inn), Route 4, 05751, tel. (802) 773-9847. 14 units. Reasonable.

Londonderry
Blue Gentia Lodge, Magic Mountain Road, 05148, tel. (802) 824-5908.

Dostal's Motor Lodge, Magic Mountain, 05148, tel. (802) 824-6700. 50 units.

Inn at Bear Creek, Route 30, Stratton Mountain, Rawsonville, tel. (802) 297-1700. 18 units.

The Inn on Magic Mountain, 05148, tel. (802) 824-6100.

The Londonderry (country inn), Route 100, South Londonderry, 05155, tel. (802) 824-5226. 25 units. Reasonable.

Magic View Motel, Route 11, 05148, tel. (802) 824-3793. 18 units.

Three Clock Inn (country inn), South Londonderry, tel. (802) 824-6327. 4 units. Reasonable. Closed Mondays.

Manchester

Aspen Motel, Box 548, Manchester Center 05255, (on U.S. 7 one mile north of junction of routes 11 and 30), tel. (802) 362-2450. Moderate.

The Barnstead Motel, Route 30 (two blocks north of junction of routes 7, 11 and 30), tel. (802) 362-1619.

Bromley Sun Lodge, Peru, 05152, tel. (802) 824-6941. 51 units.

Brook-n-Hearth, Routes 11 and 30, Box 508, Manchester Center 05255, tel. (802) 362-3604. Inexpensive.

Chalet Motel, Routes 11 and 30, 05255, tel. (802) 362-1622. Reasonable.

Four Winds Motor Inn, P.O. Box 1243, Manchester Center 05255, tel. (802) 362-1105.

Manchester View Motel, 05255, tel. (802) 362-2739.

The Marbledge Motel, U.S. 7 (five miles north of Route 11 junction), P.O. Box East, tel. (802) 362-1418.

Olympia Motor Lodge, Route 7, Manchester Center 05255, tel. (802) 362p1700.

Palmer House Best Western, Manchester Center 05255, tel. (802) 362-3600.

Snow Bound Motel, Route 7, Manchester Center 05255, tel. (802) 362-2145. Reasonable.

The Reluctant Panther (country inn), tel. (802) 362-2568. 7 units. Moderate. Closed Nov. 1 to mid-December and mid-April to Memorial Day.

Snow Bound Motel, Route 7, Manchester Center 05255, tel. (802) 362-2145. Reasonable.

Troll Hill Motor Inn, Routes 11 and 30, Manchester Center 05255, tel. (802) 362-1711.

Troll Hill Motor Lodge, Route 7, Danby, 05739, tel. (802) 293-5186. Reasonable.

The Worthy Inn (country inn), tel. (802) 362-1792. 25 units. Reasonable.

Middlebury

Blue Spruce Motel, Route 7S, 05753, tel. (802) 388-7512. 18 units.

Greystone Motel, Route 7S, 05753, tel. (802) 388-4935. 10 units. Reasonable.

Middlebury Inn (country inn), Court Square, tel. (802) 388-4961. 79 units. Reasonable.

Maple Manor Motel, Route 7S, 05753, tel. (802) 388-2193. 20 units.

Sugar House Motor Inn, Route 7, tel. (802) 388-2770. 14 units. Reasonable.

Montpelier

Lackey's Tourist Home, 153 State St., 05602, tel. (802) 223-7292.

Morrisville

Sunset Motel, junction Routes 100 and 15, tel. (802) 888-4956.

Mount Snow

Andirons Lodge, Route 100, West Dover 05356, tel. (802) 464-2114. Reasonable.

The Ironside Lodge, Route 100, Box 308VC, 05356, tel. (802) 464-3796. Moderate.

Kitzhof, Route 100, West Dover 05356, tel. (802) 464-8310.

The Lodge at Mount Snow, Route 100, Box 775, West Dover 05356, tel. (802) 451-4289, (802) 464-5112. Moderate.

Snow Den Inn, Route 100, Box 615, West Dover 05356, tel. (802) 464-9355. Moderate.

Snow Lake Lodge, 241B Mountain Road, 05356, tel. (802) 464-3333, (800) 451-4211. 105 units. Moderate.

Tollhouse Inn, Route 100, 05356. Moderate.

Waldwinkel Inn, Route 100, Box VCC, 05356, tel. (802) 464-5426.

Weathervane Lodge, 200 Dorr Fitch Road, West Dover 05356. Inexpensive.

West Dover Inn (country inn), tel. (802) 464-5207. 12 units. Reasonable.

Newfane

The Four Columns Inn (country inn), tel. (802) 365-7713. 12 units. Moderate. Closed in April and November, and Tuesdays year-round.

Norwich

Inn at Norwich, 225 Main St., tel. (802) 649-1143. 22 units. Moderate.

Pittsfield

Pittsfield Inn, Route 100, tel. (802) 746-8943. 10 units. Reasonable.

Plymouth

Farmbrook Motel, Route 100A, 05056, tel. (802) 672-3621. 10 units. Reasonable.

Pownal

Ladd Brook Motor Inn, Route 7, tel. (802) 823-7341. 27 units.

Putney

Putney Motor Inn, 05346 (I-91, Exit 4), tel. (802) 387-5517.

Quechee

Quechee Gorge Motel, P.O. Box Q, 05059, tel. (802) 295-7600. 36 units.

The Quechee Inn at Marshfield Farm (country inn), Box 747V, 05059, tel. (802) 295-3133. 22 units. Expensive.

Rochester

Harvey's Mountain View Inn and Farm (country inn), 05767, tel. (802) 767-4273. Reasonable.

Rochester Inn (country inn), P.O. Box 58, 05767, tel. (802) 767-4711. 15 units.

Rutland

Best Western Hogge Penny Motor Inn, route 4W, Box 914, 05701, tel. (802) 773-3200.

Green Mont Motel, 138 N. Main St., 05701, tel. (802) 775-2575. 30 units. Reasonable.

Mendon Motel and Chalets, Route 4, 05701, tel. (802) 773-2424. Reasonable.

Royal Motel, 115 Woodstock Ave., 05701, tel. (802) 773-9176, (800) 631-1601.

Rutland Motel, 125 Woodstock Ave., 05701, tel. (802) 775-4348. 37 units.

Rutland Travelodge, 253 S. Main St., 05701, tel. (802) 773-3361. 76 units.

Star Lite Motel, Route 7, North Clarendon, 05759, tel. (802) 773-3714.

Woodstock East Motel, 154 Woodstock Ave., 05701, tel. (802) 773-2442. Reasonable.

Shaftsbury

Hillbrook Motel, Route 7A, 05262, tel. (802) 442-4095.

Iron Kettle Motel, Route 7A, Box 195, 05262, tel. (802) 442-4316.

Stowe

Alpine Motor Lodge, Mountain Road, 05672, tel. (802) 253-7700.

Andersen Lodge, Route 108, 05672, tel. (802) 253-7336.

Buccaneer Motel and Ski Lodge, Mountain Road, 05672, tel. (802) 253-4772. Reasonable.

Bunker Hills Resort Motor Inn, Box 1309, 05672, tel. (802) 888-7771. 20 units.

Butternut Inn and Chalets, tel. (802) 253-4277. 18 units. Inexpensive.

Charda Inn (country inn), tel. (802) 253-4598. 11 units. Inexpensive. Closed Thanksgiving to Christmas and mid-April to late May.

Edson Hill Manor, Edson Hill Road, 05672, tel. (802) 253-7371, (802) 253-9797. 15 units. Moderate. Closed in November and mid-May to mid-June.

Fiddler's Green Inn, Mountain Road, 05672, tel. (802) 253-8124. Inexpensive.

Golden Kitz Lodge and Motel, RD#1, Box 2980, Mountain Road, 05672, tel. (802) 253-4127.

Grey Fox Inn, RD#1, Box 400, 05672, tel. (802) 253-8921. Reasonable.

Hob Knob Inn Motel and Restaurant, Mountain Road, Route 108, 05672, tel. (802) 253-8549. 16 units.

The Inn at the Mountain, Route 108, 05672, tel. (802) 253-7311. 33 units. Expensive.

Innsbruck Inn, Mountain Road, 05672, tel. (802) 253-8582. Reasonable.

Mountain Road Motel, Route 108, Box 8, 05672, tel. (802) 253-4566.

Mountaineer Motor Inn, Mountain Road, ;5672, tel. (802) 253-7525. 50 units. Reasonable.

Salzburg Inn, Mountain Road (Route 108), tel. (802) 253-8541. 51 units. Reasonable.

Siebeness Lodge, Mountain Road, 05672, tel. (802) 253-8942.

Spruce Pond Inn (country inn), tel. (802) 253-4828. 16 units. Reasonable. Closed Easter to May 15 and Oct. 20 to Dec. 1.

Stowe-Away, RD#1, 1360 Mountain Road, 05672, tel. (802) 253-8972.

Stoweflake Resort Motor Inn, Route 108, 05672, tel. (802) 253-7355. Moderate.

Stowehof Inn, Edson Hill Road, 05672, tel. (802) 253-9722. Expensive.

Stowe Motel, RD#1, Box 3020, 05672, tel. (802) 253-7629. Moderate.

Trapp Family Lodge, Stowe; tel. (802) 253-8511.

Tuckaway Lodge, P.O. Box 5, 05672, tel. (802) 253-9777.

Stratton

Stratton Mountain Inn, 05155, tel. (802) 297-2500. 95 units. Expensive.

Waitsfield

Tucker Hill Lodge, Route 17, tel. (802) 496-3983, (800) 451-4580. 20 units. Moderate.

Wallingford

The Wallingford Inn (country inn), tel. (802) 446-2849. 6 units. Reasonable. Closed Mondays and first two weeks of November.

Weathersfield

The Inn at Weathersfield, Route 106 near Perkinsville, tel. (802) 263-9217. 9 units. Moderate.

Weston

The Inn at Weston, Route 100, tel. (802) 824-5804. 13 units. Reasonable.

Hermitage Inn, Coldbrook Road, off Route 100, tel. (802) 464-3511. 16 units. Moderate.

Wilmington

The White House (country inn), tel. (802) 464-2135. 8 units. Moderate. Closed in April and May.

Woodstock

Braeside Motel, Route 4, Box 411, 05091, tel. (802) 457-1366. Reasonable.

Shire Motel, 46 Pleasant St., 05091, tel. (802) 457-2211. 15 units. Reasonable.

Woodstock Inn and Resort, 14 The Green, 05091, tel. (802) 457-1100. 120 units. Expensive.

Restaurants

CONNECTICUT

Avon

Chez Serge, Avon Park North (behind town hall), tel. (203) 678-0175. French. Tuesday through Saturday, 11:30 a.m. to 2 p.m., 6 to 10 p.m. Reservations required, jacket at dinner.

Bantam

New Bantam Inn, Main Street (Route 202), tel. (203) 567-8561. Continental. Wednesday through Sunday, 5 to 9 p.m., Saturday to 10 p.m., Sunday noon to 8 p.m. Reasonable.

Chester

The Inn at Chester, 318 W. Main St., tel. (203) 526-9541. American regional. Daily 6:30 to 9:30 a.m., noon to 2 p.m., 6 to 10 p.m. Sunday brunch 11 a.m. to 2:30 p.m. Jacket at dinner.

East Haddam

Gelston House, Route 82, Goodspeed's Landing, tel. (203) 873-8257, (203) 873-9300. Continental. Daily 11:30 a.m. to 2:30 p.m., 5:30 to 9 p.m., Friday and Saturday 5 to 10 p.m., Sunday noon to 8 p.m. Reasonable.

Essex

Fine Bouche, 78 Main St., tel. (203) 767-1277. French. Tuesday through Saturday 11:30 a.m. to 2 p.m., 6 to 9 p.m., patisserie 10 a.m. to 5 p.m. Moderate. Reservation required.

Griswold Inn, Main Street, tel. (203) 767-0991. Daily noon to 2 p.m., 6 to 9 p.m., Saturday 5:30 to 9:30 p.m., Sunday 5 to 9 p.m. Sunday brunch 11:30 a.m. to 2:30 p.m. by reservation only. Entertainment.

Tumbledown's Cafe, 29 Main St., tel. (203) 767-0233. Daily noon to 3 p.m., 5:30 to 10 p.m., Sunday to 9:30 p.m. Inexpensive.

Glastonbury
Blacksmith's Tavern, 2300 Main St., tel. (203) 659-0366. Continental. Daily 11:30 a.m. to 4 p.m., 5 to 9 p.m., Sunday brunch 11 a.m. to 2:30 p.m. Moderate. Jacket requested.

The Market Restaurant, 39 New London Turnpike Extension, tel. (203) 633-3832. Daily except holidays 11:30 a.m. to 3 p.m., 5 to 9:30 p.m., Friday and Saturday to 11 p.m., Sunday brunch 11 a.m. to 3 p.m.

Greenwich
Cinquante-cinq, 55 Arch St., tel. (203) 869-5641. French. Monday through Saturday noon to 2 p.m., 6 to 9:30 p.m., Friday and Saturday to 10 p.m. Formal dress at dinner.

Groton
Bootlegger, 359 Thames St., tel. (203) 448-1617. Seafood. Daily 11:30 a.m. to 3 p.m., 5 to 9:30 p.m., Sunday to 9 p.m.

Guilford
Apple Doll House, 12 Durham Road, tel. (203) 453-2933. Open weekdays year-round, Saturdays except January-February, 11 a.m. to 2 p.m.

Century House, 2455 Boston Post Road (I-95, Exit 56 or 57), tel. (203) 453-2216. Continental. Daily except Monday noon 5 to 2 p.m., 6 to 9 p.m., Friday and Saturday to 10 p.m., Sunday brunch noon to 3 p.m. Formal dress at dinner.

Hartford
Last National Bank, 752 Main St., tel. (203) 246-5387. Steak and seafood. Daily from 11 a.m., dinner 5 p.m. to midnight, Sunday brunch 11 a.m. to 2:30 p.m. Reasonable.

Summit Hotel, Constitution Plaza, tel. (203) 278-2000. **Green House** (coffee house), 6:30 a.m. to 12 midnight. **Palm Court Lobby**, 7 a.m. to 8 p.m. **Zero's Pub**, weekdays 11:30 a.m. to 1 p.m. Rib Room, 12 noon to 3 p.m. and 6 to 10 p.m., moderate, jacket and tie required.

Mystic
The Inn at Mystic, junction routes 1 and 27, tel. (203) 536-9604. **Flood Tide Restaurant**, daily 7:30 to 10:30 a.m., 11:30 a.m. to 2:30 p.m., 5 to 9:30 p.m., Sunday brunch 11 a.m. to 2:30 p.m., dinner from 3 p.m.

Seamen's Inne at Mystic Seaport, 65 Greenmanville Road, tel. (203) 536-9649. Seafood. Daily 11:30 a.m. to 3 p.m., 5 to 10 p.m., Sunday dinner from 3 p.m.

Steak Loft of Mystic, Olde Mystick Village, I-95, Exit 90, tel. (203) 536-2661. Daily 11:30 a.m. to 2:30 p.m., 4:30 to 10 p.m., Friday and Saturday to 11 p.m.

Steamboat Cafe, 73 Steamboat Wharf, tel. (203) 536-1975. Seafood. Daily 11:30 a.m. to 3 p.m., 5:30 to 9 p.m., Friday and Saturday to 10 p.m. Reasonable.

Whaler's Inne, 20 E. Main St., tel. (203) 536-1506, (800) 243-2588. **The Binnacle Restaurant**, daily 6 a.m. to 9 p.m., seafood specialties.

New Canaan
Fat Tuesday, 105 Elm St., 972-0445. Continental. Daily noon to 3 p.m. (Sunday 11 a.m. to 4 p.m.), dinner from 6 p.m. (Sunday from 5 p.m.).

Mr. Lee, 64 Main St., tel. (203) 966-3686. Szechuan Chinese. Daily noon to 10:30 p.m., weekends to 11:30 p.m. Reservations preferred.

New Haven
L'Avventura, 9 Elm St., tel. (203) 773-3457. Italian. Daily 11:30 a.m. to 2:30 p.m., 5:30 p.m. to 10 p.m., Friday and Saturday to 11 p.m., Sunday to 9 p.m. Cafe open weekdays 11:30 a.m. to 1 a.m., Saturday 5 p.m. to 2 a.m., Sunday 4 p.m. to 12 midnight.

Basel's, 991 State St., tel. (203) 624-9361. Greek. Daily (except first three weeks of August) 11:30 a.m. to 2 p.m., 5 to 9 p.m., Thursday through Saturday to 1 a.m., closed for dinner Monday. Live music and dancing. Reservation required Friday and Saturday.

Elm City Diner, 1228 Chapel St., tel. (203) 776-5050. Daily except Monday 7:30 a.m. to 11 p.m., Saturday 9:30 a.m. to 11 p.m., Sunday brunch 9:30 a.m. to 3 p.m.

Fitzwilly's, 338 Elm St., tel. (203) 624-9438. Daily 11:30 a.m. to midnight.

Gentree, Ltd., 194 York St., tel. (203) 562-4864. Prime rib. Daily 11:30 a.m. to 11 p.m., Sunday from 5 p.m., late-night menu to 2 a.m.

Leon's Restaurant, Long Wharf, tel. (203) 789-9049. Seafood. Open May, June, August and September, noon to 2:30 p.m., 5 to 10 p.m., Sunday noon to 9 p.m. Reasonable.

Louis' Lunch, 261-263 Crown St. (between College and High streets), tel. (203) 562-5507. Daily (except August to mid-September) weekdays 9 a.m. to 4:30 p.m. No smoking.

Mamoun's Falafel Restaurant, 85 Howe St., tel. (203) 562-8444. Middle Eastern. Daily 11 a.m. to 3 a.m. Inexpensive.

New Haven Restaurant, 986 Chapel St., tel. (203) 777-1272. Daily 11:30 a.m. to 10 p.m., Friday and Saturday to midnight, Sunday 4 to 9 p.m.

Old Heidelberg, 1151 Chapel St., tel. (203) 777-3639. Italian, French, steak, seafood. Daily (except summer Sundays) 11:30 a.m. to 11 p.m., Thursday to midnight, Friday and Saturday to 1 a.m., Sunday 2 to 10 p.m.

Pepe's, Wooster Street, tel. (203) 865-5762. Pizza. Daily except Tuesday and two weeks in September, 4 to 10:30 p.m. weekdays, 11:30 a.m. to midnight on Friday and Saturday, 2:30 to 10:30 p.m. Sunday.

Viva Zapata, 161 Park St., tel. (203) 562-2499, (203) 288-3784. Mexican. Daily except Sunday 11:30 a.m. to midnight.

Old Saybrook
Cuckoo's Nest, 1712 Boston Post Road, tel. (203) 399-9060. Mexican. Daily noon to 2:30 p.m., 5 to 10 p.m., Friday and Saturday to 11 p.m., Sunday 4 to 10 p.m. Inexpensive.

Stafford Springs
Chez Pierre, 179 W. Main St., tel. (203) 684-5826. French. Tuesday through Saturday, 5 to 9:30 p.m. Reservations required. Formal dress.

Stratford

Temiko's, 520 Sniffens Lane, tel. (203) 375-3986. Japanese. Daily except Tuesday, 11 a.m. to 2 p.m. (weekdays), 4 to 10 p.m., Sunday to 11 p.m.

Westport

Allen's Clam and Lobster House, Hillspoint Road, tel. (203) 226-4411. Daily March through November, 11 a.m. to 2 p.m., dinner from 5 p.m.

Willimantic

Clark's Restaurant, 32–34 North St., tel. (203) 423-1631. Daily except holidays 11:30 a.m. to 3 p.m. (weekdays), 5 to 8:30 p.m., Friday to 9 p.m., Saturday to 10 p.m., Sunday noon to 8:30 p.m. Reasonable.

MAINE

Bath

Kristina's, 160 Center St. (off Route 209), tel. (207) 442-8577. Whole foods. Daily 7 a.m. to 9 p.m., Sunday brunch 9 a.m. to 2 p.m. Inexpensive.

Kennebunkport

Bartley's Dockside, Route 9 by the bridge, tel. (207) 967-4798. Seafood. Daily 7 a.m. to 10 p.m.

Whistling Oyster, Perkins Cove. Daily noon to 2:30 p.m., 6 to 9:30 p.m. Moderate.

White Barn Inn, Beach Street, tel. (207) 967-2321. French-American. Daily March through December, 8 a.m. to noon, 5:30 to 9:30 p.m. Entertainment. Moderate.

New Harbor

Gosnold Arms, Northside Road, tel. (207) 677-3727. Seafood, steaks. Daily mid-June through Labor Day, 7:30 to 9 a.m., 5:30 to 8 p.m., Sunday brunch 11 a.m. to 1 p.m.

North Wells

Bull 'n' Claw House, Route 1, tel. (207) 646-8467. Seafood. April through December, daily 11 a.m. to 9 p.m. Inexpensive.

Portland

Seamen's Club Restaurant, 375 Fore St., tel. (207) 772-7311. Soup, sandwiches. Daily 11 a.m. to 2:30 p.m., 5:30 to 10 p.m. Reasonable.

Woolwich

Montsweag Restaurant, Route 3, tel. (207) 443-6563. Seafood, steaks. Daily 11:30 a.m. to 8 p.m., summer to 9 p.m.

York Harbor

Bill Foster's Down East Lobster and Clambake, Route 1A, tel. (207) 363-3255. Open June through Labor Day, Wednesday through Sunday; dinner at 7 p.m., Sunday at 5 p.m. Call for off-season schedule. Reservations required.

MASSACHUSETTS

Amherst

Amherst Chinese Food, 62–64 Main St., tel. (413) 253-7835. Mandarin and Szechuan cuisines. Daily 11:30 a.m. to 2:30 p.m., 4:30 to 10 p.m. Inexpensive.

Boston

Another Season, 97 Mt. Vernon St., tel. (617) 367-0880. International. Daily except Sunday, 5:45 to 10:30 p.m. Moderate.

Anthony's Pier 4 Restaurant, 140 Northern Ave., tel. (617) 423-6363. Seafood and regional. Daily 11:30 a.m. to 11 p.m., Sundays and holidays 12:30 to 10:30 p.m.

The Bay Tower Room, 60 State St., tel. (617) 723-1666. French. Daily except Sunday 6 to 10 p.m., Friday and Saturday to 11 p.m. Dancing nightly. 33rd floor panorama. Moderate.

Boston Park Plaza Hotel, 64 Arlington St., tel. (617) 426-2000. **Lobby Garden Lounge**, daily, 7 a.m. to 8 p.m. **Plaza Pub**, Monday through Friday, 7 a.m. to 2 a.m. **Cafe Rouge**, daily 7 a.m. to midnight, Sunday brunch 10:30 a.m. to 3 p.m.; continental; informal.

Chadwick Park, 184 High St., tel. (617) 542-0841. Continental. Monday through Friday, 11:30 a.m. to midnight. Reasonable.

Charley's Eating and Drinking Saloon, 344 Newbury St., tel. (617) 266-3000. Victorian saloon. Daily 11:30 a.m. to 1 a.m.

China Pearl, 9 Tyler St., tel. (617) 426-4338. Chinese. Daily 11:30 a.m. to 1:45 a.m. Reasonable.

Cityside Restaurant and Bar, 262 Quincy Market, Faneuil Hall Marketplace, tel. (617) 742-7390. Salads, sandwichs, specials. Daily 11 a.m. to 2 a.m. Reasonable.

The Colonnade Hotel, 120 Huntington Ave., tel. (617) 424-7000. **The Cafe Promenade**, daily 7 a.m. to midnight; continental; moderate. **Zachary's**, daily except Sunday 5:30 to 11 p.m., Saturday to midnight; continental; expensive.

Copley Plaza Hotel, 138 St. James Ave., tel. (617) 267-5300. **Cafe Plaza**, daily except Sunday 5:30 to 11 p.m.; continental; expensive. **Copley's**, daily 11:30 a.m. to midnight; international; moderate. **The Tea Court**, daily 7 a.m. to 5 p.m.

Cricket's, South Market Building, Faneuil Hall Marketplace, tel. (617) 227-3434. International. Daily 11 a.m. to 2 a.m.

Davio's Ristorante, 269 Newbury St., tel. (617) 262-4810. Italian. Lunch Monday to Saturday from noon; dinner daily from 5 p.m. Moderate.

DuBarry French Restaurant, 159 Newbury St., tel. (617) 262-2445. Daily 11:30 a.m. to 2:30 p.m. and 5:30 to 9:30 p.m.; closed Sunday lunch and Sundays in July and August. Moderate.

Durgin Park, 340 N. Market St., Faneuil Hall Marketplace, tel. (617) 227-2038. Yankee cooking, oyster bar. Daily 11:30 a.m. to 10 p.m., Sunday noon to 9 p.m. Moderate. Informal.

Hampshire House, 84 Beacon St., tel. (617) 227-9600. Continental. Monday to Friday 11:45 a.m. to 2:30 p.m., daily 6 to 10:30 p.m., Saturday and Sunday brunch 11 a.m. to 3 p.m. Entertainment. Moderate.

Harvard Book Store Cafe, 190 Newbury St., tel. (617) 536-0095. European and Mediterranean. Tuesday through Saturday 8 a.m. to 11 p.m., Monday 10 a.m. to 6 p.m., closed Sunday.

J.C. Hillary's, 793 Boylston St., tel. (617) 536-6300. American. Daily 11:30 a.m. to midnight, Friday and Saturday to 12:30 a.m., Sunday noon to 11:30 p.m.

Houlihan's Old Place, 60 State St., tel. (617) 367-6377. Daily 11:30 a.m. to 2 a.m., Sunday brunch 11 a.m. to 4 p.m. Moderate.

Houndstooth, 150 Boylston St., tel. (617) 482-0722. Continental. Monday through Friday 11:30 a.m. to 2:30 p.m., daily except Sunday 5:30 p.m. to 11 p.m. Entertainment. Moderate. Pub open daily except Sunday 11:30 a.m. to 2 p.m.; inexpensive fare.

Jason's, 131 Clarendon St., tel. (617) 262-9000. Continental. Sunday through Friday 11:30 a.m. to 3 p.m., daily 5 p.m. to midnight. Dancing nightly. Moderate.

Jimmy's Harborside Restaurant, 242 Northern Ave., tel. (617) 423-1000. Seafood. Daily except Sunday, 11:30 a.m. to 9:30 p.m. Moderate.

Joseph's, 279 Dartmouth St., tel. (617) 536-4200. Continental. Daily except Sunday 11:30 a.m. to midnight. Expensive.

Ken's at Copley, 549 Boylston St., tel. (617) 266-6149. Deli menu. Daily 7 a.m. to 3 a.m. Inexpensive.

Landmark Inn, 300 Faneuil Hall Marketplace, tel. (617) 227-9660. **Flower Garden Cafe**, 11:30 a.m. to 2 a.m.; entertainment; reasonable. **The Wild Goose**, Monday through Friday noon to 3 p.m., daily 6 to 11 p.m., Sunday 4 to 10 p.m.; rotisserie; moderate. **Thompson's Chowder House**, daily 11:30 a.m. to 3 p.m., 5 to 11 p.m., Sunday 4 to 11 p.m.; seafood; moderate.

Lechners, 21 Broad St., tel. (617) 523-1016. Continental. Weekdays 11:30 a.m. to 3 p.m., daily except Sunday 5 to 10 p.m. Moderate.

Legal Sea Foods, Boston Park Plaza Hotel, tel. (617) 426-4444. Daily except Saturday 11 a.m. to 10 p.m., Sunday from noon. Reasonable. Also **Fish Market Restaurant**, Statler Office Building, tel. (617) 426-5566. Same hours and prices.

Lenox Hotel, 710 Boylston St., tel. (617) 536-2200. **Delmonico's Restaurant**, daily except Sunday 5:30 to 10 p.m., Saturday to 11 p.m.; continental; moderate.

Lily's, 29 Quincy Market Building, Faneuil Hall Marketplace, tel. (617) 227-4242. Continental. Lunch and dinner.

Locke-Ober, 3–4 Winter Place, tel. (617) 542-1340. International. Daily except Sunday 11 a.m. to 10 p.m., Saturday to 10:30 p.m. Expensive.

Maison Robert, 45 School St., tel. (617) 227-3370. French. Daily 11:30 a.m. to 2:30 p.m., 5:30 to 10:30 p.m. Moderate.

Marliave Restaurant, 11 Bosworth St., tel. (617) 423-6340. Italian and American. Daily except Sunday, 11 a.m. to 10 p.m. Reasonable.

Meridien Hotel, Pearl and Franklin streets, tel. (617) 451-1900. **Cafe Fleuri**, daily breakfast to midnight. Julien, daily lunch and dinner; French.

Midtown Hotel, 220 Huntington Ave., tel. (617) 262-1000. **The Colony Room**, daily 7 a.m. to 9 p.m.; Continental and regional; reasonable.

Newbury's Steak House, 94 Massachusetts Ave., tel. (617) 536-0184. Daily noon to midnight. Reasonable.

Parker House, 60 School St., tel. (617) 227-8600. **Parker's**, Monday through Friday 11:30 a.m. to 3 p.m., 5:30 to 10 p.m., Saturday 5:30 to 10:30 p.m., Sunday 11:30 a.m. to 2:30 p.m., 5:30 to 9 p.m.; continental; expensive. **Last Hurrah**, daily 11:30 a.m. to midnight; American and seafood; music and dancing. **Cafe Tremont**, daily from 6:30 a.m.; continental.

Ramada Inn Restaurant (Boston Airport), 225 William F. McClellan Hwy., tel. (617) 569-5250. Prime rib and seafood. Daily 6 a.m. to 10 p.m. Reasonable.

The Ritz-Carlton Hotel, 15 Arlington St., tel. (617) 536-5700. Cafe, daily 7 to 11:15 a.m., 11:45 a.m. to 4 p.m., 5:30 p.m. to midnight, Sunday brunch 11:45 a.m. to 4 p.m.; American and continental; moderate. Dining room, daily noon to 2:30 p.m. and 6 to 10 p.m., Friday and Saturday to 11 p.m., Sunday brunch to 4 p.m.; continental; expensive.

Satch's Restaurant, 43 Stanhope St., tel. (617) 266-2929. Regional cuisine. Daily except Monday 11:30 a.m. to 3 p.m., 5 to 10 p.m., Friday and Saturday to 11 p.m., Sunday 4 to 8 p.m. Entertainment. Moderate.

Seaside Restaurant and Bar, 188 Faneuil Hall Marketplace, South Market Building, tel. (617) 742-8728. Daily 11:30 a.m. to 2 a.m. Reasonable.

Stella of Boston, 74 E. India Row, tel. (617) 227-3559. Italian. Daily 11:30 a.m. to 11:30 p.m. (weekdays), Saturday from 4:30 p.m., Sunday and holidays noon to 10:30 p.m. Live music and dancing. Moderate.

Stouffer's Top of the Hub, 800 Boylston St., Prudential Center, tel. (617) 536-1775. Daily 11:30 a.m. to 2:30 p.m., 5:30 to 10 p.m., Friday and Saturday to 11 p.m., Sunday brunch 11 a.m. to 2 p.m. Entertainment and dancing. 52nd floor panorama.

Joe Tecce's Ristorante, 53 N. Washington St., tel. (617) 742-6210. Italian. Daily 11:30 a.m. to 4 p.m. (weekdays), 4 to 11:30 p.m.

Union Oyster House, 41 Union St., tel. (617) 227-2750. Seafood. Daily 11:30 a.m. to 9:30 p.m., Friday and Saturday to 10 p.m. Moderate.

Villa Francesca, 150 Richmond St., tel. (617) 367-3948. Northern Italian. Daily 5 to 10:30 p.m., Friday and Saturday to 11 p.m. Moderate.

Wok In, 166 Tremont St. (opposite Boston Common), tel. (617) 482-6581; also 845 Boylston St. (opposite Prudential Center), tel. (617) 536-9181. Chinese fast food. Daily 11:30 a.m. to 9:30 p.m., Friday and Saturday to 11 p.m. Inexpensive.

Cambridge

Averof Restaurant, 1924 Massachusetts Ave., tel. (617) 354-4500. Greek and Middle Eastern. Daily 11 a.m. to 1 a.m. Reasonable.

Hyatt Regency Cambridge, 575 Memorial Dr., tel. (617) 492-1234. **Empress**, daily 6 to 11:30 p.m., Sunday brunch 11 a.m. to 3 p.m.;

Chinese and continental; moderate. **Jonah's on the Terrace**, daily 7 a.m. to midnight; seafood; moderate. **The Spinnaker**, daily 11:45 a.m. to 2 a.m., Saturday from 5 p.m., Sunday 10 a.m. to 1 a.m.; expensive.

Sheraton Commander Hotel, 16 Garden St., tel. (617) 354-1234. **Dertads**, daily 6 to 11 p.m.; French; expensive.

Concord
Colonial Inn, 48 Monument Square, tel. (617) 369-9200. Continental. Daily 7 to 10 a.m., 11:30 a.m. to 2:30 p.m., 6 to 9 p.m., Sunday noon to 8:30 p.m.

Duxbury
The Chart House, 500 Congress St. (Route 14), tel. (617) 834-9395. Steak, seafood. Daily 6 to 10 p.m., Friday 5:30 to 11 p.m., Saturday 5 to 11 p.m., Sunday 5 to 10 p.m.

Gloucester
The Easterly Restaurant, 87 Atlantic Road, tel. (617) 283-0140. Seafood, regional. Daily late April through October, 11:30 a.m. to 10 p.m., Sunday from noon. Entertainment. Moderate.

Gloucester House, Seven Seas Wharf, tel. (617) 283-1812. Daily 11:30 a.m. to 10 p.m., weekends to 11 p.m.

Lexington
Restaurant Le Bellecour, 10 Muzzey St., tel. (617) 861-9400. French; game in season. Daily except Sunday 11:30 a.m. to 2 p.m. (weekdays), 6 to 10 p.m. Reservation advised. Formal.

Northampton
Beardsley's Cafe-Restaurant, 140 Main St., tel. (413) 586-2699. Continental lunch, French dinner. Daily 11:30 a.m. to 5 p.m., 5:30 to 10 p.m., Sunday brunch 10:30 a.m. to 3 p.m. Reservation advised.

Hotel Northampton, 36 King St., tel. (413) 584-3100. **Wiggins Tavern**, daily 11:30 a.m. to 2:30 p.m. (Sunday from noon), 5 to 9 p.m. Reservation advised.

Northampton Hilton Inn, junction I-91 and Route 5, tel. (413) 586-1211. **Page's Loft**, daily 7 to 11 a.m., noon to 5 p.m., 5:30 to 10 p.m., Sunday 7 a.m. to 9 p.m. Reservation advised.

North Truro
Mediterrañee, Pond Road, tel. (617) 487-1881. French. Daily except Monday, June through September, 6 to 9:30 p.m.

Pittsfield
Yellow Aster, 1015 South St., tel. (413) 443-2506. Daily except Tuesday, April through December, noon to 2:30 p.m., 5 to 10 p.m., Sunday noon to 9 p.m. Reservation advised.

Stockbridge
Le Country Restaurant, 101 North St., tel. (413) 458-4000. Continental. Daily except Monday, 11:30 a.m. to 2 p.m. (weekdays), 5 to 9 p.m. Reservation advised. Formal.

1896 House, Route 7, tel. (413) 458-8123. Daily 4:30 to 10 p.m., Sunday 1 to 9 p.m.

Williams Inn, on the green, tel. (413) 458-9371 Daily 7 a.m. to 2:30 p.m., 5:30 to 9:30 p.m.

Woods Hole
Landfall Restaurant, Water Street, tel. (617) 548-1758. Seafood. Daily mid-June through mid-September, 11 a.m. to 10 p.m. Moderate.

Yarmouthport
Old Yarmouth Inn, 223 Main St. (Route 6A), tel. (617) 362-3191. Regional. Daily April through December, 7:30 to 10:30 a.m. (October through December 8 to 10 a.m.), noon to 3 p.m., 5 to 9:30 p.m.

NEW HAMPSHIRE

Bedford
Marketplace Restaurant, South River Road (junction I-93 and Route 101), tel. (603) 622-3754. Daily 11:30 a.m. to 2:30 p.m., 5 to 10 p.m., Friday and Saturday to 11 p.m., Sunday 1 to 10 p.m.

Bennington
Alberto's, Mill Road (off route 202), tel. (603) 588-6512. Italian. Daily except Sunday from 5 p.m. Reservation advised.

Bretton Woods
Mount Washington Hotel, Route 302, tel. (603) 278-1000. Daily 8 to 9:30 a.m., 11:30 a.m. to 5 p.m., 7 to 8:30 p.m. Reservation advised.

Charlestown
Indian Shutters Inn, Route 12, tel. (603) 826-4445. Regional. Daily 11:30 a.m. to 2:30 p.m., 5 to 8 p.m., Friday and Saturday to 10 p.m., Sunday noon to 8 p.m. Reasonable.

Concord
Red Blazer Restaurant, 72 Manchester St., tel. (603) 224-7779. Daily 11:30 a.m. to 4 p.m., 4:30 to 10 p.m., Sunday 4 to 9 p.m. Reasonable.

Thursday's, 6 Pleasant St., tel. (603) 224-2626. Whole foods, seafood. Daily 11:30 a.m. to 3 p.m., 5 to 9 p.m., Friday and Saturday 11:30 a.m. to 10 p.m., Sunday brunch 10 a.m. to 3 p.m.

Dixville Notch
The Balsams Grand Resort Hotel, tel. (603) 225-3400. Daily June through October, 8 to 9:30 a.m., 12:30 to 2 p.m., 7 to 8:30 p.m. Reservation required. Jacket after 6 p.m.

Exeter
Exeter Inn, 90 Front St., tel. (603) 772-5901. Seafood. Daily 7 a.m. to 2 p.m., 5 to 10 p.m. Reasonable. Reservation advised. Jacket.

Fitzwilliam Inn, tel. (603) 585-9000. Regional. Daily 8 to 9:30 a.m., noon to 2 p.m., 6 to 9 p.m., Sunday noon to 8 p.m. Reasonable.

Francestown
Grandmother's House, Mountain Road (off Route 47), tel. (603) 588-2355. European and American. Daily except Monday, noon to 2 p.m., 6 to 9 p.m., Sunday 1 to 6 p.m. Reservation appreciated.

Gilford
B. Mae Denny's Eating, Drinking, and Lodging Establishment, junction route 11 and 11B tel. (603) 293-4351. Daily 11:30 a.m. to 3 p.m., 5 to 10 p.m., Sunday noon to 10 p.m. Reasonable.

Glen
The Bernerhof, tel. (603) 383-4414. Continental. Daily noon to 3 p.m., 6 to 9:30 p.m. Reasonable.

Hampton
Ashworth by the Sea, 295 Ocean Blvd., tel. (603) 926-6762. Steaks, seafood. Daily 7 a.m. to 2:30 p.m., 5 to 9 p.m., Sunday 10 a.m. to 9 p.m. Reservation advised.
The Galley Hatch Restaurant, 285 Lafayette Road, (Route 1), tel. (603) 926-6152. Daily 11 a.m. to 10 p.m., weekends to 12:30 a.m. Reservation advised.
Sheraton Lamie's, 490 Lafayette Road (Route 1), tel. (603) 926-8911. Regional. Daily 7 to 11 a.m., noon to 3 p.m., 5 to 10 p.m., Sunday 7 a.m. to 9 p.m. Reasonable.

Hanover
The Hanover Inn, at Dartmouth College. Regional and continental. Daily 7 to 10:30 a.m., 11:30 a.m. to 2 p.m., 6 to 9 p.m., Sunday brunch 11:30 a.m. to 2:30 p.m. Entertainment. Moderate.

Jackson
Christmas Farm Inn, Route 16B, tel. (603) 383-4313. Daily 8 to 9:30 a.m., 6 to 9 p.m. Moderate.
Dana Place Inn, Route 16, tel. (603) 383-6822. Daily except in May and November, 8 to 9:30 a.m., 6:30 to 9 p.m., Sunday brunch June through October 12:30 to 2 p.m.
Eagle Mountain House, Route 16, tel. (603) 383-4347. Steaks, seafood, game. Daily 7:30 to 9:30 a.m., 11:30 a.m. to 2:30 p.m., 6 to 9 p.m., weekends to 10 p.m. Moderate. Reservation required.

New London
Pleasant Lake Inn, North Pleasant Street, tel. (603) 526-6271. Daily 8 to 9 a.m., 11:30 a.m. to 2 p.m., 5 to 9 p.m., Friday and Saturday to 9:30 p.m. Reservation advised.

North Conway
Eastern Slope Inn, Main Street, tel. (603) 356-5680. American, Mexican, French. Daily 8 to 10:30 a.m., 11:30 a.m. to 10 p.m., Sunday brunch 10 a.m. to 2 p.m.
Fox Ridge Resort, Route 16, tel. (603) 356-3151. Regional. Daily 7:30 to 11 a.m. (Sunday to noon), 6 to 9:30 p.m. (Friday to 10 p.m.)

North Sutton
Follansbee Inn, Keysar Street, tel. (603) 927-4221. Seafood. Daily except Monday 8 to 9:30 a.m., 5:30 to 9 p.m., Sunday to 8 p.m. Moderate.

Ossipee
Sunny Villa Restaurant, Route 16, tel. (603) 539-2252. Daily except early December, 11 a.m. to 8 p.m., Saturday 8 a.m. to 9 p.m., Sunday 8 a.m. to 8 p.m.

Petersborough
Folkway Restaurant, 85 Grove St. (off Route 101), tel. (603) 924-7484. Tuesday through Saturday, 11:30 a.m. to 10 p.m., Sunday brunch 10 a.m. to 2 p.m., closed Monday. Folk entertainment weekends. Reservations advised.

Portsmouth
Blue Strawbery Restaurant, 29 Ceres St., tel. (603) 431-6420. Daily dinner sittings at 6 p.m. (Sunday 3 and 6 p.m.) for six-course *prix fixe* dinner. Reservation required.
Dolphin Striker Restaurant, 15 Bow St., tel. (603) 431-5222. Seafood. Daily 11:30 a.m. to 3 p.m. (except Saturday), 5:30 to 9:30 p.m. Moderate. Reservation advised.
Pier II Restaurant, State Street (under bridge), tel. (603) 436-0669. Daily except January 11:30 a.m. to 11 p.m. Reservation advised.

Snowville
Snowvillage Inn, off Route 153 near Eaton Center, tel. (603) 447-2818. Daily 8 to 9:30 a.m., 6:30 to 7:30 p.m. (except Sunday). Moderate.

Sugar Hill (Franconia)
Polly's Pancake Parlor, tel. (603) 823-5575. Daily late May through mid-October, 7 a.m. to 7 p.m. Reservation advised Sunday.
Sunset Hill House. Route 117, tel. (603) 823-5522. Regional specialties. Daily 7:30 to 9:30 a.m., noon to 2 p.m. (poolside to 3 p.m.), 6:30 to 9 p.m. Moderate. Jacket and tie required.

Swanzey Center
The Alps, Route 32, tel. (603) 352-5868. German. Daily except Monday (closed two weeks in June), noon to 2 p.m., 5 to 8:30 p.m., Saturday to 9:30 p.m., Sunday noon to 7:30 p.m. Reservation required weekends.

West Rindge
The Old Forge, Route 202, tel. (603) 899-3322. European. Daily (except closed Mondays, November to May), noon to 3 p.m., 5 to 9 p.m.

Whitefield
The Playhouse Motor Inn, Route 3, tel. (603) 837-2527. French. Daily dinner cabaret July and August. Jacket preferred after 6 p.m.
Spalding Inn Club, Mountain View Road, tel. (603) 837-2572. British and continental. Daily late May through late October, 8 to 9 a.m., 12:30 to 2 p.m., 7 to 8:30 p.m. Expensive. Reservation advised. Jacket required.

Wilton
The Ram in the Thicket, Maple Street (off Route 101), tel. (603) 654-6440. Wednesday through Friday 11:30 a.m. to 2 p.m., daily from 5 p.m.

VERMONT

Bennington
Publyk House Restaurant, Harwood Hill (Route 7A), tel. (802) 442-8301. Daily 5 to 9 p.m., Friday and Saturday to 10 p.m.

Bondville
Tumbledown's Restaurant, Route 30, tel. (802) 297-1234. Daily 11:30 a.m. to 3 p.m., 5:30 to 10 p.m., Sunday noon to 3 p.m., 5:30 to 9 p.m.

Chittenden
Mountain Top Inn, Mountain Top Road, tel. (802) 483-2311. Regional and continental. Daily May 27 through Oct. 24 and Dec. 15 through April 15, 8 to 10 a.m., noon to 2 p.m., 6 to 10 p.m., Sunday brunch 11:30 a.m. to 2 p.m. Moderate. Reservation required. Formal.

Killington
Grey Bonnet Inn, Route 100N, tel. (802) 775-2537. Continental. Daily July through March, 7:30 to 10 a.m., 6 to 9 p.m. Reservation advised.
Hemingway's, Route 4, tel. (802) 422-3886. Fish and game specialties. Daily except Tuesday (closed May and November), 6 to 10 p.m. Reservation advised.
The Vermont Inn, Route 4, tel. (802) 773-9847. Regional and continental. Daily June through October, 8:30 to 9:30 a.m., 6 to 9 p.m. Reservation advised.

Marlboro
Skyline Restaurant, Route 9, tel. (802) 464-5535. Daily 8 a.m. to 8 p.m. Reasonable.

Middlebury
Dog Team Tavern, off Route 7, tel. (802) 388-7651. Daily except Monday, 5 to 9 p.m., Sunday noon to 8 p.m. Reasonable.
Middlebury Inn, Court Square, tel. (802) 388-4961. Regional. Daily 7:30 to 10 a.m., noon to 2 p.m., 6:30 to 8 p.m. Reasonable.
Sugar House Motor Inn, Route 7, tel. (802) 388-2770. Daily 7 a.m. to 2 p.m., 5 to 9 p.m. Reasonable.

Newfane
Four Columns Inn, 230 West St., tel. (802) 365-7713. Nouvelle French cuisine. Lunch daily except Tuesday, July through October, noon to 2 p.m. Dinner daily except Tuesday (closed April and November), 6 to 9 p.m. Expensive. Reservations advised.

Norwich
Inn at Norwich, 225 Main St., tel. (802) 649-1143. Daily 7:30 to 9:30 a.m., noon to 2 p.m., 6 to 9 p.m., Friday and Saturday to 10 p.m. Reservation advised.

Pittsfield
Pittsfield Inn, Route 100, tel. (802) 746-8943. French country cuisine. Daily (except closed briefly in April and November), noon to 2 p.m., 6 to 9 p.m. Reservation advised.

Quechee
The Quechee Inn at Marshland Farm, Clubhouse Road, tel. (802) 295-3133. Continental. Wednesday through Sunday, except closed April and December, 6 to 9 p.m. Expensive. Reservation required.

Shelburne
Cafe Shelburne, Route 7, tel. (802) 985-3939. French and continental. Daily except Sunday, lunch from 11:30 a.m. (not Monday), 6 p.m. to midnight. Moderate. Reservation advised.

South Londonderry
The Londonderry Inn, Route 100, tel. (802) 824-5226. Continental and America. Daily except Tuesday (closed April and November), lunch May to October noon to 3 p.m., dinner 6:30 to 9:30 p.m.
Three Clock Inn, tel. (802) 824-6327. Fish and game specialties. Daily except Monday, late May through mid-October, 6 to 9:30 p.m. Moderate. Reservation advised. Jacket required.

Stowe
The Inn at the Mountain, Mountain Road (Route 108), tel. (802) 253-7311. **Fireside Tavern**, daily June through October, late November through April 1; 7:30 to 9:30 a.m. (summer 8 to 10 a.m.), noon to 2 p.m. (summer and fall only), 6:30 to 9 p.m.; reservation advised; semiformal.
Salzburg Inn, Mountain Road (Route 108), tel. (802) 253-8541. American and continental. Daily mid-June to mid-October and December to mid-April, 7:45 to 9:30 a.m., 6 to 9:30 p.m. Moderate.

Waitsfield
Tucker Hill Lodge, Route 17, tel. (802) 496-3983. Continental. Daily (closed May and November), 7:45 to 9:30 p.m., Sunday brunch from noon. Moderate. Reservation required weekends.

Weathersfield
The Inn at Weathersfield, Route 106 near Perkinsville, tel. (802) 263-9217. Nouvelle cuisine. Daily 8 to 10 a.m., 6 to 9 p.m. Reservation required.

West Brattleboro
Jolly Butcher's Tavern, Route 9, tel. (802) 254-6043. Steaks, seafood. Daily 11:30 a.m. to 2:30 p.m., 5 to 10 p.m., Sunday noon to 9 p.m. Reasonable.

Weston
The Inn at Weston, Route 100, tel. (802) 824-

5804. Daily Memorial Day through October, 8 to 9:30 a.m., 6 to 8 p.m., Sunday brunch noon to 2 p.m. Reasonable. Reservation advised.

West Dover (Mount Snow)

Hermitage Inn, Coldbrook Road (off Route 100), tel. (802) 464-3511. Game specialties. Daily noon to 2 p.m. (weekdays in season), 11 a.m. to 3 p.m. weekends all year, 5 to 11 p.m. Reservation preferred.

Von Schrener's Delectables, Route 100 and Coldbrook Road, tel. (802) 464-5695. Ice cream and gifts. Daily noon to 8 p.m., weekends and July 4 to Labor Day to 11 p.m.

Woodstock

Woodstock Inn and Resort, 14 The Green, tel. (802) 457-1100. American and continental. Daily 7 to 11 a.m. (Sunday to 10 a.m.), noon to 2 p.m., 6:30 to 9 p.m., Sunday brunch 11 a.m. to 1 p.m. Moderate. Reservation and jacket required.

Suggested Readings

General

Peirce, Neal R. *The New England States*. New York: 1976.

Vaughan, Alden T. *New England Frontier*. Boston: 1965.

Wilson, Harold Fisher. *The Hill Country of Northern New England*. New York: 1967.

Geography

Chamberlain, Barbara B. *These Fragile Outposts: A Geological Look at Cape God, Martha's Vineyard and Nantucket*. New York: Natural History Press, 1964.

Jorgensen, Neil. *A Guide to New England's Landscape*. Barre, Vermont: Barre Publishers, 1971.

History

Brooks, Van Wyck. *The Flowering of New England*. New York: 1936.

Brooks, Van Wyck. *New England: Indian Summer, 1865-1915*. New York: 1940.

Brown, Richard. *Massachusetts: A History*. New York: W.W. Norton, 1978

Clark, Charles E. *Maine: A History*. New York: W.W. Norton, 1978.

Holand, Hjalmas R. *Explorations in America Before Columbus*. New York: 1958.8

McLoughlin, William G. *Rhode Island: A History*. New York: W.W. Norton,- 1978.

Morison, Elizabeth Forbes, and Elting E. Morison. *New Hampshire: A History*. New York: W.W. Norton, 1978.

Morrissey, Charles T. *Vermont: A History*. New York: W.W. Norton, 1978.

Rosenberry, Lois Kimball Mathews. *The Expansion of New England: The Spread of New England Settlement and Institutions to the Mississippi*. New York: Russell R. Russell, 1962.

Roth, David M. *Connecticut: A History*. New New York: W.W. Norton, 1978.

Intellectual

Miller, Perry. *The New England Mind: From Colony to Province*. Cambridge: 1953.

Archival

Bryant, William Cullen. *A Popular History of the United States*. New York: Charles Scribner's Sons, 1878.

Christiania, N. Nicolaysen. *The Viking Ship From Gokstad*. Alb. Cammermeyer, 1882.

Dawson, Henry B. *Battles of the United States by Sea and Land*. New York: Johnson, Kry, 1858.

Drake, Samuel Adams. *Nooks and Corners of the New England Coast*. New York: Harper and Bros., 1875.

King, Moses. *King's Handbook of Boston*. Cambridge: the author, 1878.

Lossing, Benson J. *Our Country: A Household History*. New York: Johnson & Miles, 1876.

Smith, Captain John. *A Description of New England*. Boston: 1865.

Sylvester, Nathan Bartlett. *History of the Connecticut Valley in Massachusetts*. Philadelphia: 1879.

By Way of Introduction

Continued from page v

second and third editions of that book. After finishing their Apa assignment in New Hampshire, the Sibleys settled in Fairfield County, Connecticut, where they are engaged in a variety of writing, photography and graphic projects. In addition to Norman's article, both Sibleys contributed a number of photographs to this book.

Mark Silber is a true Maine-iac. He has hiked every trail in Acadia National Park, conquered Mount Katahdin, and spent an entire summer working on tiny Sutton Island, south of Mount Desert. While researching this book's in-depth look at Maine, Silber was stranded in Baxter State Park for four days — a sort of commitment that has kept him employed as a reporter for, among others, the *Middlesex Daily News* in Marlboro, Massachusetts; *The Harvard Lampoon* at Cambridge; and the *Columbia Journalism Review* in New York as a special intern.

Bryan Simmons, whose writings on New England academia and folklore were developed into "The Puritans' Intellectual Legacy," was born in Memphis, Tennessee. He soon made his way north to receive an absolutely classical New England education, attending Phillips Exeter Academy in New Hampshire and proceeding to Harvard. He burst upon the Cambridge scene as a member of the Krokodiloes, a singing group, and as president of the prestigious Signet Society. A child violin prodigy, Simmons also plays piano and viola. At present he is with the Strayton Corporation, a public relations firm in Boston.

The Guide in Brief was assembled by **Andrew Herwitz**, yet another of the Harvard graduates associated with this book. Herwitz currently resides in New York, where he is still searching for a truly interesting career.

In addition to this volume's principal photographers, several others contributed wonderful images. They include **Jim McElholm** of Oxford, Mass.; **Dean Abramson** of Raymond, Maine; **William Waterfall** of Honolulu, Hawaii; **Fredrik Bodin** of Boston; **Jim Jeffers** of Plainsboro, N.J.; and **Nevin Shalit** of New York, who took a special trip for Apa between visits to Nicaragua where he was on assignment for *The Village Voice*. Additional photos were by Orin Cassill, Kay Cassill, Robert Wenkam, Ronni Pinsler, C.A. Browning, Alison Shaw and Hans Hoefer, as well as several provided courtesy of the Rhode Island Department of Economic Development.

For Hoefer, Apa's founder-publisher, *New England* is another major step toward establishing *Insight Guides* in the awareness of the American traveling public. A graduate of printing, book production, design and photography studies in Krefeld, West Germany, Hoefer is a disciple of the Bauhaus tradition of graphic arts. He established Apa Productions in the Southeast Asian island nation of Singapore with the publication of his guide to *Bali* in 1970. Since then, under his creative direction, the *Insight Guides* series has won worldwide recognition for its sensitive cultural portrayals of leading travel destinations.

The *New England* book was especially gratifying for Anderson, Apa's managing editor, who guided the project through its birth and production phases. He attended grammar school in New England and vacationed from Stowe to Cape Cod to Moosehead Lake as a youngster; but not since his family moved from Wilbraham, Massachusetts, to Eugene, Oregon, in 1960, had he been back to his childhood home. A five-day New York-to-Boston excursion with Itzkowitz in June 1983 gave him an opportunity to reminisce down Brookside Drive, where he found many of the same neighbors still living in the same houses. Only the trees were bigger. Anderson, formerly a reporter and editor for *The Honolulu Advertiser* and the *Seattle Post-Intelligencer*, joined Apa in 1981 upon completion of the Gannett Fellowship program at the University of Hawaii.

Associate publisher **Adam Liptak** offered a watchful eye and a tempered touch of Yale conservatism to the final stages of the book's production. Liptak worked with *Business Week* and *The New Yorker* before joining Apa. **Nancy Brokaw**, a Brown University graduate who works as a magazine editor in New York, assisted with copy editing. The index was prepared in Singapore by **Julie Catterson**, a Wellesley College student in the Boston area. The color maps were produced by cartographers under the direction of **Günter Nelles** and **Kaj Berndtson** in Munich, West Germany.

Most if not all of the historial reproductions in this book were photographed by **Bruce Bernstein**. The Princeton and Harvard university libraries were generous in opening' their fine collections to the producers of this book.

Many people contributed to making this book possible. Thanks are especially owed to Margot Dougherty, Mark Edwards, Lisa Henson, David Kuhn, Gloria and Mike Levitas, Thomas McCaghren, David O'Dell, John Marquand, Paul Sax, Irene Sax, Anne Keaney, Tobey Sanford, Marilyn Wood, John Paul Ziaukis, Louisa Campbell, Lorcan O'Neil, Karen Barnes, Harriet Yassky, Jim Jeffers, Hsiao-lan and Fritz Mote, Fred Bernstein, Michael Small, Eric Rayman, Tibor Kalman, "Bunny" Weil, Jonathan Kane Collier, Romolo del Deo and Professor Willard A. Hanna. Thanks also to the *Harvard Lampoon*.

The editor would personally thank the people closest to him and the project: Professor Norman Itzkowitz, Leonore Itzkowitz and Karen Itzkowtiz. He would also like to offer a special *chunmi* to all-time *prem* Pria Chatterjee.

When work on a book is completed, the work of getting it to the readers begins. It would be impossible to list all of the thousands of individual bookshop owners, travel agents and special sales representatives whose multiple efforts carry this book into private homes and offices in 30 countries around the world. We wish to acknowledge with thanks their individual and collective contributions. In particular, we wish to thank New England native Michael Hunter, head of the general publishing division of Prentice-Hall Inc., and his team of sales representatives.

To each and every one, a tip of the Pilgrim hat.

— Apa Productions

ART/PHOTO CREDITS

cover	Carole M. Allen		
cover	Ping Amranand (leaves),		
corner	Joseph F. Viesti (church)		
3	William Waterfall	38	*dustries* by Frederic Peck and Henry Earl (Fall River, 1877)
5	Carole M. Allen		
6-7	Carole M. Allen	38	From Peck and Earl's *Fall River*
8-9	William Waterfall	39	From Peck and Earl's *Fall River*
10-11	Joseph F. Viesti	41	From Lossing's *Our Country, History of the Connecticut Valley in Massachusetts* by Nathan Bartlett Sylvester (Philadelphia: 1879), and *Illustrated History of Kennebec, Maine* by Henry Kingsburg and Simon Deyo (New York: H.W. Blake & Co., 1892)
12-13	Hisham Youssef		
14	Carole M. Allen		
16-17	From *A Description of New England* by Captain John Smith (Boston: 1865)		
18	From *A Popular History of the United States* by William Cullen Bryant (New York: Charles Scribner's Sons, 1878)		
19	From Bryant's *History*	42	From *King's Handbook of Boston* (Cambridge: Mosses King, publisher, 1878)
20	From *Our Country: A Household History* by Benson J. Lossing (New York: Johnson & Miles, 1876)	43	From *All Along Shore* by M.F. Sweetser (Boston & Maine RR, 1889)
22	From *The Viking Ship From Gokstad* by N. Nicolaysen Christiania (Alb. Cammermeyer, 1882)	44	K.J. Croke
		45	Fredick D. Bodin
		46-47	Carole M. Allen
		48	Carole M. Allen
23	From Lossing's *Our Country*	49	Greta Diemente Sibley
24-L	From *Nooks and Corners of the New England Coast* by Samuel Adams Drake (New York: Harper & Bros., 1875)	50	Carole M. Allen
		51-L	Dean Abramson
		51-R	Carole M. Allen
		52-L	Carole M. Allen
24-R	From Bryant's *History*	52-R	Carole M. Allen
26	From Drake's *Nooks*	53	Joseph F Viesti
27	Joseph F. Viesti	54	Carole M. Allen
28	From Lossing's *Our Country*	55-L	Hisham Youssef
29	From Drake's *Nooks*	55-R	Carole M. Allen
30-31	Joseph F. Viesti	56-L	Carole M. Allen
32	From *Battles of the United States by Sea and Land* by Henry B. Dawson, illustrated by Alonzo Chappel (New York: Johnson, Kry, 1858)	56-R	Kay Cassill
		57	James Jeffers
		58	James Jeffers
		59	Carole M. Allen
		60-61	Joseph F. Viesti
33	From *Canadian Pictures* by The Marquis of Lorne, K.T. (New York: J. Nelson & Sons, 1883)	62-63	Carole M. Allen
		64-65	Joseph F. Viesti
		66	Joseph F. Viesti
		70-71	Joseph F. Viesti
34	From *Boston Illustrated*	72	Joseph F. Viesti
35	Joseph F. Viesti	73	From Drake's *Nooks*
36	From Drake's *Nooks*	74	From Lossing's *Our Country*
37	From *Fall River and Its In-*	75	From *Boston Illustrated*
		77	William Waterfall
		81	Hisham Youssef
		82	Hisham Youssef
		83	Hisham Youssef
		84	Hisham Youssef
		85	Hisham Youssef
		86	Hisham Youssef
		87	Hisham Youssef
		88	Hisham Youssef
		89	Hisham Youssef
		90	Fredick D. Bodin
		91	Fredick D. Bodin
		92	Hisham Youssef
		93	Hisham Youssef
		94	Carole M. Allen
		96	Hisham Youssef
		97	Ping Amranand
		99	Ping Amranand
		100	From *History of Newburyport* by Mrs. E. Vale Smith (Newburyport: 1854)
		101	Hisham Youssef
		102	Hisham Youssef
		103	Ping Amranand
		104	Hisham Youssef
		105	Hisham Youssef
		106-L	William Waterfall
		106-R	From Bryant's *History*
		107	Carole M. Allen
		108	Carole M. Allen
		109	From Lossing's *Our Country*
		110	Joseph F. Viesti
		111	Dean Abramson
		112-113	Hisham Youssef
		114	Carole M. Allen
		115	Ping Amranand
		117	Ping Amranand
		118	Ronni Pinsler
		119	Orin Cassill
		120	Ping Amranand
		121	Ping Amranand
		122	Ping Amranand
		123	Ping Amranand
		124	Ping Amranand
		125	William Waterfall
		126	Jim McElholm
		129	Jim McElholm
		130	Jim McElholm
		131	Jim McElholm
		132	Jim McElholm
		134	Jim McElholm
		135	Jim McElholm

INDEX